Fodor's

CANCÚN & THE RIVIERA MAYA

Welcome to Cancún and the Riviera Maya

Mexico's Yucatán Peninsula remains enduringly popular with travelers, and there's little wonder why. Stellar attractions include the region's magnificent beaches and the extensive reefs off Cozumel and the southern Yucatán coast, as well as myriad Maya ruins, the remains of a vast empire that ruled here long before the Spanish. Limestone pools called *cenotes*, great for a swim or dive, dot the countryside, even in Playa del Carmen. All-inclusive resorts predominate in Cancún, but luxurious retreats and simple guesthouses also offer different kinds of hospitality.

TOP REASONS TO GO

★ **Coral Reefs:** Cozumel's are among the best, drawing both divers and snorkelers.

★ **Beaches:** Cancún's are busy and beautiful; the Riviera Maya's are sugary soft and quieter.

★ **Maya Ruins:** The pyramids of Chichén Itzá soar; Tulum overlooks a perfect beach.

★ **Nightlife:** Cancún and Playa del Carmen range from raucous to sophisticated.

★ **Spas:** Almost every big resort has a spa, and many are notable for their pampering.

★ **Nature:** Pockets of pristine beauty remain, despite widespread development.

Contents

Fodor's Features

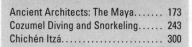

MAPS

EXPERIENCE CANCÚN & THE RIVIERA MAYA

20 ULTIMATE EXPERIENCES

Cancún offers terrific experiences that should be on every traveler's list. Here are Fodor's top picks for a memorable trip.

1 Marvel at Tulum's Seaside Ruins

While Tulum doesn't have the highest pyramids or the largest ruins, its cliff-side setting above the turquoise Caribbean sea is absolutely breathtaking—and a great backdrop for photos.

2 Float Your Way Through Xcaret

Part Maya ruins, part aquatic theme park, this enormous development has amusement rides, cultural shows, spa treatments, zip-lining, snorkeling, and more.

3 Wander the Cobblestone Streets of Valladolid

This small city is a great base for exploring the Yucatán, with colonial churches, Mexico's largest private collection of folk art, and a cenote right in the middle of town.

4 Eat Traditional Yucatecan Cuisine

Try Caribbean and Maya dishes like *cochinita pibil*, marinated roast pork often served on tortillas.

5 Indulge at a Luxury All-Inclusive Resort

With food, nightlife, activities, and spas all within the hotel, you can indulge in the art of laziness.

6 Scuba and Snorkel the Barrier Reef

Sea turtles, lobsters, moray eels, and barracudas congregate around Cozumel, all visible in the clear waters.

7 Sip Mezcal and Tequila

Mexico is the land of agave plants, and at tequila and mezcal distilleries, you can learn about the production process and pick up some useful souvenirs.

8 Explore Ancient Maya Ruins

There are over three dozen Maya ruins in the Yucatán Peninsula, including Chichén Itzá's iconic pyramids.

9 Flock with Flamingoes

One of North America's largest flamingo colonies holds court at the Ría Celestún Biosphere Reserve west of Mérida on the Gulf of Mexico from November through March.

10 Climb a Maya Pyramid at Cobá

Cobá is one of just a few places in Mexico where you can actually climb on the ruins—at your own risk.

11 Sunbathe at Sian Ka'an Biosphere Reserve

Sixty miles of coastline make up this undeveloped stretch of tropical forest framed by white-sand beaches and turquoise water.

12 Peruse Underwater Art

At this underwater museum, more than 400 statues sculpted by six artists have been installed over three sites, and the works have turned into a habitat for marine life.

13 Party Like a Spring-Breaker

College students on spring break descend on Cancún for several weeks during March and April, but the party season never pauses here.

14 Chill Out on Isla Mujeres

Golf carts are the main mode of transportation on this sleepy island full of rocky cliffs, blue-green water, and sugar sand.

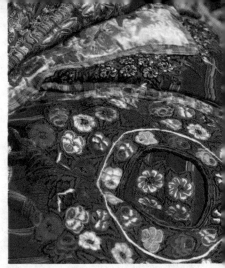

15 Shop 'til You Drop in Mérida

In Mérida, shops around the main square sell pottery, hand-embroidered clothing, and leather goods.

16 Escape to Isla Holbox

This under-the-radar island destination is full of boutique hotels, open-air restaurants, and water that's the perfect shade of seafoam green.

17 Eat at Tulum's Trendiest Restaurants

Tulum has turned into one of the chicest destinations in Mexico, with hip dining spots like Hartwood and Gitano.

18 Explore the Colorful City of Izamal

This sleepy town in the Yucatán Peninsula is like a ray of sunshine, with every building (including the impressive convent at the center of town) painted a vibrant yellow.

19 Stay at a Hacienda Hotel

Agave plantations dotted the Yucatán during the colonial era, and many of these haciendas, or ranches, have been repurposed into snazzy places to stay, like the modern Chablé resort.

20 Swim in a Cenote

There are almost 3,000 underground freshwater lagoons in the Yucatán Peninsula, offering a refreshing dip. The Maya believed these were passages to the spirit world.

WHAT'S WHERE

1 Cancún. This thriving coastal city (sometimes called the "Spring Break Capital of the World") is Mexico's most popular beach destination and the gateway to the Riviera Maya. In the waterfront area known as the Zona Hotelera, high-rise resorts offer creature comforts; inland at Cancún's downtown El Centro, accommodations are reasonably priced and offer a more authentic Mexican experience.

2 Isla Mujeres. A quick jaunt across the water from Cancún, Isla Mujeres is light-years away in temperament. This fairly quiet island is made up of dirt roads generally traveled by golf cart, moped, or bike. It's more laid-back, less crowded, and cheaper than almost anywhere on the mainland.

3 The Riviera Maya. The dazzling white sands and glittering blue waters here beckon everyone from snorkelers and sunbathers to spa goers. Most travelers come for the sugary beaches, but the seaside ruins of Tulum, the jungle-clad pyramids of Cobá, and the sidewalk cafés of

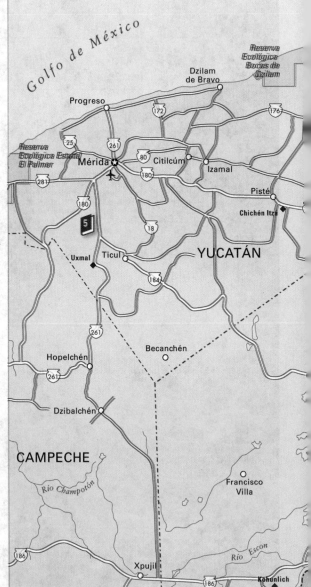

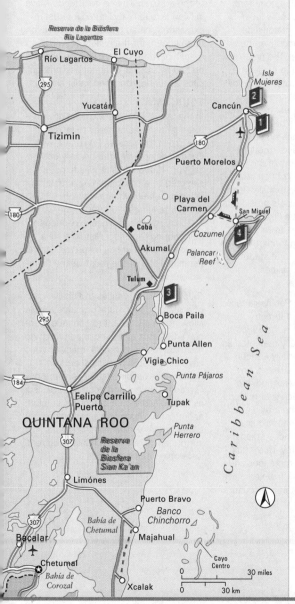

Playa del Carmen are also enticing. Numerous theme parks, dolphin programs, and hidden cenotes cater to families. Farther south, the Costa Maya offers the ultimate in isolation.

4 Cozumel. The island is hugely popular with scuba divers and cruise-ship passengers. Ever since Jacques Cousteau first made Cozumel's interconnected series of coral reefs famous in the 1960s, divers and snorkelers have flocked here. Giant ships ferry day-trippers to Cozumel. Avoid the crowds by visiting the island's windward side in search of crumbled monuments to the goddess Ixchel.

5 Yucatán State. Mérida, the capital city of Yucatán, is the cultural hub of the entire peninsula. Known for its weekend festivals, Mérida's restaurants, hotels, shops, and museums bring visitors back year after year. Near the remote north coast, you'll find shell-strewn beaches and charming villages. The area's major claim to fame, however, is its spectacular Maya architecture, including sites at Chichén Itzá and Uxmal.

Yucatán Peninsula Today

GOVERNMENT

Quintana Roo, Yucatán, and Campeche are 3 of the 31 states (plus one federal district) that make up Mexico's federal republic. The government consists of three branches: the executive, the legislative, and the judicial. The president of Mexico is elected to a onetime, six-year term by popular vote, and holds such extensive power that the position has been coined "the six-year monarchy." Each of Mexico's states is headed by a governor who also serves a single term that cannot exceed six years. Though elected by a simple majority of the populace, the actual selection of nominees for state governors has historically been largely controlled by Mexico's presidents. Much of Yucatán's revenue (like those of the other states) comes from the federal government. Such funding is then channeled to the mayors for distribution to their respective municipalities.

ECONOMY

Before 1970, the Yucatán Peninsula relied on agriculture, fishing, and forestry to support its economy, but in the 1980s, the region was successfully marketed as a travel destination, especially Cancún and the Riviera Maya. As a result, tiny fishing villages were transformed into bustling beach towns. Each year millions of tourists are drawn to the area's waterfront resorts and archaeological sites; these attractions inject a steady cash flow into the economy. This influx of mass tourism created more jobs and a higher standard of living. Travelers have also shown more interest in local culture.

This has spurred the development of historical museums, including the state-of-the-art Gran Museo del Mundo Maya in Mérida, and reawakened interest in exquisite Yucatán crafts, which have long been known for the quality of workmanship. The Yucatán's economy is also helped by exports of henequen products such as twine, rugs, and wall hangings.

TOURISM

In the late 1960s, the Mexican government launched a strategy to increase tourism in the Yucatán Peninsula, with Cancún selected as the primary destination. (Cancún's site was famously selected by a computer.) As a result, the city's population increased from 18,000 in 1976 to almost 900,000 in the early 2020s. Growth has since expanded to neighboring regions, creating a solid infrastructure that has made the Yucatán Peninsula one of the most visited destinations in Mexico.

Today the country faces the challenge of protecting its natural resources while allowing development to continue. Cancún's beaches alone are lined with more than 150 towering hotels, many of which have contributed to coastal erosion. Fortunately, building restrictions are now in place in neighboring communities such as Puerto Morelos. Ecotourism in Tulum and most of Costa Maya has helped protect area wildlife and the natural surroundings, although Tulum is currently developing at a rapid pace.

RELIGION

Although Mexico has no official religion, 83% of the population consider themselves Roman Catholic. Second only to Brazil, Mexico has more Catholics than anywhere else in the world, even though less than half attend church. Only 8% of the population call themselves Protestant, followed by Eastern Orthodox, Seventh-Day Adventists, Jehovah's Witnesses, and members of the Church of Jesus Christ of Latter-day Saints. (The Yucatán Peninsula counts the highest number of non-Catholic believers in Mexico.) Very few Maya people in the Yucatán Peninsula still practice traditional rituals of offerings and sacrifices of small animals. Central to the Maya religion is the idea of the duality of the soul, one part eternal, and the other supernatural.

SPORTS

Soccer (or *fútbol*) is the most popular sport in Mexico, and people here take the game extremely seriously. Second to soccer is boxing, with Mexico's biggest knockout rival being Puerto Rico. After the United States, Mexico has produced the most boxing world champions. Baseball rivals soccer in popularity in this region of this country. Sixteen teams compete in the Liga Mexicana de Béisbol (Mexican Baseball League), with the Quintana Roo Tigres (tigers), based in Cancún and the Yucatán Leones (lions), based in Mérida, always fierce cross-peninsula rivals. With more than 150 fairways dotting the country, golfing has gained attention and has helped promote tourism with five professional tournaments, including the PGA Tour's Mayakoba Golf Classic. More traditional sports include Mexican wrestling (also known as *lucha libre*), and *charrería*, based on a series of Mexican equestrian events.

CASH CROPS

Although tourism is the Yucatán Peninsula's main source of income, both agriculture and fishing are also great economic contributors. Until 1960 the main crop was henequen, an indigenous plant that produces sisal fiber used to make rope. The henequen here once had a global reputation of being "green gold." The advent of similar man-made fibers destroyed the international market, but henequen is still manufactured in the north-central region. The peninsula's eastern area raises 65% of the state's livestock, while the southern region, near Peto and Tzucacab, is known for corn, citrus, sugarcane, and cattle. Today the Yucatán Peninsula exports more than 1,500 products, ranging from sponges and oranges to furniture and chocolates.

Best Beaches in Cancún and the Riviera Maya

PLAYA GAVIOTA AZUL

In Punta Cancún, at Km 9.5 of the Caribbean side of Cancún's Hotel Zone beach strip, Playa Gaviota Azul (also known as Playa Forum) is one of the area's most popular public access beaches. It's also conveniently located near both Coco Bongo and Mandala, with their especially lively weekends making it perfect for partygoers. (Ch. 3)

PLAYA TULUM

The Yucatán's quintessential town-slash-ruins are stunning. Tulum's main beach extends for seven miles. Just north of town lies the so-called Tulum Ruins Beach with its Maya ruins near the water's edge. Visiting this sector is possible only by paying the admission fee to the ruins complex. (Ch. 5)

PLAYA NORTE

At the northern tip of Isla Mujeres, just a 20-minute boat ride from Cancún, Playa Norte has loungers, palms, and practically transparent waters, plus beach bars galore. Make the most of a full day there or visit in the evening for one of the few over-the-ocean sunsets in the region. (Ch. 4)

PLAYA LANGOSTA

Like most of the north zone beaches, Playa Langosta is easily accessible on public transport and an ideal spot to enjoy with kids. It's also situated close to the ferry dock—similarly to Playa Tortugas—which makes it an excellent jumping-off point for excursions and tours. The ocean here is swimmable. (Ch. 3)

PLAYA DELFINES

Moving down the Caribbean coastline—to km 19.5 of the Hotel Zone, to be precise—you'll find perhaps the most quintessential of all Cancún beaches: Playa Delfines. While admittedly not great for swimming—steer clear if you're in Cancún with little kids—it's the perfect place to lounge on the sand. (Ch. 3)

PLAYA CHAC MOOL

Next door to the rather vivacious Playa Gaviota Azul, you'll find the understated and casual Playa Chac Mool. It's not quite as busy as other central Cancún beaches despite sharing the same white sand, green-blue waters, and spectacular views over the Cancún Hotel Zone. (Ch. 3)

Tulum

PLAYA PUNTA NIZUC
If you're looking for a beach with great underwater attractions, Playa Punta Nizuc is the place. Situated at the extreme south of the Hotel Zone's Caribbean stretch, here you'll find shallow waters and coral reefs, making it the ideal place to practice kayaking, snorkeling, and plain ol' swimming. Look out for the underwater sculpture known as *The Gardener of Hope* by Jason deCaires Taylor that makes up part of the MUSA collection. (Ch. 3)

PUERTO MORELOS
Sticking to the mainland but moving down the coast somewhat, you'll find the Puerto Morelos beach. Perfect for when you tire of the pristine Cancún coastline, Puerto Morelos offers swimmable surf, more affordable bars and restaurants—don't miss the ceviche—and boats that will shuttle you out to snorkel or scuba dive in the nearby coral reefs. Hole up at one of the many beach clubs which line the shore for waiter service and shaded seating. (Ch. 5)

ISLA BLANCA
If you want to really escape the crowds of Cancún's Hotel Zone beaches but aren't convinced about heading to a nearby town or island, Isla Blanca makes for an ideal middle ground. Around 30 minutes north of the Cancún epicenter, this overlooked peninsula is dominated by jungle, sand, and the Chacmu-chuk Lagoon. While you'll probably need to rent a car to get there—there's no public transport, unfortu-nately—it's worth the trip. (Ch. 3)

Top Maya Ruins

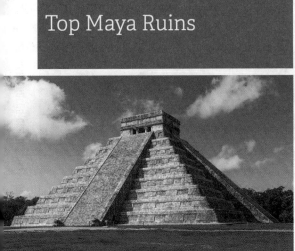

SAYIL
South of Uxmal—
sometimes referred to as a
"suburb" of the larger site—
the centerpiece of the "place
of the red ants" is its Gran
Palacio ("great palace") a
three-story Late Classic-
period structure perched
on top of a hill. Animals and
masked figures represent-
ing the Maya rain god,
Chaac, adorn the palace's
walls. (Ch. 7)

CHICHÉN ITZÁ
The most famous of the region's sites features the
enormous, oft-photographed El Castillo (Kukulcán)
pyramid. One of the Mayan world's largest and most beautiful cities makes for the peninsula's quintessential day trip
from Cancún or Mérida. (Ch. 7)

KOHUNLICH
Giant stucco masks that are
about 6 feet tall adorn this
site's main structure, the
Edificio de los Mascarones
("mask building"). There are
14 buildings showcasing a
mix of architectural styles
to visit; it is thought that
many more are yet to be
excavated among the many
burial mounds here. (Ch. 5)

**RESERVA DE LA
BIÓSFERA CALAKMUL**
Thousands of structures lie
buried under the profuse
greenery of Mexico's largest
eco-corridor at the Calakmul Biosphere Reserve.
The reserve's centerpiece
is the magnificent Templo
II pyramid, the Yucatán's
tallest Maya structure.
(Ch. 5)

COBÁ
The impressive temples
and palaces of inland
Cobá perpetually live in
the shadow of nearby
and better-known Tulum.
Its many fans are just
as happy to keep things
that way, although the
sprawling forested lakeside
site's visitor numbers are
growing. Only a small
portion of Cobá's estimated
6,000 structures are open to
visitors. Three cenotes are
nearby. (Ch. 5)

UXMAL

Along the Ruta Puuc you'll find the most elegant of the peninsula's ruins. Uxmal's perfectly proportioned buildings of the Cuadrángulo de las Monjas (Nun's Quadrangle) make a beautiful "canvas" for facades carved with snakes and the fierce visages of Maya gods. (Ch. 7)

EK BALAM

At the less visited Ek Balam, just north of Valladolid, huge monster masks guard the mausoleum of Mayan ruler Ukit Kan Lek Tok. On the amazing friezes, winged figures dressed in full royal regalia gaze down. Visitors usually mistake them for angels, but the personages more likely portray Mayan nobility. (Ch. 7)

TULUM

Tulum is the Yucatán's most visited archaeological site. Although the ruins here aren't as architecturally arresting, their spectacular location on a cliff overlooking the blue-green Caribbean makes Tulum unique. (Ch. 5)

MUYIL AT SIAN KA'AN

Translating to "where the sky is born," Sian Ka'an's spectacular and undeveloped coastline is home to a 1.3 million acre reserve with coastal lagoons, mangrove swamps, wildlife, and 22 Maya ruin complexes. Photogenic Muyil sits at the reserve's northern end and is the largest of these. Like nearby Tulum, it's perched on the Caribbean coast. Muyil's 57-foot Castillo is its largest structure. (Ch. 5)

CHACCHOBEN

This once thriving ancient city—its name translates to "land of the red corn"—dates from AD 200, but it remained forgotten until its rediscovery in 2005. The site's main structure is Templo I, which was dedicated to the Maya sun god, Itzamná, and once housed a royal tomb, found to be looted when excavated. Pending further exploration, much of the site is closed. (Ch. 5)

What to Eat and Drink in Cancún and the Riviera Maya

SOPA DE LIMA

The slight sourness of Yucatán lime soup gives an additional flavor profile to the chicken tortilla soup made elsewhere in Mexico. In this version, shredded chicken, tortilla strips, and local limes are the staple ingredients. The soup is reputed to be an effective hangover cure.

PIBIL

Pibil-style cooking creates what are arguably the Yucatán's signature dishes. Traditionally, *pollo* (chicken) or *cochinita* (a suckling pig) were slow-roasted in banana leaves in a pit; these days, the process more likely takes place in a standard oven, with pork shoulder or loin replacing the whole pig. Key to the recipe are the Yucatecan sour orange and achiote, a smoky, peppery tropical spice that imparts an orange color to the meat.

PAPADZULES

These enchilada-like treats compete with the pibil for a dish that says "quintessential Yucatán." (Papadzules have been around much longer.) Tortillas are dipped in a pumpkin-seed sauce, then hard-boiled eggs are folded inside before baking. They're usually topped with tomato sauce. The end result is a savory, creamy dish, much milder than your standard Mexican enchilada. Almost all establishments, from upscale local restaurants to market vendors, makes and serves them, usually three to four to a plate.

POC CHUC

You might dismiss poc chuc as nothing more than pork and onions, but the process and additional ingredients make it so much more than that. A sour-orange marinade gives the meat a real tang and a sprinkling of habanero salsa adds just a bit of fire. It's cooked over a grill (the name translates to "roasting on charcoal," after all) and is usually served with sides of pickled onions and cabbage. Black beans and avocados give the plate some color contrast.

CAPIROTADA

Mexican bread pudding, traditionally eaten during Lent, is made from French bread soaked in syrup, sugar, cheese, raisins, and walnuts, and it's downright delicious.

PAN DE CAZÓN

The name of this traditional casserole dish from Campeche state translates to "shark bread." (Don't worry, it won't bite). It looks like lasagna, but instead of pasta, corn tortillas (usually four at a time) are layered between shredded dogfish- or blacktip-shark meat. Refried black beans and various vegetables form the other layers. It's all covered with tomato sauce, resulting in a distinctive dish little known outside the region.

DULCE DE PAPAYA

The locally grown papaya is the star of this sweet dessert, in which the orange fruit is transformed into a compote of sorts. It's soaked in water and lime, then boiled with sugar and cinnamon. The resulting syrupy, caramel-coated treat is usually topped with a dollop of whipped cream.

Papadzules

XTABENTÚN

Comparable to Greek ouzo or the Italian sambuca, this thick and aromatic honey-anise liqueur has been distilled in the Yucatán since ancient Maya times. It's usually ordered straight, on the rocks, or as a shot in sparkling water, coffee, or tequila. Casa D'Aristi in Mérida is the largest distiller. Pronounce the name like *shtab-en-TOON*.

MARQUESITAS

Crepes are fried, rolled like a waffle cone, and filled with shredded cheese and jam or caramel in this sweet treat, once the exclusive province of the children of Yucatán nobility. (A marquis nobleman was a *marqués* in Spanish and his daughters were *marquesitas*.) These days, it's a popular street snack. Dutch Edam, incredibly popular in this region of Mexico, almost always makes up the cheese part of the filling.

QUESO RELLENO

The rind of Edam cheese, so popular here, is stuffed with ground beef, olives, raisins, and steamed in a banana leaf to form a messy but tasty dish, one of the peninsula's most popular. What is the Mexican-Dutch cheese connection? Theories abound. Henequen traders likely brought the Dutch cheese back from trips to Europe. It caught on, and Edam has been a favorite in this region of Mexico ever since.

NARANJADA

The Yucatán sour orange (*naranja agria*), an essential ingredient in pibil-style cooking, is mixed with sparkling water and sugar to make this fresh, sour juice—more like a glass of lemonade than your sweet morning OJ. The thick-rind oranges with large seeds originated in Southeast Asia, and the Spanish introduced the fruit to the region in the 16th century.

HUEVOS MOTULEÑOS

Ever ordered huevos rancheros? In the Yucatán variation, eggs are fried, sunny side up, with ham and cheese, and served with a side of black beans, plantains, and tortillas. The dish originated in the town of Motul, east of Mérida, and while the average home serves this dish only on special occasions, it is a morning restaurant staple all over the Yucatán. It promises to fortify you for a morning of sightseeing.

Best Snorkeling and Diving in Cancún and the Riviera Maya

CENOTES

Yucatán is noted for its cenotes, or limestone sinkholes, thought by the Maya to be the gateway to the underworld. The stalactites and stalagmites of the Gran Cenote, near Tulum, make it the most famous. (Ch 3–7)

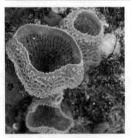

SANTA ROSA WALL

Here is Cozumel's best-known site for experienced divers. The wall here drops steeply and the normally mild current can change at a moment's notice. The reward for braving the strong conditions is the sight of sea turtles and grouper swimming along with you among caves and tunnels. (Ch. 6)

MANCHONES

Off the southwest coast of Isla Mujeres lies this dive site known for its coral reef and a sunken one-ton bronze cross (Cruz de la Bahia) that has spurred new coral growth. Shallow conditions make this one of the area's best locations for beginning divers and snorkelers. (Ch. 4)

PALANCAR REEF

Calm waters, terrific visibility, and proximity to Cozumel make this the Yucatán's ultimate wall dive for beginners. Eagle rays and nurse sharks are among the astounding variety of marine life that hides in the colorful coral reef's cracks, crevices, and tunnels. "Reefs" plural is a better way to describe Palancar, since there are technically four sectors, named "gardens," "caves," "bricks," and "horseshoe." (Ch. 6)

COLUMBIA REEF

Grouper, sea turtles, eagle rays, and barracuda populate this sector of reef and its canyons, ravines, and tall coral "pillars." The site, off the southwest coast of Cozumel, has two sections designated "Colombia Shallow" and "Colombia Deep." Both are best suited for experienced divers, and they offer some of the best conditions for underwater photography. (Ch. 6)

TORMENTOS REEF

The brightly colored section of coral reef here makes a stunning backdrop for underwater photography. Conditions are occasionally good for beginners, but most dive outfitters regard Tormentos as an intermediate dive, thanks to sudden changes in current. Barracuda, nurse sharks, and angelfish make up the underwater life you'll see here. (Ch. 6)

Museo Subacuático de Arte

PARAÍSO REEF

Another great beginner dive, especially for first-time night divers, "Paradise Reef" has two coral ridges off the west coast of Cozumel. Its crystal-clear waters are known to teem with angelfish, sea eels, and yellow rays. The shallower north ridge provides optimal conditions for beginners. (Ch. 6)

ISLA CONTOY

Experienced divers won't want to miss the Cave of the Sleeping Sharks at this island 20 miles north of Isla Mujeres. Here, at 150 feet, you can see the otherwise dangerous creatures "dozing" in a state of relaxed nonaggression. From June to mid-September, divers and snorkelers can swim with docile whale sharks, which can grow up to 50 feet in length. Manta rays, lobster, and barracuda round out Contoy's offerings. (Ch. 4)

MUSEO SUBACUÁTICO DE ARTE

Unusual underwater sculptures populate this art gallery's three installations, two near Cancún and one off the coast of Isla Mujeres. The sculptures, the most whimsical of which is a life-size VW Beetle, form an artificial reef that attracts marine life. Not into diving or snorkeling? The works are in shallow enough water that you can also see them clearly from glass-bottom boats. (Ch. 4)

PARED VERDE

One of the healthiest sections of reef in the region lies off Playa del Carmen and is home to lobsters, king crabs, and sting rays. The medium to strong current here makes the "Green Wall" a site for advanced divers only. (Ch. 5)

Day Trips Around Cancún and the Riviera Maya

Cancún might have powdery white sands, legendary nightlife, and some of the most luxurious resorts in Mexico, but you're missing out if you don't ditch the pool and the piña coladas for a day trip or two while you're in the region. Whether you're looking to relax on a Caribbean island—there are plenty to choose from—travel back in time at one of the area's many Maya ruins, or make a splash in a freshwater cenote, here are 10 day trips from Cancún you should consider.

MAYA RUINS

Chichén Itzá is by far the most well-known and popular of the Maya ruins within day-trip distance from Cancún. But is this iconic New Wonder of the World the best destination for archaeology buffs? Perhaps. As long as you get there before the busloads of tourists descend for the day, that is. If you want a quieter experience though, don't overlook Cobá. At this writing, climbing pyramids is prohibited at all Maya sites, a wise decision, we think, that preserves both your safety and the ruins' structural integrity.

TULUM

Long since overtaken by North American weekenders and Instagram influencers, Tulum is no longer the somewhat secret paradise it once was, but the white sand and palapas remain. Now thronged with uber-exclusive restaurants, jungle cocktail bars, and boutique hotels, Tulum is an ideal day trip if you're looking for somewhere with a distinctly different vibe to Cancún. Stop by the beaches, clifftop ruins and take a detour to the cool waters of nearby cenotes if you start to feel the heat.

CENOTES

Speaking of cenotes, if you're sick of the salty ocean (remember: while Cancún's beaches look beautiful, they often harbor a nasty undertow) take a trip to some cenotes. These freshwater sinkholes which were sacred to the Maya speckle the peninsula, so you won't have trouble finding a good one and the entrance fees are usually well under $10 per person. One of the region's most popular is the Gran Cenote, just outside Tulum, although Zazil-Ha, with its aquamarine waters and the made-for-Instagram appeal is a closer-to-Cancún alternative.

VALLADOLID

When the party atmosphere of Cancún all gets just too much, take a break in the colonial city of Valladolid. There, you'll find 16th-century convents, super snackable street foods (be sure to seek out the chocolate and cheese-filled marquesita) and two cenotes in which to cool off— Cenote Zaci and the recently discovered Cenote Chukum-Ha (they really are everywhere).

SIAN KA'AN BIOSPHERE RESERVE

There are close to 50 Protected Biosphere Reserves in Mexico and Sian Ka'an in Quintana Roo is widely considered to be one of the best. (As if that wasn't enough, it was also one of the first UNESCO-recognized attractions in the country.) Knotted with mangroves and dotted with lagoons, Sian Ka'an is home to dense jungles, diverse creatures, and even archaeological ruins. At three and a half hours from Cancún, it's not the most convenient day trip, but it's worth the effort.

RÍO LAGARTOS BIOSPHERE RESERVE

Made famous a few years ago thanks to the cotton-candy pink waters of Los Colorados, the Río Lagartos Biosphere Reserve is another striking natural attraction just over three hours outside of Cancún. Although you can no longer swim in them, the pink waters are what often draw people but the incredible diversity of the Biosphere Reserve itself is where the real appeal lies. Look out for the flamboyant flamingos in particular.

THE CARIBBEAN ISLANDS

Flee the mainland and make for a Caribbean island off the coast of Cancún. Isla Holbox, known for its laidback, desert island vibes is a great place to swim with whale sharks from May to September, while Cozumel is a popular cruise-ship stop and still one of the top diving destinations in the country. Over on Isla Mujeres—which is just a 20-minute ferry ride from Cancún—you'll find glorious beaches and plenty of opportunities to snorkel with sea turtles. Finally, the tiny Isla Contoy (which only accepts 200 visitors a day) is a haven for bird watchers.

PLAYA DEL CARMEN

When discussing vacations in Quintana Roo, you'll often hear people debating whether to go to Cancún or Playa del Carmen, but why not do both? Just one hour apart from one another, these two cities are a little like eyebrows—sisters, not twins. While Cancún has better nightlife and beaches, Playa is great for shopping and has a more Mexican feel to it. Stroll Quinta Avenida, hang out on Playacar, and catch a Voladores de Papantla performance in Parque Fundadores.

FISHING VILLAGES

If you remain unmoved by the bright lights of Playa del Carmen, ambivalent in the face of Tulum and reluctant to move inland for your Cancún day trip, consider a visit to one of the region's small(er) coastal towns: Akumal and Puerto Morelos. The former is probably best known for sea turtles, but you can also enjoy a quiet waterfront lunch, windsurfing lessons, and even fishing excursions. Meanwhile, Puerto Morelos is a tranquil gateway to the Mesoamerican Barrier Reef with several nearby cenotes, including the lush Verde Lucero.

ECO THEME PARKS

If you're traveling with children (or just remain young at heart), the trio of water parks which surround Cancún—Xel Há, Xcaret, and Xplor—are unmissable. Visit one or all three during your vacation but remember that they're all between one and one and a half hours away from Cancún and share similar attractions—think freshwater rivers, cenotes, jungle walkways, and massive evening spectaculars. However, true adrenaline chasers may prefer Xplor, families will probably be best suited to Xcaret, and Xel-Há is all about the water activities.

Most Romantic Experiences in Cancún

JOURNEY ALONG THE RÍO SECRETO

Everyone knows secret underground rivers are the very essence of romance. Okay, maybe not. But they are pretty spectacular and make for a cool place to explore alongside your partner while in Cancún. Ideal for adventurous couples, Río Secreto—where you can admire sparkling minerals and dramatic stalactites before biking, hiking, and swimming along the length of this hidden natural phenomenon—offers a more intimate experience than places like Xcaret and Xel-Há.

HANG OUT AT A BEACH CLUB

Get out of the resort for the day and hang out at one of Cancún's many beach clubs. Mandala Beach Club—attached to the popular Mandala nightclub—is a favorite of fun-loving friends and couples alike. Grab a poolside lounger and enjoy the live DJ sets, sleek feel, and beachfront pools. Alternatively, for a more low-key, romantic beach club experience, head to Coco's Beach Club. There, snag a private beach bed (or upgrade to the VIP-only lounge) and make the most of the inventive cocktails and refreshing seafood dishes as you admire the ocean views.

GIVE BOB SNORKELING A GO

See the best of the underwater world off the coast of Cancún during a BOB experience. The lovechild of a scuba suit and a submarine, BOBs—also known as breathing observation bubbles—allow you to submerge and scoot around below water sans all the faff of actual scuba diving, while getting more up-close-and-personal with the Cancún marine life than you could while snorkeling.

TAKE A ROMANTIC DINNER CRUISE

You can't go wrong with a sunset dinner cruise when on a romantic vacation for two and Cancún has a wealth of evening sailing options for loved-up holidaymakers. Take a Columbus Lobster Dinner Cruise on the Nichupte Lagoon, listen to live music, and make metaphorical heart eyes at your beloved as you enjoy your titular lobster dinner and drinks.

ESCAPE THE CROWDS ON A CARIBBEAN ISLAND

There's little point traveling to Cancún just to stay in Cancún the whole time, so definitely venture to one of the nearby Caribbean islands. While popular Isla Mujeres has more of a family-friendly vibe, Isla Holbox—toward the tip of the Yucatán Peninsula—is the ideal place for an intimate day trip for two. Car-free and still hovering under the radar of your average traveler, Holbox is a ready-made romantic idyll where you can sip coconut water and even swim with whale sharks. Meanwhile, animal-loving couples shouldn't pass up the opportunity to visit Isla Contoy, a protected national park which only permits access to 200 travelers per day.

INDULGE IN A COUPLES SPA TREATMENT

If you can't relax while on vacation with your significant other, then when can you? In Cancún, home to some of the best spas in Mexico, take the time to pamper yourself with facials, hydrotherapy circuits, and full-body massages alongside your partner. While there are plenty of places to choose from—your resort may even have its own onsite spa—the private couples' suites at Nizuc Spa are incredibly intimate, as are the spa's other state-of-the-art facilities. Similarly, Le Blanc Spa is a treat for fans of a good massage—opt for the relaxing Aroma Essence Massage.

DINE IN STYLE OVERLOOKING THE WATERFRONT

Cancún may not have the culinary reputation of Mexico City but the capital of Quintana Roo has no shortage of fine-dining establishments and waterfront restaurants at which lovestruck holidaymakers can indulge. Go all out with lobster everything overlooking the Nichupte Lagoon at Lorenzillo's, an iconic Cancún restaurant which specializes in lobster or—if you're more of an equal opportunity seafood enthusiast—visit Fred's House instead. Prefer turf to surf? Tuck into Kobe sliders at Harry's Prime Steakhouse.

TAKE A DIP IN A CENOTE

You can't come to Cancún without visiting a cenote (or two, or three). These freshwater natural sinkholes revered by the Maya are found across the Peninsula, although you'll need to travel outside Cancún proper to find some of the best and most easily accessible. Skip the more popular and family-friendly cenotes—such as Cenote Azul and the Gran Cenote–unless you enjoy being splashed by errant toddlers. Instead, combine a trip to Chichén Itzá with a stop at the nearby Cenote Yokdzonot or stay (slightly) closer to Cancún at Cenote Yalahau.

CATCH A SUNSET OVER THE LAGOON

A pesky problem with vacationing on the eastern coastline of Mexico is that the sun sets in the west. Simply put, you can only enjoy a Cancún sunset overlooking the Nichupte Lagoon rather than the Caribbean ocean. Don't let that deter you though—make a well-timed booking at one of the many waterfront restaurants and enjoy dinner as the sun goes down. And what if you and your partner are early risers? Well then, make your way down to the beach before the rest of Cancún shakes off its hangover and snatch a rare moment of tranquility as the sun comes up over the sea.

LEARN TO DANCE AT GRAND MAMBO CAFÉ

Few dances are quite as seductive as a well-practiced bachata and even salsa can get steamy when done properly. So, before heading out to one of the biggest clubs in Cancún, dedicate an hour or two to picking up the basics of merengue, salsa, or bachata at the Grand Mambo Café during your romantic couples-only vacation. The live music from Wednesday to Saturday should help you find your rhythm, and a shot of tequila will probably help too.

Weddings and Honeymoons

Imagine exchanging vows on a white sandy beach against a backdrop of swaying palms and the turquoise waters of the Caribbean. Your dream wedding can become a reality as long as you know the necessary steps to take when saying "I do" in Mexico.

All marriage in Mexico is civil and must be performed by a judge from the state Oficina de Registro Civil (Civil Registry Office). You may hold a religious wedding or a ceremony of your own design, but without the judge, it won't be legal. You can take care of the legalities at the registry office, or the judge can come to your ceremony. The judge's formalities will be fixed and will be in Spanish, although an interpreter can be supplied. Quintana Roo and Campeche states recognize same-sex marriage; Yucatán state does not.

Couples need to bring passports, original birth certificates, tourist cards, and results of blood tests taken in Mexico 14 days before the wedding. Most clinics charge MX$3,000 per couple for the required RPR, HIV, and blood-type tests. A judge's fee of MX$8,000 must be paid in advance, and, if all documents are not presented, the judge will not perform the ceremony.

You also must have four witnesses at the ceremony, all of whom must be over 18 and have passports. If either of the couple was previously married, the divorce decree or death certificate of the former spouse must be translated into Spanish and notarized. In such cases, you must wait a full year to remarry. There is no way around this arcane requirement, designed to ensure no pregnancy lingers from a prior marriage. It doesn't matter if you are 25 or 75.

BEAUTIFUL BACKDROPS

The Yucatán Peninsula is one of the most sought-after spots for destination weddings. In fact, this growing trend in beachside nuptials has increased by 200% in the last decade. It's no wonder: the Caribbean coast not only makes for an incredible backdrop, but it's also a great way to combine a wedding and honeymoon.

Surprisingly, exchanging vows in Mexico can be much cheaper than a traditional wedding back home. Some smaller hotels can organize beautiful ceremonies, including food and music, for under $5,000. If you book your entire wedding party at the hotel, special rates and upgrades are generally available, and you can have the entire place to yourselves. Between May and November, rates are at their lowest, but you might end up with a soggy ceremony, especially during prime hurricane period—July through September.

There are dozens of wedding planners and professional photographers in Cancún, Cozumel, Isla Mujeres, Mérida, and Playa del Carmen. Whether you choose a white sandy beach in Cozumel or a colorful hacienda in Mérida, there's no shortage of ceremony settings for your big day.

HONEYMOONS

The peninsula's countless treasures, ranging from Maya ruins to fishing villages, make it a haven for honeymooners. Beach-bound newlyweds have plenty of resort options along the Riviera Maya, many of which have luxury spas with treatments for two. Ideal for both weddings and honeymoons, Tulum offers ancient ruins, beautiful beaches, and dozens of eco-lodges willing to host simple weddings with vegetarian buffets and yoga classes between events.

Kids and Families

The Yucatán Peninsula has plenty of activities for the entire family. The warm Caribbean waters are ideal for water sports such as swimming, snorkeling, and kayaking, and some areas even have roped-off sections designated for children. If you're vacationing in Cancún, beaches facing Bahía de Mujeres tend to have calmer waters and softer sand than those facing the Caribbean. Farther out, there may be undertows or riptides, so take note of warning signs and colored flags posted daily.

KID-FRIENDLY ACTIVITIES

For teens, there are adrenaline-pumping water activities like Jet Skiing, banana boat rides, parasailing, and diving. Smaller children may prefer interactive programs like those available at Dolphin Discovery, with locations in Isla Mujeres, Cozumel, Playa del Carmen, Costa Maya, Akumal, and Puerto Aventuras; the tour includes encounters with manatees and sea lions, plus a chance to swim with the dolphins.

For parents wanting to introduce their children to history, combine a tour of the Tulum ruins with a day at the beach, or opt for the Cobá ruins, where your entire family can explore jungle trails by mountain bike. Cancún's all-inclusive resorts have plenty to keep the kids busy, including swimming pools, children's programs, and on-site water sports. Nearby La Isla Shopping Village has an interactive aquarium. Also located in Zona Hotelera is Plaza Kukulcán, an upscale mall with a food court and play area on the second floor. In the Riviera Maya, Joyà by Cirque du Soleil is a whimsical show filled with entertainment and acrobatics for the entire family.

Isla Mujeres is home to Garrafón Natural Park, where you can go snorkeling, swimming, hiking, or biking. To blend nature and education, visit the island's turtle farm, where you can see rescued turtle hatchlings.

CHOOSING A DESTINATION

Just 16 km (10 miles) south of Tulum, the Reserva de la Biósfera Sian Ka'an has hundreds of species of wildlife in their freshwater lagoons, mangrove swamps, and tropical forests. The beaches here are excellent for swimming, snorkeling, and camping.

The colorful city of Mérida has folkloric shows, free concerts, and open-air markets where local crafts are sold. South of Mérida are the impressive Grutas de Loltún, one of the largest cave systems on the Yucatán Peninsula.

The quaint fishing villages of Puerto Morelos and Puerto Aventuras are excellent for families and close to the 250-acre ecological theme park, Xcaret. Here families can experience a butterfly pavilion, aviary, and dozens of water activities. Catering to adventure seekers, the neighboring Xplor lets you swim in a stalactite river, ride in an amphibious vehicle, or soar across the park on 14 zip lines. At the entrance to Puerto Morelos is Croco Cun, an animal farm where you can feed monkeys and hold baby crocodiles.

To escape the heat, families can visit Xel-Há (the natural aquarium park) or take a dip in one of the hundreds of cenotes that dot the peninsula. These freshwater pools are ideal for snorkeling and swimming.

The People of the Yucatán Peninsula

The Maya people, whose ancient ruins have made the Yucatán a world-renowned attraction, also make up the bulk of the peninsula's population.

The Maya are the single largest indigenous group on the entire North American continent. Although predominantly located in Yucatán state, members of this group have also settled in other Mexican states such as Campeche, Quintana Roo, Tabasco, and Chiapas. Outside Mexico, the Maya can be found in Guatemala, Belize, Honduras, and El Salvador. Their total population is estimated at about 6 million, with 1.2 million living on the Yucatán Peninsula. Linguists have associated 32 distinct indigenous languages among the Maya. Most of the Maya in this area speak "Yucatec Maya" and might be able to use Spanish only as a second language. While neighboring Guatemala makes a big deal of identifying its Maya population by different ethnic subdivisions, Mexico's corresponding population typically self-identifies as simply "Maya." Guatemala's program of genocide against its highland indigenous population in the 1980s caused the flight of much of its Maya population to Mexico and resulted in an increased number of non-Yucatec speakers.

The Maya are rightfully proud of their history, which dates back to a period immediately following the rise of the Olmec culture. After the fall of the Olmecs, the Maya rose to power and settled in the Yucatán Peninsula, where they developed several city-states including that of Chichén Itzá. Mayan architecture, much of it ceremonial in nature, has been archaeologically classified as dating back some 3,000 years. Well-preserved hieroglyphics found in the Yucatán trace the presence of the Maya to 200 BC or before. More than 100 ancient Maya ruins still exist today, many of them drawing travelers from around the world to the Yucatán each year.

The Spanish fought to colonize the Yucatán well into the 1500s, achieving victory by the middle of that century. But long before the Spanish arrived, the once-powerful Mayan civilization was already in decline, and no one really knows why—possibly disease, war, or famine. But while historians speak of the "waning" of Mayan society, that pertains only to the military power it once wielded over Mesoamerica. The Maya have evolved and adapted to modern civilization.

The Maya continue to blend the elements of their ancient worship practices and rituals (minus the live sacrifice) with more contemporary religious practices. While Catholicism still dominates the Yucatán Peninsula as it does elsewhere in the country, this is a less Catholic region of Mexico, with evangelical and Pentacostal denominations having made big inroads in the Maya population. Many people here still wear traditional clothing, and construct the oblong, thatch-roof houses of their forebears. The Mayan passion to preserve its long history can be seen in the highly valued handicrafts that they create with the same skill and artistry as their ancestors. We recommend any excursion that allows you to experience this fascinating history and culture. Even if you're ensconced at a flashy beach resort, Mayan villages and ruins are never far away.

Chapter 2

TRAVEL SMART

Updated by
Jeffrey Van Fleet

★ **MAJOR CITIES:**
Cancún, Playa del Carmen, Mérida

♛ **POPULATION:**
Quintana Roo state 1.86 million; Yucatán state 2.32 million

💬 **LANGUAGE:**
Spanish; English spoken in tourism industry

$ **CURRENCY:**
Peso

☎ **COUNTRY CODE:**
52

⚠ **EMERGENCIES:**
911

🚗 **DRIVING:**
On the right

⚡ **ELECTRICITY:**
120–220 v/60 cycles; plugs have two or three rectangular prongs

🕐 **TIME:**
Quintana Roo state: winter, same as New York; summer 1 hour behind New York. Yucatán: 1 hour behind New York

🌐 **WEB RESOURCES:**
www.visitmexico.com

✈ **AIRPORT:**
Cancún (CUN), Cozumel (CZM), Mérida (MID)

Know Before You Go

Is it safe? Can you drink the water? Do you need special documents to enter the country? You may have a few questions before your trip to Mexico. We've got answers and a few insider tips to help you make the most of your visit, so you can rest easy in paradise.

HEED THE DOCUMENTS YOU NEED TO ENTER (AND LEAVE) THE COUNTRY.

You must have a valid passport to enter Mexico and to reenter the United States. Before landing in Mexico, you'll be given an FMM (tourist permit) to be stamped at immigration. This allows you to stay in the country for 180 days. Keep this card safe, because you'll need to present it on departure. If you lose your FMM card (or overstay your time), you will need to visit an immigration office and pay a fine before leaving the country.

IT'S A CINCH TO GET AROUND.

It's relatively easy to travel around the Yucatán, thanks to improved roadways and infrastructure. Mexico's bus system is an excellent way to travel around the country. Deluxe buses are more expensive, but have air-conditioning, reclining seats, movies, and fewer stops. Intercity transportation (used mainly by locals) is extremely reliable, and a great way to experience Mexican culture. Compared to other parts of Mexico, the roads in the Yucatán Peninsula are safe, flat, and well maintained. The main highway between Cancún and Belize, known as Carretera 307, is clearly marked and well paved. Toll road 180D runs between Cancún and Mérida—you can do it in four hours—and is by far your safest, fastest east–west option. Even most secondary roads are in decent shape, but tend to get pitted with potholes during and after the rainy season. Only in remote areas like Punta Allen will you find major potholes. Throughout the peninsula, beware of unmarked *topes* (speed bumps) that can leave you airborne. Although road conditions have improved tremendously, avoid driving at night, since most areas lack street lighting.

YOU MUST TAKE THE CAR INSURANCE.

Regardless of what coverage you have from your credit card or travel insurance, you must (by law) have additional Mexican auto insurance to rent a car. Average daily insurance rates start around $45, which is often more than the daily rental fee if you happened to find a good deal online. When renting a car, make sure that your insurance coverage includes an attorney and claims adjusters who will come to the scene of an accident.

CONSIDER AN ALL-INCLUSIVE PACKAGE.

Cancún and the Riviera Maya pioneered the all-inclusive concept in Mexico. Fly in planeloads of visitors for a week or two, house them at a flashy beach resort, throw in all (or most) of their food and drink, and provide them with all the activities they could desire. (Rest assured that if you seek a relaxing vacation, you can eschew your lodging's activities.) The resorts here do it well and they roll everything into a fair price. You'll find even the toniest Cancún beach property more reasonably priced than comparable facilities on a Caribbean island. We do recommend getting off the resort a time or two during your stay and sampling the region's many offerings.

BUT OTHER PLACES, DO IT À LA CARTE.

The farther you get from the beach, the scarcer the all-inclusive options become, and that's okay too. Mérida, Valladolid, Campeche, and the towns of the peninsula are the province of small but stylish colonial-era inns that once served as palaces, convents, and haciendas.

Something lurks behind those walls and the gates; it takes peering inside to see the sumptuous rooms and lovely gardens. Rates include breakfast, but rarely other meals. Check out our local recommendations for lunch and dinner.

DON'T FORGET TO PAY THE VISITAX.

Quintana Roo state debuted a new visitor tax in 2021. All travelers to the state four years and over must pay MX$224 (approximately US$11). You may pay online (⊕ www.visitax.gob.mx) prior to arrival or during your stay, but definitely by the time pass through passport exit control on departure at the airport.

EXPAND YOUR DEFINITION OF MEXICAN FOOD.

Tacos, enchiladas, fajitas, nachos, burritos...they're all here for your dining pleasure, but Yucatecan cooks will give you a whole new notion of what south-of-the-border cuisine looks like and tastes like. Your morning *huevos rancheros* give way here to *huevos motuleños*, eggs with ham and cheese, black beans and plantains. *Pibil*-style cooking, a Mayan specialty, bakes chicken (*pollo*) or pork (*cochinita*) in an oven or casserole with fruits and spices. Top off your evening with a standard Mexican tequila, but fortify it with a dash of *xtabentún*, a honey-anise liqueur distilled here since ancient Mayan times.

YOU SHOULD CARRY SOME CASH.

Outside of remote areas like Xcalak and Mahahual, most tourist-oriented businesses accept Visa and Master-Card, but some places charge 5% to 10% more for credit-card payments to help offset high processing fees. It's always a good idea to have at least some cash on hand. Remember: if you plan to bargain in a traditional market, cash gives you better leverage. A merchant likely won't give you a price break if you wish to pay by card. Most ATMs in Mexico accept U.S. credit and debit cards. Before your trip, make sure your PIN has only four numbers, since ATMs in Mexico do not recognize more digits. Foreign transaction fees can be high, as much as MX$150 per withdrawal.

THE "IS MEXICO SAFE?" QUESTION DOESN'T HAVE AN EASY ANSWER.

We've all heard the accounts of Mexico's drug-cartel violence. They've put once-popular travel spots in the northern part of the country off limits, and they have even affected travel to storied destinations such as Acapulco. The occasional drug-related killing grabs headlines here, but the Yucatán has largely been spared such problems and remains one of the safest regions of the country. Let common sense be your guide: leave the flashy jewelry at home, use ATMs during the day, store valuables in hotel safes, keep an eye on your

belongings, watch your drink in public, and avoid Cancún's center city late at night. You should have a safe and enjoyable time here.

MEXICO AND COVID-19

Mexico was praised and panned for its official, self-described "non-coercive" approach to tourism during the pandemic. Land borders closed to all but essential travel for extensive periods in 2020 and 2021. Air travel, albeit lessened by lower demand, never stopped and was never restricted. The country has yet to require COVID testing or quarantines of visitors. You'll see nothing more than a temperature check and the filling-out of a health questionnaire on arrival. The hotel industry itself *has* stepped up to the plate with appropriate safety measures.

Helpful Phrases in Spanish

BASICS

Hello	Hola	**oh**-lah
Yes/no	Sí/no	see/no
Please	Por favor	pore fah-**vore**
May I?	¿Puedo?	**Pweh**-doh
Thank you	Gracias	**Grah**-see-as
You're welcome	De nada	day **nah**-dah
I'm sorry	Lo siento	lo see-**en**-toh
Good morning!	¡Buenos días!	**bway**-nohs **dee**-ahs
Good evening!	¡Buenas tardes! (after 2pm)	**bway**-nahs-**tar**-dess
	¡Buenas noches! (after 8pm)	**bway**-nahs **no**-chess
Good-bye!	¡Adiós!/¡Hasta luego!	ah-dee-**ohss/ah**-stah **lwe**-go
Mr./Mrs.	Señor/Señora	sen-**yor**/sen-**yohr**-ah
Miss	Señorita	sen-yo-**ree**-tah
Pleased to meet you	Mucho gusto	**moo**-cho **goose**-toh
How are you?	¿Cómo estás?	**koh**-moh ehs-**tahs**

NUMBERS

one	un, uno	oon, **oo**-no
two	dos	dos
three	tres	tress
four	cuatro	**kwah**-tro
five	cinco	**sink**-oh
six	seis	saice
seven	siete	see-**et**-eh
eight	ocho	**o**-cho
nine	nueve	new-**eh**-vey
ten	diez	dee-**es**
eleven	once	**ohn**-seh
twelve	doce	**doh**-seh
thirteen	trece	**treh**-seh
fourteen	catorce	ka-**tohr**-seh
fifteen	quince	**keen**-seh
sixteen	dieciséis	dee-es-ee-**saice**
seventeen	diecisiete	dee-**es**-ee-see-**et**-eh
eighteen	dieciocho	dee-**es**-ee-**o**-cho
nineteen	diecinueve	dee-**es**-ee-new-**ev**-eh
twenty	veinte	**vain**-teh
twenty-one	veintiuno	**vain**-te-**oo**-noh
thirty	treinta	**train**-tah
forty	cuarenta	kwah-**ren**-tah
fifty	cincuenta	seen-**kwen**-tah
sixty	sesenta	sess-**en**-tah
seventy	setenta	set-**en**-tah
eighty	ochenta	oh-**chen**-tah
ninety	noventa	no-**ven**-tah
one hundred	cien	see-**en**
one thousand	mil	meel
one million	un millón	oon meel-**yohn**

COLORS

black	negro	**neh**-groh
blue	azul	ah-**sool**
brown	café	kah-**fehg**
green	verde	**ver**-deh
orange	naranja	na-**rahn**-hah
red	rojo	**roh**-hoh
white	blanco	**blahn**-koh
yellow	amarillo	ah-mah-**ree**-yoh

DAYS OF THE WEEK

Sunday	domingo	doe-**meen**-goh
Monday	lunes	**loo**-ness
Tuesday	martes	**mahr**-tess
Wednesday	miércoles	me-**air**-koh-less
Thursday	jueves	hoo-**ev**-ess
Friday	viernes	vee-**air**-ness
Saturday	sábado	**sah**-bah-doh

MONTHS

January	enero	eh-**neh**-roh
February	febrero	feh-**breh**-roh
March	marzo	**mahr**-soh
April	abril	ah-**breel**
May	mayo	**my**-oh
June	junio	**hoo**-nee-oh
July	julio	**hoo**-lee-yoh
August	agosto	ah-**ghost**-toh
September	septiembre	sep-tee-**em**-breh
October	octubre	oak-**too**-breh
November	noviembre	no-vee-**em**-breh
December	diciembre	dee-see-**em**-breh

USEFUL WORDS AND PHRASES

Do you speak English?	¿Habla Inglés?	**ah**-blah in-**glehs**
I don't speak Spanish.	No hablo español	no **ah**-bloh es-pahn-**yol**
I don't understand.	No entiendo	no en-tee-**en**-doh
I understand.	Entiendo	en-tee-**en**-doh
I don't know.	No sé	no **seh**
I'm American.	Soy americano (americana)	soy ah-meh-ree-**kah**-no (ah-meh-ree-**kah**-nah)
What's your name?	¿Cómo se llama?	koh-mo seh **yah**-mah
My name is . . .	Me llamo . . .	may **yah**-moh
What time is it?	¿Qué hora es?	keh **o**-rah es
How?	¿Cómo?	**koh**-mo
When?	¿Cuándo?	**kwahn**-doh
Yesterday	Ayer	ah-**yehr**
Today	hoy	oy
Tomorrow	mañana	mahn-**yah**-nah
Tonight	Esta noche	es-tah **no**-cheh
What?	¿Qué?	keh

What is it?	¿Qué es esto?	keh es **es**-toh
Why?	¿Por qué?	pore **keh**
Who?	¿Quién?	kee-**yen**
Where is . . .	¿Dónde está . . .	**dohn**-deh es-**tah**
. . . the bus station?	la central de autobuses?	lah sehn-**trahl** deh ow-toh-**boo**-sehs
. . . the subway station?	estación de metro	la es-ta-see-**on** del **meh**-tro
. . . the bus stop?	la parada del autobus?	la pah-**rah**-dah del ow-toh-**boos**
. . . the terminal? (airport)	el aeropuerto	el air-oh-**pwar**-toh
. . . the post office?	la oficina de correos?	la oh-fee-**see**- nah deh koh-**rreh**-os
. . . the bank?	el banco?	el **bahn**-koh
. . . the hotel?	el hotel?	el oh-**tel**
. . . the museum?	el museo?	el moo-**seh**-oh
. . . the hospital?	el hospital?	el ohss-pee-**tal**
. . . the elevator?	el elevador?	ehl eh-leh-bah-**dohr**
Where are the restrooms?	el baño?	el **bahn**-yoh
Here/there	Aquí/allí	ah-**key**/ah-**yee**
Open/closed	Abierto/cerrado	ah-bee-**er**-toh/ ser-**ah**-doh
Left/right	Izquierda/derecha	iss-key-**eh**-dah/ dare-**eh**-chah
Is it near?	¿Está cerca?	es-**tah** sehr-kah
Is it far?	¿Está lejos?	es-**tah leh**-hoss
I'd like . . .	Quisiera . . .	kee-see-**ehr**-ah
. . . a room	un cuarto/una habitación	oon **kwahr**-toh/**oo**-nah ah-bee-tah-see-**on**
. . . the key	la llave	lah **yah**-veh
. . . a newspaper	un periódico	oon pehr-ee-**oh**- dee-koh
. . . a stamp	un sello de correo	oon **seh**-yo deh korr-**eh**-oh
I'd like to buy . . .	Quisiera comprar . . .	kee-see-**ehr**-ah kohm-**prahr**
. . . soap	jabón	hah-**bohn**
. . . suntan lotion	bronceador	brohn-seh-ah-**dohr**
. . . envelopes	sobres	so-brehs
. . . writing paper	papel	pah-**pel**
. . . a postcard	una postal	oo-nah pohs-**tahl**
. . . a ticket	un billete (travel)	oon bee-**yee**-teh
	una entrada (concert etc.)	oona en-**trah**-dah
How much is it?	¿Cuánto cuesta?	**kwahn**-toh **kwes**-tah
It's expensive/ cheap	Es caro/barato	es **kah**-roh/ bah-**rah**-toh
A little/a lot	Un poquito/mucho	oon poh-**kee**-toh/ **moo**-choh
More/less	Más/menos	mahss/**men**-ohss
Enough/too (much)	Suficiente/	soo-fee-see-**en**-teh/
I am ill/sick	Estoy enfermo(a)	es-**toy** en-**fehr**-moh(mah)

Call a doctor	Llame a un medico	**ya**-meh ah oon **med**-ee-koh
Help!	Ayuda	ah-**yoo**-dah
Stop!	Pare	**pah**-reh

DINING OUT

I'd like to reserve a table . . .	Quisiera reservar una mesa . . .	kee-**syeh**-rah rreh-sehr-**bahr oo**-nah **meh**-sah . . .
. . . for two people.	para dos personas.	**pah**-rah dohs pehr-**soh**-nahs
. . . for this evening.	para esta noche.	**pah**-rah **ehs**-tah **noh**-cheh
. . . for 8 PM	para las ocho de la noche.	**pah**-rah lahs **oh**-choh deh lah **noh**-cheh
A bottle of . . .	Una botella de . . .	**oo**-nah bo-**teh**-yah deh
A cup of . . .	Una taza de . . .	**oo**-nah **tah**-sah deh
A glass of . . .	Un vaso (water, soda, etc.) de...	oon **vah**-so deh
	Una copa (wine, spirits, etc.) de...	oona **coh**-pah deh
Bill/check	La cuenta	lah **kwen**-tah
Bread	Pan	pahn
Breakfast	El desayuno	el deh-sah-**yoon**-oh
Butter	mantequilla	man-teh-**kee**-yah
Coffee	Café	kah-**feh**
Dinner	La cena	lah **seh**-nah
Fork	tenedor	ten-eh-**dor**
I don't eat meat	No como carne	noh koh-moh **kahr**-neh
I cannot eat . . .	No puedo comer . . .	noh **pweh**-doh koh-**mehr**
I'd like to order . . .	Quiero pedir . . .	**kee**-yehr-oh peh-**deer**
I'd like . . .	Me gustaría . . .	Meh goo-stah-**ee**-ah
I'm hungry/thirsty	Tengo hambre/sed	**Tehn**-goh **hahm**-breh/seth
Is service/the tip included?	¿Está incluida la propina?	es-**tah** in-cloo-**ee**-dah lah pro-**pee**-nah
Knife	cuchillo	koo-**chee**-yo
Lunch	La comida	lah koh-**mee**-dah
Menu	La carta, el menú	lah **cart**-ah, el **meh**-noo
Napkin	servilleta	sehr-vee-**yet**-ah
Pepper	pimienta	pee-mee-**en**-tah
Plate	plato	
Please give me . . .	Me da por favor . . .	meh dah pohr fah-**bohr**
Salt	sal	sahl
Spoon	cuchara	koo-**chah**-rah
Sugar	ázucar	ah-**su**-kar
Tea	té	teh
Water	agua	ah-**gwah**
Wine	vino	**vee**-noh

Getting Here and Around

Air

Cancún is 4½ hours from New York and Chicago, 5 hours from Los Angeles, 3 hours from Dallas, and 2 hours from Miami. Flights to Cozumel and Mérida are comparable in length, but many fewer in number. There are direct flights to Cancún from hub airports such as New York, Newark, Boston, Washington, D.C., Houston, Dallas, Miami, Chicago, Los Angeles, Orlando, Fort Lauderdale, Charlotte, Phoenix, Atlanta, and Toronto. You can reach it from other locales on connecting flights; some arrive via Mexico City, where you must pass through immigration and customs before transferring to a domestic flight to Cancún.

Charter flights, especially those leaving from Cancún, are notorious for last-minute changes. Be sure to ask for an updated telephone number from your charter company before you leave, so you can verify departures times. Most recommend that you call within 48 hours of departure. Commercial airlines usually have more dependable departure times; any changes are usually due to weather conditions.

AIRPORTS

The Yucatán Peninsula has international airports in Cancún, Mérida, and Cozumel. Domestic airports are in Campeche and Chetumal.

The Aeropuerto Internacional de Cancún (CUN) is the area's major gateway and offers the best selection of flights and fares. Several North American hubs also offer nonstop flights to the Aeropuerto Internacional de Cozumel (CZM). The inland Aeropuerto Internacional Manuel Crescencio Rejón (MID), in Mérida, is smaller but closer to most major Mayan ruins. Campeche (CPE) and Chetumal (CTM) have very small airports served primarily by domestic carriers.

It's 20 to 30 minutes from the Zona Hotelera to the Cancún airport or from downtown Mérida or Campeche to theirs. Allow 1½ hours from Playa del Carmen to the Cancún airport. The Cozumel airport is less than 10 minutes from downtown Cozumel.

AIRPORT TRANSFERS

As you exit the Cancún airport, transportation operators can be overwhelming as they eagerly wave signs and yell names to arriving passengers. All four terminals have an ADO kiosk (the name of the company) outside selling bus tickets into the city. A bus leaves every hour from the airport to the ADO terminal in downtown Cancún.

It's not uncommon to be told that you just missed the last bus, taxi, or van to your destination. This is actually a ploy to get you to use the transportation company that is "assisting" you. Ask around if you're not entirely sure. Always arrive with small bills for taxi or bus fare; otherwise, you're liable to get ripped off. Check the identification of transportation operators and don't allow anyone to "help" you with your luggage. Many people perform this task on commission for specific transportation companies. Worse yet, they might end up disappearing into the crowd with your baggage.

Some of the major hotels send shuttles to pick up arriving guests; it's worth checking before you arrive at the airport. Private taxis from the airport charge reasonable rates within Cancún. Airport shuttle vans, which charge set rates based on your destination, are another option; however, they sometimes take forever before filling up and getting under way. There are taxi and shuttle desks in the baggage-claim area, just before you exit the terminal. Go to the ones with posted prices, but keep in mind that rates are much higher for last-minute bookings as opposed to prearranged ground transportation reserved online. For round-trip transportation from the airport to the Riviera Maya, it's worth looking for a shuttle service, as a private taxi can be prohibitively expensive. Some can be arranged beforehand by phone or online. Cancún Valet rents per van, rather than per person, for up to 10 passengers, making it a good value for couples, families, and groups. Prices from the airport to the Hotel Zone, Playa del Carmen, and Tulum, as well as intermittent points are reasonable: MX$800 to Cancún (MX$1,400 round-trip) or MX$1,500 to Playa del Carmen (MX$2,700 round-trip), for example. Van Travel charges MX$700 per couple or individual, one way, to the Hotel Zone (MX$1,100 round-trip) or MX$1,200 to Playa del Carmen (MX$2,200 round-trip). Despite their names, anyone may use the services of USA Transfers and Canada Transfers. Both companies get high marks for dependable service. Expect to pay MX$1,000 one way to Cancún's hotel zone and MX$1,900 to Playa del Carmen.

The ride-sharing service Uber operates illegally in Cancún. That status makes it nearly impossible to use to get to and from the airport.

FLIGHTS

International, national, and regional carriers serve the Yucatán Peninsula. The most convenient flight from the United States is nonstop on either a U.S. or Mexican airline. Flying within the Yucatán is neither cost-effective nor time-efficient. Given the additional time needed for check-in, you might as well drive or take a bus to your destination, unless you're continuing on by plane.

Since all the major airlines listed here fly to Cancún—and often have the cheapest and most frequent flights there—it's worthwhile to consider it as a jumping-off

point even if you don't plan on visiting the city. At this writing, more than 450 flights land daily in Cancún. Airlines that serve it include Aeroméxico, Air Canada and Air Canada Rouge, Alaska, American, Delta, Frontier, JetBlue, Southwest, Spirit, United, Viva Aerobús, Volaris, and WestJet. Air Canada Rouge, American, Delta, Frontier, Southwest, United, Volaris, and WestJet also fly to Cozumel. Aeroméxico, American, United, Viva Aerobús, and Volaris fly to Mérida. Mayair offers domestic flights from Cancún to Chetumal, Cozumel, and Mérida.

When you arrive at the airport, hang onto your FMM (Forma Migratoria Múltiple para Extranjeros, or "tourist permit") because you'll need it again on departure.

⊙ Boat

The Yucatán is served by a number of ferries and boats. Most popular are the efficient speedboats that run between Playa del Carmen and Cozumel or from Puerto Juárez, Punta Sam, and Isla Mujeres. Vessels also run from Chiquila to Isla Holbox. Most carriers follow set schedules, with the exception of those going to the smaller, less visited islands. But departure times can vary with the weather and with the number of passengers. Visitcancun.com, travelyucatan.com, and granpuerto.com.mx have information on water taxis and ferries, though you should always confirm the details before heading down to the docks.

⊙ Bus

The extensive Mexican bus network is a great means of getting around. Service is frequent, and tickets can be purchased on the spot (except during holidays and on long weekends, when advance

Getting Here and Around

purchase is crucial). Bring something to eat on long trips in case you don't like the restaurant or market where the bus stops. Bring toilet tissue and wear a sweater, as the air-conditioning is often set on high. Most buses play videos or television until midnight, so bring earplugs if you're bothered by noise. Smoking is prohibited on Mexican buses.

Bus companies here offer several classes of service: first-class (*primera clase*), deluxe or executive class (*de lujo* or *ejecutivo*), and second class (*segunda*). First-class and executive-class buses are generally punctual and have comfortable air-conditioned coaches with bathrooms, movies, reclining seats with seat belts, and refreshments. They take the fastest route (usually on safer, well-paved toll roads) and make few stops between points. Less desirable, second-class vehicles connect smaller, secondary routes; they also run along some long-distance routes, often taking slower, local roads. They're tolerable, but are usually cramped and make many stops. The class of travel will be listed on your printed ticket—if you see *"económico"* printed next to *"servicio,"* you've been booked on a second-class bus. At many bus stations, one counter will represent several lines and classes of service, and mistakes do happen. ADO is the Yucatán's principal first-class bus company, and Mayab (operated by ADO) is the second-class line. Most bus tickets, including first-class (or executive) and second-class, can be reserved ahead of time in person at ticket offices. ADO also allows you to reserve tickets online 48 hours in advance.

If you're staying in the Riviera Maya, *colectivos* (minibuses) run along Carretera 307 from Cancún to Tulum. Although affordable, traveling by bus means you'll have to either walk or organize additional transportation from the bus stop.

Bus travel in the Yucatán, as throughout Mexico, is inexpensive by U.S. standards, with rates averaging MX$80 per hour depending on the level of luxury (or lack of it). Schedules are posted at bus stations; the bus leaves more or less around the listed time. Occasionally, if all the seats have been sold, the bus will leave early.

Typical times and fares on first-class buses are: Cancún to Mérida, 4 hours, MX$525; Mérida to Campeche, 2½ hours, MX$290; and Cancún to Mexico City, 28 hours, MX$1,730.

🚗 Car

Few people travel all the way to the Yucatán Peninsula by car, especially with the risks involved just south of the U.S. border. Those who do so will need a valid driver's license, a temporary car-importation permit, a car registration, a copy of the car title, and an FM-T form.

The most practical way to explore the Yucatán Peninsula is to fly to your region and rent a car for the duration of your stay. The best flight deals, however, usually arrive and depart from the Cancún airport. Mexican auto insurance is mandatory here, regardless of what travel-insurance package you have back home or what your credit card provides.

However, you may not have to rent a vehicle at all. Your itinerary may not require one. Rental prices are expensive in and around Cancún. If you're not traveling far afield, don't bother to rent, as you'll be able to arrange taxi service to nearby sights through your hotel. If you are nervous about driving, first-class buses make the cheapest way to get around.

The luxury liners of ADO (⊕ *www.ado. com.mx*) travel throughout the Yucatán Peninsula. *Colectivos* (minibuses) run along Carretera 307 from Cancún to Tulum. Although affordable, traveling by bus means you'll have to either walk or organize additional transportation from the bus stop. Taxis will cost you about $30 per hour.

You won't need a car on Isla Mujeres or Isla Holbox, which are too small to make driving practical. (Electric golf carts are a popular way to get around Isla Mujeres, and you can rent one.) Playa del Carmen's downtown area is quite compact and the main street is blocked off to vehicles. Cars can feel like a burden in Mérida and Campeche City, because of the narrow cobbled streets and the lack of parking spaces. You'll need a car in Cozumel only if you wish to explore the less-developed eastern side of the island.

However, taxis for longer trips—to Playa del Carmen, for instance—can be pricey, so renting a car for a day or two of exploring may be more economical. As a rule, local agencies might have better rates than major companies, but if you're looking for a reliable car, it's best to stick with a brand you recognize. You can get the same kind of midsize and luxury cars in Mexico that you can rent in the United States. Economy usually refers to a small car barely fitting four passengers, which may or may not come with air-conditioning. Pancake-flat Yucatán makes for fairly easy driving, although side roads may have inadequate (or no) signposting; four-wheel-drive vehicles aren't necessary unless you plan on traveling to sites far off the beaten path in rainy season. If you'll require a child's car seat, request one when booking.

Car-rental agencies in Mexico require you to purchase a CDW or Collision Damage Waiver (starting at $30 per day), and

Mexico Liability Auto Insurance (starting at $15 per day). Regardless of any coverage afforded by your credit-card company, you must purchase liability insurance. If you are caught without coverage, fines start at $200. Keep in mind that although you might have reserved a rental car for only $20 per day, full coverage insurance will cost you about $50 per day. Additional theft protection and personal injury policies are optional. Since most U.S. insurance policies are not recognized in Mexico (including those purchased online at time of booking), it is best to buy insurance directly at the counter with the rental car provider.

Be sure that you've been provided with proof of such insurance; if you drive without it, you're not only liable for damages, but you're also breaking the law. If you're in a car accident and you don't have insurance, you may be placed in jail until you're proven innocent. If anyone is injured you'll remain in jail until you make retribution to all injured parties and their families—which will likely cost you thousands of dollars. Mexican laws seem to favor nationals.

Even if you're absolutely certain you're fully covered by your credit-card company, we recommend you purchase full coverage insurance in Mexico. Getting into a car accident in Mexico would be harrowing enough without having to navigate the bureaucracy of your credit-card company to clear things up with Mexican authorities. Make sure that your insurance covers the cost for an attorney and claims adjusters who will come to the scene of an accident. Buying insurance makes renting a car in Mexico one of the most expensive parts of the trip, but in this case it's better to be safe than frugal.

Before setting out on any car trip, check your vehicle's fuel, oil, fluids, tires,

Getting Here and Around

windshield wipers, and lights. It's even a good idea to check the stereo if you are planning a long road trip. Don't forget to pack an adapter for your phone if you want to listen to your own music. Gas stations and mechanics can be hard to find off the beaten path. Consult a map and have your route in mind as you drive.

Be aware that Mexican drivers often think nothing of tailgating, speeding, and weaving in and out of traffic. Drive defensively and keep your cool. When stopping for traffic or at a red light, always leave sufficient room between your car and the one ahead so you can maneuver to safety if necessary. On the highway, a left-turn signal in Mexico means the driver is signaling those behind that it's safe to pass. Blinking hazard lights means that traffic is stopped up ahead and to slow down. Always aim to be at your destination by sunset because roads may be pitted with potholes and void of streetlights and signs. In Mexico the minimum driving age is 18, but most rental-car agencies have a minimum age requirement between 21 and 25; some have a surcharge for drivers under 25. Your own driver's license is acceptable; there's no reason to get an international driver's license.

GASOLINE

Pemex, Mexico's government-owned petroleum monopoly, franchises all gas stations, so prices throughout the Yucatán—and the country—are the same. Overall, gas prices run around 25% higher than in the United States. Gas is always sold in liters. High-octane unleaded (called *premium*), the red pump, and regular unleaded (*magna*), the green pump, are available nationwide. Fuel quality is generally lower than that in the United States and Europe, but it has improved enough so that your car will run acceptably.

Some stations accept credit cards and a few have ATMs, but don't count on it— make sure you have pesos handy. When paying by credit card, don't be surprised if the gas attendant makes a photocopy of your passport since this is a normal practice. It is best to pay in cash since attendants have been known to run credit cards through twice, claiming it didn't work the first time, thus leaving you with two charges on your statement. Ask for a *recibo* (receipt) just in case you need to present it to your credit card company for evidence. A few stations in Cancún accept U.S. dollars, but most do not. Plan to pay in pesos.

There are no self-service stations in Mexico. Ask the attendant to fill your tank (*"lleno* [YAY-noh], *por favor"*) or ask for a specific amount in pesos to avoid being overcharged. Check to make sure that the attendant has set the meter back to zero and that the price is shown. Watch the attendant check the oil as well—to make sure you actually need it—and watch while they pour it into your car. Never pay before the gas is pumped, even if the attendant asks you to. Always tip your attendant a few pesos. Finally, keep your gas tank full, because gas stations are not plentiful in this region. If you run out of gas in a small village and there's no gas station for miles, ask if there's a store that sells gas from containers. Do everything you can to avoid having to use this option; you run a risk of such gas being less clean.

PARKING

A circle with a diagonal line superimposed on the letter *E* (for *estacionamiento*) means "no parking." A red curb means parking is restricted at all times, and a white curb is designated for loading and unloading only. A blue curb is for handicap parking, a green curb allows parking during specific hours, and a yellow curb means that the parking space is private.

If you're ticketed, your license plate will be taken to a nearby police station and will only be returned upon payment of the infraction. Never park overnight on the street, and never leave anything of value in an unattended car.

When in doubt, choose a parking lot; it will probably be safer anyway. Lots are plentiful, though not always clearly marked, and fees are reasonable—as little as MX$60 for a half day. Sometimes you park your own car; more often, though, you hand the keys over to an attendant. Tip him and ask that he look after your vehicle.

ROAD CONDITIONS

Compared to other parts of Mexico, the roads in the Yucatán Peninsula are nicely paved. Carretera 307 serves as the coastal route between Cancún and the Belize border, but this stretch of highway is known for its speed traps and large *topes* (speed bumps). Toll road 180D, the four-lane highway from Cancún to Mérida, is nicely paved, sometimes with long stretches between off-ramps. The colonial city of Valladolid and the Mayan ruins of Chichén Itzá have their own exits. From Cancún, you can reach Mérida in about four hours. You will pay MX518 in tolls, an excellent investment in terms of time and ease of driving. (Tolls must be paid in cash in pesos.) A free section of Highway 180 continues southwest to Campeche and the rest of Mexico. From Mérida, the winding, more scenic Carretera 261 also leads to some of the more off-the-beaten-track archaeological sites on the way south to Campeche and Escárcega, where it joins Carretera 186 going east to Chetumal. These highways are two-lane roads. Carretera 295 (from the north coast to Valladolid and Felipe Carrillo Puerto) is also a good two-lane

road. Regardless of where you drive, be sure to arrive by sunset.

Many secondary roads are in bad condition—unpaved, unmarked, and full of potholes. If you must take one of these roads, the best course is to allow plenty of daylight hours and never travel at night. Slow down when approaching towns and villages—which you're forced to do by the *topes* (speed bumps)—and because of the added presence of people and animals. Locals selling oranges, candy, or other food will almost certainly approach your car.

MEXICAN DRIVERS

Mexicans are generally skilled drivers, but they do drive quite fast, even on twisting or extraordinarily dark roads. That said, Mexicans motorists are in some ways more courteous than U.S. ones—it's customary, for example, for drivers to put on their hazard lights to warn the cars behind them of poor road conditions, slow-downs, or upcoming speed bumps; oncoming cars may flash their lights at you for the same reasons.

ROADSIDE EMERGENCIES

The Mexican Tourism Ministry operates a fleet of some 1,800 pickup trucks, known as Angeles Verdes, or the Green Angels, an organization in existence since the early 1960s that assists motorists on major highways. Dial 078 from any cell phone or Telmex phone booth and your call will be routed to the Green Angels' dispatch office. The bilingual drivers provide mechanical help, first aid, radio-telephone communication, basic supplies and small parts, towing, and tourist information. Services are free, and spare parts, fuel, and lubricants are provided at cost. Tips are always appreciated, and are sometimes openly solicited.

The Green Angels patrol fixed sections of the major highways twice daily 8 am to

Getting Here and Around

dusk, later on holiday weekends. If your car breaks down, pull as far as possible off the road, lift the hood, hail a passing vehicle, and ask the driver to notify the patrol. Most bus and truck drivers will be quite helpful. Don't accept rides from strangers. If you witness an accident, don't stop to help since witnesses are often detained for questioning for long periods of time. Instead find the nearest official.

RULES OF THE ROAD

There are two absolutely essential points to remember about driving in Mexico. First and foremost is to carry Mexican auto insurance. If you injure anyone in an accident, you could well be jailed—whether it was your fault or not—unless you have insurance. Second, if you enter Mexico with a car, you must leave with it. In recent years the high rate of U.S. vehicles being sold illegally in Mexico has caused the Mexican government to enact stringent regulations for bringing a car into the country. You must be in your foreign vehicle at all times when it's driven. You cannot lend it to another person. Do not, under any circumstances, let a national drive your car. It's illegal for Mexicans to drive foreign-owned cars; if a national is caught driving your car, the car will be impounded by customs and you will receive a stiff fine. Newer models of vans, SUVs, and pickup trucks can be impossible to get back once impounded.

You probably won't be driving to the Yucatán Peninsula from the United States. On the rare chance you do, you must cross the border with the following documents: title or registration for your vehicle, a valid passport, proof of insurance, a credit card (MasterCard or Visa only), and a valid driver's license with a photo. You'll also need a temporary car-importation permit and an FMM (tourist permit). The title-holder, driver,

and credit-card owner must be one and the same—that is, if your spouse's name is on the title of the car and yours isn't, you cannot be the one to bring the car into the country. For financed, leased, rental, or company cars, you must bring a notarized letter of permission from the bank, lien holder, rental agency, or company. When you submit your paperwork at the border and pay the approximate US$60 charge on your credit card, you'll receive a car permit and a sticker to put on your vehicle. The permit is valid for the same amount of time as your tourist visa, which is up to 180 days. You may go back and forth across the border during this six-month period, as long as you check with immigration and bring all your permit paperwork with you. If you're planning to stay and keep your car in Mexico for longer than six months, however, you'll have to get a new permit before the original one expires. In addition to the permit fee, your credit card will be charged a deposit based on the age of your car. This fee is to guarantee return of the vehicle to U.S. territory. If your car is older than 2000, you'll pay $200; cars between 2001 and 2006 will be charged $300; and anything newer than 2007 will cost $400. This amount is refunded in full 24 hours after you cancel your permit, unless you have passed the expiration date or left your car in Mexico. Upon your departure from Mexico, the permit for temporary importation must be cancelled at Customs or you will not receive your refunded deposit.

One way to minimize hassle when you cross the border with a car is to have your paperwork done in advance at a branch of Sanborn's Mexico Auto Insurance; you'll find an office in almost every town on the U.S.–Mexico border. Average daily insurance rates start around $45. The fact that you drove in with a car is stamped on your tourist card, which you must give to immigration authorities at departure. If an emergency arises and you must fly home, there are complicated customs procedures to face.

When you sign up for Mexican car insurance, you should receive a booklet on Mexican rules of the road. It really is a good idea to read it to avoid breaking laws that differ from those of your country. If an oncoming vehicle flicks its lights at you in the daytime, slow down: it could mean trouble ahead. When approaching a narrow bridge, the first vehicle to flash its lights has right of way. One-way streets are common. One-way traffic is indicated by an arrow; two-way, by a double-pointed arrow. Other road signs follow the widespread system of international symbols.

Mileage and speed limits are given in kilometers: 100 kph and 80 kph (60 mph and 50 mph, respectively) are the most common maximums. A few of the toll roads allow 110 kph (65 mph). In cities and small towns, observe the posted speed limits, which can be as low as 20 kph (12 mph). Seat belts are required by law throughout Mexico.

Drunk-driving laws are harsh in Mexico, and if you're caught you'll go to jail immediately. Quintana Roo, Yucatán, and Campeche states impose a blood-alcohol limit of 0.08, but transit police often apply that number more strictly. The best way to avoid any problems is simply not to drink and drive. Designate a driver if you're with a group. Right turns on red are not allowed, and phoning or texting while driving is not permitted. Foreigners must pay speeding penalties on the spot, which can be steep. Some minor traffic violations can be dismissed until you return your rental car by simply showing your "Tourist Traffic Card" available from several car-rental agencies.

If you encounter a police checkpoint, stay calm. These are simply routine checks for weapons and drugs; customarily they'll check out the car's registration, look in the back seat, the trunk, and at the undercarriage with a mirror. Basic Spanish does help during these stops, though a smile and polite demeanor will go a long way.

SAFETY ON THE ROAD
Never drive at night in remote and rural areas. Although there are few *bandidos* on the roads here, more common problems are large potholes, free-roaming animals, cars with no working lights, and road-hogging trucks. Getting assistance is difficult. If you must travel at night, use the toll roads whenever possible; although costly, they're much safer.

Some of the biggest hassles on the road might be from police who pull you over for supposedly breaking the law, or for being a good prospect for a scam. Remember to be polite—displays of anger will only make matters worse—and be aware that a police officer might be pulling you over for something you didn't do. Although efforts are being made to fight corruption, it's still a fact of life in Mexico. The MX$100 (and up) it costs to get your license back is definitely supplementary income for the officer who pulled you over with no intention of taking you down to police headquarters.

ⓦ Cruise
As a popular cruise destination on western Caribbean itineraries, many travelers arrive by ship at the ports of Cancún, Cozumel, Calica, Costa Maya, and Progreso. A few cruise lines include multiple stops in Cancún, Playa del Carmen, and Cozumel.

Getting Here and Around

Cozumel is technically three separate ports—Punta Langosta, Puerto Maya, and the International Terminal—each catering to its own cruise lines. Large ships dock in Calica, south of Playa del Carmen, although a few call at Carmen's small downtown port itself. Mahahual (commonly known as Puerto Costa Maya) is a self-contained port facility. Progreso (near Mérida) is known for its five-mile pier, reputedly the world's longest.

🚗 Ride-Sharing

Uber operates in a few localities here, albeit illegally in all of them. Whose fault that is depends on who's talking: Uber blames the powerful taxi unions for keeping it out of the open market; taxi drivers complain that Uber doesn't procure proper government permits. Both statements are true. Tales abound of Uber drivers not being able to enter Cancún airport or the hotel zone and having to drop off travelers several blocks away, or of authorities stopping and seizing vehicles with passengers inside. Until the situation is resolved, we advise against using the service.

🚕 Taxi

Taxis are ubiquitous in both cities and larger towns. The standard taxi is a mid-size, four-door sedan. Drivers generally speak English, either enough to negotiate the fare or, in some cases, enough for a lively discussion of national politics.

In addition to private taxis, many cities have bargain-price collective taxi services using minibuses and sedans. The service is called *colectivo* or *pesero*. Such vehicles run along fixed routes, and you hail them on the street and tell the driver where you're headed. He charges you based on how far you're going on that route. Note that drivers often run out of change, so being able to pay the exact amount can help make your ride smoother.

AIRPORT TAXIS

For safety, you should only take the authorized taxi service from most airports. A metered taxi has a *taxímetro,* and if a cab has one, ask the driver what the rates are. Most taxis, particularly those in resort areas, are unmetered. Always confirm the fare before setting out. Major hotels post rate sheets, or you can ask a concierge or front-desk person what the rates should be. Note that even the posted rates are inflated, so always try to negotiate a slightly better price. Clearly, if any cabbie asks for more than the posted fare you're being grossly overcharged.

A surcharge of 20% to 40% may be added at night, usually after 11 pm.

If a driver doesn't know the address you give him, he'll radio either a dispatcher or other cabbie to get the info, or drive to the neighborhood and ask around. When you've negotiated the fare before starting, you needn't pay extra if the cabbie has to drive around a bit to find the address.

Tipping isn't customary, unless the driver helps you with your bags.

Essentials

🍽 Dining

If you're here on an all-inclusive package, your meals will likely be covered (though you should check carefully for exclusions). The downside is that you may feel locked into your dining options. We recommend enjoying a meal or two outside your resort to experience Cancún and the Riviera Maya's amazing dining scenes.

PAYING

Most small restaurants do not take credit cards. Larger restaurants and those catering to tourists typically accept MasterCard and Visa.

RESERVATIONS AND DRESS

During high season, it's a good idea to make a reservation if you can. In Cancún, for example, they're expected at the nicer restaurants. Some restaurants accept online reservations, although it's always wise to confirm by phone. We mention them specifically only when reservations are essential (there's no other way you'll ever get a table) or when they're not accepted. Large parties should always call ahead to check the reservations policy. We mention dress only when men are required to wear a jacket.

MEALS AND MEALTIMES

Desayuno can be either a breakfast sweet roll and coffee or milk or a full breakfast of an egg dish such as *huevos a la mexicana* (scrambled eggs with chopped tomato, onion, and chiles), *huevos rancheros* (fried eggs on a tortilla covered with salsa), or *huevos con jamón* (scrambled eggs with ham), plus juice and toast or tortillas. Some cafés don't open until 8 or 8:30, in which case hotel restaurants are the best bets for early risers. *Panaderías* (bakeries) open early and provide the cheapest breakfast you'll find—a bag of assorted rolls and pastries will likely cost less than MX$60.

Traditionally, lunch is called *comida* or *almuerzo* and is the biggest meal of the day. Most restaurants start serving lunch no earlier than 1 pm and traditional businesses close between 2 pm and 4 pm for this meal. It usually includes soup, a main dish, and dessert. Regional specialties include *pan de cazón* (baby shark shredded and layered with tortillas, black beans, and tomato sauce) in Campeche; *pollo pibil* (chicken baked in banana leaves) in Mérida; and *tikin xic* (fish in a sour-orange sauce) on the coast. Restaurants in tourist areas also serve American-style food such as hamburgers, pizza, and pasta. The evening meal is called *cena*, which is sometimes replaced by *merienda*, a lighter meal between lunch and dinner.

Most restaurants are open daily for lunch and dinner during high season (late November through April), but hours may be reduced during the rest of the year. It's always a good idea to phone ahead.

Unless otherwise noted, the restaurants listed in this guide are open daily for lunch and dinner.

WINES, BEER, AND SPIRITS

Almost all restaurants in the region serve beer and some Mexican spirits. Larger restaurants have beer, wine, and spirits. Some of the more expensive all-inclusive resorts offer top-shelf international liquor brands but will serve them only if you specifically request the brands by name (otherwise, expect a hangover). The Mexican wine industry is relatively small, but notable producers include L.A. Cetto, Bodegas de Santo Tomás, Casa Pedro Domecq, and Monte Xanic, all based in the northern Baja Peninsula on the opposite end of the country. As well as offering Mexican vintages, restaurants may offer Chilean, Spanish, Italian, and French wines at reasonable prices.

Essentials

You pay more for imported liquor such as vodka, brandy, and whiskey; some brands of tequila and rum are less expensive. Take the opportunity to try some of the higher-end, small-batch tequila—it's a completely different experience from what you might be used to. Some small lunch places called *loncherías* don't sell alcohol. Almost all corner stores sell beer, brandy, cheap wine, and tequila. Grocery stores carry all brands of beer, wine, and spirits. Liquor stores are rare and usually carry specialty items. You must be 18 or older to buy liquor.

⚠ Emergencies

It's helpful, albeit daunting, to know ahead of time that you're not protected by the laws of your native land once you're on Mexican soil. However, if you get into a scrape with the law, you can call the Citizens' Emergency Center in the United States. In Mexico, you can also call INFOTUR, the 24-hour English-speaking hotline of the Mexico Ministry of Tourism (Sectur). The hotline can provide immediate assistance as well as general, nonemergency guidance. Mexico uses a 911 emergency number nationwide for police, fire, and ambulance. Operators speak Spanish and English.

✚ Health

According to the U.S. government's Centers for Disease Control and Prevention (CDC) there's a limited risk of malaria in certain rural areas of the Yucatán Peninsula, in the states of Campeche and Quintana Roo. Dengue fever is also a limited risk along the Caribbean Coast. Travelers in mostly urban areas need not

worry, nor do travelers who rarely leave resort environs.

To safeguard yourself against mosquito-borne diseases like malaria and dengue, use mosquito nets (provided at most beach and jungle properties), wear clothing that covers the body, apply repellent containing DEET, and use spray for flying insects in living and sleeping areas. The CDC recommends mosquito avoidance for this region of Mexico rather than a regimen of antimalarial-preventive pills. There's no vaccine to combat dengue.

In Mexico the biggest health risk is traveler's diarrhea caused by consuming contaminated fruit, vegetables, water (ice included), and unpasteurized milk or milk products.

Drink only bottled water or water that has been boiled for at least 10 minutes, even when you're brushing your teeth. At restaurants off the beaten path, be sure to ask for *agua mineral* (mineral water) or *agua purificada* (purified water). When ordering cold drinks at questionable establishments, skip the ice: *sin hielo.* (You can usually identify ice made commercially from purified water by its uniform barrel shape and the hole in the center.) Hotels with water-purification systems will post signs to that effect in the rooms; even then, be wary. Although salads in tourist-oriented areas have usually been hygienically prepared, when in doubt don't eat any raw vegetables or fruits that haven't been, or can't be, peeled (e.g., lettuce and tomatoes). In coastal towns like Celestún, the shrimp may be fresh, but it has been known to cause traveler's diarrhea for travelers with sensitive stomachs.

Mild cases of diarrhea may respond to Imodium (known generically as loperamide) or Pepto-Bismol (not as strong), both of which you can buy over the counter. Keep in mind, though, that these drugs can complicate more serious illnesses. Drink plenty of bottled water or tea. Chamomile tea (*té de manzanilla*) is a good remedy, and it's readily available in restaurants throughout Mexico.

In severe cases, hydrate with Gatorade or a salt-sugar solution (½ teaspoon salt and 4 tablespoons sugar per quart of water). You can also balance out your pH levels by drinking a glass of water with a tablespoon of baking soda, which acts as a natural antacid. If your fever and diarrhea last more than three days, see a doctor—you may have picked up a parasite that requires prescription medication.

It's best to be cautious and go indoors at dusk (called the "mosquito hour" by locals). An excellent brand of *repelente de insectos* (insect repellent) called Autan is readily available; don't use it on children under age two. If you want to bring a mosquito repellent from home, make sure it has at least 20% DEET or it won't be effective. If you're hiking in the jungle or near standing water, wear repellent and/or long pants and sleeves; if you're camping in the jungle, use a mosquito net and invest in a package of mosquito coils (sold in most stores). Isla Holbox is often riddled with tiny mosquitoes and "no-seeums" after the rains. Island locals use baby oil as a natural repellent. If you plan on visiting one of the many cenotes (subterranean water bodies) throughout the Yucatán, be sure to bring waterproof insect repellent.

Another local flying pest is the *tabaño*, a type of deer fly, which resembles a common household fly with yellow stripes. Some people swell up after being bitten, but taking an antihistamine can help. Watch out for the small red ants, as their bites can be quite irritating.

Scorpions also live in the region; their sting is similar to a bee sting. They're rarely fatal, but can cause strong reactions in small children and the elderly. Clean all cuts carefully (especially those produced by coral), as the rate of infection is much higher here.

The Yucatán has many poisonous snakes. The coral snake, easily identified by its black and red markings, should be avoided at all costs since its bite is fatal. If you're planning any jungle hikes, be sure to wear hard-sole shoes and stay on the path. For more remote areas, hire a guide and make sure there's an antivenom kit accompanying you on the trip.

More common hazards to travelers in the Yucatán are sunburn and heat exhaustion. The sun is strong here; it takes fewer than 20 minutes to get a serious burn. When practical, avoid the sun between 11 am and 3 pm. Wear a hat and use sunscreen, preferably something with zinc oxide. You should drink more fluids than you do at home—Mexico is probably hotter than what you're used to and you'll perspire more. Rest in the afternoon and stay out of the sun to avoid heat exhaustion. The first signs of dehydration and heat exhaustion are dizziness, extreme irritability, and fatigue.

If you aren't interested in purchasing comprehensive trip coverage, consider buying medical-only travel insurance. Neither Medicare nor some private insurers cover medical expenses anywhere outside the United States. Medical-only policies typically reimburse you for medical care (excluding that related to preexisting conditions), hospitalization abroad, and provide for evacuation. You still have to pay the bills and await reimbursement from the insurer, though.

Another option is to sign up with a medical-evacuation assistance company.

Essentials

A membership in one of these companies gets you doctor referrals, emergency evacuation or repatriation, 24-hour hotlines for medical consultation, and other assistance. International SOS and AirMed provide evacuation services and medical referrals. Medjet offers medical evacuation.

COVID-19 brought all travel to a virtual standstill in 2020, and interruptions to travel have continued into 2021. Although the illness is mild in most people, some experience severe and even life-threatening complications. Once travel started up again, albeit slowly and cautiously, travelers were asked to be particularly careful about hygiene and to avoid any unnecessary travel, especially if they are sick.

Older adults, especially those over 65, have a greater chance of having severe complications from COVID-19. The same is true for people with weaker immune systems or those living with some types of medical conditions, including diabetes, asthma, heart disease, cancer, HIV/AIDS, kidney disease, and liver disease. Starting two weeks before a trip, anyone planning to travel should be on the lookout for some of the following symptoms: cough, fever, chills, trouble breathing, muscle pain, sore throat, new loss of smell or taste. If you experience any of these symptoms, you should not travel at all.

And to protect yourself during travel, do your best to avoid contact with people showing symptoms. Wash your hands often with soap and water. Limit your time in public places, and, when you are out and about, wear a face mask that covers your nose and mouth. Indeed, a mask may be required in some places, such as on an airplane or in a confined space like a theater, where you share the space with a lot of people. You may wish to bring extra supplies, such as disenfecting wipes, hand sanitizer (12-ounce bottles were allowed in carry-on luggage at this writing), and a first-aid kit with a thermometer.

Given how abruptly travel was curtailed at the onset of COVID-19, it is wise to consider protecting yourself by purchasing a travel insurance policy that will reimburse you for any cancellation costs related to COVID-19. Not all travel insurance policies protect against pandemic-related cancellations, so always read the fine print.

🛡 Immunizations

At this writing, no immunizations are required for travel between the United States and Mexico. How implementation of a future COVID-19 vaccine passport will play out is not yet known. The CDC has given a tentative go-ahead (with proper precautions) for international travel to people who have passed completion of the vaccine series by at least two weeks. The CDC also recommends being up to date on all routine immunizations (tetanus, mumps, measles, varicella, seasonal flu).

🛏 Lodging

The price and quality of accommodations in the Yucatán Peninsula vary from luxury resorts and coastal villas to seedy hostels and eco-friendly cabanas. Near Mérida and Campeche, many historic haciendas have been converted into luxury accommodations. You may find bargains while you're on the road, but if your comfort threshold is high, look for an English-speaking staff, guaranteed dollar rates, and toll-free reservation numbers. Mexico doesn't have an official star-rating system, but the usual number of stars (five being the ultimate) denotes the most luxury and amenities, while a two-star hotel might have a ceiling fan and TV with local channels only. "Gran turismo" is a special category of hotel that may or may not have all the accoutrements of a five-star hotel (such as minibars) but is nonetheless at the top of the heap, both in price and level of service and sophistication. All-inclusive hotels are a good option for families since the price of the room usually includes children's activities and meals.

APARTMENT AND HOUSE RENTALS

Local agencies that specialize in renting out apartments, condos, villas, and private homes can be found in many tourist locales. International agencies are another option, and rental websites such as ⊕ *www.airbnb.com* or ⊕ *www.homeaway.com* are increasingly popular.

HOTELS

Hotel rates are subject to the 16% value-added tax, in addition to a 2% (Yucatán and Campeche states) to 3% (Quintana Roo state) hotel tax. Service charges and meals generally aren't included in the quoted rates. Make sure to ask if tax is included and take this into account when comparing properties.

High- and low-season rates can vary significantly. In the off-season, Cancún hotels can cost one-third to one-half what they cost during peak periods. Keep in mind, however, that this is also the time that many hotels undergo necessary repairs or renovations.

Hotels in this guide have private bathrooms with showers, unless stated otherwise; bathtubs aren't common in inexpensive hotels and properties in smaller towns.

Reservations are easy to make online. If you choose this route, be sure to book at least two days in advance of your stay,

and always print out your confirmation. Although major resorts are generally efficient at keeping up with online bookings, there's often a lag, and the reservation desks that handle such things may be closed on weekends. If you prefer to make phone reservations, hotels in the larger urban areas will have someone on staff who speaks English. In smaller destinations, you'll have to make your reservations in Spanish. In more remote areas (like Xcalak), you'll have to make reservations by email since most properties don't have telephones.

It's essential to reserve in advance if you're traveling to the resort areas in high season (late November through Easter), and it's recommended, though not always necessary, to do so elsewhere during high season. Resorts popular with college students tend to fill up in the summer months and during spring break (generally March through April). Overbooking is a common practice in some parts, especially in Cancún. To protect yourself, get a written confirmation via email.

$ Money

Mexican currency is the peso. Like many countries, Mexico uses the $ sign to designate prices. You will see *MX$* (the notation we use), *MP$*, and *Mex$* too. When in doubt, ask which currency is being displayed.

Exchange rates have hovered in the US$1 = MX$ 18-22 in recent years. Lop off the last digit of the peso price and divide in half. You'll get a pretty good dollar estimate.

When you arrive, it's a good idea to have smaller bills to pay for tips, bus fare, or taxis. Avoid having anything larger than a MX$50, since change is sometimes

Essentials

difficult to find. Do not accept damaged pesos, which are of no value to merchants or banks.

Traveler's checks have become increasingly difficult to cash in Mexico. We advise against taking them along. They might be exchanged at some banks for a processing fee and a hefty chunk of your time. A passport is required when exchanging U.S. dollars or traveler's checks. Foreign travelers may not exchange more than $1,500 U.S. dollars (cash) per person per month into Mexican pesos. However, credit card transactions, traveler's checks, and non-U.S. foreign currencies are not affected by this law.

ATMs are the most convenient ways to get cash, are readily available, and charge the official exchange rate. Make sure your PIN has only four numbers, and inquire about foreign transaction fees processed by your U.S. bank. Larger resorts have ATMs on the premises, and most large hotels will exchange dollars for pesos.

Most businesses accept major credit cards but may add a surcharge to compensate for their own hefty processing fee. In Mexico, American Express, Discover, and Diner's Club are not as readily accepted as Visa or MasterCard.

Because the value of the currency fluctuates, and since most hotels quote rates in U.S. dollars, we've listed hotel prices in this book in both dollars and pesos; all other prices are listed in Mexican pesos.

U.S. dollar bills (but never coins) are widely accepted in many tourist destinations of the Yucatán, particularly in Cancún and Cozumel; however, you may get your change back in pesos. Many restaurants, tourist shops and market vendors, as well as virtually all hotel service personnel, also accept dollars. Wherever you are, though, watch out for bad exchange rates—you'll generally do better paying in pesos. Note that many smaller businesses and highway toll booths accept only pesos.

ATMS AND BANKS

Foreign travelers may not exchange more than US$1,500 (cash) per person, per month into Mexican pesos. Mexican travelers are also limited to US$1,500 cash per person, per month, with the added restriction of no more than US$300 cash per day. Other methods of payment including credit cards, traveler's checks, and non-American foreign currencies are not affected by this law.

When exchanging foreign currency at banks and hotels in Mexico, you must show your passport. ATMs (*cajeros automáticos*) are commonplace in key tourist areas. All airports and many gas stations have them, but many bus stations do not. Rural locales also often lack ATMs (truly remote ones, like Xcalak near Belize, don't have ATMs or banks, and businesses there don't accept credit cards). Unless you're in a major city or resort area, treat ATMs as you would gas stations—don't assume you'll be able to find one in a pinch. In smaller towns, even when they're present, machines are often out of order or out of cash.

Cirrus and Plus are the most frequently found networks. Your own bank will probably charge a transaction fee for withdrawing money in Mexico (up to $8 a pop); the foreign bank you use may also charge a fee. Before you leave home, ask your bank if they have an agreement with a Mexican counterpart to waive or charge reduced fees for cash withdrawals. For example, Bank of America has such an agreement with Scotiabank. Regardless of the fee, you'll usually get a better rate of exchange at an ATM than you will at a currency-exchange office or even when changing money in a bank.

PINs with more than four digits are not recognized at ATMs in Mexico. If your PIN has five or more numbers, get it changed before you leave.

CREDIT CARDS

Throughout this guide, it's safe to assume that businesses accept major credit cards unless the service information reads ⊟ *No credit cards.*

It's a good idea to inform your credit-card company before you travel to Mexico, especially if you don't travel internationally very often. Otherwise, the credit-card company might put a hold on your card owing to unusual activity—not a good thing halfway through your trip. Record all your credit-card numbers—as well as the phone numbers to call if your cards are lost or stolen—in a safe place, so you're prepared should something go wrong.

Note that some credit-card companies *and* the banks that issue them add substantial percentages to all foreign transactions. Check on these fees before leaving home, so there won't be any surprises when you get the bill.

Credit cards are accepted in most tourist areas. Smaller, less expensive restaurants and shops, however, tend to take only cash. In general, credit cards aren't accepted in small towns and villages. The most widely accepted cards are MasterCard and Visa; American Express is not widely accepted in Mexico except at large international chain hotels and resorts. When shopping in traditional markets, you can usually get better prices if you pay with cash.

In Mexico the decision to pay cash or use a credit card might depend on whether the establishment in which you're making a purchase finds bargaining for prices acceptable. To avoid fraud, it's wise to make sure that "pesos" or the initials *M.N.* (*moneda nacional,* or

national currency) is clearly marked on all credit-card receipts, unless the charge was made in U.S. dollars.

CURRENCY AND EXCHANGE

Check with your bank, the financial pages of your local newspaper, or online for current exchange rates.

Mexican currency comes in denominations of 20-, 50-, 100-, 200-, 500-, 1000-, and 2000-peso bills. The latter are not commonly seen, and many establishments refuse to accept them due to a lack of change. Coins officially come in denominations of 1, 2, 5, and 10 pesos, although you will likely not see anything less than a 5. Many of the coins are very similar, so check carefully.

Most banks change money only on weekdays until noon (though they stay open until 5), whereas *casas de cambio* (private exchange offices) generally stay open until 6 or 9 and often operate on weekends. Bring your passport when you exchange money. Bank rates are regulated by Mexico's federal government but vary slightly from bank to bank, while casas de cambio have slightly more variable rates.

Many shop and restaurant owners are unable to make change for large bills. Enough of these encounters may compel you to request *billetes chicos* (small bills) when you exchange money.

⊙ Packing

Pack lightly, because you may want to save space in your suitcase for purchases. The Yucatán is filled with bargains on clothing, leather goods, jewelry, and other crafts. If you purchase pottery or ceramics, make sure they're carefully wrapped in your check-in luggage since

Essentials

a few airlines prohibit these items from being in your carry-on.

Bring lightweight clothes, bathing suits, sun hats, and cover-ups for the Caribbean beach towns, but also pack a light jacket or sweater to wear in chilly, air-conditioned restaurants, or to tide you over during a rainstorm or an unusual cool spell. For trips to rural areas or Mérida, where dress is typically more conservative and shorts are considered inappropriate, make sure you have at least one pair of slacks. Comfortable walking shoes with rubber soles are a good idea, both for exploring ruins and for walking around cities. Lightweight rain gear and an umbrella are a good idea during the rainy season. Cancún is the dressiest spot on the peninsula; however, even fancy restaurants there don't usually require men to wear jackets, opting instead for a "resort elegant" dress code.

Pack sunscreen and sunglasses for the Yucatán's strong sun. Other handy items—especially if you're using budget hotels and restaurants or going off the beaten path—include toilet paper, hand sanitizer, facial tissues, a plastic water bottle, and a flashlight (for occasional power outages). Snorkelers should consider bringing their own equipment unless traveling light is a priority; reef shoes with rubber soles for rocky underwater surfaces are also advised. To avoid problems at customs, bring your prescription drugs in the original pill bottle or with a current prescription. Don't count on purchasing necessary OTC or prescription meds (such as sleeping pills); the same brands are not always available in Mexico.

🛂 Passports and Visas

A tourist visa (FMM) and valid passport are required for all visitors to Mexico traveling by air. If you're arriving by plane, the standard tourist visa forms will be given to you while you're on board. They're also available through travel agents and Mexican consulates and at the border if you're entering by land. In addition to having your visa form, you must prove your citizenship.

You're given a portion of the FMM upon entering Mexico. Keep track of this document throughout your trip: you will need it when you depart. You'll be asked to submit it, along with your ticket and passport, to airline representatives at the gate when boarding for departure.

If you lose your tourist card, plan to spend some time (and about US$80) sorting it out with Mexican officials at the immigration office before your flight home.

➕ Safety

Unfortunately, Mexico as a whole has seen a dramatic increase in violence over the past few years, but most of this has been concentrated along border zones and in less touristed areas. Sporadic murders have taken place around Cancún and the Riviera Maya—all of which were drug related. Nevertheless, the Yucatán Peninsula remains one of the safest regions of the country.

With that said, you should always use common sense. Take advantage of hotel safes when available, and carry your own baggage whenever possible unless you're checking into a hotel. Leave expensive jewelry at home, since it often entices thieves and will mark you as a *turista* who can afford to be robbed.

When traveling with all your money, be sure to keep an eye on your belongings at all times and distribute your cash and any valuables between different bags and items of clothing. Do not reach for your money stash in public. If you carry a purse, choose one with a zipper and a thick strap that you can drape across your body; adjust the length so that the purse sits in front of you at or above hip level.

There have been reports of travelers being victimized after imbibing drinks that have been drugged in Cancún night-clubs and even in a few of the resorts here. Never drink alone with strangers, watch your drink being poured, and keep your eye on it at all times. Avoid driving on desolate streets, don't travel at night, and never pick up hitchhikers or hitchhike yourself.

Use ATMs during the day and in big com-mercial areas. Avoid the glass-enclosed street variety where you may be more vulnerable to thieves who force you to withdraw money for them.

Cancún's *Zona Hotelera* (Hotel Zone) is a high-trafficked tourist area, making it extremely safe for those who want to relax at the beach or explore the string of shops and restaurants that line Boulevard Kukulcán. Security has increased on this main strip, which means you'll most likely see armed tourist police driving up and down the boulevard. There is also a security checkpoint that marks the entrance to the Zona Hotelera on Boule-vard Kukulcán in front of Playa Delfines. Tourists are rarely stopped here. Less visited by tourists, El Centro (downtown Cancún) should be avoided late at night. Video cameras survey activity in strategic points throughout the city.

Bear in mind that reporting a crime to the police is often a frustrating experience unless you speak excellent Spanish and have a great deal of patience. If you're victimized, contact your local consular agent or the consular section of your country's embassy in Mexico City.

A woman traveling alone will be the subject of much curiosity, since it is uncommon in Mexico. Don't walk on deserted beaches alone, and make sure your hotel room is securely locked when you retire.

Part of the machismo culture is being flir-tatious and showing off, and lone women are likely to be subjected to catcalls, although this is less true in the Yucatán than in other parts of Mexico. It's best not to enter into a discussion with harassers, even if you speak Spanish. When the suitor is persistent say "no" to whatever is said, walk briskly, and leave immediately for a safe place, such as a nearby store. Dressing conservatively may help, and note that Mexico has laws against topless sunbathing on public beaches.

Distribute your cash, credit cards, IDs, and other valuables between a deep front pocket, an inside jacket or vest pocket, and a hidden money pouch. Don't reach for the money pouch once you're in public.

BEACHES

Empty coastlines can be susceptible to car break-ins and theft. Most resorts notify beachgoers of coastal conditions by displayed colored flags.

Don't swim when the black danger flag flies; a red or yellow flag indicates that you should proceed with caution, and a green flag means the waters are safe.

You will seldom see the green flag—even when the water is tranquil—so swim

Essentials

cautiously. Beware: the calmest-looking waters can still have currents and riptides. Ignoring these warning flags has resulted in at least one tourist drowning each season.

If visiting isolated beaches, bring sunscreen and drinking water to avoid overexposure and dehydration. Take note that waves are most powerful during December, and that hurricane season lasts from June through November.

📦 Shipping

Mail can be sent from your hotel or the *oficina de correos* (post office). Be forewarned, however, that mail service to, within, and from Mexico is notoriously slow and can take anywhere from 10 days to, well, never. Don't send anything of value to or from Mexico via mail, including cash, checks, or credit-card numbers.

Hotel concierges can recommend international carriers, such as DHL, Estafeta, or FedEx, which give your package a tracking number and ensure its arrival back home.

💲 Taxes

An air-departure tax of around US$65 is almost always included as part of your ticket price (check with your airline if you're unsure); in the rare case it's not included, you must pay the tax in cash at the airport.

Mexico has a value-added tax (V.A.T.), or IVA (*impuesto al valor agregado*), of 16%. Many establishments already include the IVA in their quoted price. When comparing rates, it's important to know whether yours does. Occasionally (and illegally) it may be waived for cash purchases; this is nothing for you to worry about. Hotel taxes also apply. The amount is the V.A.T. plus 3% in Quintana Roo, plus 2% in the states of Yucatán and Campeche.

Quintana Roo state (Cancún, Cozumel, Isla Mujeres, Riviera Maya) implemented a new tourist tax in 2021. The so-called Visitax is a separate unbundled fee of MX$224 (approximately US$11) that must be paid for each visitor four years old and over. Payment can be made online (🌐 *www.visitax.gob.mx*) before arrival or during your stay. A few hotels will collect the tax on your behalf. The deadline for payment is when you pass through airport security upon departure. A QR code on your smartphone is your receipt to present to airport authorities.

If you depart Mexico by air or cruise ship, you are eligible for partial reimbursement of the value-added tax you paid on items bought in participating Mexican stores. A private company called MoneyBack administers the tax-refund scheme. Look for its orange-white-black logo in stores. The refund pertains only to items you take out of Mexico; taxes on hotel and restaurant bills do not apply. There are, of course, some restrictions. You must have paid by a Visa or MasterCard issued outside Mexico, or cash, and your purchases must have totaled at least MX$1,200 per individual receipt. While making purchases, you must show your passport and get a receipt and refund form. On departure, you can visit a MoneyBack kiosk at the Cancún, Cozumel, or Mérida airports or a cruise port to receive about half the tax (8.9%) credited to your credit card, a step that takes 45 days. Some visitors have reported problems with the system, and for small purchases, it is probably not worth your time.

💵 Tipping

When tipping in Mexico, remember that the minimum wage is only about $5 a day and that many in the tourism industry don't earn much more. Many tourism workers think in dollars and know, for example, that in the United States porters are tipped $1 to $2 a bag. They therefore expect the peso equivalent from visitors. Though dollars are widely accepted in Cancún and Cozumel, you should always tip using local currency whenever possible, so that service personnel aren't stuck going to the bank to exchange dollars for pesos. Never leave U.S. coins; they are worthless here.

What follows are some guidelines. Naturally, larger tips are always welcome: porters and bellhops, MX$20 per bag at airports and moderate and inexpensive hotels and MX$40 per person per bag at expensive hotels; maids, MX$20 per night (all hotels); waiters, 15% to 20% of the bill, depending on service, and less in simpler restaurants (anywhere you are, make sure a service charge hasn't already been added, a practice that's particularly common in resorts); bartenders, 15% to 20% of the bill, depending on service (and, perhaps, on how many drinks you've had); taxi drivers, MX$20 only if the driver helps you with your bags. Tipping cabbies isn't usual, and they sometimes overcharge tourists when possible. Tip tour guides MX$100 per half day, MX$200 for a full day; drivers about half as much. Gas-station attendants expect MX$10 unless they check the oil, tires, and so on, in which case tip more; parking attendants, MX$10 to MX$20, even if it's for valet parking at a theater or restaurant that charges for the service. For spa attendants, plan on tipping 15% to 20% of the total bill.

🧭 Tours

Old standby Gray Line Cancún covers the entire peninsula with a broad range of packages for both day trips and overnight junkets. It can deliver most experiences on the typical tourist wish list. Mérida-based Ecoturismo Yucatán leads guided tours that hit the region's archaeological and cultural highlights; other options focus on nature, cuisine, and active pursuits. Alltournative is recommended for sustainable adventure tours on the coast; it specializes in archaeological and eco-oriented excursions. EcoColors runs single- and multiday trips to the wildlife reserves at Isla Holbox and Sian Ka'an, and to remote Mayan ruin sites; bird-watching and biking excursions are also available. The California Native includes guide service, accommodations, breakfast, and most lunches in its seven-day trip with stops at Mérida, Izamal, Chichén Itzá, Ek Balam, Uxmal, and Edzná.

🇺🇸 U.S. Embassy/Consulate

The work of the United States Embassy in Mexico City is supplemented by 10 consulates around the country, one of which is in Mérida and serves this region. Mérida, in turn, operates two branch consular agencies (Cancún and Playa del Carmen) which keep shorter hours and can tend to routine matters.

📍 Visitor Information

ONLINE TRAVEL TOOLS

The official website for Mexico tourism has information on tourist attractions and activities, plus an overview of Mexican history and culture. The state of Quintana Roo maintains an informative website

Essentials

(⊕ *www.mexicancaribbean.travel*)
devoted to tourism. Yucatán state does
the same (⊕ *www.yucatan.travel/en*). The
online and print newspaper Yucatán Today
(⊕ *www.yucatantoday.com/en/*) has
comprehensive information on nightlife,
hotel listings, archaeological sites, area
history, maps, and more. We also like the
private sites ⊕ www.cozumelmycozumel.
com and ⊕ www.isla-mujeres.net.

🗓 When to Go

Low Season: You can save 20% to 50%
during low season (the day after Easter
to late November).

Shoulder Season: Post-Easter through the
end of May still offers plenty of morning
sunshine.

High Season: High season lasts from late
November through Easter, with Christmas and Holy Week holiday prices being
up to 50% above regular rates. Beach
resorts—particularly in Cancún—tend to
fill up with college students during summer months and spring break (primarily
March and April). European travelers
flock here during the summer months
too.

WEATHER

November through March, winter
temperatures hover around 27°C (80°F).
Occasional winter fronts called *nortes*
can bring blustery skies and sharp winds
that make air temperatures drop and
swimming unappealing. The spring (especially April and May) sees a period of
intense heat that tapers off in June. The
most active part of hurricane season—
July through the end of September—is
also hot and humid.

Great Itineraries

Cancún and Day Trips

Cancún is the place where you'll likely start your visit. If sunbathing, water sports, and parties that last until the wee hours of the morn are what you're after, you won't need to set foot outside the Zona Hotelera (or even your resort). If you're staying for a week or so, though, you should definitely check out some of the attractions that are an easy day-trip from Cancún.

Driving is the best way to see the peninsula, especially if your time is limited. However, there's nothing in this itinerary that can't be accessed by either bus or taxi.

DAYS 1 AND 2: ARRIVAL AND CANCÚN

After arriving at your hotel, spend your first day or two doing what comes naturally: lounging at the hotel pool, playing in the waves, and going out for dinner and drinks. If you start to feel restless your second day, you can head to El Rey ruins, go tequila tasting at La Destilería, or take a ride into El Centro (downtown Cancún) to browse the shops and open-air markets along Avenida Tulum and grab some real Mexican food.

DAY 3: COZUMEL OR ISLA MUJERES

Spend the day visiting one of the islands off Mexico's Caribbean coast. If beach-combing and a laid-back meal of fresh seafood under a *palapa* (thatch roof) sound appealing, take a ferry from the Embarcadero Dock at Playa Linda and make the 30-minute trip to Isla Mujeres. If you like underwater sea life, drive or take a bus south from Cancún to Playa del Carmen, where you can catch a boat over to Cozumel. There are more than 100 scuba and snorkeling outfits on the island, all of which run trips out to the spectacular Mesoamerican Barrier Reef.

DAY 4: PLAYA DEL CARMEN AND XCARET

In the morning, pack your bathing suit and take a bus from your hotel to the magical Xcaret nature park. You can easily spend an entire day here snorkeling through underwater caves, visiting the butterfly pavilion, sea-turtle nursery, and reef aquarium, and bonding with dolphins (if you reserve a spot early). Alternatively, get up early and take a rental car south along Carretera 307 toward Playa del Carmen, about 1½ hours away. Once you arrive, head to Avenida 5, where you can choose from dozens of waterfront lunch spots. Then spend the afternoon either wandering among the shops and cafés or relaxing at a beach club. Since Xcaret is only a 10-minute drive south, ambitious types can tick that box, too.

DAYS 5 AND 6: TULUM AND COBÁ

If you have the time, it's worth spending a day at each of these beautiful Maya ruins south of Playa del Carmen; they are entirely different from one another. Cobá, which is about a half-hour's drive west of Tulum, is a less visited but spectacular ancient city that's completely surrounded by jungle. Tulum, the only major Mayan site built right on the water, has less stunning architecture but a dazzling location overlooking the Caribbean. After picking through the ruins, you can take a path down from the cliffs and laze for a while on the fabulous beach below. Be warned, though: since Tulum is just a 45-minute drive south from Playa, it's the Yucatán's most popular Mayan site.

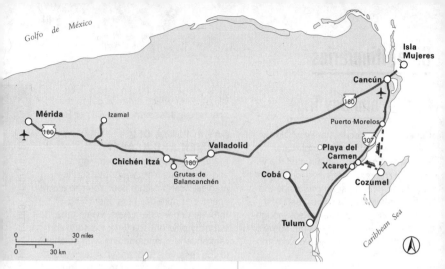

Yucatán and the Mayan Interior

If you have more than a week to spend on the peninsula, you're in luck. You'll have time to visit some of the most beautiful—and famous—ruin sites in the country, and to explore some authentically Mexican inland communities that feel worlds away from the more touristy coast.

If you travel November–March, remember that the places in this itinerary are one hour earlier than Cancún. The rest of the year, they share the same time.

DAY 7: VALLADOLID AND CHICHÉN ITZÁ

Get up early, check out of your hotel, and make the drive inland along Carretera 180D toward the world-renowned Chichén Itzá ruins. Stop en route for a late breakfast or early lunch in Valladolid, about 2½ hours from Cancún. One of the best places to go is the casual eatery at Cenote Zaci, where you can also swim in the lovely jade-green cenote. Continue another half hour to Chichén Itzá and check into one of the area hotels (the Hacienda Chichén is a terrific choice), then spend the afternoon exploring the site before it closes at 5 pm. Visit El Castillo; check out the former marketplace,

steam bath, observatory, and temples honoring formidable Mayan gods; then turn in after dinner at your hotel.

DAYS 8 AND 9: WEST TO MÉRIDA

Either take an easterly detour for an on-the-hour tour at the limestone caverns of Grutas de Balancanchén, or head immediately west on Carretera 180D for the 1½-hour drive to Mérida. After checking into a hotel in the city (Casa Azul is an especially delightful option), wander the *zócalo* (main plaza) and surrounding streets. Spend the next day shopping, visiting museums, and enjoying Mérida's vibrant city scene.

DAYS 10 AND 11: EAST TO CANCÚN AND DEPARTURE

The drive from Mérida back to Cancún will take you about four hours, so if you're flying out of Cancún airport the same day, get an early start. Otherwise, if you can afford to take your time, stop at Izamal on the way back. At this charming town, famous for its bright yellow buildings, you can take a horse-drawn carriage tour of artisans' shops, visit the stately 16th-century church, and check out the crumbling Kinich Kakmó pyramid. Arrive in Cancún in the afternoon, take a last swim on the sugar-sand beach before dinner, and get a good night's sleep at your hotel before your departure the next day.

Contacts

✈ Air

AIRPORTS Aeropuerto Internacional Alberto Acuña Ongay. *(Campeche Aeropuerto Internacional).* ✉ *Av. Lopez Portillo s/n, Campeche City* ☎ *981/823–4059* ⊕ *www. aeropuertosasa.mx.* **Aeropuerto Internacional de Cancún.** ✉ *Carretera Cancún-Chetumal, Km 22, Cancún* ☎ *998/848–7200* ⊕ *www.asur.com.mx.* **Aeropuerto Internacional de Chetumal.** ✉ *Prolong Av. Efrain Aguila, Chetumal* ☎ *983/834–5013* ⊕ *www. aeropuertosasa.mx.* **Aeropuerto Internacional de Cozumel.** ✉ *Av. 65 and Blvd. Aeropuerto, Cozumel* ☎ *987/872–2081* ⊕ *www. asur.com.mx.* **Aeropuerto Internacional Manuel Crescencio Rejón.** *(Mérida Aeropuerto Internacional).* ✉ *Av. Itzáes, Km 14.5, Mérida* ☎ *999/940–6090* ⊕ *www.asur.com.mx.*

TRANSFERS Canada Transfers. ☎ *998/478–2994, 866/751–7012 in USA and Canada* ⊕ *www. canadatransfers.com.* **Van Travel.** ☎ *998/210–3317* ⊕ *www.cancuntransfers.com.* **Cancún Valet.** ☎ *888/479–9095 in the U.S. and Canada, 998/848–3634* ⊕ *www. cancunvalet.com.* **USA Transfers.** ☎ *998/914–0290, 209/382–7587 in USA and Canada* ⊕ *www.usa-transfers.com.*

🚌 Bus

ADO. ☎ *55/5784–4652 in Mexico City* ⊕ *www.ado. com.mx.*

🚗 Car

REGIONAL CAR RENTAL CONTACTS Adocar Rental. ✉ *Cancún* ☎ *998/253–6113* ⊕ *www.adocarrental. com.* **U-Save Car Rental.** ☎ *800800/438–2390 in the U.S. and Canada, 998/886–2393* ⊕ *www. usave.com.*

MAJOR CAR RENTAL CONTACTS Alamo. ☎ *855/533–1196* ⊕ *www.alamo.com.* **Avis.** ☎ *888/583–6369 in the U.S. and Canada, 01800/288–8888 toll-free in Mexico* ⊕ *www.avis. com.* **Budget.** ☎ *877/467–7518 in the U.S. and Canada* ⊕ *www.budget. com.* **Hertz.** ☎ *800/654–3001 in the U.S. and Canada* ⊕ *www.hertz. com.* **National Car Rental.** ☎ *800/227–7368 in the U.S. and Canada* ⊕ *www. nationalcar.com.*

EMERGENCY SERVICE CONTACTS Angeles Verdes. *(Green Angels).* ☎ *078* ⊕ *av.sectur.gob.mx.*

INSURANCE Sanborn's Mexico Auto Insurance. ☎ *800/222–0158 in the U.S. and Canada* ⊕ *www. sanborns.com.*

🛏 Lodging

APARTMENT AND HOUSE RENTALS Akumal Villas. ☎ *866/535–1324 in the U.S. and Canada, 984/875–9088* ⊕ *www. akumal-villas.com.* **Caribbean Realty.** ☎ *910/543–0019* ⊕ *www.puertoaventuras-rentals.com.* **Cozumel Villas.** ☎ *866/564–4427 in the U.S. and Canada, 406/686–9169* ⊕ *www. cozumelvillas.com.* **Lost Oasis.** ☎ *998/887–0951, 226/298–0504 in the U.S. and Canada* ⊕ *www. lostoasis.net.* **Real Estate Yucatán.** ☎ *999/944–1315* ⊕ *www.realestateyucatan.com.* **Turquoise Water Rentals.** ☎ *877/254–9791 in the U.S. and Canada* ⊕ *www.turquoisewater. com.* **Villas & Apartments Abroad.** ☎ *212/213–6435* ⊕ *www.vaanyc.com.* **Villas of Distinction.** ☎ *800/289–0900 in the U.S. and Canada* ⊕ *www.villasofdistinction.com.*

🏛 Embassy

U.S. Consular Agency Cancún. ✉ *Blvd. Kukulcán, Km 13, Zona Hotelera* ☎ *999/316–7168.* **U.S. Consular Agency Playa del Carmen.** ✉ *Plaza Progreso, Carretera Puerto Juárez-Chetumal 2933, Playa del Carmen* ☎ *999/316–7168.* **U.S. Consulate.** ✉ *Calle 60*

Contacts

No. 338, Col. Alcala Martin, Centro ☎ 999/316–7168 ⊕ mx.usembassy.gov/embassy-consulates/merida.

➕ Health

MEDICAL-ONLY INSURERS International Medical Group. *(IMG).* ☎ 263–0669 in the U.S. and Canada, 31717/655–9796 ⊕ www.imglobal.com. **Wallach & Company.** ☎ 800/237–6615 in the U.S. and Canada, 540/687–3166 ⊕ www.wallach.com.

MEDICAL ASSISTANCE COMPANIES AirMed. ☎ 205/443–4840, 800/356–2161 in the U.S. and Canada ⊕ www.airmed.com. **International SOS.** ☎ 215/942–8226 ⊕ www.internationalsos.com. **Medjet.** ☎ 800/527–7478 in the U.S. and Canada, 205/595–6626 ⊕ www.medjetassist.com.

🧭 Tours

RECOMMENDED COMPANIES Alltournative. ✉ Carretera Cancún-Tulum Juarez, Km 287, Playa del Carmen ☎ 01800/466–2848 toll-free in Mexico, 877/437–4990 in the U.S. and Canada ⊕ www.alltournative.com. **The California Native.** ☎ 800/926–1140 in the U.S. and

Canada ⊕ www.calnative.com. **EcoColors.** ✉ Calle Camaron 32, Smz 27, El Centro ☎ 998/884–3667 in Mexico ⊕ www.ecotravelmexico.com. **Ecoturismo Yucatán.** ✉ Calle 3 No. 235, between 32A and 34, Col. Pensiones, Mérida ☎ 999/920–2772 ⊕ www.ecoyuc.com.mx. **Gray Line Cancún.** ☎ 01800/719–5465 toll-free in Mexico, 877/240–5864 in the U.S. and Canada ⊕ www.graylinecancun.com.

📍 Visitor Information

Mexico Tourism Board. ⊕ www.visitmexico.com/en.

On the Calendar

January

El Día de los Tres Reyes. (Three Kings Day) Tradition says the Three Kings brought gifts to the infant Jesus on January 6. So, too, do families present gifts to their children to mark what is almost a "second Christmas." Christmas Eve gift-giving has taken hold as Mexico has started to adopt global customs, but traditional families wait until the 6th. Look for Magi processions and the *rosca*, a traditional sweet fruit bread.

February

Carnaval. Festivities take place the week before Lent, with parades, floats, outdoor dancing, music, and fireworks. They're especially spirited in Mérida, Cozumel, Isla Mujeres, and Campeche. Depending on the calendar, Carnaval could occur in March.

March

Equinoccio de Primavera. (Spring Equinox) The Maya were meticulous astronomers, and they constructed Chichén Itzá's Kukulkán (El Castillo) pyramid to display a twice-a-year optical illusion. As spring begins, a mirage of a serpent shadow "descends" the pyramid. The serpent is said to fertilize the land when it reaches the ground. Visitors come to Chichén Itzá from around the world to witness the spectacle. See the event in September if you can't make it in March; it's just as cool.

Spring Break. No place does spring break quite like Cancún does. Drunken revelry increases markedly, and the scene is legendary. Depending on your proclivities, you might think "Thanks for the warning!" or "Let's party!" Staggered mid-semester breaks on North American college campuses mean drinking, dancing, and debauchery roll through March and early April. (Mexico's drinking age is 18.)

April

Semana Santa is the most important religious week in Mexico. Reenactments of the Passion, family parties and meals, and religious services are held during the week leading up to Easter Sunday. For many Mexicans this means a holiday at the beach, resulting in crowded or booked oceanside hotels. Depending on the calendar, Holy Week could occur in March.

August

Founder's Day. In mid-August, Isla Mujeres celebrates its founding with six days of races, folk dances, music, and regional cuisine.

September

Día de Independencia (Independence Day) is celebrated throughout Mexico with fireworks and parties beginning at 11 pm on September 15, and continuing on the 16th.

Fiesta del Cristo de las Ampollas (Feast of the Christ of the Blisters) is an important religious event that takes place in late September or early October. People dress in traditional clothing and partake in daily mass and processions. Dances, bullfights, and fireworks take place in Ticul and other small villages.

On the Calendar

October

Fiesta del Cristo de Sitilpech. Ten days of festivities and a solemn parade mark this religious event, during which the Christ image of Sitilpech village is carried to Izamal. The biggest dances (with fireworks) are toward the culmination of the festivities on October 28.

November

Día de los Muertos (Day of the Dead), called Hanal Pixan in Mayan, is a joyous holiday during which graves are refurbished and symbolic meals are prepared to welcome the spirits of family members back to Earth for the day. Deceased children are associated with All Saints Day, November 1, while adults are feted on All Souls Day, November 2.

December

Navidad. Among the many Christmas events are *posadas,* during which families gather to eat and sing, and lively parades with colorful floats and brass bands, culminating December 24, on **Nochebuena** (Christmas Eve).

Chapter 3

CANCÚN

Updated by
Dana Freeman

◉ Sights	🍴 Restaurants	🛏 Hotels	🛍 Shopping	🍸 Nightlife
★★★★☆	★★★★★	★★★★★	★★★★☆	★★★★★

WELCOME TO CANCÚN

TOP REASONS TO GO

★ **Dancing the night away:** Salsa, cumbia, reggae, mariachi, hip-hop, and electronic music dizzy the air of the Zona Hotelera's many nightclubs.

★ **Exploring the nearby Maya ruins:** Trips to remarkable sites like Tulum, Cobá, and Chichén Itzá can easily be accomplished in a day.

★ **Getting wild on the water:** Rent a Wave Runner, jungle boat, stand-up paddleboard, or kayak, then skim across the sea or Laguna Nichupté.

★ **Browsing for Mexican crafts:** The colorful stalls of Mercado Veintiocho and Coral Negro will certainly hold something that catches your eye.

★ **Indulging in local flavor:** Dishes like lime soup and *poc chuc* (pork in a sour orange sauce) and drinks like tamarind margaritas pay respect to traditional cuisine.

Over the past five decades, Cancún has turned into the Miami of the south, with international investors pouring money into property development. The main attractions for most visitors lie along the Zona Hotelera, a barrier island shaped roughly like the number 7. To the east is the Caribbean, and to the west you'll find a system of lagoons, the largest of which is Laguna Nichupté. Downtown Cancún—aka El Centro—is 4 km (2½ miles) west of the Zona Hotelera on the mainland.

1 El Centro. Cancún's mainland commercial center provides an authentic glimpse into modern-day Mexico and a colorful alternative to the Zona Hotelera. Many of the restaurants scattered throughout this downtown area offer surprising bursts of culture and Mexican flavor. With more than 800,000 permanent residents, Cancún is full of shops, cafés, and open-air markets that cater mainly to locals. Although the majority of tourists choose to bask on the beaches, those who venture into the heart of El Centro will be glad they did—prices are much more reasonable and the food is outstanding.

2 Punta Sam. A separate strip called Punta Sam, north of Puerto Juárez, is sometimes billed as the Zona Hotelera Norte (Northern Hotel Zone) or Playa Mujeres. This area is quieter than the main Zona, but there are some newer resorts, marinas, restaurants, and a golf course. This is also a good launch point for those heading to the nearby Isla Mujeres.

3 Zona Hotelera. The Hotel Zone is structured along a 25-km (15½-mile) stretch known as Boulevard Kukulcán. On the Caribbean side, dozens of resorts and condominiums tightly line the beachfront like a row of Legos. On the inland side, Laguna Nichupté is home to water sports, shopping malls, restaurants, and golf courses. At the northern tip of this main thoroughfare, near Punta Cancún, is a pack of nightclubs, discos, and bars—a nighttime favorite for those who like to party. For quieter accommodations, opt for a hotel near Punta Nizuc (at the southern tip of Kukulcán Boulevard) or PokTaPok (a small inlet halfway between Punta Cancún and El Centro).

2 PUNTA SAM

Punta Sam

ISLA MUJERES

0   2 miles

0   2 kilometers

Puerto
Juárez

1 EL CENTRO

Av. Uxmal

Av. Bonampak

**Mercado
Veintiocho**

Av. López Portillo

← TO COBA AND
CHICHÉN ITZÁ

Av. Cobá

TO
ISLA MUJERES

Bahía de Mujeres

Laguna
Morales

Blvd. Kukulcán

Playa las Perlas

Playa Linda

Playa Langosta

Playa Pez Volador

Playa
Tortugas

Playa
Caracol

Punta
Cancún

Coral Negro

Laguna
Bojórquez

Playa Gaviota Azul

Playa Chacmool

**ZONA
3 HOTELERA**

Laguna
Nichupté

Playa Marlin

Caribbean Sea

Blvd. Kukulcán

Playa
Ballenas

Av. Tulum

Laguna
Río
Inglés

Playa Delfines

Playa
Punta Nizuc

Punta Nizuc

Paseo Kukulcán

TO TULUM

MEXICAN FOOD PRIMER

Regional culinary characteristics make it difficult to define "Mexican food" as a whole. Its complexity is a direct result of the different ingredients that are available within each region.

Still, there are overlapping items used throughout much of the county. The most frequently used spices are chile powder, cumin, oregano, cilantro, epazote, cinnamon, and cocoa. Chipotle, a smoke-dried jalapeño chile, is common, as are tomatoes, garlic, onions, and peppers. Rice is the most common grain, but corn, beans, and chiles are considered the cornerstones of Mexican cuisine.

The Spanish introduced rice, wheat, olive oil, nuts, cinnamon, wine, and parsley, and a variety of animals including cattle, chickens, goats, sheep, and pigs. These ingredients were incorporated with indigenous corn-based dishes, beans, turkey, fish, vanilla, chocolate, and fruits such as guava, pineapple, and papaya, giving us what we now know as Mexican food.

JUST DESSERTS

Locally grown fruits like mango, mamey, cherimoya, pomegranate, *tuna* (cactus apple), and strawberries are delicious alone or served with a dollop of cream and sugar. Stewed peaches and guavas are refreshing on a hot summer day, especially with a side of *nieves* (sherbet or sorbet). Among Mexico's most common desserts are *tres leches* (sponge cake soaked in three types of milk), churros (fried-dough pastry), and *arroz con leche* (rice cooked in milk with sugar and cinnamon).

Regional Cuisines

Mexican food is much more than burritos, tacos, and rice and beans. Traditional recipes reach far beyond these stereotypical dishes, varying by region as a result of the climate, geography, local ingredients, and cultural differences among the inhabitants.

Yucatán Peninsula. The cuisine of the Yucatán Peninsula has both strong European and Mayan influences. Specialties of the region include *cochinita pibil* (seasoned pork colored with annatto seed and wrapped in banana leaves), turkey with black stuffing, and *papadzules* (tortillas filled with hard-boiled eggs and topped with a pumpkin-seed sauce). Unique to Yucatán's cooking is the earthen pit oven where meats are slowly cooked with *recado negro* or *chilmole* (a blend of dried chiles that are set aflame and ground with spices to create a paste).

Mexico City and Environs (including Puebla). Largely influenced by the rest of the country, Mexico City still has original dishes such as *carnitas* (braised or roasted pork), *menudos* (tripe stew), and *pozole* (pork and hominy soup). Mexico City is also known for its incredible cheeses, tamales, and yellow-corn

White pozole

tortillas. The favored *mixiote* (mutton wrapped in maguey leaves) is slowly steam-baked in a pit oven. Puebla produces various species of cacti including maguey and nopal, which can be eaten as a vegetable (de-spined, of course) or used to make juices and sorbets. Puebla is best known for *mole poblano* (thick, chocolate-tinged sauce).

Oaxaca. With a strong pre-Hispanic influence, the state of Oaxaca has the second-highest percentage of indigenous residents in Mexico, exceeded only by the Yucatán. *Gusanos de maguey* (worms) and *chapulines* (grasshoppers), originally indigenous foods, are fried and eaten like roasted peanuts or sprinkled onto tacos. Oaxaca takes pride in its assortment of chiles, including yellow and black *chilhuacles, costeños,* and light-green *chiles de agua.*

Veracruz. Spanning the coast of the Gulf of Mexico, the cuisine here is characterized geographically by fish and seafood. It is also one of the most versatile agricultural regions of Mexico. Nut- and seed-based sauces are very popular, as are spicy chicken and vegetable dishes.

Cochinita pibil tacos

Cancún is a great place to experience 21st-century Mexico, because it has everything you'd want in a vacation: shopping, sports, spas, and beaches. Here you'll find five-star resorts, exceptional food, Mexican culture, and natural beauty, all within day-trip distance of the world-famous Maya ruins.

The locals—most of whom have embraced the accoutrements of urban middle-class life—typically live on the mainland in a part of the city called El Centro, but they work in the Zona Hotelera's tourist hub. The zone's main drag is Boulevard Kukulcán, and kilometer markers along it indicate where you are, from Km 1 near El Centro to Km 25 at the southern tip of Punta Nizuc. The area in between consists entirely of hotels, restaurants, shopping complexes, marinas, and time-share condominiums. Most travelers base themselves in this 25-km (15½-mile) stretch of paradise.

The party atmosphere of Zona Hotelera has inevitably earned it the title "Spring Break Capital of the World." Dozens of bars and nightclubs cater to college students just south of Punta Cancún at Km 9. Fortunately, this late-night/early-morning scene is contained within a small area, far from the larger resorts. Cancún, though, isn't just a magnet for youth on the loose. Adults with more sophisticated tastes appreciate its posh restaurants and world-class spas, while families are drawn to the limitless water sports and a plethora of children's activities.

If you believe that local flavor trumps the Zona Hotelera's pristine beaches, El Centro beckons. Although less visited by vacationers, the downtown area holds cultural gems that will remind you that you really are in Mexico. Hole-in-the-wall cantinas promise authentic regional food; evocative markets offer bargain-priced goods; and the hotels, while much more modest in terms of scale and amenities, provide true Mexican ambience for more modest prices, too.

Planning

Timing

There's a lot to see and do in Cancún—if you can force yourself away from the beach, that is. Understandably, many visitors stay here a week, or longer, without ever leaving the silky sands and seductive comforts of their resorts. If you're game to do some exploring, though, allow an extra two or three days for day trips to nearby eco-parks and archaeological sites.

When to Go

The sun shines an average of 253 days a year in Cancún. During high season (late November to April), the weather is nearly perfect, with temperatures hovering around 29°C (84°F) during the day and 18°C (64°F) at night. Hotel prices hit their peak between December 15 and January 5. If you plan to visit during Christmas, spring break, or Easter, you should book at least three months in advance.

Vacationers with travel-date flexibility can avoid the crowds and save 20% to 50% on accommodations during the remaining months. Be advised, though, that May through September are hot and humid, with temperatures that can top 36°C (97°F). The rainy season starts in mid-September and lasts until mid-November, bringing afternoon downpours that can last anywhere from 30 minutes to two hours. El Centro's streets often get flooded during these storms, and traffic can grind to a halt.

Getting Here and Around

AIR

Located 16 km (9 miles) southwest of the heart of Cancún and 10 km (6 miles) from the Zona Hotelera's southernmost point, Cancún Aeropuerto Internacional (CUN) receives direct scheduled flights from many cities, including New York, Washington, D.C., Houston, Dallas, Miami, Chicago, Los Angeles, Orlando, Fort Lauderdale, Charlotte, Atlanta, Toronto, and Montreal. An increasing number of direct charter flights from other locales are also available. Hourly buses link the airport to downtown Cancún; taxis, *colectivos* (minibuses), hotel shuttles, and rental cars are other options.

(Check out our Travel Smart chapter for more on air travel and ground transportation.)

BICYCLE

Cancún is not the sort of place you can get to know on foot, although there's a cycling and walking path that starts downtown at the beginning of the Zona Hotelera and continues through to Punta Nizuc. The beginning of the path parallels a grassy strip of Boulevard Kukulcán decorated with reproductions of ancient Mexican art.

BUS

For travel within the Zona Hotelera, buses R1, R2, R15, and R27 stop every five minutes along Boulevard Kukulcán and cost a flat MX$10 no matter where you get on or off. The R2 and R15 continue to El Centro's Walmart and Mercado Veintiocho; the R1 goes as far as Puerto Juárez and the main bus terminal in El Centro.

Buses for farther-flung destinations leave from El Centro's terminal. One of the oldest bus lines in Mexico, ADO has first-class buses that make stops in Puerto Morelos, Playa del Carmen, Tulum, Felipe Carrillo Puerto, Limones, and Chetumal; the full trip (concluding in Chetumal) takes five hours and 45 minutes and costs MX$354. Fifteen buses make the trip daily, departing between 6 am and midnight. Mayab, a division of ADO, has second-class buses leaving for destinations along the Riviera Maya every hour.

BUS CONTACTS ADO. ☎ *555/133–2424* ⊕ *www.ado.com.mx.* **Terminal de Autobuses.** ⊠ *Corner of Avs. Tulum and Uxmal, El Centro* ☎ *998/884–5552.*

CAR

If you are planning to visit only Cancún, you don't need to (and probably shouldn't) rent a car. But if you want to explore the region, a car can be convenient if expensive. Be sure to read our extensive guidelines regarding road conditions, insurance requirements, and costs *(see Car in Travel Smart)* so that you can make an informed decision.

TAXI

It's easy and cheap to get around Cancún by bus; if you prefer traveling by taxi, however, you can always find one. Cab rides cost MX$135–MX$270 within the Zona Hotelera and MX$67–MX$135 within El Centro. Fares between the two run around MX$270. A ride to the ferries at Punta Sam or Puerto Juárez will set you back MX$330 or more. Make sure you check the fare before accepting a ride; a list of rates can be found in the lobby of most hotels or you can ask the concierge.

The ride-hailing service Uber operates in Cancún, albeit illegally. Accounts abound of its drivers unable to enter the airport and the Zona Hotelera, leaving passengers stranded. Until Uber and the authorities work out their differences, we recommend not using its services.

Beaches

All beaches can be reached by public transportation; just let the driver know where you are headed. Those not maintained by hotels will have seaweed on their shores. If you're traveling with young children, it's best to choose beaches facing Bahía de Mujeres at the top of the "7." They tend to be less crowded and more sheltered than ones on the Caribbean side. Wide beaches and shallow waters make the northern tip ideal for those wanting to snorkel or swim. Forming the right side of the "7" are beaches facing the Caribbean Sea. Here riptides and currents can be somewhat dangerous, especially when the surf is high. For snorkeling, it's best to head to the southern end of Boulevard Kukulcán near the Westin Hotel. In the saltwater lagoon, jungle boats and Wave Runners rule the waters by day and adult crocodiles wade the banks by night.

Don't swim when the black danger flag flies; a red or yellow flag indicates that you should proceed with caution; and a green flag means the waters are calm. Most likely, you will always see a red or yellow flag posted on the shores.

Hotels

You might find it bewildering to choose among Cancún's many hotels, not least because brochures and websites make them sound—and look—almost exactly alike. For luxury and amenities, the Zona Hotelera is the place to stay. If you want to be in the heart of the action, northern hotels near Punta Cancún are within walking distance of the nightclubs. Quieter properties are located at the southern end of Boulevard Kukulcán and in the residential streets between El Centro and the Zona Hotelera at Laguna Nichupté near the PokTaPok Golf Course. In the modest Centro, local color outweighs facilities. Downtown hotels here are more basic and much less expensive than those in the Zona.

Many hotels have all-inclusive packages, as well as theme-night parties complete with food, beverages, activities, and games. Take note: generally the larger the all-inclusive resort, the blander the food (and the more watered-down the cocktails). For more memorable meals, you may need to dine off-site and essentially pay for food you're not consuming.

Many of the larger and more popular all-inclusives will not guarantee an ocean-view room when you make your reservation. If this is important to you, check that all rooms have ocean views at your chosen hotel, or book only at places that will guarantee one. Be sure to bring your confirmation information with you to prove you paid for an ocean-view room. Also be careful about lost wristbands and unreturned towels, since many resorts charge up to $150 per day for the former and $25 for the latter. When checking out, make sure the hotel hasn't tacked on excessive phone or minibar charges, as a few tend to do.

At check-in, ask if your all-inclusive rate includes tips—some resorts automatically add 15% gratuities—and resort fees, which tend to be hidden supplementary charges.

While Cancún is the consummate spring-break destination, many lodgings here will not accept partying college students as guests, no matter what the time of year.

Hotel reviews have been condensed for this book. For expanded reviews, facilities, and current deals, visit Fodors.com.

Nightlife

We're not here to judge: we know that most people come to Cancún to party. If you want fine dining and dancing under the stars, you'll definitely find it here. But if your tastes run more toward bikini contests, all-night chug-a-thons, or cross-dressing Cher impersonators, rest assured: Cancún has plenty of those, too. For all its raucous reputation, Cancún concentrates its party-hearty nightlife along a relatively small strip of the Zona Hotelera, south of the convention center. It's as easy to avoid as it is to find.

Indoor areas of all venues are no-smoking. Carrying open containers of alcohol outside bars and restaurants is against the law.

If you want to avoid rowdy spring breakers, stay clear of "open-bar" establishments and chain restaurants like Señor Frog's. They'll likely be packed with party animals on the loose.

Restaurants

Why dine out in Cancún if you've already paid for meals at your all-inclusive resort? Even at all-inclusives, some resort restaurants may not be included in your rate, and the city has one of Mexico's great dining scenes, so you'll be amply rewarded if you leave your hotel grounds. Large breakfast and brunch buffets are among the most popular meals in the Zona Hotelera, with prices ranging from MX$200 to MX$400 per person. El Centro, downtown Cancún, offers an impressive selection of restaurants, all just a taxi ride away from the Zona Hotelera. Most local restaurants open for lunch around 2 pm and generally stay open until midnight. When choosing one, be aware that those lining Avenidas Tulum and Yaxchilán are often noisy and crowded, and gas fumes make it hard to enjoy meals alfresco. Many of the finer options are on Avenida Bonampak. Eateries in the Parque de las Palapas, just off Avenida Tulum, serve expertly prepared Mexican food. Deeper into the city center, you can find fresh seafood and traditional fare at Mercado Veintiocho (Market 28). Dress is casual in Cancún, but many restaurants do not allow bare feet, short shorts, or bathing suits. Even at the fanciest places, suggested attire is "resort elegant," meaning long pants, collared shirts, and closed shoes for gentlemen. For women, a dress or skirt and blouse with chichi sandals or heels will suffice.

Upscale resorts in the Zona Hotelera typically purify their tap water; however, ask in advance whether it's safe to drink.

The indoor portions of all restaurants are no-smoking.

WHAT IT COSTS in Dollars and Pesos			
$	$$	$$$	$$$$
RESTAURANTS			
under MX$135	MX$135–MX$200	MX$201–MX$350	over MX$350
HOTELS IN DOLLARS			
under $100	$100–$200	$201–$300	over $300
HOTELS IN PESOS			
under MX$1,450	MX$1,450–MX$2,900	MX$2,901–MX$4,400	over MX$4,400

Safety

Cancún is one of the safest cities in Mexico. Reported violence generally takes place 2,090 km (1,300 miles) from Cancún on the northern border of Mexico, the same distance from New York to Texas. Don't be surprised to see Tourist Police patrolling the Zona Hotelera, especially during the holidays and high season when security is increased. The C4 Surveillance and Rescue Center monitors the tourist area through video cameras installed at strategic points throughout the city, and an emergency 911 call center is available. Visitors are still advised to exercise caution and use common sense while traveling.

Shopping

The *centros comerciales* (malls) in Cancún are fully air-conditioned and as well kept as similar establishments in the United States or Canada. Like their northerly counterparts, they also sell just about everything: designer clothing, beachwear (including raunchy T-shirts aimed at the spring break crowd), sportswear, jewelry, music, electronics, household items, shoes, and books. Some even have the same terrible mall food that's standard north of the border. Prices are fixed in shops. They're also generally—but not always—higher than in the markets, where bargaining is a given. Perfumes in Cancún are considerably less expensive than at home (and even than at the duty-free shops at the airport). Tequila is a bargain here as well, but make sure you buy at the supermarket rather than at a souvenir shop.

There are many duty-free stores selling designer goods at reduced prices, sometimes as much as 30% or 40% below retail. You can find handwoven textiles, leather goods, and handcrafted silver jewelry, although prices are higher than in other cities and the selection is limited.

Monday through Saturday, shopping hours are generally 10–1 and 4–7, although more stores stay open throughout the day rather than closing for siesta. Many open on Sunday as well. Centros comerciales tend to be open daily from 9 or 10 am to 8 or 9 pm.

Sights

Taxis from the Zona Hotelera to El Centro cost around MX$240 each way. An inexpensive option is to take a northbound public bus to the Kukulcán–Bonampak intersection, which marks the beginning of El Centro (MX$10). From here, you can explore by foot or flag down a taxi to your area of choice. If you want to get a taste of downtown culture, start at the colorful Mercado Veintiocho or Parque de las Palapas. To return to the Zona Hotelera, take a taxi to the Chedraui on Avenida Tulum and then catch the bus that passes every few minutes toward the Zona. (Don't be alarmed if a man in a clown suit roams the aisle in search of tips: at night the buses come alive with all sorts of amateur performers, from accordionists to jugglers, hoping to earn a few pesos.)

South of Punta Cancún, Boulevard Kukulcán becomes a busy road and is difficult for pedestrians to cross. It's also punctuated by steeply inclined driveways that turn into the hotels, most of which are set back at least 100 yards from the road. The lagoon side of the boulevard consists of scrubby stretches of land alternating with marinas, shopping centers, and restaurants.

Because there are so few sights, there are no orientation tours of Cancún: just do the local bus circuit to get a feel for your surroundings. Buses run until midnight, and you'll rarely have to wait more than five minutes.

You might find El Centro's downtown layout confusing at first—it's based on a circular pattern rather than a grid. The whole city is divided into districts called Super Manzanas (abbreviated "Sm"), each with its own central square or park. In general, walks through downtown are somewhat unpleasant, with whizzing cars, corroded pathways, and overgrown weeds. Sidewalks sometimes disappear, forcing pedestrians to cross grassy inlets and thin strips of land separating four lanes of traffic. Few people seem to know exactly where anything is, even those who live in El Centro. When exploring on foot, expect to get lost at least once. Taxis are always a good bet for exploring downtown Cancún.

Tours

GENERAL TOURS
Gray Line Cancún
Cancún's Gray Line office can customize your vacation, offering everything from luxury airport transportation and dolphin adventures to sunset dinner cruises and tours of Chichén Itzá. ☎ *877/240–5864, 998/887–2495, 01800/719–5465 toll-free in Mexico* ⊕ *www.graylinecancun.com* ✉ *From MX$680.*

Olympus Tours
Specializing in outings around Cancún, this agency's options run the gamut from ATV and horseback tours to cenote excursions and cultural encounters. It will also book reservations for Xcaret, Xel-Há, and other area adventure parks. ⊠ *Av. Yaxchilán, Sm. 17, Lote 13, Mza 2, El Centro* ☎ *998/881–9030, 786/338–9358 in the U.S.* ⊕ *www.olympus-tours.com* ✉ *From MX$750.*

BOAT TOURS
AquaWorld
In addition to Nichupté lagoon tours and Isla Mujeres day trips, AquaWorld's sightseeing menu includes unusual options like the B.O.B. Adventure. Short for Breathing Observation Bubble, B.O.B. lets you steer through the reefs on a machine that resembles an underwater motor scooter (a pressurized helmet allows for normal breathing). Tours on the Paradise SubSee are another alternative. This "floating submarine" is a glass-bottom boat that submerges halfway into the water. On the short journey to Punta Nizuc, you'll see turtles, fish, coral, and a few statues in the Underwater Museum. ⊠ *Blvd. Kukulcán, Km 15.2, Zona Hotelera* ☎ *998/689–1013, 866/201–1236 in the U.S.* ⊕ *www.aquaworld.com.mx* ✉ *B.O.B. MX$920; SubSee Explorer from MX$544; other tours from MX$817.*

Asterix Tours
This is one of the few companies permitted to depart from the Zona Hotelera on tours to Isla Contoy and the underwater gardens of Isla Mujeres. Trips to the former leave at 9 am and return at 5 pm on Tuesday, Thursday, and Saturday; ones to the latter leave on Wednesday and Friday. Day- and nighttime fishing trips run three times a week. ⊠ *Blvd. Kukulcán, Km 5.5, Zona Hotelera* ☎ *998/886–4270* ⊕ *www.contoytours.com* ✉ *Isla Contoy tours MX$1,900.*

Kolumbus Tours
Excursions to Isla Contoy are available daily on a double-decker trawler, less frequently during the May–October low season. You can also choose a catamaran tour that combines Isla Contoy and Isla Mujeres. ⊠ *Punta Conoco 36, Sm 24, El Centro* ☎ *998/885–5333* ⊕ *www.kolumbustours.com* ✉ *From MX$1,294.*

Sea Passion Catamaran
Day trips to Isla Mujeres (which include a buffet lunch, open bar, and snorkel equipment) are available by reservation. ⊠ *Chac-Chi Marina, Blvd. Kukulcán, Km 3.2, Zona Hotelera* ☎ *998/849–4940* ⊕ *www.seapassion.mx* ✉ *From MX$1,089.*

ECOTOURS
Eco Colors
Bike tours, butterfly- and bird-watching adventures, as well as kayaking, diving, and eco-oriented snorkeling trips can be booked through Eco Colors. It also

specializes in cultural programs and volunteer opportunities. ✉ *Calle Camarón 32, Sm 27, El Centro* ☎ *998/884–9580* ⊕ *www.ecotravelmexico.com* ✉ *From MX$1,361.*

Visitor Information

Cancún Convention & Visitors Bureau. (CVB) ✉ *Zona Hotelera, Blvd. Kukulcán, Km 9, Cancun Center* ☎ *998/881–2745* ⊕ *www.mexicancaribbean.travel/cancun.*

El Centro

There really is a downtown Cancún, although you'll never see it if you confine yourself to your resort in the Zona Hotelera. El Centro's malls and markets offer a glimpse of Mexico's urban lifestyle. Avenida Tulum, the main drag, is marked by a huge sculpture of shells and starfish in the middle of a traffic circle. This iconic Cancún sight, which locals refer to as El Ceviche, is particularly dramatic at night when the lights are turned on. El Centro is also home to many restaurants and bars. (We recommend taking a taxi to and from at night.) You'll also find Mercado Veintiocho (Market 28), an enormous crafts market just off Avenidas Yaxchilán and Sunyaxchén, and the nearby Mercado Veintitres (Market 23) for a fun look at a local produce market. For bargain shopping, hit the stores and small strip malls along Avenida Tulum.

The built-up area in the Zona Hotelera near the convention center at the sharply angled bend of Boulevard Kukulcán is not El Centro.

 Restaurants

Bandoneón

$$$$ | **ARGENTINE** | Entering Bandoneón you might think you're in Buenos Aires. The broad menu features starters like smoked marlin and charcoal-grilled provolone cheese; mains include pasta, fish, and chicken—but steak is the star. **Known for:** cool Argentine atmosphere; impeccably prepared steaks; enormous wine selection. $ *Average main: MP406* ✉ *Av. Bonampak at Nichupté, El Centro* ☎ *998/889–9500, 998/889–9911* ⊕ *www.bandoneonrestaurantes.com.*

Café con Gracia

$$ | **CAFÉ** | This adorable downtown café with an outdoor garden is a local favorite for breakfast. They serve an extensive selection of coffees alongside yummy pancakes, crepes, bagels, waffles, and paninis. **Known for:** hot and cold drinks; all-day breakfast menu; informal café setting. $ *Average main: MP200* ✉ *Avenue Tankah 69, Mza 1 Lot 24, El Centro* ☎ *998/884–9850, 998/734–4218 WhatsApp* ⊕ *cafecongracia.com.*

El Cejas

$ | **SEAFOOD** | The clientele is lively and the seafood is fresh at this open-air eatery, located at the bustling Mercado Veintiocho. The kitchen serves crab (stuffed, steamed, or fried) and whole fried fish that's crispy outside and moist inside. **Known for:** quality crab and fried fish; fun atmosphere in a local market; strolling musicians. $ *Average main: MP130* ✉ *Mercado Veintiocho, Sm. 26, Loc 90–100, El Centro* ✛ *Inside Market 28* ☎ *998/884–0401* ⊕ *elcejas.negocio.site.*

El Oasis

$$ | **SEAFOOD** | This aptly named eatery is a welcome respite from El Centro's busy streets. House specials include grilled seafood with rice, fish fillet with coconut cream, and smaller dishes like ceviche or *aguachiles* (spicy lime shrimp). **Known for:** dishes grilled to perfection; colorful decorations; relaxing setting. $ *Average main: MP140* ✉ *Av. Yaxchilan, Sm 17, Mza 2, Lote 3, across from Costco, El Centro* ☎ *998/884–1140, 998/294–0128 WhatsApp* ⊕ *www.eloasismariscos.com* ⊘ *No dinner.*

★ La Dolce Vita

$$$ | **ITALIAN** | The grande dame of Cancún restaurants delivers on the promise of its name. The fare includes homemade pizzas and pastas such as Bolognese-style lasagna; veal scaloppine and calamari steak in shrimp and lobster sauce are other options. **Known for:** excellent wine list; chocolate desserts; slow service. [$] *Average main: MP338* ✉ *Av. Cobá 87, Sm 3, El Centro* ☎ *998/884–3393* 🌐 *www.ladolcevitacancun.com.*

La Habichuela

$$$ | **CARIBBEAN** | The much-loved Green Bean has an elegant yet cozy indoor dining room plus an outdoor area full of Mayan sculptures and local flora. The seafood lover in you can satisfy your cravings with Caribbean lobster tail or giant shrimp prepared 10 different ways. **Known for:** lush surroundings; ample seafood portions; cozy elegance. [$] *Average main: MP271* ✉ *Av. Margaritas 25, Sm 22, El Centro* ☎ *998/884–3158* 🌐 *www.lahabichuela.com.*

La Parrilla

$$$ | **MEXICAN** | With its flamboyant live mariachi music and energetic waiters, this place is a Cancún classic. The menu isn't fancy, but it offers good, basic Mexican food—including sizzling fajitas, thick burritos, and 30 different taco dishes. **Known for:** solid Mexican menu; showy service; great tequila selection. [$] *Average main: MP216* ✉ *Av. Yaxchilán 51, Sm 22, El Centro* ☎ *998/287–8118* 🌐 *www.laparrilla.com.mx.*

Locanda Paolo

$$$ | **ITALIAN** | Flowers and artwork lend warmth to this sophisticated Italian restaurant, where the cuisine includes linguine with lobster, angel-hair pasta with seafood, specialty lasagnas, plus assorted meat and fish dishes. The waiters are laid-back and seem to know everyone who walks in the door. **Known for:** terrific international wine menu; careful attention to Italian dishes; friendly service in formal setting. [$] *Average main: MP270* ✉ *Av. Bonampak 145, Sm. 3, corner of Calle Jurel, El Centro* ☎ *998/887–2627, 998/884–8396* 🌐 *www.locandapaolo.com.*

100% Natural

$$ | **CAFÉ** | Start the day at this open-air restaurant with a signature omelet and a *bebida inteligente* ("intelligent drink") which combines fruit juice with ginseng. Sandwiches, soy burgers, and stuffed pitas are prepared with fresh-baked breads. **Known for:** vegetarian cuisine; fresh fruit juices; relaxing, plant-filled surroundings. [$] *Average main: MP135* ✉ *Av. Sunyaxchén 62, Sm 25, El Centro* ☎ *998/884–0102* 🌐 *www.100natural.com.*

★ Peter's Restaurant

$$$ | **INTERNATIONAL** | Although it has only six tables, Peter's Restaurant has an impressive menu that gives international dishes a Mexican twist—think foie gras with hibiscus or grilled salmon with potato-chipotle mash. Portions are generous, flavors are outstanding, and prices aren't too bad. **Known for:** cozy, intimate atmosphere; key lime pie; expat hangout. [$] *Average main: MP271* ✉ *Av. Bonampak, Sm. 3, between Robalo and Sierra, El Centro* ☎ *998/251–9310* ⏲ *Closed Mon. June–Nov. No lunch.*

Rolandi's Pizzeria

$$ | **PIZZA** | This Cancún landmark since almost the beginning draws crowds with its scrumptious wood-fired pizzas. The most popular, Pizza del Patrón, is topped with tomatoes, prosciutto, arugula, and mascarpone cheese. **Known for:** calzones with fresh ingredients; friendly service; 20 pizza varieties. [$] *Average main: MP189* ✉ *Av. Cobá 12, Sm. 5, El Centro* ☎ *998/884–4047* 🌐 *rolandispizzeria.mx.*

Ty-Coz

$ | **CAFÉ** | The inexpensive croissants and freshly brewed coffee make a delicious breakfast combo at this place tucked behind the Comercial Mexicana grocery store on Avenida Tulum. At lunchtime, stop in for a huge sandwich stuffed with

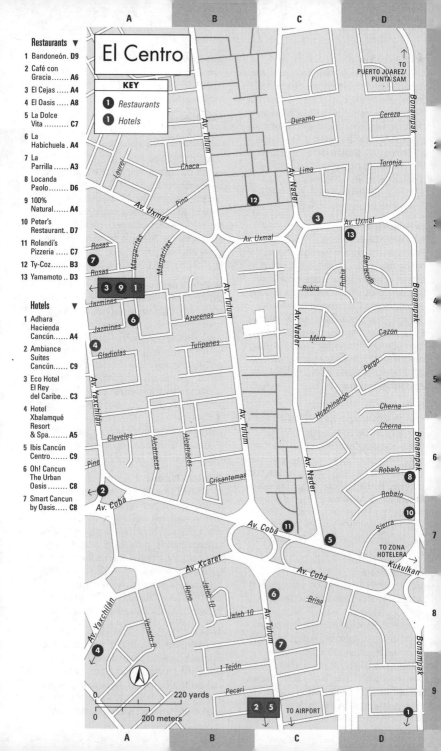

El Centro

Restaurants ▼

1 Bandoneón. **D9**
2 Café con Gracia....... **A6**
3 El Cejas **A4**
4 El Oasis **A8**
5 La Dolce Vita **C7**
6 La Habichuela . **A4**
7 La Parrilla **A3**
8 Locanda Paolo **D6**
9 100% Natural **A4**
10 Peter's Restaurant. **D7**
11 Rolandi's Pizzeria **C7**
12 Ty-Coz **B3**
13 Yamamoto .. **D3**

Hotels ▼

1 Adhara Hacienda Cancún...... **A4**
2 Ambiance Suites Cancún...... **C9**
3 Eco Hotel El Rey del Caribe... **C3**
4 Hotel Xbalamqué Resort & Spa.... **A5**
5 Ibis Cancún Centro....... **C9**
6 Oh! Cancun The Urban Oasis **C8**
7 Smart Cancun by Oasis..... **C8**

KEY

🔴 Restaurants
🔴 Hotels

TO PUERTO JUÁREZ/ PUNTA SAM

Av. Tulum

Laurel

Chaca

Av. Uxmal

Pino

Rosas

Margaritas

Rosas

Margaritas

Jazmines

Jazmines

Azucenas

Av. Tulum

Tulipanes

Gladiolas

Av. Yaxchilán

Claveles

Alcatraces

Alcatraces

Pino

Crisantemas

Av. Cobá

Av. Tulum

Av. Xcaret

Reno

Jaleb 10

Jaleb 10

Av. Tulum

Venado 8

1 Tejón

Pecari

Av. Cobá

Av. Cobá

Brisa

Av. Yaxchilán

TO AIRPORT

Durazno

Av. Lima

Av. Nader

Av. Uxmal

Av. Uxmal

Rubia

Rubia

Av. Nader

Mero

Huachinango

Av. Nader

Cereza

Toronja

Barracuda

Cazon

Pargo

Cherna

Cherna

Robalo

Robalo

Sierra

Bonampak

Bonampak

TO ZONA HOTELERA

Kukulkan

Bonampak

0   220 yards
0   200 meters

all the deli classics, but be prepared to wait awhile since lines are long. **Known for:** dirt-cheap prices; local atmosphere; monster sandwiches. $ *Average main: MP81* ⊠ *Av. Tulum, Sm 2, El Centro* ☎ *998/884–6060* ⊗ *Closed Sun.*

Yamamoto

$$$ | JAPANESE | The oldest Japanese restaurant in Cancún serves the best sushi and sashimi in El Centro with a menu of traditional Japanese dishes like chicken teriyaki and tempura for those who prefer their food cooked. Large groups can order combination platters of sushi, sashimi, kushikatsu, and gyoza. **Known for:** delivery to El Centro hotels; Japanese decor; terrific sushi variety. $ *Average main: MP230* ⊠ *Av. Uxmal 31, Sm. 3, El Centro* ☎ *998/887–3366* ⊕ *www. yamamoto-cancun.com.*

🛏 Hotels

Adhara Hacienda Cancún

$$ | HOTEL | A stimulating change from the street on which it sits, this hacienda-style building is strikingly hip and sleek. **Pros:** business center; one handicapped-accessible unit; beach shuttle; state-of-the-art gym equipment. **Cons:** east-facing rooms tend to have street noise; popular buffet breakfast not included in room rate; lights in rooms are movement triggered. $ *Rooms from: $100* ⊠ *Av. Náder 1, El Centro* ☎ *998/881–6500, 998/122–1861 WhatsApp* ⊕ *www.adharacancun.com* ⇆ *Adhara 173 rooms, Margaritas 74 rooms* ⏉ *No Meals.*

Ambiance Suites Cancún

$ | HOTEL | Branding itself as "your home and office," this modern hotel caters mostly to business executives. **Pros:** good value; convenient El Centro location. **Cons:** unfriendly staff; far from the beach. $ *Rooms from: $88* ⊠ *Av. Tulum 227, Sm. 20, El Centro* ☎ *998/892–0392* ⊕ *www.ambiancecancun.com* ⇆ *48 rooms* ⏉ *Free Breakfast.*

Eco Hotel El Rey del Caribe

$ | HOTEL | Thanks to the use of solar energy, a water-recycling system, and composting toilets, this tranquil hotel has little impact on the environment—and its luxuriant garden blocks the heat and noise of downtown. **Pros:** free Wi-Fi; walking distance to El Centro's shops and restaurants; eco-friendly; affordable spa. **Cons:** simple and musty rooms; alcohol is not served at the hotel restaurant; mosquitoes in common areas. $ *Rooms from: $92* ⊠ *Av. Uxmal 24, Sm. 2A, at Náder, El Centro* ☎ *998/884–2028, 800/508-1864 In USA* ⊕ *www.elrey-delcaribe.com* ⇆ *31 rooms* ⏉ *Free Breakfast* ⏴ *Visa and Mastercard only, no American Express.*

Hotel Xbalamqué Resort & Spa

$ | HOTEL | This refreshing retreat from El Centro's bustling streets reflects Mayan culture through murals, statues, and reliefs; it forms part of a complex that also includes two restaurants and a snack shop, which are open to the general public. **Pros:** kids under 11 stay free; small on-site spa and beauty salon; good El Centro location. **Cons:** intermittent hot water; street noise audible from front rooms; patchy Wi-Fi. $ *Rooms from: $75* ⊠ *Av. Yaxchilan 31, Sm. 22, Mza 18, El Centro* ☎ *998/892–3377, 998/283–3353 Reservations* ⊕ *www.xbalamque.com* ⇆ *81 rooms, 10 suites* ⏉ *No Meals.*

Ibis Cancún Centro

$ | HOTEL | Within walking distance of Las Américas Shopping Center and next to a grocery store, this hotel is perfect for mixing business with pleasure at a very reasonable price. **Pros:** car rental agency and tour operator on-site; clean, bright rooms; free underground parking. **Cons:** mainly caters to business and budget travelers; no pool; hotel will not sell alcohol on Sunday. $ *Rooms from: $67* ⊠ *Avs. Tulum and Nichupté, Sm 11, El Centro* ☎ *998/272–8500* ⊕ *all.accor.com/ hotel/7118/index.en.shtml* ⇆ *190 rooms* ⏉ *No Meals.*

Oh! Cancun The Urban Oasis

$$ | HOTEL | This fresh, hip hotel greets guests with a pop art–style lobby and vibrant hallways, which lead to guest rooms with marble floors, iPod docks, 42-inch flat-screen TVs, minibars, and small balconies. **Pros:** lovely pool area; adults-only. **Cons:** not on the beach; no spa; not suitable for families. [$] *Rooms from: $110 ⊠ Av. Tulum, Sm 4, corner of Brisa, El Centro ☎ 998/848–8600, 800/446–2747 USA/Canada, 998/287–4478 WhatsApp ⊕ www.oasishotels.com ⤴ 55 rooms, 7 suites ⦾ Free Breakfast.*

Smart Cancun by Oasis

$ | HOTEL | Oasis Smart caters mainly to business travelers, with its El Centro location just 20 minutes from the airport and 10 minutes from Hotel Zone. **Pros:** walking distance from main avenues; free shuttle to sister properties in Zona Hotelera; peaceful atmosphere. **Cons:** seemingly safe but old elevators; small bathrooms. [$] *Rooms from: $80 ⊠ Av. Tulum and Calle Brisa, Lote 113, Sm 4, El Centro ☎ 998/848–8600, 800/446–2747, 998/287–4478 WhatsApp ⊕ www.oasishotels.com ⤴ 119 rooms ⦾ Free Breakfast.*

🌟 Nightlife

Laser Hot Bar

BARS | The oldest gay bar in Cancún has been operating for over 15 years. Doors open at 10 pm, but don't expect things to get underway until midnight. There's no cover here. ⊠ *Plaza Galerias, Av. Tulum 20, Sm 5, El Centro ☎ 998/860–0426, 998/366–1560.*

Parque de las Palapas

GATHERING PLACES | To mingle with locals and hear great music for free, head to the Parque de las Palapas. Every Friday night at 7:30 there's live music that ranges from jazz to salsa; lots of locals show up to dance. On Sunday afternoon the Cancún Municipal Orchestra plays.

⊠ *Bordered by Avs. Tulum, Yaxchilán, Uxmal, and Cobá, Sm 22, El Centro.*

🛍 Shopping

There are lots of interesting shops downtown along Avenida Tulum between Avenidas Cobá and Uxmal; for the most part, however, stores in El Centro are geared toward the needs of locals rather than tourists. The most interesting shops for travelers may be in Plaza Bonita; otherwise, there are better options available in the Zona Hotelera.

GROCERY STORES

Chedraui

CHAIN | With several locations in El Centro, this popular superstore—think a Mexico-wide version of Walmart—has a large selection of local and American products. ⊠ *Av. Tulum 57, at Av. Cobá, El Centro ☎ 998/884–1024, 555/563–2222 Main Number ⊕ www.chedraui.com.mx.*

Mega Comercial Mexicana

CHAIN | One of the major Mexican grocery-store chains, Mega Comercial Mexicana has multiple locations. The most convenient is at Avenidas Tulum and Uxmal, across from the bus station; its largest store, farther north on Avenida Kabah, is open 24 hours. ⊠ *Avs. Tulum and Uxmal, Sm 2, El Centro ☎ 998/884–3330 ⊕ www.comercialmexicana.com.mx.*

Súper Akí

CHAIN | This is a smaller grocery store downtown. ⊠ *Av. Centenario, Sm. 227, Lote 083, Mza 73, El Centro ☎ 998/889–5034 ⊕ www.superaki.mx.*

MARKETS AND MALLS

★ Mercado 28

MARKET | Mercado Veintiocho is Cancún's largest open-air market. In addition to a few small restaurants, it has about 100 stalls where you can buy many of the same items found in the Zona Hotelera at a fraction of the cost. Expect to be bombarded by aggressive vendors trying to coax you into their shop. This is a great place to haggle, and usually you can end up paying half of the initial asking price. ✉ *Xel-ha Mz 13, 28, El Centro* 🌐 *market-28cancun.negocio.site.*

Mercado Veintitres (*Mercado 23*)
MARKET | If Mercado Veintiocho is El Centro's large local Mexican crafts market, Mercado Veintitres goes more local still. Here's where the typical Cancunese comes to shop for produce, although you'll find a selection of souvenirs here, too. This market provides a healthy dose of local color, but Spanish is a must here. ✉ *Ciricote 23, at Cedro, El Centro.*

Plaza Las Américas
MALL | This is the largest shopping center in downtown Cancún. Its 100-plus shops, three restaurants, two movie theaters, video arcade, fast-food outlets, and several big department stores will—for better or worse—make you feel right at home. The mall is intolerably crowded on weekends. ✉ *Av. Tulum, Sm 4 and Sm 9, El Centro* ☎ *998/887–3863.*

Punta Sam

Sights

★ Cancún Underwater Museum (*Museo Subacuático de Arte*)
NAUTICAL SIGHT | Locally known as MUSA, Cancún's Underwater Museum is made up of more than 400 lifelike statues sculpted by six artists. The stunning artworks, located off the shores of Punta Sam, Punta Nizuc, and Manchones Reef near Isla Mujeres, create an artificial habitat for marine life that can be viewed by divers, snorkelers, and passengers on glass-bottom-boat tours. The sculptures at the Manchones site are 26 feet deep, best observed on a scuba dive. Two sites closer to Cancún, at half that depth or less, can easily be viewed by snorkelers. ✉ *Punta Cancún, Punta Nizuc, and Manchones Reef in Isla Mujeres, Cancún* ☎ *1998/206–0182* 🌐 *musamexico.org* 🎟 *Free.*

Hotels

The area north of Cancún is slowly being developed into an alternative hotel zone, known informally as the Zona Hotelera Norte or Playa Mujeres. (This term has nothing to do with the island of Isla Mujeres.) This is an ideal area for a tranquil beach vacation, because the shops, eateries, and nightlife of Cancún are about 30 minutes away by cab. If you decide against an all-inclusive plan, be sure to factor in about MX$540 in cab fees (each way) from Punta Sam to Cancún restaurants.

★ Beloved Playa Mujeres
$$$$ | **RESORT** | One of the region's few boutique-style all-inclusives, this modern sugar-cube-like structure is stylishly decorated in creams and whites, and offers the perfect balance of luxury and comfort. **Pros:** personalized service; great food; tequila tastings; Wi-Fi signal reaches beach. **Cons:** one-way cab fare to Cancún is an additional cost; narrow beach lined with sea grass; swim-up bar is in the shade. [$] *Rooms from: $529* ✉ *Vialidad Paseo Mujeres, Sm 3, Mza 1, Lote 10, Punta Sam* ☎ *998/872–8730, 866/540–2585* 🌐 *www.belovedhotels.com* 🛏 *109 rooms* 🍴 *All-Inclusive.*

Excellence Playa Mujeres
$$$$ | **ALL-INCLUSIVE** | Onyx pillars rising from two-tone marble floors, overshadowed only by a massive stained-glass ceiling illuminated from above, are your first indication of luxury at this adults-only resort. **Pros:** doesn't operate as a time-share; beautiful property; never feels crowded. **Cons:** 15-minute drive to El Centro, 30-minute drive to Zona Hotelera; $40 charge for spa facilities; no children under 18. [$] *Rooms from: $620* ✉ *Prolongacíon Bonampak s/n, Sm 003, Mza 001, Lote Terrenos 001, Punta Sam* ☎ *866/540–2585 in the U.S.,*

998/872–8600 🌐 *www.excellenceresorts.com* 🛏 *450 rooms* 🍴 *All-Inclusive.*

Villa del Palmar

$$$$ | **RESORT** | **FAMILY** | This five-star resort, which blends Mayan and modern architecture, makes you feel right at home. **Pros:** complimentary Cancún shuttle; walking distance to Isla Mujeres ferry; on-site minimart; free nonmotorized sports equipment; great service. **Cons:** mosquitoes; seaweed in water. [$] *Rooms from: $311* ✉ *Carretera Punta Sam, Km 5.2, Punta Sam* ☎ *1998/193–2600, 877/845–3795 in the U.S.* 🌐 *www.villapalmarcancun.com* 🛏 *125 rooms, 290 suites* 🍴 *No Meals.*

★ TRS Coral Hotel

$$$$ | **ALL-INCLUSIVE** | A member of The Leading Hotels of the World, expect 5-star service at this adults-only Palladium Hotel Group property. **Pros:** free access to the wet areas of the spa; attentive staff; Rafa Nadal tennis centre. **Cons:** property is spread out. [$] *Rooms from: 475 Vialidad Paseo Mujeres MZ 1, Punta Sam* ☎ *984/873–4825* 🌐 *www.palladiumhotelgroup.com* 🛏 *469 suites* 🍴 *All-Inclusive.*

Zona Hotelera

Sights

Cancún Scenic Tower (*Torre Escénica de Cancún*)

OBSERVATORY | This 262-foot rotating tower has a bird's-eye view of Cancún and the bay. The experience, which includes ascent, a few rotations at the top, and descent, takes about 10 minutes and is accompanied by Spanish-English narration. ✉ *Blvd. Kulkulcán, Km 4.5, Zona Hotelera* ☎ *998/849–5582, 855/326–0682 USA* 🌐 *www.xcaret.com* 🎫 *MX$300; MX$360 for day and night ride.*

Interactive Aquarium Cancún (*Acuario Interactivo de Cancún*)

AQUARIUM | The enthusiastic staff at this small aquarium incorporate concern for the environment into their presentations, and the animals are well looked after. For added fees, guests can participate in an aquarium trek, dolphin presentation, or swim with dolphins. ✉ *La Isla Shopping Village, Blvd. Kukulcán, Km 12.5, Zona Hotelera* ☎ *998/251–6581* 🌐 *www.interactiveaquariumcancun.com* 🎫 *$15.*

Ruinas el Rey

RUINS | Large signs on the Zona Hotelera's lagoon side, roughly opposite Playa Delfines, point out the so-called Ruins of the King, though the noble who held court here may or may not have been a king. Although much smaller than famous archaeological sites like Tulum and Chichén Itzá, this site, commonly called El Rey, is worth a visit and makes for an interesting juxtaposition of Mexico's past and present. First entered into Western chronicles in a 16th-century travelogue, the ruins weren't explored by archaeologists until 1910, and excavations didn't begin until 1954. In 1975, archaeologists began restoration work on the 47 structures with the help of the Mexican government. Dating to the 3rd to 2nd century BC, El Rey is notable for having two main plazas bounded by two streets. (Most other Maya cities contain only one plaza.) Originally named Kin Ich Ahau Bonil, Mayan for "king of the solar countenance," the site was linked to astronomical practices. The pyramid is topped by a platform, and inside its vault are paintings on stucco. Skeletons interred at the apex and at the base indicate the site may have been a royal burial ground. In 2006, workmen unearthed an ancient Maya skeleton on the outskirts of the park. ✉ *Blvd. Kukulcán, Km 17, Zona Hotelera* ☎ *998/849–2880, 983/837–2411* 🌐 *www.inah.gob.mx* 🎫 *MX$55.*

Yamil Lu'um

RUINS | Located on Cancún's highest point (the name means "hilly land"), this archaeological site is on the grounds of the Park Royal Cancún and Westin Lagunamar, which means that nonguests can visit only from the beachside. The concierges at either hotel may let you enter through their property if you ask nicely, but otherwise head to Playa Marlín and admire the ruins from a distance. Although it consists of two structures—one probably a temple, the other probably a lighthouse—this is the smallest of Cancún's few archaeological sites. Discovered in 1842 by John Lloyd Stephens, the ruins date from the late 13th or early 14th century. Keep an eye out for roaming iguanas. ⊠ *Blvd. Kukulcán, Km 12, Zona Hotelera* 🎫 *Free.*

🌣 Beaches

Playa Ballenas

BEACH | Also known as Whale Beach, this Blue Flag Beach is a raw stretch of sand and crystal water at Km 14.5 between the Hard Rock Hotel and Secrets The Vine. Jet Skiers often zoom through the water, and the strong wind makes the surf rough. The beach is open to the public; parking and beach access are at Calle Ballenas. Food and drinks are available at any of the resorts along this stretch, including the Hard Rock, Secrets The Vine, and Sandos Cancún—but keep in mind these all-inclusives cater only to hotel guests. **Amenities:** parking (free); water sports. **Best for:** sunrise; walking; windsurfing. ⊠ *Blvd. Kukulcán, Km 14.5, Zona Hotelera.*

Playa Caracol

BEACH | The last "real beach" along the east–west stretch of the Zona Hotelera is near Plaza Caracol and the Xcaret dock. Located at Km 8.5, the whole area has been eaten up by development, in particular the high-rise condominium complex next to the entrance. Playa Caracol (*caracol* means snail) is also hindered by the rocks that jut out from the water to mark the beginning of Punta Cancún, where Boulevard Kukulcán turns south. There are several hotels along here and a few sports rental outfits. It's also the launching point for trips to Contoy Island. Closer to the Fiesta Americana Grand Coral Beach hotel, the water is calm because of the jetty that blocks the wind and waves. **Amenities:** food and drink; water sports. **Best for:** swimming; windsurfing. ⊠ *Blvd. Kukulcán, Km 8.5, Zona Hotelera.*

Playa Chac Mool

BEACH | Located at Km 10 on Boulevard Kukulcán, this Blue Flag Beach can be accessed through the beach entrance across the street from Señor Frog's. As at Playa Caracol, development has greatly encroached on the shores here. There are a lot of rocks, but the water is a stunning turquoise; moreover, the beach is close to shopping centers and the party zone, so you'll find plenty of restaurants nearby. The short stretch to the south has gentler waters and fewer rocks. Public changing rooms and limited free parking are also available. The clear, shallow water makes it tempting to walk far out, but be careful—there's a strong current and undertow. Lifeguards are on duty until 5 pm. The closest hotel to Playa Chac Mool is Le Blanc Resort. **Amenities:** food and drink; lifeguards; parking (free); toilets. **Best for:** partiers; sunrise. ⊠ *Blvd. Kukulcán, Km 10, Zona Hotelera.*

Playa Delfines (*Dolphins Beach*)

BEACH | Near Ruinas del Rey, where Boulevard Kukulcán curves into a hill, this local favorite is one of the last before Punta Nizuc. Hotels have yet to dominate this small section of coastline that's considered a Blue Flag Beach. ("Yet" is, unfortunately, the operative word here.) Delfines showcases an incredible lookout and the iconic sign with large letters painted in bright colors that spell "Cancún." It's a popular photo op, so you may have to wait in line to get a picture.

The sand is darker and more granular here than on other Cancún beaches, and on a clear day you can see at least four shades of blue in the water. Swimming is treacherous unless a green flag is posted, but you'll find plenty of sand and waves. It's one of the few places in Cancún you'll see a surfer, though even during hurricane season, waves seldom hit "epic" status; at best, you might find choppy, inconsistent surf. **Amenities:** lifeguard; parking (free); toilets. **Best for:** sunrise; surfing. ⊠ *Blvd. Kukulcán, Km 18, Zona Hotelera.*

Playa Gaviota Azul (*Blue Seagull Beach*)
BEACH | Heading down from Punta Cancún onto the long, southerly stretch of the island, Playa Gaviota Azul (meaning Blue Seagull Beach, but also commonly called City Beach or Forum Beach) is the first on the Caribbean's open waters. Closer to Km 9, the waves break up to 6 feet during hurricane season, making it one of the few surfing spots in Cancún; lessons are offered by the 360 Surf School (⊕ *www.360surfschoolcancun.com*). If you'd rather just relax, ascend a short flight of steps to Mandala Beach Club at Km 9.5, where you can enjoy the full resort experience without booking into a hotel. There is paid parking at Plaza Forum plus minimal street parking. The closest hotels—Krystal Grand Punta Cancún and Aloft—are across the street from the beach. **Amenities:** food and drink; parking (fee); toilets; water sports. **Best for:** partiers; sunrise: surfing; swimming. ⊠ *Blvd. Kukulcán, Km 9.5, Zona Hotelera.*

Playa Langosta
BEACH | FAMILY | Small, placid Lobster Beach has safe waters and gentle waves that make it a popular swimming spot for families and spring breakers alike. On weekends, you'll be lucky if you can find a space on the sand. There's an entrance to the beach at Boulevard Kukulcán's Km 5. A dock juts out in the middle of the water, but swimming areas are marked off with ropes and buoys. Next to the

beach is a small building with a restaurant, an ice-cream shop, and an ATM. **Amenities:** food and drink; toilets. **Best for:** swimming. ⊠ *Blvd. Kukulcán, Km 5, Zona Hotelera.*

Playa Las Perlas
BEACH | FAMILY | Pearl Beach is the first heading east from El Centro along Boulevard Kukulcán. Located at Km 2.5, between the Cancún mainland and the bridge, this Blue Flag Beach is a relatively small beach on the protected waters of the Bahía de Mujeres, and is popular with locals. There are several restaurants lining the sand, but most of the water-sports activities are only available to those staying at the nearby lodgings like the Imperial las Perlas. There's a small store beside that resort where you can buy sandwiches and drinks if you want to have a beach picnic. Parking is limited. **Amenities:** food and drink; parking (free); lifeguards; water sports. **Best for:** swimming. ⊠ *Blvd. Kukulcán, Km 2.5, Zona Hotelera.*

Playa Linda
BEACH | At Km 4 on Boulevard Kukulcán, Pretty Beach is where the ocean meets the freshwater of Laguna Nichupté to create the Nichupté Channel. Restaurants and changing rooms are available near the launching dock. Playa Linda is situated between the Barceló Costa Cancún and Sotavento Hotel. There's lots of boat activity along the channel, and the ferry to Isla Mujeres leaves from the adjoining Embarcadero marina, so the area isn't safe for swimming. It is, however, a great place to people-watch, with a 300-foot rotating scenic tower nearby that offers a 360-degree view. **Amenities:** food and drink; parking (free); toilets. **Best for:** solitude. ⊠ *Blvd. Kukulcán, Km 4, Zona Hotelera.*

Playa Marlín
BEACH | Accessible via a road next to Kukulcán Plaza, Marlin Beach is a seductive stretch of sand in the heart of the Zona Hotelera at Km 13. Despite its

Did You Know?

After several hurricanes seriously damaged Cancún, Cozumel, and Playa del Carmen's beautiful coast, the Mexican government instituted a beach restoration project that pumped 16,000 cubic meters of sand onto Cancún's beaches. The project cost around $70.3 million. In 2014, more than 12,000 palm trees were also planted along the shores from Punta Cancún to Punta Nizuc as part of the Beach Reforestation Program.

turquoise waters and silky sands, the waves are strong and the currents are dangerous. If this Blue Flag Beach is crowded, you can walk in either direction to find quieter spots. There's also a small tent where you can rent boogie boards, snorkel gear, and motorized sports equipment. Although there are currently no public facilities, you can always walk over to Kukulcán Plaza if you need a restroom and to the nearby Oxxo, Mexico's convenience-store chain, for a snack or beverage. **Amenities:** water sports. **Best for:** snorkeling; sunrise; surfing; walking. ✉ *Blvd. Kukulcán, Km 13, Zona Hotelera.*

Playa Pez Volador

BEACH | FAMILY | The calm surf and relaxing shallows of Playa Pez Volador—the name translates as Flying Fish Beach—make it an aquatic playground for families with young children. Marked by a huge Mexican flag at Km 5.5, the wide beach is popular with locals, as many tourists tend to head to the more active Playa Langosta. Sea grass occasionally washes ashore here, but by early morning it is cleared away by the staff of the neighboring Casa Maya Hotel. **Amenities:** none. **Best for:** swimming. ✉ *Blvd. Kukulcán, Km 5.5, Zona Hotelera.*

Playa Punta Nizuc

BEACH | You'll find Cancún's most isolated and deserted beach on the southern tip of the peninsula. Far from the crowds and party scene, Playa Punta Nizuc has few amenities other than those available to guests at the nearby Wet 'n Wild Waterpark (Km 25), Nizuc Resort (Km 21), or Club Med (Km 21.5). The lack of beach traffic helps keep the white sands clean and the waters sparkling, except when sea grass washes up. Bordered by jungle to the south, Playa Punta Nizuc can be accessed directly from Boulevard Kukulcán, so there's plenty of street parking—but make sure you bring water, snacks, sunscreen, and an umbrella for shade. This is a great place to collect shells or swim, since waves crash only on stormy days. **Amenities:** parking (free). **Best for:** solitude; snorkeling; swimming; walking. ✉ *Blvd. Kukulcán, Km 24, Cancún.*

Playa Tortugas

BEACH | Don't be fooled by the name—this spot is seldom frequented by *tortugas*. It's the opportunity to swim, snorkel, kayak, paraglide, and ride Wave Runners that really brings folks to Turtle Beach. The water is deep, but the beach itself (the nicest section of which is on the far right, just past the rocks) can get very crowded. Passengers usually grab a drink or snack here before catching the ferry to Isla Mujeres, and locals from El Centro will spend their entire weekend on the sand. If you are looking for isolation, head elsewhere. There's an over-the-water bungee-jumping tower where your head will actually touch the water. **Amenities:** food and drink; water sports. **Best for:** partiers; snorkeling; swimming. ✉ *Blvd. Kukulcán, Km 6.5, Zona Hotelera.*

🍴 Restaurants

Babel Odissea Culinaria

$$ | INTERNATIONAL | Overlooking the Nichupté Lagoon, Babel has created a new type of dining experience with one of the prettiest sunset views in all of Cancun. This gastronomic market brings together a group of award-winning international chefs to cook in 14 separate kitchens under one roof. **Known for:** vegan; artistically presented food; plenty of variety. [$] *Average main: MP300 Blvd Kukulclan, Km 13.5, Nichupté, Zona Hotelera* ☎ *998/474–2686* 🌐 *babelcancun.com.*

Cambalache

$$$ | ARGENTINE | This Argentinean steak house is rustic yet elegant, with dark wooden tables and arched brick ceilings. Not surprisingly, steak is the most popular main; however, the local fish and lamb skewers grilled over a brick fire also make good choices. **Known for:** lively—sometimes loud—surroundings;

Cancún's History

The Maya, Cancún's original inhabitants, arrived centuries ago, and their descendants live in this region to this day. During the golden age of Maya civilization, called the classic period, this part of the coast remained sparsely populated as other parts of the peninsula were developing trade routes and building enormous temples and pyramids. Consequently, Cancún never grew into a major Maya center. Excavations of ruins at El Rey in what is now the Zona Hotelera have shown that the Maya communities that lived here around AD 1200 simply used this area for burial sites. Even the name given to the area was not inspiring: Cancún means "nest of snakes" in Mayan.

When the Spanish conquistadores began to arrive in the early 1500s, much of the Maya culture was already in decline. Over the next three centuries the Spanish largely ignored coastal areas like Cancún, which consisted mainly of low-lying scrub, mangroves, and swarms of mosquitoes, and focused instead on settling inland where there was more economic promise—and shelter from pirate attacks. Although it received a few refugees from the Caste War of the Yucatán, which engulfed the entire region in the mid-1800s, Cancún remained mostly undeveloped until the last half of the 20th century.

By the 1950s, Acapulco had become the number one tourist attraction in the country—and had given the Mexican government its first taste of tourism dollars. Looking to capitalize on the tourism boom, the government hired a market-research firm to determine the perfect location for developing Mexico's next big tourist destination. The firm's computers famously evaluated various sites. Guess which one it picked? At the time, the area had just 120 residents, most of whom worked at a local coconut plantation. Five decades later, some 800,000 people call the city home and are happy to host 6 million visitors annually here in Mexico's top tourist destination.

cool Argentine atmosphere; tango music. $ *Average main: MP338* ⊠ *La Isla Cancun Shopping Village, Blvd. Kukulcán, Km 12.5, Zona Hotelera* ☎ *998/883–0902, 998/883–0897* ⊕ *www.cambalacherestaurantes.com* ☞ *Valet Parking.*

Casa Rolandi

$$$$ | **EUROPEAN** | The secret to this restaurant's success is its creative handling of Italian and Swiss cuisine—that explains why both carpaccio *de pulpo* (thin slices of fresh octopus) and cheese fondue appear on the menu. Appetizers are tempting, too: there's puff bread from a wood-burning oven plus a salad and antipasto bar. **Known for:** attentive service; pleasant dining room;

jumbo shrimp baked in banana leaves. $ *Average main: MP406* ⊠ *Plaza Caracol, Blvd. Kukulcán 7500, Zona Hotelera* ☎ *998/883–2557* ⊕ *www.gruporolandi. com.*

Casitas

$$$$ | **SEAFOOD** | Sink your toes into the sand at Cancún's only on-the-beach restaurant where impeccable service matches an incredible setting. The romantic ambiance caters to couples—silk curtains drape palapas, each centered with an illuminated table adorned with seashells—and many of the seafood dishes are created for two. **Known for:** rare beach setting; flawless service; seafood platter—shrimp, oysters, tuna tartare, king

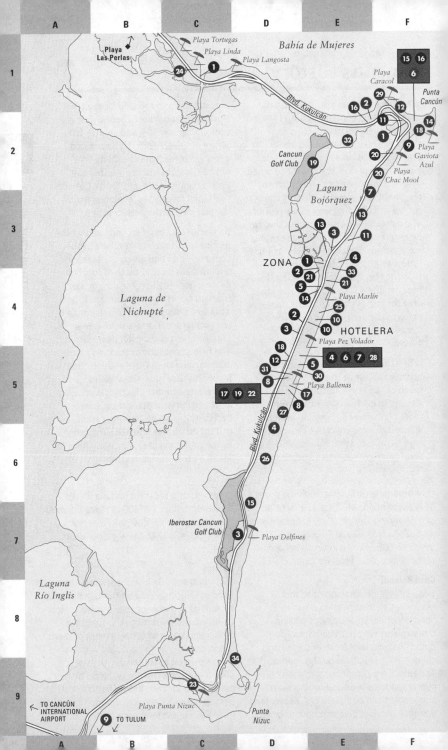

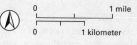

0 _____ 1 mile

0 _____ 1 kilometer

Sights ▼

1 Cancún Scenic
Tower **C1**

2 Interactive Aquarium
Cancún.................... **E4**

3 Ruinas el Rey............ **D7**

4 Yamil Lu'um.............. **E3**

Restaurants ▼

1 Cambalache.............. **E3**

2 Babel Odissea
Culinaria **D4**

3 Casa Rolandi **D4**

4 Casitas **D5**

5 Cenacolo................. **E4**

6 The Club Grill........... **D5**

7 Fantino **D5**

8 Gustino.................. **D5**

9 Hacienda el Mortero **F2**

10 Hacienda Sisal.......... **E4**

11 Hanaichi **F2**

12 Harry's **D5**

13 KAI....................... **E3**

14 La Habichuela Sunset... **E4**

15 La Joya................... **F2**

16 Le Basilic **F2**

17 Mikado.................. **D5**

18 Puerto Madero.......... **D5**

19 Sasi Thai................. **D5**

20 The Surfin' Burrito...... **F2**

21 Thai Lounge **E4**

Hotels ▼

1 Aloft Cancún **F2**

2 Beach Scape Kin-Ha
Villas & Suites........... **E2**

3 Canopy by Hilton
Cancun La Isla **E3**

4 Fiesta Americana
Condesa Cancún **D6**

5 Golden Parnassus
Resort & Spa **D5**

6 Grand Fiesta Americana
Coral Beach Cancun
All-Inclusive Spa
Resort **F2**

7 Grand Park Royal
Cancún Caribe **E3**

8 Hard Rock Hotel
Cancún.................. **D5**

9 Haven Riviera
Cancun.................. **B9**

10 Hotel Casa Turquesa **E4**

11 Hotel NYX Cancún....... **E3**

12 Hotel Riu Caribe......... **F1**

13 Hyatt Zilara Cancún **E3**

14 Hyatt Ziva Cancún....... **F2**

15 Iberostar Selection
Cancún.................. **D6**

16 InterContinental
Presidente
Cancún Resort **E2**

17 JW Marriott Cancún
Resort & Spa **D5**

18 Krystal Grand Cancun
Resort & Spa Hotel **F2**

19 Laguna Suites
Golf & Spa **E2**

20 Le Blanc Spa Resort..... **F2**

21 Live Aqua Beach
Resort Cancún **E4**

22 Marriott Cancún
Resort.................... **D5**

23 Nizuc Resort & Spa...... **C9**

24 Occidental Costa
Cancún................... **C1**

25 Occidental Tucancún ... **E4**

26 Omni Cancún
Hotel & Villas **D6**

27 Paradisus Cancún...... **D5**

28 The Ritz-Carlton,
Cancún.................. **D5**

29 Riu Palace
Las Américas............ **F1**

30 Sandos Cancún **D5**

31 Secrets The Vine
Cancún.................. **D5**

32 Sina Suites.............. **E2**

33 The Westin Lagunamar
Ocean Resort
Villas & Spa,
Cancun.................... **E4**

34 The Westin Resort
& Spa Cancún............ **C8**

Caribbean

Sea

KEY

1 *Exploring Sights*

1 *Restaurants*

1 *Hotels*

Zona Hotelera

G   H   I

crab, and lobster tail. $ *Average main: MP1299* ✉ *Ritz-Carlton Cancún, Retorno del Rey 36, off Blvd. Kukulcán, Km 13.5, Zona Hotelera* ☎ *998/881–0808* ⊕ *www. ritzcarlton.com* ⊗ *No lunch.*

Cenacolo

$$$$ | ITALIAN | Brick-oven pizza and pasta, handmade in full view, have made this fine Italian restaurant a Cancún favorite, serving stellar pasta dishes like lobster ravioli filled with ricotta cheese and served in a white-wine sauce. Appetizers include beef or octopus carpaccio that practically melts in your mouth and a light calamari. **Known for:** wine cave; romantic setting; elegant Italian cuisine. $ *Average main: MP379* ✉ *Blvd. Kukulcán, Km 12.6, Zona Hotelera* ☎ *998/885–3603, 998/885–2746 Reservations* ⊕ *www. cenacolo.com.mx.*

★ The Club Grill

$$$$ | INTERNATIONAL | Recently renovated in beautiful neutral colors, begin the evening at the Club Grill with a special cocktail at the Champagne bar. The contemporary continental menu includes starters like beef tartar and mains like roasted duck with tequila and agave honey sauce; a multicourse tasting menu, paired with boutique Mexican wines, is available, too. **Known for:** elegant, romantic surroundings (check on the dress code); chocolate soufflé; silver serving platters. $ *Average main: MP680* ✉ *Ritz-Carlton Cancún, Retorno del Rey 36, Zona Hotelera* ☎ *998/881–0822* ⊕ *www.ritzcarlton.com* ⊗ *No lunch.*

Fantino

$$$$ | MEDITERRANEAN | Expect fine dining and culinary excellence, with rich-in-flavor ingredients, at this Mediterranean restaurant; consider the tasting menu for the full Fantino experience. With synchronized precision, servers unveil each plate with beautiful, if not artistic, execution. **Known for:** ballroom setting; polished service; careful attention to ingredient selection. $ *Average main: MP1,016* ✉ *Ritz-Carlton Cancún, Blvd. Kukulcán,*

Km 13.5, Zona Hotelera ☎ *998/881–0822* ⊕ *www.ritzcarlton.com* ⊗ *No lunch* 🍴 *Long pants and shoes required for gentlemen.*

Gustino

$$$$ | ITALIAN | As soon as you walk down the dramatic staircase at this elegant restaurant, you know you're in for a memorable experience. The *gamberi saltati* (sautéed shrimp with spinach, artichoke and asiago cheese) appetizer is a standout here, as is the fettuccine carbonara in truffle sauce and risotto entrées. **Known for:** wine cellar; great Italian and seafood selections; impeccable service. $ *Average main: MP677* ✉ *JW Marriott Resort, Blvd. Kukulcán, Km 14.5, Zona Hotelera* ☎ *998/848–9600* ⊕ *www.gustinocancun.com* ⊗ *No lunch.*

Hacienda el Mortero

$$$$ | MEXICAN | The main draw at one of Cancún's first restaurants is the setting: a replica of a 17th-century hacienda, complete with courtyard fountain, flowering garden, and strolling mariachi band. The traditional Mexican menu includes tortilla soup, tasty chicken fajitas, and rib-eye steaks. **Known for:** pescado Veracruzana (grouper with olives, garlic, and tomatoes); traditional setting; astounding variety of tequila. $ *Average main: MP610* ✉ *Blvd. Kukulcán, Km 9.5, Zona Hotelera* ☎ *998/848–9800, 998/108–0628 WhatsApp* ⊕ *www.restaurantehaciendaelmortero.com* ⊗ *No lunch Mon.–Sat.*

Hacienda Sisal

$$$ | MEXICAN | Built to resemble a sprawling hacienda, this restaurant is warm and intimate, with comfortable high-backed chairs and Mexican paintings. Menu highlights include the goat-cheese-and-mango salad, Tampico chicken breast, New York steak with stuffed pepper, and annatto-seasoned grilled pork chops; a kids menu is available. **Known for:** weeknight music and dance performances; Sunday breakfast buffet; faux hacienda vibe. $ *Average main: MP338* ✉ *Blvd. Kukulcán, Km 13.5, next to Royal Sands*

Resort, Zona Hotelera ☎ *998/848–8220* ⊕ *www.haciendasisal.com* ☉ *No lunch.*

★ Hanaichi

$$$ | JAPANESE | It might look like a hole-in-the-wall, but this small Japanese restaurant has some of Cancún's best sushi. Expect sashimi, nigiri, and every type of sushi roll imaginable; house specialties include the Copán roll (deep-fried shrimp wrapped in cucumber) and the Cancún roll (stuffed with eel and scallops). **Known for:** casual surroundings; great sushi selection; inexpensive menu. ⓢ *Average main: MP203* ⊠ *Blvd. Kukulcán, Km 9, across from Plaza Caracol, Cancún* ☎ *998/883–2804.*

Harry's

$$$$ | STEAKHOUSE | High-profile locals and visitors alike are drawn to this contemporary steak house's Vegas–meets–Beverly Hills style. The spectacular menu features glazed duck, Maine lobster, and Kobe beef served with aged Vermont cheddar cheese. **Known for:** steaks grilled to perfection; atmospheric, dimly lit setting; cotton candy that comes with the check. ⓢ *Average main: MP677* ⊠ *Blvd. Kukulcán, Km 14.2, Zona Hotelera* ☎ *998/840–6550* ⊕ *www.harrys.com.mx.*

KAI

$$$$ | JAPANESE | Don't be put off by the shopping mall location or shared entrance with the Macao casino, because this modern Japanese restaurant serves the freshest sashimi and sushi with unique toppings such as miso foie grass, black truffles, and lemon caviar. Their excellently trained servers help guide you through the extensive menu and offer cocktail suggestions to complement the myriad of main courses and roll choices from uramaki to futomaki. **Known for:** excellent service; umami roll; waygu burgers. ⓢ *Average main: MP400* ⊠ *Plaza, La Isla, II, Zona Hotelera* ☎ *998/159–7999* ⊕ *kai. restaurant.*

La Habichuela Sunset

$$$$ | CARIBBEAN | Popular dishes at this bustling restaurant include soft-shell-crab tacos, garlic shrimp, and breaded fish served with tamarind and mango sauce. Cap off your meal with butterscotch crepes and Mayan coffee. **Known for:** restaurant's own archaeological dig; live show three nights weekly; fresh fish dishes. ⓢ *Average main: MP406* ⊠ *Blvd. Kukulcán, Km 12.6, Zona Hotelera* ☎ *988/840–6240* ⊕ *www.lahabichuela. com.*

La Joya

$$$$ | MEXICAN | Soaring stained-glass windows, a fountain, artwork, and beautiful furniture from the central part of the country lend drama to this restaurant in the Fiesta Americana Grand Coral Beach. Like the decor, the Mexican food is traditional but creative, with dishes like grilled Tampiqueña-style beef and sea bass wrapped in maguey leaves. **Known for:** traditional Mexican decor; Oaxacan cuisine; performances by a 10-piece Mariachi band. ⓢ *Average main: MP406* ⊠ *Grand Fiesta Americana Coral Beach Cancun, Blvd. Kukulcán, Km 9.5, Zona Hotelera* ☎ *998/881–3200* ⊕ *www. coralbeachcancunresort.com* ☉ *Closed Mon. No lunch.*

★ Le Basilic

$$$$ | MEDITERRANEAN | Arched bay windows, checkered marble floors, live jazz, and exquisite garden views create a stunning backdrop to your dining experience here. The menu changes every four months but is always comprised of fine French-Mediterranean cuisine served beneath silver domes by tuxedoed waiters. **Known for:** centerpiece gazebo with orchids; attentive service; art gallery. ⓢ *Average main: MP474* ⊠ *Fiesta Americana Grand Coral Beach, Blvd. Kukulcán, Km 9.5, Zona Hotelera* ☎ *998/881–3200* ⊕ *www.coralbeachcancunresort.com* ☉ *Closed Sun. No lunch.*

Mikado

$$$$ | **JAPANESE** | **FAMILY** | Sit around the teppanyaki tables and watch the utensils fly as the showmen chefs here prepare steaks, seafood, and vegetables. The menu includes Japanese specialties such as *futo-maki* (large sushi rolls) and pan-fried sea bass. **Known for:** family-friendly setting; sushi tempura; showy food preparation. [$] *Average main: MP610* ✉ *Marriott Cancun, Blvd. Kukulcán, Km 14.5, Zona Hotelera* ☎ *998/881–2000* 🌐 *www.marriott.com* 🕒 *No lunch.*

★ Puerto Madero

$$$$ | **STEAKHOUSE** | Modeled after the dock warehouses that have been converted into modern eateries in Argentina's Puerto Madero, this steak-and-seafood house gets rave reviews from locals. The grilled octopus seasoned with paprika is exceptional, as is the Alaskan halibut prepared with white wine, shallots, and fresh pepper. **Known for:** fun-loving staff; crackly soufflé potatoes; chic appetizers. [$] *Average main: MP474* ✉ *Blvd. Kukulcán, Km 14.1, Zona Hotelera* ☎ *998/885–2829* 🌐 *www.puertomaderorestaurantes.com.*

Sasi Thai

$$$$ | **THAI** | Six thatch-roof cabanas—each housing four tables—are staggered on a hill and dimly lit with candles and lanterns. The menu features traditional Thai cuisine such as spring rolls, pork dumplings, red duck curry, and pad Thai with chicken or shrimp. **Known for:** open-air setting; mango crème brûlée with ginger sorbet; bamboo decor. [$] *Average main: MP474* ✉ *Casa Magna Marriott, Blvd. Kukulcán, Km 14.5, Zona Hotelera* ☎ *998/881–2092* 🌐 *www.sasi-thai.com* 🕒 *No lunch.*

The Surfin' Burrito

$$ | **MEXICAN** | A truly local joint that seems out of place in the Zona Hotelera draws the crowds in the morning for its smoothie bowls and later on for tacos and burritos. Forget your own private booth at this 24-hour place: you'll eat at long tables and really get to know your fellow diners. **Known for:** friendly service; informal late-night eats; California-style burritos. [$] *Average main: MP200* ✉ *Blvd. Kukulcán Km 9.5, Zona Hotelera* ☎ *998/883–0083, 998/490–2217 WhatsApp* 🌐 *www.facebook.com/thesurfinburrito.*

Thai Lounge

$$$ | **THAI** | The individual huts with thatch roofs here at this garden oasis provide an intimate setting to sample spicy Thai dishes like roasted duck in coconut red curry or the house favorite, a deep-fried fish fillet prepared with ginger, garlic, and a tamarind-chile sauce. The menu also features such traditional items as shrimp curry, Thai salad, and spicy chicken soup. **Known for:** intimate garden setting; sunset views over lagoon; palapa casitas perched over the water. [$] *Average main: MP345* ✉ *La Isla Cancún Shopping Village, Blvd. Kukulcán, Km 12.5, Zona Hotelera* ☎ *998/176–8070* 🌐 *www.thai.com.mx* 🕒 *No lunch.*

Hotels

Aloft Cancún

$ | **HOTEL** | This hip Marriott property near the convention center has a fresh, modern concept that generates quite a social scene. **Pros:** within walking distance to main clubs; free parking and Wi-Fi; pet- and child-friendly. **Cons:** not on beach; small rooms; meals not included. [$] *Rooms from: $110* ✉ *Blvd. Kukulcán, Km 9, across from Fiesta Americana Grand Coral Beach, Zona Hotelera* ☎ *998/848–9900* 🌐 *www.marriott.com* 🛏 *177 rooms* 🍴 *No Meals.*

Beach Scape Kin-Ha Villas & Suites

$$ | **HOTEL** | **FAMILY** | This condo hotel is a wonderful place for families thanks to its tranquil beach and relaxed atmosphere. **Pros:** peaceful location; all rooms have balconies; one of Cancún's best beaches. **Cons:** three-story hotel has no elevator; no children's programs. [$] *Rooms from:*

$157 ⊠ *Blvd. Kukulcán, Km 8.5, Zona Hotelera* ☎ *998/891–5400* ⊕ *www.beach-scape.com.mx* ⌁ *49 rooms, 47 suites* ⏐❍⏐ *No Meals.*

Canopy by Hilton Cancun La Isla

$$$ | HOTEL | Shopaholics will love staying in this luxury lifestyle hotel with direct access to the high-end shops in the La Isla Entertainment Village. **Pros:** complimentary bikes; pet-friendly; rooftop pool. **Cons:** no beach not on the oceanside. $ *Rooms from: $229* ⊠ *Blvd. Kukulcan S, N-Km. 12.5, Zona Hotelera* ⊹ *adjacent to La Isla Shopping Village* ☎ *998/689–1193* ⊕ *www.hilton.com* ⌁ *174 rooms* ⏐❍⏐ *No Meals.*

Fiesta Americana Condesa Cancún

$$$$ | ALL-INCLUSIVE | FAMILY | More laid-back than the Grand Fiesta Americana Coral Beach, this sister property is easily recognized by the 118-foot-tall palapa that covers its lobby. **Pros:** scheduled activities on the hour; smaller pools designated for children; friendly staff. **Cons:** popular with convention goers and tour groups; sound carries between floors; halls get slippery when it rains. $ *Rooms from: $321* ⊠ *Blvd. Kukulcán, Km 16.5, Zona Hotelera* ☎ *998/881–4200, 800/343–7821 in the U.S.* ⊕ *www.fiestamericana.com* ⏐❍⏐ *All-Inclusive* ⌁ *502 rooms.*

Golden Parnassus Resort & Spa

$$$ | ALL-INCLUSIVE | Accommodations at this all-inclusive, adults-only resort are decorated with rich wood furnishings and a cream-and-plum palette. **Pros:** evening entertainment; great tiki bar; free shuttle to sister property Great Parnassus Resort & Spa. **Cons:** thin towels and poor lighting; no kids under 18; dated common areas; charge for Wi-Fi. $ *Rooms from: $273* ⊠ *Blvd. Kukulcán, Km 14.5, Zona Hotelera* ☎ *998/287–1400, 998/195–5665* ⊕ *www.goldenparnassusresortspa.com* ⌁ *214 rooms* ⏐❍⏐ *All-Inclusive.*

Grand Fiesta Americana Coral Beach Cancun All-Inclusive Spa Resort

$$$$ | ALL-INCLUSIVE | FAMILY | Traditional luxury lovers will feel at home in this distinctive all-suites hotel, which boasts both an award-winning restaurant (Le Basilic) and one of Latin America's largest spas (the 40,000-square-foot Gem Spa). **Pros:** enormous pool with swim-up bars; secluded beach; business center with private offices; complimentary kids' club; stellar spa and restaurant. **Cons:** pool is only heated October to March; too big for some. $ *Rooms from: $640* ⊠ *Blvd. Kukulcán, Km 9.5, Zona Hotelera* ☎ *998/991–3200, 888/830–9008* ⊕ *www.coralbeachcancunresort.com* ⌁ *602 suites* ⏐❍⏐ *All-Inclusive.*

Grand Park Royal Cancún Caribe

$$ | ALL-INCLUSIVE | You'll find a wide variety of accommodations at the Grand Park Royal, including the newest category of beachfront villas with a private beach area and personal concierge. **Pros:** excellent pool areas; most rooms face ocean; kids club. **Cons:** Wi-Fi and gym cost extra; reservations required at restaurants. $ *Rooms from: $194* ⊠ *Blvd. Kukulcán, Km 10.5, Zona Hotelera* ☎ *998/848–7800, 800/890–3798 in the U.S.* ⊕ *www.park-royalhotels.com* ⌁ *311 rooms* ⏐❍⏐ *All-Inclusive.*

Hard Rock Hotel Cancún

$$$$ | RESORT | FAMILY | This resort's focus on music and entertainment fits right into Cancún's energetic atmosphere. In keeping with Hard Rock tradition, it showcases musical memorabilia and hosts an ongoing slate of entertainment experiences and celebrity-driven soirees. **Pros:** activities for children and teens; two tennis courts; friendly staff; excellent Japanese restaurant. **Cons:** hard mattresses; no water sports; some rooms lack ocean views. $ *Rooms from: $600* ⊠ *Blvd. Kukulcán, Km 14.5, Zona Hotelera* ☎ *998/881–3600, 855/537–4606 in the U.S.* ⊕ *www.hrhcancun.com* ⌁ *625 rooms* ⏐❍⏐ *All-Inclusive.*

3

Cancún ZONA HOTELERA

Haven Riviera Cancun

$$$$ | **ALL-INCLUSIVE** | This adults-only sophisticated sanctuary is located 15 minutes south of the airport in a secluded complex. **Pros:** coffee bar and pastry shop; custom cocktails at Limes Bar; strong Wi-Fi at pool and beach. **Cons:** service is inconsistent; oceanfront swim-out suites shady in afternoon; some hallway noise carries into first floor rooms. $ *Rooms from: $464* ⊠ *Km.12.5, Blvd. Kulkulcan Lt 18, Zona Hotelera* ☎ *889–9600* ⊕ *www.havenresorts.com* ⇨ *333 suites* ¶○¶ *All-Inclusive.*

Hotel Casa Turquesa

$$$$ | **HOTEL** | Perched on a hill overlooking the ocean, this all-suites boutique hotel doubles as an impressive gallery showcasing works by famous artists. **Pros:** 24-hour room service; intimate, personalized feel; lighted tennis court. **Cons:** MX$340 charge for Wi-Fi; not child-friendly; ground-floor rooms lack full ocean views. $ *Rooms from: $320* ⊠ *Blvd. Kulkulcán, Km 13.5, Zona Hotelera* ☎ *998/193–2260* ⊕ *hotelcasaturquesa.mydirectstay.com* ⇨ *29 rooms* ¶○¶ *No Meals.*

★ Hotel NYX Cancún

$$ | **RESORT** | Here's a hotel that's funky and fun, catering to young adults with its chic lounge bar, ambient music, and hot-pink billiard tables and rugs that match the hotel's bright exterior. **Pros:** gracious staff; reasonable rates; close to shops. **Cons:** no elevator. $ *Rooms from: $152* ⊠ *Blvd. Kulkulcán, Km 11.5, Zona Hotelera* ☎ *998/848–9310* ⊕ *www.nyxhotels.com* ⇨ *196 rooms* ¶○¶ *Free Breakfast.*

Hotel Riu Caribe

$$$$ | **ALL-INCLUSIVE** | This hotel, part of a Spanish chain, proffers a modern motif that includes bright orange balconies overlooking the white pyramid-shaped lobby. **Pros:** large beach and pools; use of facilities at neighboring Riu Cancún; tennis courts. **Cons:** beach and pool areas can get crowded; minimum stay of three nights; no room service. $ *Rooms from:* *$356* ⊠ *Blvd. Kulkulcán, Km 5.5, Zona Hotelera* ☎ *998/848–7850, 888/748–4990 in the U.S.* ⊕ *www.riu.com* ⇨ *445 rooms, 61 suites* ¶○¶ *All-Inclusive.*

★ Hyatt Zilara Cancún

$$$$ | **ALL-INCLUSIVE** | Luxury is the focus at this high-end, adults-only resort, where every room has mahogany furniture, Jacuzzis, ocean views, balconies with hammocks, and "magic boxes" that allow room service to be delivered without ever opening the door. **Pros:** two-person Jacuzzis in suites; ocean view from all suites. **Cons:** sleepless nights for rooms near the pool and lobby; no children under 18; time-share sales pitch. $ *Rooms from: $472* ⊠ *Blvd. Kulkulcán, Km 11.5, Zona Hotelera* ☎ *998/881–5600, 800/323–7249 in the U.S.* ⊕ *cancun.zilara.hyatt.com* ⇨ *307 suites* ¶○¶ *All-Inclusive.*

★ Hyatt Ziva Cancún

$$$$ | **ALL-INCLUSIVE** | This luxury resort, perched at the very point where Caribbean and Gulf of Mexico meet, caters to families and adults, and manages to do so by keeping them separate. **Pros:** exclusivity of adults-only tower; teen and kids club included; impeccable service; stunning setting. **Cons:** restaurant fare is uninspiring. $ *Rooms from: $436* ⊠ *Blvd Kulkulcán, Km 8.5, Cancún* ☎ *998/848–7000, 800/323–7249 in the U.S.* ⊕ *www.hyatt.com* ⇨ *547 rooms* ¶○¶ *All-Inclusive.*

Iberostar Selection Cancún

$$$$ | **ALL-INCLUSIVE** | Located on Playa Delfines, every standard room at this all-inclusive resort has a Caribbean ocean view. **Pros:** tennis; angled pool area gets all-day sunshine; all standard rooms have ocean view. **Cons:** some villas lack ocean views; only one heated pool. $ *Rooms from: $470* ⊠ *Blvd. Kulkulcán, Km 17, Zona Hotelera* ☎ *998/881–8000* ⊕ *www.iberostar.com* ⇨ *449 rooms, 82 villas* ¶○¶ *All-Inclusive.*

Cancún's beautiful JW Marriott resort is the only local property designed to withstand a category-five hurricane.

InterContinental Presidente Cancún Resort
$$$ | **RESORT** | This landmark hotel boasts one of the best beaches in Cancún, and it has a contemporary and clean look to it that includes the swanky lobby with a mixology bar. **Pros:** virtually current-less beach is great for families; IKAL Spa offers unique massages that blend Mayan and Eastern ancient techniques; short walk to shops and restaurants. **Cons:** palm trees block ocean view in some lower-level rooms; focus on business travelers and conventions. [$] *Rooms from: $209* ✉ *Blvd. Kukulcán, Km 7.5, Zona Hotelera* ☎ *998/848–8700, 800/496–7621* 🌐 *www.presidenteiccancun.com* 🛏 *289 rooms* 🍴 *No Meals.*

JW Marriott Cancún Resort & Spa
$$$ | **RESORT** | This towering beach resort property recently received a luxurious multi-million dollar restoration that included upgrades to the ocean-facing guest rooms and suites which now feature modern elements complemented by local Mayan Flair. Oversized bathrooms have free-standing soaking tubs and luxurious rainfall showers. **Pros:** top-notch service; artificial reef; huge spa. **Cons:** extra charge for the Kids' Club; lacks the festive mood of other hotels on the strip. [$] *Rooms from: $299* ✉ *Blvd. Kukulcán, Km 14.5, Lote 40-A, Zona Hotelera* ☎ *998/848–9600, 888/813–2776* 🌐 *www.jwmarriottcancunresort.com* 🛏 *521 rooms* 🍴 *No Meals.*

Krystal Grand Cancun Resort & Spa Hotel
$$$ | **RESORT** | **FAMILY** | On the tip of Punta Cancún, this contemporary 14-story hotel offers some of the Hotel Zone's best views; west-facing rooms can enjoy the sunset and both lagoon and bay vistas, while east-facing ones can watch the sunrise over Isla Mujeres and the Caribbean. **Pros:** great restaurants; on-site beauty salon and car rental; excellent views. **Cons:** extra charge for Kids' Club; Wi-Fi isn't free; bathrooms have showers only. [$] *Rooms from: $296* ✉ *Blvd. Kukulcán, Km 8.5, Zona Hotelera* ☎ *998/891–5555* 🌐 *www.krystal-hotels.com* 🛏 *295 rooms* 🍴 *All-Inclusive.*

Laguna Suites Golf & Spa

$$$ | HOTEL | Framing the fairway of Pok-TaPok Golf Course, this tranquil resort is comprised of 12 white-stucco buildings, each housing four spacious suites that are ideal for families or groups. **Pros:** free hourly shuttle to the beach; quiet location; neighboring laundromat is convenient; all-inclusive plan available; access to golf course. **Cons:** no children's activities; bathrooms have showers only; menu is repetitive if you select all-inclusive package. $ *Rooms from: $280* ✉ *Paseo Pok Ta Pok 3, Zona Hotelera* ☎ *998/891–5252, 800/986–9359 in the U.S.* ⊕ *www.sunsetworldresorts.com* 🛏 *47 suites* ⦿ *All-Inclusive.*

★ Le Blanc Spa Resort

$$$$ | ALL-INCLUSIVE | The most upscale of the Palace Resort properties and perhaps the most luxurious all-inclusive resort in Cancún, this adults-only resort underwent a recent top-to-bottom renovation that showcases the resort's chic modern decor with elegant touches. **Pros:** complimentary use of hydrotherapy; personalized butler; great food; excellent spa. **Cons:** some rooms have small French balconies only; no kids; pricey. $ *Rooms from: $800* ✉ *Blvd. Kulkulcán, Km 10, Zona Hotelera* ☎ *998/881–4740, 888/702–0913* ⊕ *www.leblancsparesort.com* 🛏 *260 rooms* ⦿ *All-Inclusive.*

★ Live Aqua Beach Resort Cancún

$$$$ | RESORT | Benefiting from a multi-million dollar upgrade, redesigned guest rooms, remodeled dining venues, and refurbished beach and pool areas, this resort attracts luxury-minded thirtysomething sun worshippers who appreciate soothing hues, large airy rooms, and a resident DJ spinning tunes that perfect the Zen vibe. **Pros:** 24-hour in room dinning; gratuities included; huge suites; all rooms have oceanfront views. **Cons:** fee for beach or poolside cabanas; no nightly entertainment; no kids under 18; some hallway noise carries into rooms. $ *Rooms from: $550* ✉ *Blvd. Kulkulcán,*

Km 12.5, Zona Hotelera ☎ *998/881–7600, 888/782–7601* ⊕ *www.liveaqua.com* 🛏 *407 rooms* ⦿ *No Meals.*

Marriott Cancún Resort

$$$ | RESORT | FAMILY | The sweeping grounds and arched walkways that lead up to this six-story, hacienda-style building will make you forget you're at an outlet of a U.S. chain hotel. **Pros:** more culturally traditional than most Marriotts; new SacBé Beach Club; new lobby; gorgeous views from most rooms. **Cons:** Wi-Fi can be spotty; no designated children's pool; geared to groups and conventions, which account for 60% of the business. $ *Rooms from: $195* ✉ *Blvd. Kulkulcán, Km 14.5, Retorno Chac L-41, Zona Hotelera* ☎ *998/881–2000* ⊕ *www.marriottcancunresort.com* 🛏 *488 rooms* ⦿ *No Meals.*

★ Nizuc Resort & Spa

$$$$ | RESORT | Tucked away on a beach sheltered by mangroves and facing the Mesoamerican Barrier Reef, the stylish 29-acre Nizuc Resort has the most secluded location in Cancún. **Pros:** all-inclusive plan available; excellent service; only private beach in Cancún; top-tier restaurants. **Cons:** occasional airplane noise; 18% service charge added to bill; sprawling property means long walks or golf cart trips. $ *Rooms from: $560* ✉ *Blvd. Kulkulcán, Km 21.26, Zona Hotelera* ☎ *998/891–5700* ⊕ *www.nizuc.com* 🛏 *274 rooms* ⦿ *No Meals.*

Occidental Costa Cancún

$$$$ | RESORT | FAMILY | Ferries to Isla Mujeres are just steps away from this active resort near El Embarcadero; however, the location also means the beach here is quite small and there are often boats passing by. **Pros:** good watersports center; close to Embarcadero; great for kids. **Cons:** no air-conditioning in lobby; small beach area; check-in/out times can be chaotic in the lobby area. $ *Rooms from: $310* ✉ *Blvd. Kulkulcán, Km 4.5, Zona Hotelera* ☎ *998/849–7100,*

The Nizuc Resort & Spa has a beautiful infinity pool looking out onto Punta Nizuc.

800/227–2356 in the U.S. 🌐 *www.barcelo.com* 🛏 *358 rooms* 🍴 *All-Inclusive.*

Occidental Tucancún

$$$ | **RESORT** | Strategically located near a couple of shopping centers, this lively resort is an ideal location for mall addicts; however, there's enough to keep non-shoppers occupied, too—including volleyball games and water-polo matches in the activities pool. **Pros:** wide range of activities for children and adults; four handicapped-accessible rooms; near two of Cancún's biggest malls. **Cons:** chaotic lobby during check-in/check-out times; hotel feels dated; only half the rooms have water views. [$] *Rooms from: $210* ✉ *Blvd. Kukulcán, Km 14, Zona Hotelera* ☎ *998/891–5900, 800/227–2356* 🌐 *www.barcelo.com* 🛏 *316 rooms, 16 villas* 🍴 *All-Inclusive.*

Omni Cancún Hotel & Villas

$$$$ | **RESORT** | A relaxed atmosphere and accommodating staff give this 12-story all-inclusive added appeal. **Pros:** educational programs at Kid's Club; four handicapped-accessible rooms; tons of scheduled activities. **Cons:** dark lobby is uninviting; time-share sales pitches; crowded pool area. [$] *Rooms from: $395* ✉ *Blvd. Kukulcán, Km 16.5, Zona Hotelera* ☎ *998/881–0600, 888/444–6664 in the U.S.* 🌐 *www.omnihotels.com* 🛏 *228 rooms, 23 villas* 🍴 *All-Inclusive.*

★ Paradisus Cancún

$$$$ | **RESORT** | Resembling a modern Mayan temple, this enormous beachfront property comes complete with atriums topped by pyramid-shaped skylights. **Pros:** free golf course exclusively for guests; privacy of The Reserve; three play zones for babies, kids, and teens. **Cons:** top-shelf alcohol and Tempo restaurant not part of the all-inclusive plan; no children allowed at several restaurants. [$] *Rooms from: $400* ✉ *Blvd. Kukulcán, Km 16.5, Zona Hotelera* ☎ *998/881–1100* 🌐 *www.paradisus.com* 🛏 *668 suites* 🍴 *All-Inclusive.*

★ The Ritz-Carlton, Cancún

$$$$ | **RESORT** | Outfitted with crystal chandeliers, beautiful antiques, and oil paintings, this hotel's style is so European

you may forget you're in Mexico. **Pros:** cooking classes and tequila tastings; turtle-release program May–October; AAA Five Diamond restaurant with white glove service; tennis center. **Cons:** expensive; formal atmosphere; slightly dated and not up to Ritz-Carlton standards. $ *Rooms from: $725* ⊠ *Retorno del Rey 36, off Blvd. Kukulcán at Km 13.5, Zona Hotelera* ☎ *998/881–0808, 301/547–4700 in the U.S.* ⊕ *www.ritzcarlton.com* ⇨ *411 rooms* ❑ *No Meals.*

Riu Palace Las Américas
$$$$ | **ALL-INCLUSIVE** | The most upscale of Cancún's four Riu properties, this colossal eight-story resort at the north end of the Zona is visually stunning. **Pros:** spacious suites; access to sister properties in Cancún and Playa del Carmen; room service 24 hours a day. **Cons:** small pools and tiny beach; no kids under 18; not much sun by the pool or beach by late afternoon. $ *Rooms from: $410* ⊠ *Blvd. Kukulcán, Km 8.5, Zona Hotelera* ☎ *998/891–4300, 888/748–4990* ⊕ *www.riu.com* ⇨ *372 suites* ❑ *All-Inclusive.*

Sandos Cancún
$$$$ | **RESORT** | High on a hill off the main boulevard, this refined yet relaxed hotel (formerly Le Méridien Cancún) is gaining recognition for its personalized service under Sandos's management. **Pros:** near one of Cancún's best malls; all rooms have water views; good fitness facilities. **Cons:** not all rooms have balconies; shady pool by early afternoon. $ *Rooms from: $480* ⊠ *Retorno del Rey, Lote 37, Mza 53, off Blvd. Kukulcán at Km 14, Zona Hotelera* ☎ *998/881–2200, 863/223–4530 in the U.S.* ⊕ *www.sandos.com* ⇨ *214 rooms* ❑ *All-Inclusive.*

Secrets The Vine Cancún
$$$$ | **RESORT** | This adults-only resort boasts "unlimited luxury," so even butler service, international calls, 24-hour room service, taxes, and gratuities are included in the rate. **Pros:** access to Riviera Maya sister properties; no dinner buffets; great restaurants; free fitness classes. **Cons:** only suites have full ocean view; thin walls; no children under 18; understaffed. $ *Rooms from: $420* ⊠ *Retorno del Rey, Mza 13, Lote 38 & 38B, off Blvd. Kukulcán, Km 14.5, Zona Hotelera* ☎ *998/848–9400, 866/467–3273 in the U.S.* ⊕ *www.secretsresorts.com/vine-cancun* ⇨ *495 rooms* ❑ *All-Inclusive.*

Sina Suites
$ | **HOTEL** | On a quiet residential street off Boulevard Kukulcán, these economical suites are in front of Laguna Nichupté and close to the PokTaPok golf course. **Pros:** ideally situated on the lagoon; access to beach club at Ocean Spa Hotel; affordable. **Cons:** 10-minute walk from beach; no elevator; loud air-conditioning. $ *Rooms from: $82* ⊠ *Club de Golf, Calle Quetzal 33, Zona Hotelera* ✛ *Turn right at Blvd. Kukulcán, Km 7.5, after golf course* ☎ *998/883–1018* ⇨ *37 rooms* ❑ *Free Breakfast.*

The Westin Lagunamar Ocean Resort Villas & Spa, Cancun
$$$ | **RESORT** | **FAMILY** | Every room here—four-person studio or eight-person villa—is oceanfront and equipped with a washer and dryer, full kitchen, Jacuzzi tub, and modern touches like recessed lighting and built-in shelves displaying Mexican pottery. **Pros:** all the comforts of home; great for families; beautiful infinity pool. **Cons:** no all-inclusive plan; spotty Wi-Fi in areas; time-share pitch. $ *Rooms from: $275* ⊠ *Blvd Kukulcán, Km 12.5, Zona Hotelera* ☎ *998/891–4200* ⊕ *www.marriott.com* ⇨ *580 suites* ❑ *No Meals.*

The Westin Resort & Spa Cancún
$$$ | **RESORT** | **FAMILY** | Subtle hints of pampering are what make this hotel so extraordinary, like the white tea mist that periodically sprays in the lobby and the "heavenly beds," so luxurious that some guests buy them for their own homes. **Pros:** all-inclusive plan available; natural reef great for snorkeling; two beaches. **Cons:** driving distance to off-site shops and restaurants; only odd-numbered

rooms have ocean views. $ *Rooms from: $267* ✉ *Blvd. Kukulcán, Km 20, Zona Hotelera* ☎ *998/848–7400, 800/545–7964 in the U.S.* ⊕ *www.marriott.com* ⌁ *379 rooms* ⦿ *No Meals.*

Nightlife

BARS

Many of these spots daylight as restaurants, but after sunset the party kicks up with pulsating music and waiters who don't so much encourage crowd participation as demand it. Just remember: it's all in good fun.

Champions Sports Bar

LIVE MUSIC | With two giant screens and more than 22 TVs, Champions Sports Bar is a place to watch all kinds of sporting events. You can also play pool here, dig in to American-style grub, or enjoy karaoke at night. ✉ *Marriott Cancún Resort, Blvd Kukulcán, Km 14.5, Zona Hotelera* ☎ *998/881–2000* ⊕ *www.championscancun.com.*

Señor Frog's

BARS | Known for its over-the-top drinks, Señor Frog's serves up foot-long funnel glasses filled with margaritas, daiquiris, or beer, which you can take home as souvenirs once you've chugged them dry. Spring breakers adore this place and often stagger back night after night. Expect to pay a MX$500 cover or MX$1,200 for the open-bar option. ✉ *Blvd. Kukulcán, Km 9.5, across from Coco Bongo, Zona Hotelera* ☎ *998/883–5644* ⊕ *www.senorfrogs.com/cancun.*

DANCE CLUBS

Cancún wouldn't be Cancún without clubs, both glittering and raucous, which generally start jumping around midnight (though most open around 10 pm) and often carry on until 6 am. As the hours roll on, frenzied dancing seems to quake the building and the floor beneath. Most offer open-bar tickets (MX$600–MX$1,100) that cover admission and unlimited drinks until 3 am. (The fine

print usually specifies unlimited domestic—meaning Mexican—alcohol. In any case, check carefully what your ticket buys you.) If you stay past 3, however, you're on your own for beverages. You can also pay a lower cover charge of MX$200–MX$500 and buy drinks separately. Typical prices range from MX$100 for a shot to MX$200 for a cocktail. The most popular clubs include Coco Bongo, Dady'O, and The City, but every place seems to be pumping by midnight—especially during spring break.

The City

DANCE CLUBS | Open only on Friday nights, The City is a giant party complex with several large bars selling overpriced drinks and a cavernous dance floor with stadium seating. Dancing and live shows are the main draw during the legendary foam parties. This is by far the loudest club in the Zona Hotelera, so don't be surprised if you go home with your ears ringing. Doors open at 10 pm; expect to pay a MX$500 cover or MX$1,300 for open-bar entry. ✉ *Blvd. Kukulcán, Km 9.5, Zona Hotelera* ☎ *998/883–3313* ⊕ *www. thecitycancun.com.*

Coco Bongo

DANCE CLUBS | The wild, wild Coco Bongo has no chairs, but there are plenty of tables that everyone dances on and capacity for 1,800 people. There's also a popular show billed as "Las Vegas meets Hollywood," featuring celebrity impersonators and an amazing gravity-defying acrobatic performance with an accompanying 12-piece orchestra. After the shows, the techno gets turned up to full volume and everyone gets up to get down. Doors open at 10:30 pm. Tickets are MX$1,400–MX$2,600 for open bar and shows. ✉ *Forum Cancun, Blvd. Kukulcán, Km 9.5,, Zona Hotelera* ☎ *998/883–2373* ⊕ *www.cocobongo.com.*

Congo Bar

DANCE CLUBS | Brought to you by the makers of the famed Coco Bongo, Congo Bar is hard to miss. This spot stops traffic due

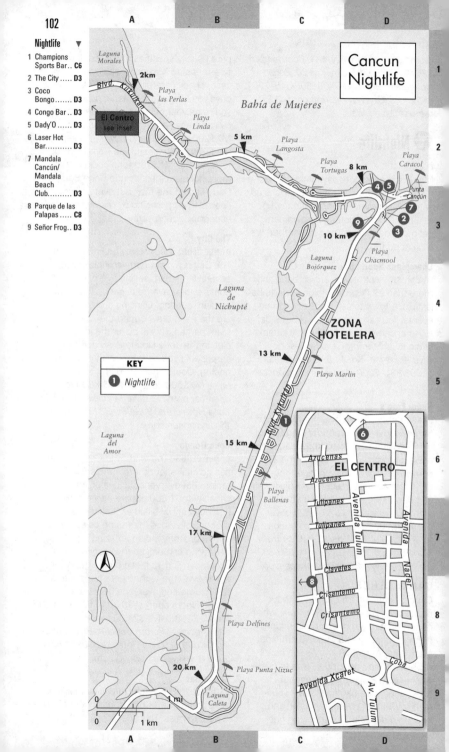

Cancun Nightlife

Laguna Morales

Blvd. Kukulkan

2km

Playa las Perlas

Playa Linda

El Centro see inset

Bahía de Mujeres

5 km

Playa Langosta

Playa Tortugas

8 km

Playa Caracol

Punta Cancún

4 5

7

2

9

3

10 km

Playa Chacmool

Laguna Bojórquez

Laguna de Nichupté

ZONA HOTELERA

13 km

Playa Marlin

Laguna del Amor

1

15 km

Playa Ballenas

17 km

Playa Delfines

20 km

Playa Punta Nizuc

Laguna Caleta

KEY

1 Nightlife

EL CENTRO

6

Azucenas

Azucenas

Tulipanes

Tulipanes

Claveles

Claveles

8

Crisantemo

Crisantemo

Avenida Tulum

Avenida Nader

Avenida Tulum

Coba

Avenida Xcaret

Av. Tulum

0 ____ 1 mi

0 ____ 1 km

to the go-go dancers who perform on open platforms lining the street. Expect Jell-O shots, confetti showers, and loud music. An open-bar ticket costs MX$600. ⊠ *Blvd. Kukulcán, Km 9, diagonally across from Coco Bongo, Zona Hotelera* ☎ *800/841–4636 toll-free in Mexico, 998/883–0563* ⊕ *www.facebook.com/ CongoBarOficial.*

Dady'O

DANCE CLUBS | Cancún's original dance club is still very "in" with the younger set. A giant screen projects music videos above the always-packed dance floor, while laser lights whirl across the crowd. During spring break, Hawaiian Bikini contests make the place even livelier. The cover charge (waived for women on Fridays) is MX$500, and the open-bar option is MX$850. ⊠ *Blvd. Kukulcán, Km 9.5, across from Coco Bongo, Zona Hotelera* ☎ *998/883–3333* ⊕ *www.dadyo-cancun.com.*

Mandala Cancún/Mandala Beach Club

DANCE CLUBS | This Balinese-style party place is a buzzing beach retreat by day and a more upscale nightclub after dark. Both have bikini contests, DJs, pool parties, and bottle service. Don't forget your swimsuit and beach-appropriate shoes. Expect to pay a MX$800 cover or MX$1,300 for an open bar. ⊠ *Blvd. Kukulcán, Km 8.5, Zona Hotelera* ☎ *998/883–3333* ⊕ *www.mandalabeach.com.*

🛍 Shopping

The few grocery stores in the Zona Hotelera tend to be expensive. It's better to shop for groceries downtown.

MARKETS AND MALLS

Coral Negro

MARKET | Next to the convention center, this open-air market has about 50 stalls selling crafts and souvenirs. Everything here is overpriced, and vendors are pushy; however, bargaining does work. Stalls deeper in the market tend to have better deals than those around the

---

Avoid Tortoiseshell

Refrain from buying anything made from tortoiseshell. The *carey*, or hawksbill turtle from which most of it comes, is an endangered species, and it's illegal to bring tortoiseshell products into the United States and several other countries. Also be aware that there are some restrictions regarding black coral. For one, you must purchase it from a recognized dealer.

---

periphery. ⊠ *Blvd. Kukulcán, Km 9, Zona Hotelera* ☎ *998/984–8531.*

Forum Cancún

MALL | This three-level entertainment and shopping plaza in the Zona features brand-name restaurants, upscale clothing boutiques, a food court, and chain stores, all in a circus-like atmosphere. For spring breakers the main draws are the nightclubs, Coco Bongo and Carlos 'n Charlie's. The bungee trampolines set up here during high season are especially popular with children. You will also find several ATMs on-site. ⊠ *Blvd. Kukulcán, Km 9.5, Zona Hotelera* ☎ *998/883–4425* ⊕ *www.forumcancun.mx.*

★ La Isla Shopping Village

MALL | The glittering, ultratrendy, and ultraexpensive La Isla Shopping Village is on the Laguna Nichupté under chic, white canopies. A series of canals and small bridges is designed to give the place a Venetian look. In addition to more than 200 designer shops, the mall has a marina, restaurants, and movie theaters. There's also an interactive aquarium where you can swim with the dolphins and feed the sharks. With the completion of Plaza La Isla II, it added a larger ferris wheel, casino, chocolate factory, and tequila museum. ✉ *Blvd. Kukulcán, Km 12.5, Zona Hotelera* ☎ *998/883–5025* ⊕ *www.laislacancun.mx.*

Plaza Caracol

MALL | North of the convention center, the two-story Plaza Caracol has chain stores, souvenir shops, jewelry boutiques, and pharmacies. If you work up an appetite, it also has a food court. Free Wi-Fi is available at the Häagen-Dazs ice cream shop. ✉ *Blvd. Kukulcán, Km 8.5, Zona Hotelera* ☎ *998/883–4760.*

Plaza Kukulcán

MALL | This mall has about 30 shops and restaurants. The mall also hosts art exhibits and other cultural events. While parents shop, kids can enjoy the game arcade and play area. ✉ *Blvd. Kukulcán, Km 13, Zona Hotelera* ☎ *998/193–0161* ⊕ *www.kukulcanplaza.mx.*

Plaza la Fiesta (*Mexican Outlet*)

MARKET | Near the convention center, Plaza la Fiesta has 20,000 square feet of showroom space and more than 100,000 different products for sale. Offering probably the widest selection of Mexican goods in the Hotel Zone, it has leather items, jewelry, clothing, handicrafts, alcohol, and assorted souvenirs. Look carefully at what you buy, though: not everything here is made in Mexico. There are some good bargains, but be prepared to pay sticker price as this is not a place to haggle. ✉ *Blvd. Kukulcán, Km 9, Zona Hotelera.*

⚡ Activities

BOATING AND SAILING

AquaWorld

WATER SPORTS | Aside from organizing assorted on-the-water excursions, this outfit rents two-person speedboats for jungle tours. Wave Runners and cool water toys like flyboards and hoverboards are available too. Ninja warrior fans will love bouncing around on their on-the-water inflatable obstacle course. ✉ *Blvd. Kukulcán, Km 15.2, Zona Hotelera*

☎ *554/166–3092, 866/210–1236 in the U.S.* ⊕ *www.aquaworld.com.mx* ✉ *Day passes from $129 USD.*

Cancun Adventures

BOAT TOURS | Cancun Adventures provides a variety of excursions in the Riviera Maya, including catamaran sailings to the Isla Mujeres. The 5.5-hour voyage departs from the Marina Cancun and includes lunch, an open bar on board, snorkeling, and free time to explore Isla Mujeres. You also have time to visit Playa Norte, one of the most beautiful beaches in Cancun. Round-trip transportation to the dock is included from select hotels if you book 24-hours in advance. Knowledgeable, bilingual guides accompany guests on every tour. ✉ *Vialidad Paseo Mujeres MZ1, Punta Sam ⊕ Condominio Playa Mujeres, Marina Cancun* ☎ *984/854–3460* ⊕ *www.cancun-adventure.com/en* ✉ *$83.*

Eco Tours Adventure

ECOTOURISM | FAMILY | Led by marine biologists and certified guides, this tour company is dedicated to delivering a fun and safe experience, without exploiting the natural environment by respecting animal rights and the conservation of nature. The Whale Shark Tour is an easy excursion that the whole family can enjoy. In addition to snorkeling with the whale sharks, there's also time to snorkel at Isla Mujeres. Breakfast, lunch, mask, fins, and safety jackets are included, as is transportation from and to any hotel. Tours are 100% guaranteed. ✉ *Carr. a Punta Sam, 84, Punta Sam* ☎ *984/147–9678, 984/114–2199* ⊕ *www. ecotoursadventure.com* ✉ *From $199* ⊗ *Closed mid-September–May.*

Marina Barracuda

WATER SPORTS | Jungle boats for two to three passengers can be rented through Marina Barracuda. Book mangrove or jungle tour. Private tours to Isla Mujeres, with a captain, and up to ten passengers can also be arranged. ✉ *Blvd. Kukulcán, Km 14.1, in front of Ritz-Carlton, Zona*

Water Sports in Cancún

With the Caribbean on one side and the still waters of Laguna Nichupté on the other, it's no wonder that Cancún is one of the world's water sports capitals. The top activities are snorkeling and diving along the coral reef just off the coast.

Kiteboarding and windsurfing are also popular, although the waves are not as constant as on Mexico's Pacific coast. For the beach-break surfer, the sandbars are best at Playa Gaviota Azul and Playa Delfines, but waves are generally choppy and created by wind swells. Thirty-two kilometers (20 miles) south of Cancún are several point breaks off the coast of Puerto Morelos and Punta Brava.

If you want to view the mysterious underwater world but don't want to get your feet wet, a glass-bottom boat or "submarine" is the ticket. You can also go fishing, parasailing, or try your balancing skills on a stand-up paddleboard. Paddleboats, kayaks, catamarans, and banana boats are readily available, too.

Because the beaches along the Zona Hotelera can have a strong undertow, always respect the flags posted in the area. A black flag means no swimming at all. A red flag means you can swim but only with extreme caution. Yellow means approach with caution, while green means water conditions are safe. You'll most likely always see a red or yellow flag, even when the water is calm.

Unfortunately, there's very little wildlife in the Laguna Nichupté, so most advertised jungle tours are glorified Jet Ski romps where you drive around fast, make a lot of noise, and don't see many animals. American crocodiles still reside in these waters though, so don't stand or swim in the lagoon.

Although the coral reef in this area is not as spectacular as farther south, there's still marine life. It's quite common to spot angelfish, parrot fish, blue tang, sea turtles, and the occasional moray eel. To be a good world citizen, follow the six golden rules for snorkeling or scuba diving:

1. Don't throw any garbage into the sea, as the marine life will assume it's food, an often lethal mistake.

2. Never stand on the coral.

3. Secure all cameras and gear onto your body so you don't drop anything onto the fragile reef.

4. Never take anything from the sea.

5. Don't feed any of the marine animals.

6. Avoid applying sunblock, tanning lotion, or mosquito repellent just before you visit the reef.

Hotelera ☎ 998/885–2444 ⊕ www.marinabarracuda.com ⊡ From $44.

DINNER CRUISES

Sunset boat cruises that include dinner, drinks, music, and sometimes dancing are popular in Cancún—especially among couples looking for a romantic evening and visitors who'd rather avoid the carnival atmosphere of the clubs and discos.

Capitán Hook

ENTERTAINMENT CRUISE | FAMILY | Watch a show aboard a replica of an 18th-century Spanish galleon, then enjoy a lobster or steak dinner and drinks as the ship cruises around at sunset. Capitán Hook's three-hour trip runs daily from 7 to 10:30 pm, but you must arrive 45 minutes before departure. ⊠ *Blvd. Kukulcán, Km 5, Zona Hotelera* ☎ *998/849–4931, 998/849–4933* ⊕ *www.capitanhook.com* 🖃 *From MX$1,400.*

Columbus Cancún

ENTERTAINMENT CRUISE | This company offers couples-only cruises on a 62-foot galleon. Advertised as a "romance tour," it has some elements of a booze cruise (including watered-down cocktails). But it's still worth it for the fresh lobster dinner and sunset views over Laguna Nichupté; afterward, the boat trip continues so you can stargaze. Departures take place at 5 and 8 pm. Families are welcome, but no children under 14 are permitted. ⊠ *Marina Aquatours, Km 6.5, Blvd. Kukulcán, Zona Hotelera* ✛ *in front of Playa Tortugas–Turtles beach also known as the Fat Tuesday beach* ☎ *866/393–5158 in the U.S., 800/727–5391 toll-free in Mexico* ⊕ *www.columbuscancun.com.mx* 🖃 *From MX$1,800.*

★ Xoximilco

ENTERTAINMENT CRUISE | Brought to you by the creators of Xcaret, this dinner cruise experience combines culture, cuisine, music, and dancing for a fiesta like no other. Set sail aboard a colorful *trajinera* (gondolalike boat) named after one of the Mexican states. (The entire setup is modeled on the famous Xochimilco floating gardens near Mexico City.) While cruising down the freshwater canals, passengers are treated to live music, an open bar (tequila and beer), and various dishes from around the country. Three-hour tours begin at 7 pm. Bring mosquito spray. ⊠ *Carretera 307, Km 338, 5 mins from Cancún Airport, Carretera Cancún-Aeropuerto* ☎ *998/883–3143 in Mexico, 855/326–0682 in the U.S.* ⊕ *www.xoximilco.com* 🖃 *From MX$1,800.*

FISHING

Some 500 species—including sailfish, wahoo, bluefin, marlin, barracuda, and red snapper—live in the waters off Cancún. You can charter deep-sea fishing boats for four to eight hours; rates generally include a captain and first mate, gear, bait, and beverages.

Charter Fishing Cancún

FISHING | This outfit offers sportfishing trips between the mainland and Isla Mujeres. Possible catches include mahimahi, sailfish, barracuda, king mackerel, wahoo, tuna, grouper, snapper, and shark. Boats, ranging in size from 31 to 54 feet, can be chartered for four, six, eight or 10 hours. Shared boats with a maximum of six anglers are also available. ⊠ *Marina Aquatours, Blvd. Kukulcán, Km 6.5, Zona Hotelera* ☎ *998/200–3240, 998/200–3240 in the U.S.* ⊕ *www.charterfishingcancun.com* 🖃 *From MX$2,900.*

Scuba Cancún

SCUBA DIVING | In addition to diving trips, Scuba Cancún offers PADI instruction certification programs. Additionally, they have whale shark snorkeling tours, trips to Isla Contoy, and deep-sea fishing expeditions that last from four to eight hours. ⊠ *Playa Langosta, Blvd. Kukulcán, Km 5, Zona Hotelera* ☎ *998/849–7508, 998/279–2199 WhatsApp* ⊕ *www.scubacancun.com.mx* 🖃 *From MX$11,800.*

GOLF

All courses here enforce a moderate dress code: collared shirts, skirts or shorts that extend to at least mid-thigh, and no jeans or swimwear.

El Tinto

GOLF | El Tinto, a challenging 18-hole course within the Cancun Country Club, is conveniently located just 10 minutes south of the Cancun Airport. Designed by world-renowned professional Nick Price, this well-maintained course has 84 bunkers, five lakes, and wide fairways. The yardage length, coupled with multiple sets of tee markers, challenges golfers of all abilities. A good value, greens fees include a mandatory golf cart, water bottle, and game accessories.

Cancún may not be the best destination for serious golfers, but it has several beautiful and challenging courses.

Additionally, there is a practice area and a golf academy on-site. *Carretera Federal 307, Chetumal Km 388,* ⊠ *Carretera Cancún-Aeropuerto* 🕾 *998/886–2815* ⊕ *www.cancuncountryclub.com* 🕾 *$180 for 18 holes* 🏌 *18 Holes, 7,435 yards, Par 72.*

★ Iberostar Cancún

GOLF | The only 18-hole championship course in Cancún is at the Iberostar. Designed by legendary golfer Isao Aoki, it lies along the Nichupté Lagoon. The course has a practice facility with driving range and putting green. Four sets of tees stretch from 5,000 yards to 6,800 yards over 150 lush acres; you're likely to see all kinds of wildlife including crocodiles, birds, and iguanas as you play. Other than a few holes lined by jungle and lagoon, the course is wide open and the fairways are fast. The 16th hole overlooks the Mayan Ruinas El Rey. The greens fee includes 10 holes, golf cart, unlimited food and beverage, and transfers between the golf course and the Cancún hotel area for a minimum of two people. Hotel guests receive 60% off greens fees. ⊠ *Iberostar, Blvd. Kukulcán, Km 17, Zona Hotelera* 🕾 *998/881–8016* ⊕ *www.iberostar.com/en/iberostar-cancun-golf-club* 🕾 *$199 for 18 holes* 🏌 *18 holes. 6735 yards. Par 72.*

Moon Spa & Golf Club

GOLF | Designed by Jack Nicklaus, this is the only exclusive 27-hole par 72 course in the Mexican Caribbean. Spread over three nine-hole courses—the Jungle, the Lakes, and the Dunes—they each have four sets of tees with mangroves, wetlands, and strategically placed bunkers. Eighteen-hole play consists of three combinations: Dunes and Jungle, Jungle and Lakes, or Lakes and Dunes. The 18-hole greens fee includes a cart, food, and drink service. If you're staying at any of the Palace Resorts, inquire about all-inclusive golf packages. Lessons are available. ⊠ *Moon Palace Golf & Spa Resort, Carretera Cancún-Chetumal, Km 340, about 15 mins from airport,* 🕾 *998/881–6100* ⊕ *www.palaceresorts.*

com ✉ *$303 for 18 holes* 🏌. *18 holes.*
7165 yards. Par 72.

Playa Mujeres Golf Club

GOLF | Playa Mujeres Golf Club is the
only golf course in Cancun designed by
Greg Norman. By rearranging the site's
native plants and indigenous foliage, the
course was carefully crafted and shaped
through the abundant fauna and environ-
mentally sensitive areas that surround
it. The front 9 holes take you on a route
between the mangroves and wetlands
of an extensive ground, adjacent to the
Chachmuchuch Lagoon. The back 9 holes
open up through natural sand dunes and
lead you to the ocean, featuring the turquoise waters of the Mexican Caribbean
Sea and a spectacular view of the Isla
Mujeres skyline. The well-kept, lush fairways and true-rolling greens of this great
resort course, are swept by daily trade
winds, which demand pinpoint accuracy
and challenge even the most experienced golfer. On the day of play, all players have access to the on-site facilities
and services, which include golf carts
with a GPS visage system plus unlimited
use of the driving range and two putting
greens. Guest of Dreams Playa Mujeres
enjoy complimentary greens fees. ✉ *Playa Mujeres Beach Resort, Prolongación
Bonampak, Punta Sam* ☎ *998/887–7322,
998/800–3892* ⊕ *www.dreamsresorts.
com* ✉ *$103 for 18 holes* 🏌. *18 holes.*
7218 yards. Par 72.

Puerto Cancún Golf

GOLF | Designed by British Open Champi-
on Tom Weiskopf, this 18-hole course is
in Puerto Cancún, midway between the
Zona Hotelera and El Centro. It stretches
over 185 acres and has ocean views plus
two holes that play on the marina. The
winding fairways will test your skills on
distance and short game swing, and the
strategically placed bunkers demand a
great deal of accuracy. Stay focused on
the final hole, as it is located on an island
in the middle of a canal. The course
offers access to the Puerto Cancún youth
golf program. ✉ *Blvd. Kulkulcan, Puerto*

Juarez, Zona Hotelera ☎ *998/898–3306*
⊕ *www.puertocancun.com/golf* ✉ *$161
for 18 holes* 🏌. *18 holes. 7241 yards. Par
72* ⊙ *Closed Mon.*

Riviera Cancún Golf

GOLF | Designed by Jack Nicklaus,
this signature 18-hole golf course has
strategic bunkering, immaculate greens,
wooden bridges, and incredible ocean
views on holes 14 and 15. Surrounded by
mangroves, dunes, bridges, and lakes,
this 7060 yards, par 72 is challenging.
Bring more balls than you think, as you'll
encounter water at nearly every hole. The
contemporary Mexican-style clubhouse
with a restaurant has fantastic views of
the 18th hole. There is a driving range,
plus putting and chipping greens. This
course is not associated with a specific hotel. ✉ *Blvd. Kulkulcán, Km 25.3,
southern end of Kukulcán near Punta
Nizuc, Zona Hotelera* ☎ *998/848–7777*
⊕ *www.facebook.com/GolfRivieraCancun*
✉ *$255 for 18 holes* 🏌. *18 holes. 7060
yards. Par 72.*

SCUBA DIVING AND SNORKELING

The snorkeling is best at Punta Nizuc,
Punta Cancún, and Playa Tortugas,
although you should be careful of the
strong currents at Tortugas. You can rent
gear from many of the diving places as
well as at many hotels.

Scuba diving is popular in Cancún,
though it's not as spectacular as in Cozumel. Look for a company that will give
you lots of personal attention. (Smaller
outfits are often better at this than larger
ones.) Regardless, ask to meet the dive
master, and check the equipment and
certifications thoroughly.

The one-hour courses that many resorts
offer for free do not prepare you to dive
in the open ocean—only in shallow water
where you can easily surface without
danger. They are meant only to whet
your appetite. If you've caught the scuba
bug and want to take deep or boat dives,
prepare yourself properly by investing in a
full certification course.

Aqua Fun

SCUBA DIVING | FAMILY | Sign on with Aqua Fun for a two-hour tour of the mangroves that includes snorkeling at the Punta Nizuc reef. Tours go Monday, Wednesday, and Friday at 10 am, 1 pm, and 3 pm. Advance reservations are required. ✉ *Blvd. Kukulcán, Km 16.5, Zona Hotelera* ☎ *998/885–2930* ⊕ *aquafun.com.mx* 💳 *MX$1,400.*

AquaWorld

SCUBA DIVING | FAMILY | If you want to visit the underwater museum, AquaWorld runs both snorkeling excursions and scuba trips to the site. Dive explorations of boat wrecks are also organized. ✉ *Blvd. Kukulcán, Km 15.2, Zona Hotelera* ☎ *998/689–1013, 866/210–1236 in the U.S.* ⊕ *www.aquaworld.com.mx* 💳 *Snorkeling trips MX$1,700; dive trips from MX$3,700.*

Marina Punta del Este

SCUBA DIVING | Located right in front of the Grand Park Royal Cancún Caribe, Marina Punta del Este has dives that last from 3½ to 4 hours. If you need a lesson, daily ones begin at 9 am and 1 pm. ✉ *Blvd. Kukulcán, Km 10.3, Zona Hotelera* ☎ *998/883–1210* 💳 *Dives from MX$2,200.*

Scuba Cancún

SCUBA DIVING | Long-established Scuba Cancún specializes in diving trips and offers PADI instruction. ✉ *Playa Langosta, Blvd. Kukulcán, Km 5, Zona Hotelera* ☎ *998/849–7508* ⊕ *www.scubacancun.com.mx* 💳 *Dives from MX$1,240.*

Solo Buceo

SCUBA DIVING | In addition to PADI instruction, Solo Buceo offers one- and two-tank dives and whale shark snorkeling. ✉ *Blvd. Kukulcán, Km 9.5, Zona Hotelera* ☎ *998/260–4995, 855/980–6736 in the U.S.* ⊕ *www.solobuceo.com* 💳 *Dives from MX$2,600; instruction from MX$1,900.*

SPAS

Aqua Spa

SPAS | It may be one of the smaller spas in the Hotel Zone, but Aqua Spa has talented, long-standing therapists who attract repeat clients from neighboring resorts. Treatments begin with a foot bath, hand massage, and your choice of chlorophyll water or green tea. A hydrotherapy ritual is included with treatments like the coffee exfoliation, coconut–chocolate wrap, and honey scrub. For the ultimate in pampering, request a diamond facial that uses over 30 botanical ingredients like Chardonnay Yawn Seed extract and a powerful deep-sea antioxidant that enhances skin firmness. ✉ *Live Aqua Beach Resort Cancun, Blvd. Kukulcán, Km 12.5, Zona Hotelera* ☎ *998/881–7600, 800/343–7821* ⊕ *www.liveaqua.com.*

BlancSpa

SPAS | This massive facility takes pampering to a whole new level. Arrive early and linger in one of the dimly lighted relaxation rooms, nibble on fresh cookies and sip *agua fresca* flavored with hibiscus or cucumber. Before your treatment utilize the hydrotherapy area with hot/cold plunge pools, sauna, herbal steam room, ice room, sauna therapy, and relaxation lounge. A vast array of treatments—from facials and body wraps to intensive four-handed couples' massages—are offered in oversized suites. Nonguests can use the resort on a day pass when booking treatments at the spa. ✉ *Le Blanc Spa Resort, Blvd. Kukulcán, Km 10, Zona Hotelera* ☎ *998/881–4740* ⊕ *www.leblancsparesorts.com.*

★ Gem Spa

SPAS | With 40,000 square feet and 26 treatment rooms, this is one of Latin America's largest spas. The experience begins with a 90-minute, 10-step hydrotherapy ritual that detoxifies the skin Incorporating an aromatherapy steam room, multi-jet shower, clay steam room, rain shower, sauna, ice room, whirlpool, cold plunge pool, and pebble walkway

3

Cancún **ZONA HOTELERA**

with warm water jets. Gem Spa treatments—ranging from a diamond-dust body exfoliation to an amber-and-gold facial—are inspired by the healing energy of gemstones. The 80-minute Seventh Wonder Luxury Massage, during which quartz crystals are placed on seven chakras, is worth the splurge. Guest must be 16 years or older. ✉ *Fiesta Americana Grand Coral Beach, Blvd. Kukulcán 9.5, Zona Hotelera* ☎ *998/881–3200* ⊕ *www.gemspacancun.com.*

JW Marriott Spa

SPAS | This 35,000-square-foot spa has breathtaking ocean views and Mayan-inspired treatments like the Mayan Treasure Hydrating Vichy Treatment. Choose from one of six invigorating facials including the aromatic comfort facial. Fitness classes are available. The spa also offers specialized treatments for men, expectant mothers, couples, and teens. ✉ *JW Marriott, Blvd. Kukulcán, Km 14.5, Cancún* ☎ *998/848–9700 Ext. 6700* ⊕ *wwww.jwmarriottcancunspa.com.*

The Ritz-Carlton Spa

SPAS | The intimate spa at The Ritz-Carlton offers a unique invigorating Zac-Xib body polish. Meaning "clean man" in Mayan, this treatment combines a vigorous body scrub with a renewing bath therapy. Essential oils and plant extracts, as prepared in ancient warrior rituals, relax muscle tension, soothe mental stress, and reduce fatigue. ✉ *The Ritz Carlton, Blvd. Kukulcán, Km 13.5, Retorno del Rey 36, Zona Hotelera* ☎ *998/881–0808* ⊕ *www.ritzcarlton.com/Cancun.*

Chapter 4

ISLA MUJERES

4

Updated by
Luis Domínguez

⊙ Sights   🍴 Restaurants   🛏 Hotels   🛍 Shopping   🍸 Nightlife

★★★★☆   ★★★★☆   ★★★★☆   ★★★☆☆   ★★★☆☆

WELCOME TO ISLA MUJERES

TOP REASONS TO GO

★ **Getting away from the crowd:** Although Isla Mujeres is just across the bay from Cancún, the peace and quiet make it seem like another universe.

★ **Exploring the southeastern coast:** Bump along in a golf cart where craggy cliffs meet the blue Caribbean.

★ **Eating freshly grilled seafood:** For some reason it always tastes best under a beachfront *palapa* (thatch roof) at lovely Playa Norte.

★ **Diving with "sleeping sharks":** Plunge into the underwater caverns off Isla, where these gentle giants sleep.

★ **Taking a boat trip to Isla Contoy:** On this even smaller island, more than 150 species of birds make their home.

Isla Mujeres is still quiet by Riviera Maya standards, with a small-town feel that makes it a great escape from Cancún. (Don't mention that to locals, who will tell you that the influx of big hotels has changed it forever.) Just 8 km (5 miles) long and 1 km (½ mile) wide, its landscapes include flat sandy beaches in the north and steep rocky bluffs to the south. The liveliest activities here are swimming, snorkeling, exploring the remnants of the island's past, drinking cold beer, eating fresh seafood, and lazing under palapas.

1 Greater Isla Mujeres. Midway along the western coast of Isla you can glimpse the lovely Laguna Makax. At the lagoon's southeastern end are the shady stretches of Playa Tiburón and Playa Lancheros. At Isla's southernmost tip is Garrafón Natural Reef Park.

2 Playa Norte. With its waist-deep turquoise waters and wide soft sands, Playa Norte is the northernmost beach on Isla Mujeres, and the most beautiful. The bulk of the island's resorts and hotels are located here, and the town center and historic cemetery are both just a short walk away.

3 El Pueblo. Directly in front of the ferry piers, El Pueblo is Isla's only town. It extends the full width of the island's northern end, sandwiched between sand and sea to the south, west, and northeast. The *zócalo* (main square) is the hub of *isleño* life.

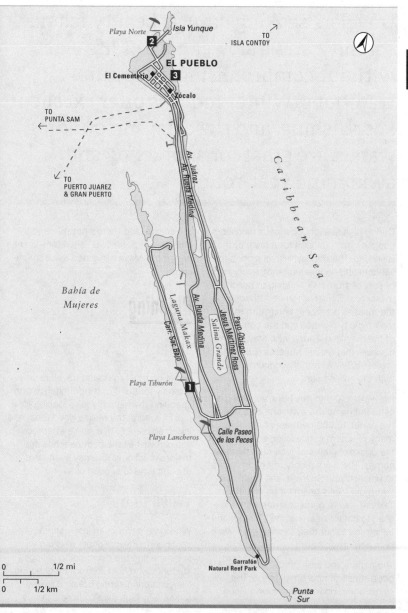

Playa Norte

Isla Yunque

2

TO
ISLA CONTOY

EL PUEBLO

El Cementerio

3

Zócalo

TO
PUNTA SAM

TO
PUERTO JUAREZ
& GRAN PUERTO

Av. Juarez

Av. Rueda Medina

C a r i b b e a n   S e a

*Bahía de
Mujeres*

Av. Rueda Medina

Laguna Makax

Carr. Sac-Bajo

Payo Obispo

Jesus Martinez Ross

Salina Grande

Playa Tiburón

1

Playa Lancheros

Calle Paseo
de los Peces

Garrafón
Natural Reef Park

*Punta
Sur*

0   1/2 mi

0   1/2 km

Once a small fishing village, colorful Isla Mujeres (meaning "Island of Women") has become a favorite for travelers seeking natural beauty, island serenity, and a slower pace of life—all without compromising its cultural traditions. Winter months offer excellent sportfishing, and the calm surrounding waters are great for snorkeling and swimming year-round.

During high season, boatloads of visitors pop over from Cancún for a taste of the island life. The midday rush is a boon for vendors and hagglers offering every kind of service from hair braiding to beach massages. By late afternoon, though, the masses disappear and return to their big-city nightlife and the comforts of the mainland. Those who stay behind discover that on Isla Mujeres (*EES-lah moo-HAIR-ays*), worldly concerns fade with the setting sun.

Isla—after 10 minutes here, you'll short-hand the name like everyone else does—has about 12,000 permanent residents, many of whom earn a living selling fish at the docks or plates of food outside their homes. There are plenty of opportunities to practice your Spanish, and you'll find that most locals beam when you try. Taxi drivers are genuinely interested in sharing details of the island's history and telling you about their families who were born and raised here.

The minute you step off the boat, you'll get a sense of how small Isla is. The sights and properties are strung along the coasts, and there's not much to the interior except for two saltwater marshes where the Maya harvested salt centuries ago.

Planning

Timing

Although most mainland travelers visit Isla only for the day, it's definitely worth spending the night if you're looking for a mix of culture, tranquility, good food, and island ambience. In a single afternoon you can visit all the best beaches and major attractions. You may even have enough time to snorkel or swim.

When to Go

When you factor in an international contingent of vacationers seeking winter sunshine and the day-tripping college students who flock in from neighboring Cancún during spring break, it's easy to see why high season here extends from late November (U.S. Thanksgiving) straight through Easter. Other months qualify as low season, and prices may be cut in half. Some of the best deals can be found from late October to mid-November, after the rainy season has passed but before the crowds have arrived.

Isla enjoys its best weather between November and May, when temperatures usually hover around 27°C (80°F). June, July, and August are the hottest and most humid months, with daytime highs routinely over 35°C (95°F). A few festivals and holidays are worth keeping in mind while you're planning your trip: Carnaval in either February or March (the week before Lent); the Sol a Sol Regatta in late April; Founder's Day on August 17; the Day of the Virgin de la Caridad del Cobre, patron saint of local fishermen, on September 8; the Day of the Dead from October 31 to November 2; and the Feast of the Immaculate Conception on December 8. Be sure to book well in advance if you're planning to visit on any of these days.

Getting Here and Around

BOAT AND FERRY

Isla ferries are typically two-story passenger cruisers that run between the mainland and the island's main dock. The ride gets a bit choppier with evening crossings.

Between 9:30 and early evening, Ultramar ferries to Isla's main dock depart from three locations in Cancún's Zona Hotelera: El Embarcadero marina complex at Playa Linda (approximately hourly), Playa Tortugas (approximately hourly), and Playa Caracol (approximately ly every two hours). The voyage costs MX$210 one way and takes about 30 minutes. Services from the hotel zone are more geared to day-trippers to and from Cancún. Local people are more apt to use the half-hourly service that departs from Cancún's Puerto Juárez

from 5 am to midnight. (You can, too.) Fares are MX$208 one way.

If you have a vehicle—and you really don't need one on the island—the Ultramar Vehicle Ferry leaves from Punta Sam, a dock north of Puerto Juárez. The ride takes about 45 minutes, and the fare is MX$400 per family car including the driver, and prices may vary for bigger cars and more passengers. If you're staying at Zoëtry Villa Rolandi or Isla Mujeres Palace, transportation by private boat is included in your room rate.

CONTACTS Ultramar. ✉ *Gran Puerto Cancún, Av. López Portillo, Sm 84, Cancún* ☎ *998/293–9092* ⊕ *www.ultramarferry. com.*

GOLF CART

Golf carts are a fun way to get around the island, especially if you're traveling with kids. Due to *topes* (speed bumps), potholes, and the occasional gusty winds when you're out on the island, they're a much safer option than exploring by moped or bike. The downside is you can't lock them. Never leave anything of value inside. There are more than a dozen rental agencies, although not all golf carts are created equal. Bypass the rusty cream-color carts, and opt for those with thick tires made by familiar brands like Jeep Wrangler. Most companies allow prebooking online and will deliver your golf cart directly to your hotel. This, however, limits your ability to haggle over the price. Rates start at approximately MX$1,200 for 24 hours, with prorated rates for shorter periods, depending on the season.

CONTACTS Golf Carts Indios. (*Apache's*) ✉ *Av. Rueda Medina, Sm 1, Mza 2, Lote 19, between Avs. López Mateos and Matamoros, Isla Mujeres* ☎ *998/274– 0392* ⊕ *www.indios-golfcarts.com.* **Isla Mujeres Golf Cart Rentals.** ✉ *Av. Martínez Ross, Lote 6, Isla Mujeres* ☎ *998/578– 5266* ⊕ *www.islamujeresgolfcartrentals.* **Pepe's Moto Rent.** ✉ *Av. Hidalgo*

19, and Ave Matamoros, Isla Mujeres ☎ *998/877–0019* ⊕ *rentadora-ppes. negocio.site.*

MOPED AND BICYCLE

If you need your own wheels—and you really don't here on Isla—we strongly recommend you rent a golf cart rather than a scooter for safety reasons. If you absolutely want two wheels rather than four, Avenida Rueda Medina, directly across from the dock, is lined with shops where you can rent mopeds. Most charge MX$600 a day, but the final price will depend on the vehicle's make and condition and your own haggling skills. Some also offer bike rentals, with daily rates starting at MX$250 for beaters and MX$350 for mountain bikes. If you are interested in cycling, be advised that it's hot here and you'll encounter plenty of speed bumps and the occasional wind gusts out on the island. Don't ride at night, since many roads don't have streetlights, and make sure your bike comes with a lock to keep it from wandering off.

Before leaving the rental agency, check your moped or golf cart for scratches and dings. You may even want to take a photo for additional proof of the original condition. Otherwise, you'll pay dearly for any damage that was not noted prior to your rental agreement.

Hotels

Hotels here range from B&Bs and boutique properties to all-inclusive resorts; even the largest of the latter are small compared to what you might find on the mainland, and, with so many restaurants around, it's not worth paying for an all-inclusive package unless you'd rather not venture off-site. Places on the north end near El Pueblo are within walking distance of shops, eateries, and the calm waters of Playa Norte; budget digs can be found in the center of town—just bear in mind they get street noise from the pedestrian traffic on Avenida Hidalgo. Lodgings elsewhere on the island are more private but aren't as convenient and might lack beaches. Many of Isla's smaller hotels don't accept credit cards, and some add a 5%–10% surcharge if you use one. Hoteliers here have also been tightening up cancellation policies, so inquire about fees for changing reservations.

Before paying, always ask to see your room to make sure everything is satisfactory—especially at the smaller hotels.

Vacation rentals are an alternative to hotels, and several agencies can help you find one: ⊕ *www.islabeckons.com*, for example, lists fully equipped apartments and houses (and also handles reservations for hotel rooms); ⊕ *www.morningsinmexico.com* offers less expensive properties.

For expanded reviews, facilities, and current deals, visit Fodors.com.

Restaurants

Dining on Isla is a casual affair, and much more affordable than in neighboring Cancún. Restaurants tend to serve simple food like seafood, pizza, salads, and Mexican dishes. Fresh ingredients and hospitable waiters make up for the island's lack of elaborate menus and master chefs. It's cash-only in most restaurants. If credit cards are accepted, you'll most likely pay an additional 5% service charge. It's customary in Mexico for the waiter to bring the bill only when you ask for it (*"la cuenta, por favor"*). Always check to make sure you didn't get charged for something you didn't order, and to make sure the addition is correct. The "tax" on the bill is often a service charge, a sort of guaranteed tip. Expect to have some of the island's stray dogs looking you in the eye if you dine outdoors. It's part of the casual life on Isla.

Though informal, most indoor restaurants do request that you at least wear a shirt and shoes. Some outdoor terrace and palapa restaurants also require shoes and some sort of cover-up over your bathing suit.

WHAT IT COSTS in Dollars and Pesos			
$	$$	$$$	$$$$
RESTAURANTS			
under MX$135	MX$135– MX$200	MX$201– MX$350	over MX$350
HOTELS IN DOLLARS			
under $100	$100– $200	$201– $300	over $300
HOTELS IN PESOS			
under MX$2,000	MX$2,000– MX$4,000	MX$4,001– MX$6,000	over MX$6,000

Banks and Currency Exchange

Isla Mujeres banks rarely change U.S. dollars into Mexican pesos, but there are many *casas de cambio* (exchange houses) that will; there's also one at the Ultramar ferry dock in Cancún if you want to come prepared. Alternatively, you can withdraw pesos at several on-island ATMs, including those at the Super Aki store on the town square, the Banamex at the corner of Juarez and Morelos, and the HSBC across from the ferry port. Note, however, that these machines tend to have long lines and can run out of money on busy weekends and holidays. While most businesses accept U.S. dollars, you should expect to get change back in pesos at a less-than-favorable exchange rate. A minority of establishments accept credit cards (mostly MasterCard and Visa, and often with a 5% service fee attached), though this number is growing.

Beaches

Despite being surrounded by water, Isla Mujeres really has only three beaches suitable for visitors: Playa Norte on the north end, and Playa Lancheros and Playa Tiburón on the west side. With its crystal clear water, Playa Norte is generally tranquil and better for swimming than eastern beaches facing the Caribbean, which are rocky and susceptible to strong winds and riptides. Western beaches always have a subtle south-to-north current, which can be dangerous if you're not alert. The southern part of the island has several secluded beaches, but they, too, have exposed reefs and strong currents and are often littered with sea grass and ocean debris.

Isla's sandy beaches have experienced erosion due to high winds and stormy seas in the past few decades and have never fully recovered. However, property owners have worked to minimize erosion with geotubes placed along Playa Norte's shores.

Nightlife

This sleepy island has a surprisingly healthy nightlife scene, with a variety of options to choose from. Most bars close by midnight, but the party continues at a few nightclubs until 2 am. The majority of venues are within downtown's four-block radius, with a few others along Playa Norte. The proximity makes barhopping on foot perilously convenient.

Isleños also celebrate many holidays and festivals in El Pueblo, usually with live entertainment. Carnaval, held annually in February or March (the week before Lent), turns sleepy Isla Mujeres into party central with music, dancing, and colorful parades in the zócalo. In Mardi Gras–like fashion, locals dressed in costumes liven up the island with decorated golf carts and dance performances. Other popular events include Founder's Day (August 17), which marks the island's official founding by the Mexican government. From October 31 to November 2, locals head to the cemetery to honor their dearly departed during Día de los Muertos (Day of the Dead) celebrations.

Safety

The presence of a Mexican naval base contributes to a sense of safety here. There's little crime on this small island, making it an excellent choice for visitors traveling alone. But common-sense precautions do apply: stay clear of drugs; don't leave personal items unattended on the beach or in a golf cart; and lock your hotel room when you leave. Dehydration is one of the biggest safety concerns, so drink plenty of bottled water and order beverages without ice unless you're at a restaurant that uses purified water. Be careful when driving along the narrow roads, especially since many have gravel surfaces and potholes.

Sights

To get your bearings, picture the island as a long fish: the head is the southeastern tip, the tail is the northwest prong. Eight kilometers (5 miles) long and 1 km (½ mile) wide, Isla Mujeres is easy to explore in a single day. If you take your time, however, you'll discover that the island is not a destination to be rushed. Mopeds and golf carts are the most popular modes of transportation on Isla's virtually car-free dirt roads. If you're staying at one of the remote hotels on the southern tip, a taxi will take you from one end of the island to the other for MX$140, or roughly MX$240 per hour.

If you're interested in taking a DIY driving tour of Isla Mujeres, start by looping the island's perimeter, stopping midway at the southernmost tip. Here you can walk down to the rocky shores where waves crash at your feet. The views from Punta Sur are magnificent, and the temple of Goddess Ixchel is worth a visit. Head back north and explore colorful neighborhoods on the outskirts of town, with a stop at the excellent Mango Cafe for lunch. If you prefer the beach, relax at peaceful Playa Lancheros on the island's west side and see the area's dolphins, turtles, or nurse sharks before enjoying a traditional Mayan lunch at Playa Tiburón. Finish your tour with a sunset cocktail at Playa Norte before going downtown for dinner and live music.

Visitor Information

CONTACTS Tourist Office. ⊠ *Av. Rueda Medina 130, Isla Mujeres* ☎ *998/877–0307* ⊕ *www.islamujeres.gob.mx.*

Greater Isla Mujeres

◉ Sights

Garrafón Natural Reef Park
REEF | FAMILY | Despite the widely publicized "Garrafón Reef Restoration Program," much of the coral at this national marine park is dead—the result of hurricanes, boat anchors, and too many careless tourists. There are still colorful fish, but many of them will come near only if bribed with food. Although there's not much for snorkelers anymore, the park—part nature, part amusement—does have kayaks, restaurants, ziplines, bathrooms, and a gift shop. Be prepared to spend over USD$60 for the basic package called Royal Garrafón, which includes snorkeling gear, breakfast, lunch, kayaks, transportation from Cancún, a bike tour, and an open bar. Another option is Dolphin Encounter (USD$116), which lets you use the park amenities and swim with dolphins. The Beach Club Garrafón de Castilla next door is a much cheaper alternative; the snorkeling is at least equal to that available in the park, and

a day pass is just MX$50. You can take a taxi from town. El Garrafón National Park is home to the Santuario Maya a la Diosa Ixchel, the sad vestiges of a Mayan temple once dedicated to a goddess Ixchel. This southern point is where the sun first rises in Mexico, meaning that thousands of travelers make a pilgrimage to the temple on New Year's to see the country awaken. A lovely walkway around the area remains, but the natural arch beneath the ruin has been blasted open and repaired with concrete badly disguised as rocks. The views are spectacular, though: you can look to the open ocean, where waves crash against dramatic cliffs on one side and the Bahía de Mujeres (Bay of Women) on the other. On the way to the temple there's a cutesy Caribbean-style shopping center selling overpriced jewelry and souvenirs, as well as a park with brightly painted abstract sculptures. The ruins (open daily 9–5) are near the old lighthouse, where the road turns northeast into the Corredor Panorámico. It costs MX$60 to visit just the ruins and sculpture park, but this is included with admission to El Garrafón. ⊠ *Punta Sur, southeast of Playa Lancheros, Carretera El Garrafón, Km 6, Sm 9, Mza 41, Lote 12, Isla Mujeres* ☎ *01800/727–5391 toll-free in Mexico, 866/393–5158 in the U.S.* ⊕ *www.garrafon.com* ⊠ *USD$62* ⊗ *Closed Mon.*

★ **Isla Mujeres Underwater Museum**

OTHER MUSEUM | Combining art and nature, sculptor Jason de Caires Taylor has created "underwater museums" off the shores of Punta Cancún, Punta Nizuc, and Manchones Reef near Isla Mujeres. Locally known as MUSA (Museo Subacuático de Arte), his main work features more than 480 lifelike statues that serve as artificial reefs to attract marine life. Within the 12 galleries is "The Silent Evolution," a 120-ton work of more than 400 individual statues, as well as "Anthropocene" a full-scale VW Beetle made from 8 tons of pH-neutral concrete. The displays have conveniently been placed in shallow

Detour: Off the Path 👁

When exploring the southeastern tip of Isla Mujeres, be sure to visit the unique shell-shape house located on Corredor Panorámico. Owned by artist Octavio Ocampo, it resembles an enormous conch shell both inside and out.

4

Isla Mujeres GREATER ISLA MUJERES

areas for viewing by divers, snorkelers, and glass-bottom boats. The unusual artificial habitat also helps restore the natural reefs that have suffered damage over the years. Most local dive shops can organize excursions to the site starting at $47 USD. ⊠ *Punta Cancún, Punta Nizuc, and Manchones Reef in Isla Mujeres, Isla Mujeres* ☎ *998/810–4508* ⊕ *musamexico.org* ⊠ *From $47 USD.*

Laguna Makax

BODY OF WATER | Pirates are said to have anchored their ships in this lagoon while waiting to ambush hapless vessels crossing the Spanish Main. Today it houses a local marina and provides a safe harbor for boats during hurricane season. ⊠ *Carretera Al Garrafon Mz 121 Lote 5, Isla Mujeres* ✛ *About 2½ km (1½ mile) south of town* ☎ *998/888–0973* ⊕ *marinamakaxcancun.com.*

Museum Capitán Dulché

HISTORY MUSEUM | The island's only museum gives a glimpse into the life of famed ocean explorers Ramón Bravo, Jacques Cousteau, and Captain Ernesto Dulché Escalante, who founded the 5th Naval Region of Isla Mujeres. A collection of photographs, model ships, anchors, buoys, lanterns, and other maritime tools also showcases Isla's seafaring history. The museum is part of a beach club, so you can reminisce about the past before enjoying the present with a cold beer under the shade of a palapa. ⊠ *Carretera*

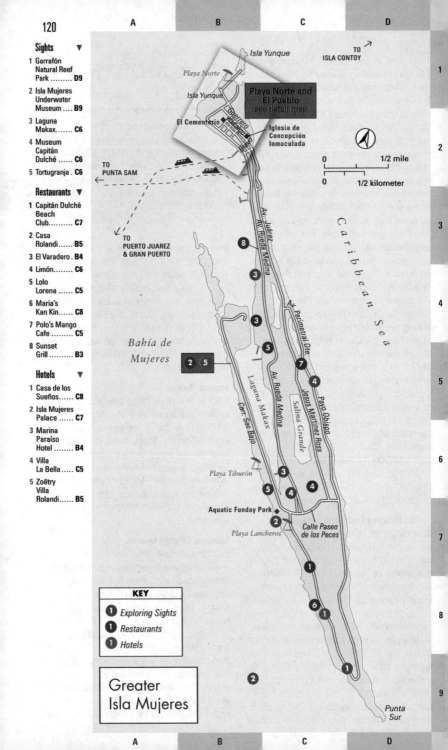

120

Greater Isla Mujeres

Who Was Ixchel?

Ixchel (ee-*shell*) is a principal figure in the pantheon of Mayan gods. Sometimes called the "Rainbow Goddess" or the "Red Goddess," she is the patroness of childbirth, fertility, and healing, and is said to control the tides and all water on Earth. Originally married to the Earth god Voltan, Ixchel fell in love with the moon god Itzamna, considered the founder of the Maya because he taught them how to read, write, and grow corn. When Ixchel became his consort, she gave birth to four powerful sons known as the Bacabs, who continue to hold up the sky in each of the four directions.

Often portrayed as a wise crone, Ixchel can be seen wearing a skirt decorated with crossbones and a crown of serpents while carrying a jug of water. The crossbones are a symbol of her role as the giver of new life and keeper of dead souls. The serpents represent her wisdom and power to rejuvenate, and the water jug alludes to her dual role as both a benign and destructive deity. Although she gives mankind the continual gift of water—the most essential element of life—according to Mayan myth Ixchel also sent floods to cleanse the Earth of wicked people who had stopped thanking the gods. She is said to give special protection to those making the sacred pilgrimage to her sites on Cozumel and Isla Mujeres.

Garrafón, Km 4.5, Isla Mujeres ☎ *998/139–5504* ⊕ *capitandulche.com* 🖃 *USD$5.*

Tortugranja (*Turtle Farm*)
WILDLIFE REFUGE | FAMILY | This scientific station, run by the Mexican government in partnership with private funding, works to conserve the endangered sea turtle. You can see rescued hatchlings in three large pools or watch larger turtles in sea pens. There's also a small section with seahorses, crabs, and other marine life. May through October, you can join the staff in collecting and hatching eggs; in the fall you can help release baby turtles. 🖃 *Carretera Garrafón Km 4 Calle Sac Bajo, Isla Mujeres* ☎ *998/888–0705* ⊕ *facebook.com/Tortugranja.mx* 🖃 *MX$30.*

 Beaches

Playa Lancheros (*Boatman's Beach*)
BEACH | FAMILY | On the western side of the island, this stretch between Laguna Makax and Garrafón Natural Reef Park is a popular spot with an open-air restaurant where locals gather to eat freshly grilled *tikin xic* (whole fish marinated with *adobo de achiote* and sour oranges, then wrapped in a banana leaf and cooked over an open flame). Playa Lancheros has grittier sand than Playa Norte but more palm trees. Calm water makes it good for children, but keep them close to shore as the bottom drops off steeply. Souvenir stands here are fairly low-key, and most bars and restaurants will give you access to their beach facilities provided you order a drink. The closest hotel is Isla Mujeres Palace, an all-inclusive resort open to hotel guests only. There's a small pen with tame *tiburones gatos* (nurse sharks). You can swim with them or just get your picture taken for a MX$20 tip. **Amenities:** food and drink; showers; toilets; water sports; parking (free). **Best for:** snorkeling; swimming; sunset. 🖃 *Carretera El Garrafón, Km 4.6, near Hacienda Mundaca, Isla Mujeres.*

Playa Tiburón (*Shark Beach*)
BEACH | FAMILY | Like Playa Lancheros, this beach on the west side of the island faces Bahía de Mujeres, so the water is exceptionally calm. Once a respite from the crowds, it has become more developed, with a large restaurant (through which you actually enter the beach) that serves burgers, hot dogs, and fish. There are several souvenir stands selling handmade seashell jewelry. On certain days you can find women who will braid your hair or give you a henna tattoo. Many people visit to swim or take photos with tame nurse sharks (MX$50), but the tiny pen entrapping the large creatures is rather sad. Although there are public restrooms, you have to pay for toilet paper. **Amenities:** food and drink; toilets; water sports; parking (free). **Best for:** snorkeling; sunset; swimming. ✉ *Carretera Sac Bajo, Isla Mujeres.*

Safety First

Unlike Cancún and Cozumel, Isla Mujeres does not use the colored safety flag system, and there are no lifeguards to keep watch over swimmers. Therefore, it's best to venture out near familiar beaches like Playa Norte, Playa Lancheros, and Playa Tiburón only on calm days when winds are light. Be wary of strong currents and riptides, especially on the east and west sides of the island. If you plan to spend a day at the beach, bring fresh drinking water and use sunscreen or wear protective clothing to avoid overexposure.

🍴 Restaurants

Capitán Dulché Beach Club
$$$ | INTERNATIONAL | Come for the art and stay for the drinks at this beach club and museum combo. The sister property of the only museum in Isla Mujeres (which holds the same name), this trendy beach club draws visitors who come all the way from Cancún via catamaran to enjoy the peaceful beach, large swimming pool, and Yucatán and international cuisine including seafood, pizza, and cocktails. **Known for:** tikin xic fish; great beach; swimming pool. [$] *Average main: MP 300* ✉ *Carr. Garrafón Km. 4,5, El Pueblo* ☎ *998/139–5504* 🌐 *capitandulche.com.*

Casa Rolandi
$$$$ | ITALIAN | This quietly sophisticated hotel restaurant has an open-air dining room connected to a deck overlooking the water. A northern Italian menu includes wonderful carpaccio *di tonno alla Giorgio* (thin slices of tuna with extra-virgin olive oil and lime juice), along with excellent pastas. **Known for:** spectacular views; fine dining; seafood risotto. [$] *Average main: MP370* ✉ *Zoëtry Villa Rolandi, Fracc. Laguna Mar, Sm 7, Mza 75, Lotes 15 and 16,* ☎ *998/999–2000, 888/496–3879* 🌐 *rolandirestaurant.com* ☞ *Reservations required.*

El Varadero
$$ | CUBAN | Located off the beaten path in a weathered, palapa-topped fisherman's cottage, this local favorite is the perfect place for delicious, reasonably priced seafood. It's known for fresh mojitos, but the family-style plates of grilled or fried fish are an even bigger draw. **Known for:** early dinners; lobster; Cuban specialties. [$] *Average main: MP195* ✉ *Calle de Septiembre Lt. 14, Isla Mujeres* ☎ *998/877–1600* 🕓 *Closed Mon.*

Limón
$$$ | MEXICAN | Inspired by "mom's recipes," chef Sergio makes freshness a top priority—nothing here is ever frozen. The Mexican-fusion menu features dishes like slightly sweet hibiscus-filled tacos and impressive zucchini towers with grilled panela cheese, and shrimp with a four-chile sauce. **Known for:** pineapple flambé; grilled fish and steaks; Mayan fusion. [$] *Average main: MP320* ✉ *Colonia*

Isla's History

The name Isla Mujeres means "Island of Women," although no one knows who dubbed it that. Many believe it was the ancient Maya, who were said to use the island as a religious center for worshipping Ixchel (the "Rainbow Goddess"), the tide-controlling Mayan patroness of fertility, childbirth, and healing. Another popular legend has it that the Spanish conquistador Hernández de Córdoba named the island when he landed here in 1517 and found hundreds of female-shape clay idols dedicated to Ixchel and her daughters. Still others say the name dates from the 1600s, when visiting pirates left women on Isla before sailing out to pillage merchant ships. (Reputedly both Henry Morgan and Jean Lafitte buried treasure here, although no one has ever found any pirate's gold.) Pick the story you like best.

Settlement began in earnest in the mid-19th century. Refugees from the Caste War of the Yucatán fled to the island and built its first official village of Dolores. By 1858, Fermín Mundaca de Marechaja, a slave trader turned pirate, began building an estate that took up 40% of the island. By the end of the century the population had risen to 650, and residents began to establish trade with the mainland, mostly by supplying fish to the owners of chicle and coconut plantations on the coast. In 1949, the Mexican navy built a base on Isla's northwestern coast. Around this time the island also caught the eye of some wealthy Mexican sportsmen, who began using it as a vacation spot.

Tourism flourished on Isla during the latter half of the 20th century, partly due to the island's most famous resident, Ramón Bravo (1927–98). A diver, cinematographer, ecologist, and colleague of Jacques Cousteau, Bravo was the first underwater photographer to explore the area. He contributed to the discovery of the now-famous Cave of the Sleeping Sharks and produced dozens of underwater documentaries for American, European, and Mexican television. Bravo's efforts to maintain the ecology on Isla have helped keep development here to a minimum. Even today, Bravo remains an iconic figure to many *isleños* (ees- *lay*-nyos); his statue can be found where Avenida Rueda Medina becomes the Carretera El Garrafón, and there's a museum named after him on nearby Isla Contoy.

la Gloria, Calle Lizeta 159, near Super Express, Isla Mujeres ☎ 998/130–1924 💳 No credit cards ⏲ Closed Sun. No lunch.

★ Lolo Lorena

$$$$ | MEDITERRANEAN | Join the dinner party at Lolo's, where the multicourse, prix-fixe menu varies each night, but might include lobster carpaccio or gnocchi with truffle sauce, served in an outdoor courtyard. A few catches: you bring your own wine—there's no corking fee; dining is at communal tables; you must make reservations. **Known for:** Lolo, a local celebrity; unique dining experience; strict reservation policy. [$] *Average main: MP700 ✉ Av. Rueda Medina, Isla Mujeres ☎ 998/704–4392 🌐 facebook.com/lololorena ⏲ Closed June–Aug. No lunch.*

Maria's Kan Kin

$$$ | SEAFOOD | The difference between a memorable evening here and an unforgettable one is reserving a table for two

Playa Norte is a superb beach for strolling in the sun.

at the water's edge—otherwise, you'll be sitting beneath a palapa roof overlooking an infinity pool and the crystal bay, which is, of course, a spectacular runner-up. The minimal menu presents the best local seafood in dishes like red snapper with herb sauce; shrimp skewers with lime; and grouper with tomatoes, olives, and basil. **Known for:** unbelievable setting; caramel lava cake; grilled lobster. $ *Average main: MP290* ✉ *Carretera El Garrafón, Km 4.5, Isla Mujeres* ☎ *998/877–0733* ⊕ *www.mariaskankin.com.*

★ Polo's Mango Cafe

$ | **ECLECTIC** | **FAMILY** | Warm and inviting with wooden tables and colorful chalkboards announcing the day's *agua frescas*, this 10-table hot spot is a must if you're looking for an unbeatable breakfast or lunch. Standouts are traditional chiles rellenos, fish tacos, and delicious French toast. **Known for:** vegan menu; massive portions; Mexican-inspired classics. $ *Average main: MP140* ✉ *Payo Obispo, Lot 1, No 725, Isla Mujeres*

☎ *998/274–0118* ⊕ *facebook.com/mango-cafeisla* ⊗ *No dinner.*

Sunset Grill

$$$ | **SEAFOOD** | With an enormous menu to appease every appetite, this elegant palapa restaurant is the perfect place to savor the sunset. The wide range of dinner dishes includes grilled tuna, coconut shrimp, paella, and grouper in a creamy dill-and-wine sauce; homemade coconut pie provides a sweet finish. **Known for:** fresh seafood; oceanfront dining; romantic ambience. $ *Average main: MP260* ✉ *SM 002 Mz 88 Lote 9, Av. Rueda Medina, Isla Mujeres* ☎ *998/865–4148* ⊕ *www.sunsetgrill.com.mx.*

🛏 Hotels

★ Casa de los Sueños

$$$ | **HOTEL** | Walking into the open-air sunken lobby of this gorgeous hotel feels like walking into a friend's fabulous vacation hacienda; it's colorful and cozy, yet modern and chic. **Pros:** three swimming pools; exceptional breakfast served until

noon; intimate atmosphere. **Cons:** no beach; far from town; not child-friendly. **$** *Rooms from: $140* ✉ *Fracc. Turquesa, Lote 9 A and B, Isla Mujeres* ☎ *998/877–0708* ⊕ *www.hotelcasasuenos.com* ⇨ *12 rooms* ⦿ *Free Breakfast.*

Isla Mujeres Palace

$$$$ | RESORT | Fine all-inclusive dining, a blissful beach, and pool, plus an on-site spa and dive center make Palace's island outpost a tempting vacation choice. **Pros:** comfortable rooms; great service; large pool. **Cons:** restrictions apply for boat transfers; no children under 18; far from downtown. **$** *Rooms from: $430* ✉ *Carretera Garrafón, Km 4.5, Sm 7, Mza 63, Isla Mujeres* ☎ *998/999–2020, 800/986–5632 in the U.S. and Canada* ⊕ *islamujeres.palaceresorts.com* ⇨ *62 rooms* ⦿ *All-Inclusive.*

Marina Paraíso Hotel

$$ | HOTEL | Far enough away to feel secluded but within walking distance of El Pueblo, this hotel—made up of white two-story buildings—has a private marina, an infinity pool, and a well-regarded restaurant (Barlito). **Pros:** excellent restaurant; accommodating staff; caters to divers. **Cons:** lower rates require three-night minimum stay; Wi-Fi in common areas only; not all rooms have ocean views. **$** *Rooms from: $150* ✉ *Av. Rueda Medina, Prol. Aeropuerto 491, Isla Mujeres* ☎ *998/877–0252* ⊕ *facebook.com/MarinaParaisoHotelIslaMujeres* ⇨ *20 rooms* ⦿ *No Meals.*

Villa La Bella

$$ | B&B/INN | This romantic, laid-back B&B on the east coast has fantastic sea views and funky designs—bungalow rooms are equipped with king-size beds, conch showerheads, and bamboo faucets; rooms with palapa roofs have beds swinging from ropes, and the grounds feature remarkable stonework. **Pros:** relaxing atmosphere; tasty breakfasts; welcoming owners. **Cons:** no in-house restaurant; kids under 18 not allowed; taxi ride from downtown. **$** *Rooms from:* *$220* ✉ *Carretera Perimetral al Garrafón SM 4, MZ 91, Isla Mujeres* ☎ *998/888–0342* ⊕ *www.villalabella.com* ⇨ *6 rooms* ⦿ *Free Breakfast.*

Zoëtry Villa Rolandi

$$$$ | HOTEL | The luxury starts with a private yacht that delivers you to this all-inclusive hotel from Cancún's Embarcadero Marina, and it continues throughout your stay. **Pros:** luxurious amenities; great views; attentive staff. **Cons:** must drive to main town; expensive; children under 13 not allowed. **$** *Rooms from: $500* ✉ *Fracc. Laguna Mar, Sm 7, Mza 75, Lotes 15 and 16, Isla Mujeres* ☎ *998/999–2000, 888/496–3879 in the U.S. and Canada* ⊕ *www.zoetryresorts.com/mujeres* ⇨ *35 suites* ⦿ *All-Inclusive.*

Playa Norte

⦿ Sights

El Cementerio

CEMETERY | Isla's cemetery is on Avenida López Mateos, the road that runs parallel to Playa Norte. Many of the century-old gravestones are covered with carved angels and flowers, with the most elaborate and beautiful marking the graves of children. Hidden among them is the tomb of the notorious Fermín Mundaca de Marechaja, a 19th-century slave trader—often billed more glamorously as a pirate—who carved his own skull-and-crossbones gravestone with the ominous epitaph: "As you are, I once was; as I am, so shall you be." Ironically, his remains actually lie in Mérida, where he died. The monument is tough to find, so ask a local to point out the marker. ✉ *Av. López Mateos, Supmza.001, Isla Mujeres* ☎ *998/877–0082* ⊕ *islamujeres.gob.mx* ⦿ *Free.*

El Malecón

PROMENADE | FAMILY | To enjoy the drama of Isla's western shore while soaking up some rays, stroll along this 1½-km-long

Isla's Salt Mines [👁]

The ancient salt mines in Isla's interior were worked during the postclassic period of Mayan history (roughly AD 1000–1500). Salt was an important commodity for the Maya, who used it not only for preserving and flavoring food but also for making armor. Since the Maya had no metal, they soaked cotton cloth in salt until it formed a hard coating.

There's little to see today: simply two shallow marshes called Salina Chica (Small Salt Mine) and Salina Grande (Big Salt Mine) with murky water and quite a few mosquitoes at dusk. But since both of the island's main roads (Avenida Rueda Medina and the Corredor Panorámico) pass by them, you can have a look on your way to other parts of Isla.

(1-mile-long) boardwalk. It runs from the Ultramar pier to Playa Norte and has several benches and lookout points. Check out El Monumento dal Marlin Azul y la Barracuda (Blue Marlin and Barracuda Monument) along the way. ✉ *Isla Mujeres* 🎫 *Free.*

⛱ Beaches

★ Playa Norte (*North Beach*)
BEACH | FAMILY | North Beach is easy to find: simply head north on any of the north–south streets in town until you hit it. The turquoise sea is as calm as a lake here, though developers have built along most of the coast. The small cove between Mia Reef Resort and the Caribbean is the nicest section. Relatively shallow, the water flows directly from the open sea, so it's clean and good for snorkeling; tour guides often lure the fish with food. A food or drink purchase from Cafe del Mar gives you access to beach beds and changing facilities at Privilege Aluxes Resort. Alternately, you can enjoy a libation at one of the palapa bars where wooden swings take the place of bar stools; Buho's is especially popular, as MX$90 lounge chairs and MX$200 beach beds come with a free drink ticket. At Sunset Grill, lounge chairs, umbrellas, towels, toilets, and showers are included when you spend MX$300 on food or drink. **Amenities:** food and drink; showers; toilets; parking. **Best for:** snorkeling; sunset; walking; swimming. ✉ *Calle Zazil-Há, along the northern end of the island, just before Mia Reef Resort, Isla Mujeres* 🎫 *Free.*

🛏 Hotels

Ixchel Beach Hotel
$$ | HOTEL | With a location—on a beach with clear, calm water—that can't be beat, this property consists of two condo-style buildings that face one another: the slightly newer, five-story East Wing has 48 units; the six-story West Wing has 69 units. **Pros:** reasonable rates; on-site restaurant; beachfront. **Cons:** small pool; no meals; some rooms are very humid. [$] *Rooms from: $227* ✉ *Playa Norte, Calle Guerrero, Sm 1, Isla Mujeres* ☎ *998/999–2010, 800/638–5061 in the U.S. and Canada* 🌐 *www.ixchelbeachhotel.com* 🛏 *117 rooms* 🍴 *No Meals.*

El Pueblo

👁 Sights

Aquatic Funday Park
WATER PARK | FAMILY | As its name suggests, this water park is the way to spend a fun day by the beach. Play beach volleyball, ride a bike through the quaint streets of Isla, explore the calm waters

of the Caribbean in a kayak, or let the adrenaline pump through your veins as you slide down one of four slides that end directly in the sea. All the while, you can enjoy a good buffet and an even better open bar. The place is in constant renovation, so note that while some areas are top-notch, others are in need of a face-lift. ✉ *Carr. Longitudinal Km 4 Lote 8-A, Sac Bajo, El Pueblo* ☎ *998/123–7310* 🌐 *aquaticfundaypark.com* 🎟 *From USD$25.*

Iglesia de Concepción Inmaculada (*Church of the Immaculate Conception*)
CHURCH | In 1890 local fishermen landed at a deserted colonial settlement known as Ecab, where they found three identical statues of the Virgin Mary, each carved from wood with porcelain face and hands. No one knows where the statues came from, but it's widely believed they were gifts from the Spanish during a visit in 1770. One statue went to the city of Izamal in the Yucatán, and another was sent to Kantunikin in Quintana Roo. The third remained on the island. It was housed in a small wooden chapel while this church was being built; legend has it that the chapel burst into flames when the statue was removed. Some islanders still believe the statue walks on the water around the island from dusk until dawn, looking for her sisters. You can pay your respects daily 10–11:30 am and 7–9 pm, or attend mass, mostly in Spanish, with a few services in English throughout the week. ✉ *Avs. Morelos and Bravo, Isla Mujeres* 🎟 *Free.*

🍴 Restaurants

Amigos
$$ | ECLECTIC | This easy-to-miss eatery offers a little bit of everything from fish and meat to pastas and vegetarian dishes, but it's best known for its superb pizza. Breakfasts, featuring delicious omelets and strong coffee, are also served. **Known for:** big portions; street-side dining; local vibe. [$] *Average main: MP155* ✉ *Av. Hidalgo 19, between Avs. Matamoros and Abasolo, Isla Mujeres* ☎ *998/877–0624* 🌐 *facebook.com/Restaurantbaramigos.*

Angelo
$$$ | ITALIAN | FAMILY | Named for its Italian chef Angelo Sanna, this charming bistro on Hidalgo's busy main strip is done up with soft lighting and a wood-fired oven. Come for the pizza; they have a thin crispy crust and are quite delicious. **Known for:** late-night pizza; friendly atmosphere; Italian classics. [$] *Average main: MP300* ✉ *Av. Hidalgo 14, Isla Mujeres* ☎ *998/877–1273* 🕒 *Closed Sept. No lunch.*

Café Cito
$ | CAFÉ | Cheery, seashell-decorated Cito was one of Isla's first cafés, and it's still among the best breakfast spots on the island. The menu includes pancakes, waffles, fruit-filled crepes, and egg dishes, as well as great cappuccino and espresso. **Known for:** homemade coffee; Mexican breakfasts; fresh-squeezed orange juice. [$] *Average main: MP90* ✉ *Avs. Juárez and Matamoros, Isla Mujeres* ☎ *998/877–1470* 🕒 *No dinner.*

Café Mogagua
$$$ | ECLECTIC | FAMILY | Whether you come for breakfast or lunch, you'll enjoy the relaxed vibe at this open-air café. Its menu ranges from Mexican classics like chilaquiles and *huevos divorciados* (eggs with chile sauce), to pizza, grilled meats, and fish later in the day. **Known for:** delicious chilaquiles; friendly service; organic coffee. [$] *Average main: MP250* ✉ *Av. Juárez at Madero, El Pueblo* ☎ *998/877–0127* 🌐 *www.facebook.com/cafe.mogagua.*

Chaya & Cacao
$$ | MEXICAN FUSION | This farm-to-table, gluten-free, and vegan- and kosher-friendly restaurant is a hidden gem in the heart of Isla Mujeres. Owner and Chef Lori Dumm offers a dynamic menu featuring ingredients that are always fresh,

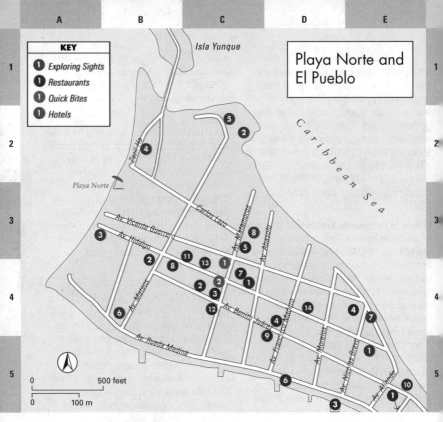

Playa Norte and El Pueblo

organic, and ethically sourced from the local community. **Known for:** smoothies; organic food; local fermented kombucha. [$] *Average main: MP 200* ✉ *Matamoros s/n Supmza.001, Matamoros s/n Supmza.001, Downtown* ☎ *998/164–4977* 🌐 *facebook.com/chayaandcacao* 💳 *No credit cards* ⏲ *Closed Sun.*

Cocktelería Picus

$$ | **SEAFOOD** | Kick off your shoes and settle back with a beer at this charming beachside restaurant near the ferry docks, where you can watch the fishing boats come and go while you wait for some of the island's freshest seafood. The grilled fish and lobster with garlic butter are both excellent, as are the shrimp fajitas—but the real showstopper is the ceviche, which might include conch, shrimp, abalone, fish, or octopus. **Known for:** waterfront location; Yucatecan pescado tikin-xic; ceviche. [$] *Average main: MP195* ✉ *Av. Rueda Medina, 1 block northwest of ferry docks, Isla Mujeres* ☎ *998/120–6258* ⏲ *No dinner.*

El Patio

$$$ | **ECLECTIC** | This low-key establishment is a peaceful oasis in the heart of El Pueblo, with chit palms and ocean grape trees decorating the open-air restaurant, each branch wrapped in fairy lights and adorned with seashell lanterns. House specialties like chicken mole and grilled octopus are served with a choice of two side dishes. Head to the rooftop lounge for live music and frozen mojitos. **Known for:** frozen mojitos; live music; happy hour. [$] *Average main: MP300* ✉ *Av. Hidalgo 17, El Pueblo* ☎ *207/514–3385* 🌐 *facebook.com/ElPatioIslaMujeres.*

Fredy's Restaurant & Bar

$$ | **MEXICAN** | This family-run restaurant specializes in simple fish, seafood, and Mexican dishes like fajitas and oven-baked shrimp. There isn't much here in the way of decor, but the staff is friendly, the food is fresh, the beer is cold, and the value is good. **Known for:** seafood dishes; local vibe; famous margaritas. [$] *Average main: MP275* ✉ *Av. Hidalgo 13, between Avs. Matamoros and López Mateo, Isla Mujeres* ☎ *998/877–1339* 🌐 *facebook.com/restaurantfredys* ⏲ *Closed Tues. May–Oct. No lunch.*

Javi's Cantina

$$$ | **AMERICAN** | There's nothing fancy about one of Isla's most popular restaurants—think plastic tables and chairs with bright tablecloths and furnishings—but Javi's captures that island informality perfectly. Seafood is the specialty here, with cilantro-chile-lime shrimp, grilled octopus, or Alfredo lobster as the dishes you don't want to miss. **Known for:** outstanding seafood; live music; courtyard dining. [$] *Average main: MP340* ✉ *Av. Juárez, between Av. Madero and C. Abasolo, El Pueblo* ☎ *998/274–4097* 🌐 *www.javiscantina.com* ⏲ *Closed Wed. No lunch.*

La Lomita

$$ | **MEXICAN** | This hole-in-the-wall, with its red plastic tables and chairs, is a perennial local favorite. Expect enormous portions of the beloved *sopa de frijoles* (black bean soup made with onions, tomatoes, lime, and fresh cheese) and chile relleno: stuffed chiles lightly battered, fried, and served with a side of pickled cabbage and rice. **Known for:** no-frills setting; best chicken mole on the island; seafood dishes. [$] *Average main: MP120* ✉ *Av. Juárez Sur 25-B, at Av. Allende, El Pueblo* ☎ *998/939–2331* 🌐 *facebook.com/RestaurantLaLomita* ⏲ *Closed Sun.*

Lola Valentina

$$$ | **CARIBBEAN** | Chef Lori Dumm provides a unique take on Caribbean-fusion cuisine here, creating all of her own recipes and making every menu item from scratch. Starters like blue corn empanadas served with tamarind dipping sauce make way for shrimp-stuffed red snapper topped with creamy poblano peppers, or chicken kabobs bathed in a peanut-coconut sauce. **Known for:** Cuban salsa; passion fruit salmon; decadent breakfasts.

$ Average main: MP280 ⊠ North Av. Hidalgo 27, Isla Mujeres ☎ 998/129–7544 ⊕ facebook.com/lolavalentinaislamujeres ▭ No credit cards.

★ Olivia

$$$ | MEDITERRANEAN | The delightful dishes at this Mediterranean restaurant are combinations of Moroccan, Greek, and Turkish flavors based on owners Lior and Yaron Zelzer's family recipes. Start with the Greek or Moroccan tapas and move onto house favorites like the shawarma pita wrap filled with grilled chicken, hummus, tahini, and fried eggplant, or the *mafrum*, a blend of potatoes stuffed with ground beef in a Moroccan red sauce. **Known for:** romantic setting; cherry ice cream; homemade pastries. $ Average main: MP240 ⊠ Matamoros 11, between Avs. Juárez and Rueda Medina, El Pueblo ☎ 998/877–1765 ⊕ www.olivia-isla-mujeres.com ▭ No credit cards ⊘ Closed Sun. No lunch.

Qubano

$$ | CUBAN | This delightful restaurant has a good reputation for delicious Cuban food. The grilled *tostones* sandwiches, which use fried plantains instead of bread, are topped with a finger-licking onion-and-orange sauce. **Known for:** vegetarian options; Cuban food; amazing mojitos. $ Average main: MP150 ⊠ Av. Hidalgo, across from Angelo, Isla Mujeres ☎ 998/214–2118 ⊕ facebook. com/qubanorestaurant ⊘ Closed Sun.

Sardinian Smile

$$$ | ITALIAN | FAMILY | Despite the cheesy name, this cozy spot on busy Avenida Hidalgo is the island's most authentic Italian restaurant, serving handmade pastas like fettuccine with clams or lobster ravioli to happy crowds. Pesto linguine, misto del mar, and rich tiramisu dusted with cocoa powder make it hard to forget that you're not in Italy. **Known for:** Italian wine list; authentic handmade pasta; Sardinian-style seafood. $ Average main: MP250 ⊠ Av. Hidalgo 103, near the zócalo, El Pueblo ☎ 998/163–6850

⊕ facebook.com/sardiniansmilepage ⊘ Closed Mon.

☕ Coffee and Quick Bites

Aluxes Bar, Grill & Coffee Shop

$$ | CAFÉ | With its long hours, this spot is equally good for a midday cappuccino, afternoon tea, or nighttime cocktail. It also has terrific smoothies and bakery items (the New York–style cheesecake and triple-fudge brownies are especially decadent). **Known for:** sports events on TV; Caribbean cuisine; daily specials. $ Average main: MP250 ⊠ Av. Matamoros 316, between Avs. Hidalgo and Guerrero, Isla Mujeres ☎ 998/218–5843 ⊕ facebook.com/ivanaluxes ⊘ Closed Tues.

Gelateria Montebianco

$ | ITALIAN | FAMILY | Run by an Italian couple who have lived on the island since 2005, Gelateria Montebianco serves a wide variety of gelatos, as well as tasty desserts like tiramisu. It's the place to take a break and enjoy what many consider the best ice cream on the island. **Known for:** zuppa inglese; variety of gelatos; tiramisu. $ Average main: MP100 ⊠ Av. Matamoros 316, Isla Mujeres ☎ 998/149–3109.

🛏 Hotels

★ Casa El Pío

$ | HOTEL | Off the town square, this boutique hotel is bursting with character, charm, and creativity, ideally suited for independent travelers who don't need 24-hour service, but appreciate value, comfort, and modern design. **Pros:** excellent rates; spotless property; unlimited fresh drinking water. **Cons:** reception closes at 1 pm; adults only; no meals. $ Rooms from: $95 ⊠ Av. Hidalgo 3, between Bravo and Allende, ☎ 998/152–8669 ⊕ www.casaelpio.com ⇗ 5 rooms ⦿ No Meals.

In Search of the Dead

El Día de los Muertos (the Day of the Dead) is often described as a Mexican version of Halloween, but it's much more than that. The festival, which runs from October 31 to November 2, is a hybrid of pre-Hispanic and Christian beliefs that honors the cyclical nature of life and death. Local celebrations are as varied as they are dynamic, often laced with warm tributes and dark humor.

To honor departed loved ones at this time of year, families and friends create *ofrendas*, altars adorned with photos, flowers, candles, liquor, and other items whose colors, smells, and potent nostalgia are meant to lure spirits back for a family reunion. The favorite foods of the deceased are prepared with extra spice so that the souls can absorb the essence of the offerings. Although the ofrendas and the colorful *calaveritas* (sugar skulls and skeletons) are common everywhere, the holiday is observed in so many ways that a definition of it depends entirely on what part of Mexico you visit. In the Yucatán Peninsula, the cultural center of Mérida is where most people gather to honor the dead.

On Isla Mujeres, reverence is paid at the historic cemetery, where locals like Marta rest on a fanciful tomb in the late-afternoon sun. "She is my sister," Marta says, motioning toward the teal-and-blue tomb. "I painted this today." Instead of mourning, she's smiling, happy to be spending the day with her sibling.

Nearby, Juan puts the final touches—vases made from shells he's collected—on his father's colorful tomb. A glass box holds a red candle and a statue of the Virgin Mary, her outstretched arms pressing against the glass as if trying to escape the flame. "This is all for him," Juan says, motioning to his masterpiece, "because he is a good man."

Hotel Secreto

$$$ | **HOTEL** | Intimate and contemporary, Hotel Secreto is one of Isla's few luxury boutique hotels. **Pros:** great fitness center; private and secure; pool overlooks ocean. **Cons:** property could use renovation; rocky beach; no elevator or restaurant. [$] *Rooms from: $200* ✉ *Half Moon Beach, Sección Rocas, Lote 11, Isla Mujeres* ☎ *998/877–1039* 🌐 *www.hotelsecreto.com* 🛏 *12 rooms* 🍴 *Free Breakfast.*

Na Balam

$$ | **HOTEL** | Elegant without being pretentious, this tranquil hotel is a true sanctuary with sandy pathways winding through a jungle setting that spills onto the beach. **Pros:** 24-hour security; beautiful beach; good restaurant. **Cons:** not all rooms are on the beach; Wi-Fi in common areas only; lots of mosquitoes. [$] *Rooms from: $150* ✉ *Calle Zazil-Ha 118, Isla Mujeres* ☎ *998/881–4770, 866/719–2138 in the U.S. and Canada* 🌐 *www.nabalam.com* 🛏 *35 rooms* 🍴 *Free Breakfast.*

Playa la Media Luna Hotel

$$ | **HOTEL** | This breezy palapa-roofed hotel on Half Moon Beach has rooms decorated in bright Mexican colors, with hammocks, king-size beds, and balconies or terraces overlooking the pool and ocean beyond. **Pros:** some deluxe rooms have Jacuzzis; balconies with hammocks; nearby beach is calm and shallow. **Cons:** no elevator; a few rooms could stand renovating; pool bar seldom open. [$] *Rooms from: $125* ✉ *Half Moon Beach,*

Sección Rocas, Lote 9/10, Isla Mujeres ☎ *998/877–0759* 🌐 *www.playamedialuna.com* 🛏 *33 rooms* 🍴 *Free Breakfast.*

Privilege Aluxes

$$$ | **ALL-INCLUSIVE** | Perched on the sugary shores of Playa Norte, this five-story resort is one of the island's largest and one of the few to offer an all-inclusive plan. **Pros:** spa and gym; excellent location; Wi-Fi on the beach. **Cons:** standard rooms lack tubs; some rooms have cemetery views; adults only. [$] *Rooms from: $168* ✉ *Playa Norte, Av. López Mateos, Isla Mujeres* ☎ *998/848–8470, 877/635–5293 in the U.S. and Canada* 🌐 *www.privilegehotels.com* 🛏 *124 rooms* 🍴 *All-Inclusive.*

Rocamar Hotel Panorámico

$$ | **HOTEL** | You can smell, hear, and see the ocean from the starkly minimalist, blue-and-white rooms at this hotel: located right on the eastern *malecón* (boardwalk), it's one of the few on the island that overlooks the Caribbean. **Pros:** steps from the water; communal lounge with TV and library; helpful staff. **Cons:** no elevator; Wi-Fi in common areas only; no kids under five. [$] *Rooms from: $135* ✉ *Avs. Nicolas Bravo and Abasolo, Isla Mujeres* ☎ *998/877–0101* 🌐 *www.rocamar-hotel.com* 🛏 *32 rooms* 🍴 *No Meals.*

Selina Isla Mujeres PocNa

$$ | **HOTEL** | Formerly known simply as PocNa, this was the first hostel in Latin America and still carries that aura of Caribbean legend. **Pros:** daily entertainment activities; on the beach; coworking area. **Cons:** dorms of up to 12 people; some rooms share bathroom; no restaurant. [$] *Rooms from: $120* ✉ *Matamoros 15, El Pueblo* ☎ *998/224–1155* 🌐 *www.selina.com* 🛏 *84 rooms* 🍴 *Free Breakfast.*

Nightlife

Fayne's Bar and Grill

LIVE MUSIC | Best known for its terrific cocktails and live music, Fayne's is a brightly painted place with a hip, energetic personality. The party kicks off nightly at 8 pm with everything from American rock to Caribbean rhythms providing the soundtrack. Bring your dancing shoes. ✉ *Av. Hidalgo 12A, between Avs. Mateos and Matamoros, Isla Mujeres* ☎ *998/877–0525* 🌐 *facebook.com/faynesbar.*

Jax Bar & Grill

BARS | When you're looking for live music, cold beer, good bar food, and a satellite TV that's always tuned to the current game, make tracks for Jax, open daily until 11 pm. ✉ *Av. Adolfo Mateos 42, near lighthouse, Isla Mujeres* ☎ *998/877–1218* 🌐 *facebook.com/jaxislamujeres.*

La Adelita Tequileria

BARS | Connoisseurs can sample an amazing variety of tequilas at this fun, popular spot. ✉ *Av. Hidalgo Norte 12A, Isla Mujeres* ☎ *998/877–0528.*

Playa Norte Beach Club

BARS | This architecturally modern bar plays chill-out music by day and has live music at night. The fish tacos are a perfect cerveza accompaniment. Try to stop by for the gorgeous sunset. ✉ *Av. López Mateos, Isla Mujeres* ☎ *998/848–8470* 🌐 *privilegehotels.com/en/beach-club/.*

Shopping

Although Isla produces few local crafts, the streets are filled with souvenir shops selling cheap T-shirts, garish ceramics, and seashells glued onto a variety of objects. Amid all the junk you may find good Mexican folk art, hammocks, textiles, and silver jewelry. Most stores are small family operations that don't take credit cards, but almost everyone gladly accepts U.S. dollars at a slightly disadvantageous exchange rate. Stores that do take credit cards often tack on a fee to offset the commission they must pay. Hours are generally Monday through Saturday 10–1 and 4–7, although many stores stay open during the midday siesta.

CLOTHING
Gladys Galdamez Isla Mujeres

CRAFTS | Galdamez's eponymous shop carries Isla-designed and manufactured clothing and accessories for both men and women, as well as bags and jewelry. Select something off the rack, or bring a photograph of your dream bikini and she'll sew a bespoke version for you. ⊠ *Caracol, entre Tortuga y Manatí, Isla Mujeres* ⊹ *Punta Sur* ☎ *998/147–1115* ⊕ *www.gladysgaldamez.com.*

CRAFTS
Isla Mujeres Artist Fair

MARKET | Held every Thursday from November through April, this community event profiles the work of resident artists, designers, authors, and even palm readers. It's a great place to find jewelry, clothing, and artwork, while benefiting local nonprofits. Food vendors and musicians also take part in the fair, which runs from 3 to 8 pm. ⊠ *Casa de la Cultura, Abasolo s/n, Isla Mujeres* ☎ *998/157–7298* ⊕ *facebook.com/islamujeresartistfair2* ⊗ *Closed Fri.–Wed.*

Women's Beading Cooperative (*Taller Artesanias de Mujeres*)

JEWELRY & WATCHES | Nearly 60 local women are part of this beading cooperative, which creates handcrafted jewelry for a very reasonable price. It's worth the drive to the middle of the island to see these talented artisans at work. ⊠ *Colonia La Gloria, Paseo de los Peces Mz 160 Lt 5, La Gloria, Isla Mujeres* ☎ *998/161–9659* ⊕ *facebook.com/IslaMujeresBeadingCoop* ⊗ *Closed Sun.*

GROCERY STORES
Chedraui

SUPERMARKET | Selling everything from food and clothing to appliances and medicine, and keeping long hours, this Mexican grocery chain is about as close as you can get to the Walmart experience. You'll find the island's best selection of groceries here. ⊠ *Mid-island, at Salina Chica, Rueda Medina, south*

of the hospital, near the baseball field, ☎ *998/888–0175* ⊕ *chedraui.com.mx.*

Mercado Municipal (*Mercado Audomaro Magaña*)

MARKET | For fresh produce, the Mercado Municipal is your best bet. It's open daily from 6 am until 2 pm. A second market (Mercado Javier Rojo Gomez) operates during the same hours on Avenida Guerrero between Mateos and Matamoros. ⊠ *Guerrero, Supmza. 001, Isla Mujeres.*

Super Aki

SUPERMARKET | One of two main grocery stores on the island, Super Aki is well stocked with all the basics and is a good in-town option if you can't make it out to Chedraui. ⊠ *Av. Morelos 3, between Avs. Hidalgo and Guerrero, El Pueblo* ☎ *998/877–1092.*

JEWELRY

Jewelry on Isla ranges from tasteful to tacky. Bargains are available, but beware of street vendors—most of their wares, especially the amber, are fake.

Galería de Arte Mexicano

JEWELRY & WATCHES | Bypass the street vendors and come directly to this lovely shop for the best quality silver in town. It also sells Talavera and custom-made jewelry at amazing prices. Don't be afraid to haggle. ⊠ *Av. Guerrero 3, El Pueblo* ☎ *998/877–1272* ⊕ *facebook.com/GaleriaDeArteMexicano* ⊗ *Closed Sun.*

Galería Elemento Arte

CRAFTS | For authentic made-in-Isla gifts—including wooden boxes, hand-carved sculptures, and ceramics—head to Galeria L'Mento Arte. Jewelry is another top draw: pick your stone, setting, and clasp, then watch the masters make a custom piece before your eyes. ⊠ *Av. Hidalgo, at Plaza los Almendros, Isla Mujeres* ☎ *998/214–0664* ⊕ *facebook. com/galeriaLmentoarte.*

Some impressive catches are to be had off the coast of the island.

🏃 Activities

FISHING

Cooperativa Isla Mujeres

FISHING | This fishermen's cooperative rents boats for a maximum of four hours and six people; tours to the underwater museum (lunch included) are also available. ✉ Pier 7, Av. Rueda Medina, Isla Mujeres ☎ 998/196–6250 ⊕ islamujeres-tours.com.mx ⛵ Off shore sport fishing from USD$750.

Keen M International Blue Water Encounters

FISHING | Captain Anthony Mendillo Jr. runs specialized fishing trips from December to June aboard several vessels, which range from 34 to 41 feet. ✉ Sección Rocas, Punta Norte, Lote 10, Int. B2, Isla Mujeres ☎ 998/877–0759 ⊕ www.islamujeressportfishing.com ⛵ From USD$900 for up to 4 anglers.

Sea Hawk Divers

FISHING | If you're interested in either offshore or deep-sea fishing, try Sea Hawk Divers. It offers trips daily from 9 am to 1 pm. Scuba diving and snorkeling tours are also available. ✉ Av. Arq. Carlos Lazo Mza.30 Lt.19, near Playa Norte, Isla Mujeres ☎ 998/877–1233 ⊕ www.seahawkislamujeres.com ⛵ Off shore fishing from USD$350.

SNORKELING AND SCUBA DIVING

There are numerous dive spots on the island but make sure you follow local laws and rules to help preserve them. Coral reefs at Garrafón Natural Reef Park have suffered tremendously from a variety of factors, some unavoidable (hurricanes) and some all-too-avoidable (boats dropping anchors onto soft coral, a practice now outlawed). Some good snorkeling can be found near Playa Norte on the north end.

Isla is a good place for learning to dive, since dive areas are close to shore. Offshore, there is excellent diving and snorkeling at Xlaches (pronounced ees-lah-chays) reef, due north on the way to Isla Contoy. One of Contoy's most alluring dives is a cave full of sharks off the northern tip. Discovered in 1969 by a local fisherman, the cave was extensively explored by Ramón Bravo, a local diver,

Shhh... Don't Wake the Sharks

The underwater caverns off Isla Mujeres attract reef sharks, a dangerous species. Once the sharks swim into the caves, though, they enter a state of relaxed nonaggression seen nowhere else. Naturalists have two explanations, both involving the composition of the water inside the caves, which contains more oxygen, more carbon dioxide, and less salt than usual.

According to the first theory, the decreased salinity causes the parasites that plague sharks to loosen their grip, allowing the remora fish (sharks' personal vacuum cleaners) to eat the parasites more easily. Perhaps the sharks relax to make the cleaning easier, or maybe it's the aftereffect of a good scrubbing. Another theory is that the caves' combination of fresh- and saltwater produces a euphoria similar to the "nitrogen narcosis" scuba divers experience on deep dives.

Whatever the sharks experience while "sleeping" in the caves, they pay a heavy price for it. A swimming shark breathes automatically and without effort as water flows through its gills, but a stationary shark must laboriously pump water to continue breathing. If you dive in the Cave of the Sleeping Sharks, be cautious: many are reef sharks, the species responsible for the largest number of attacks on humans. Dive with a reliable guide and be on your best underwater behavior.

cinematographer, and Mexico's foremost expert on sharks. It's a fascinating 150-foot dive for experienced divers only.

At 30–40 feet deep and 3,300 feet off the southwestern coast, the coral reef known as **Manchones** is a good dive site. During the summer of 1994, an ecological group hoping to divert divers and snorkelers from Garrafón commissioned a 1-ton, 9¾-foot bronze cross, which was later sunk here. Named the Cruz de la Bahía (Cross of the Bay), it's a tribute to everyone who has died at sea. Another option is the Barco L-55 and C-58 dive, which visits World War II boats 20 minutes off Isla Mujeres's coast.

Most dive shops offer a variety of packages with rates depending on the time of day, location, and the number of tanks.

Carey Diving
DIVING & SNORKELING | You can sign on for one-tank reef dives, deep dives, and two-tank cenote dives at this popular PADI dive shop. Whale-watching, fishing, and snorkeling excursions are offered as well. ⊠ Av. Matamoros 13-A, off Av. Juárez, Isla Mujeres ☎ 998/877–0763 ⊕ careydivecenter.com ⊠ Dives from USD$70.

Isla Whale Sharks
DIVING & SNORKELING | Venture into the heart of whale shark territory with Isla Whale Sharks from June 1 to September 15. Owner Ramón Guerrero García is a professional diver who has dedicated more than 20 years to researching these gentle giants. Included in the boat trip are beverages, a light snack, snorkel gear, and time at the reef and beach. Tours last approximately five hours and must be prebooked online. ⊠ Adrian's Internet Cafe, Av. Morelos, between Avs. Guerrero and Hidalgo, Isla Mujeres ☎ 998/196–1994 ⊕ www.islawhalesharks.com ⊠ Dives from MX$1,800.

Sea Hawk Isla Mujeres
SCUBA DIVING | In addition to highly regarded PADI courses, Sea Hawk Divers offers one- and two-tank dives plus special excursions to the more exotic shipwrecks and underwater museum. For nondivers, snorkel trips depart daily at 8:30 and 2:30. ⊠ Av. Arq. Carlos

Lazo, near Playa Norte, Isla Mujeres
☎ *998/877–1233* ⊕ *www.seahawkislamujeres.com* ✉ *Dives from USD$70.*

Squalo Adventures

DIVING & SNORKELING | One of the more experienced dive shops on the island, this PADI-certified outfit offers full scuba courses, as well as one- and two-tank dives to local sites including the underwater museum. ✉ *Av. Hidalgo, Sm 1, Isla Mujeres* ☎ *998/274–1644* ⊕ *www.squaloadventures.com* ✉ *Dives from USD$115.*

Side Trip to Isla Contoy

30 km (19 miles) north of Isla Mujeres.

The national wildlife park and bird sanctuary of Isla Contoy (Isle of Birds) is just 6 km (4 miles) long and less than 1 km (about ½ mile) wide. The whole island is a protected area, with visitor numbers carefully regulated to safeguard the flora and fauna. Isla Contoy has become a favorite among nature lovers who come to enjoy its unspoiled beauty. Sand dunes rise as high as 70 feet along the east coast, which is edged by black rocks and coral reefs. The west coast is fringed with sand, shrubs, and coconut palms.

More than 150 bird species—including gulls, pelicans, petrels, cormorants, cranes, ducks, flamingos, herons, doves, quail, spoonbills, and hawks—fly this way in late fall, some to nest and breed. Although the number of species is diminishing, partly as a result of human traffic, Isla Contoy remains a treat for bird-watchers.

The island is rich in sea life as well. Snorkelers will see brilliant coral and fish, while 5-foot-wide manta rays are visible in the shallow waters. All around the island are large numbers of shrimp, mackerel, barracuda, flying fish, and trumpet fish. In December, lobsters pass through in great (though diminishing) numbers on their southerly migration.

GETTING HERE AND AROUND

The trip to Isla Contoy takes 45 minutes to 1½ hours, depending on the weather and the boat, and costs MX$1,017. Everyone landing has to purchase a MX$80 authorization ticket, though this is usually included in the price of a guided tour. The standard excursion begins with a fruit breakfast on the boat and a stopover at Xlaches reef on the way to Isla Contoy for snorkeling (gear is included). As you sail, your crew trolls for the lunch it will cook on the beach: anything from barracuda to snapper (beer and soda are also included). While the catch is being barbecued, you have time to explore the island, snorkel, check out the small museum and biological station, or just laze under a palapa.

The island is officially open to a maximum of 200 visitors daily 9–5:30; overnight stays aren't allowed. Other than the birds and the dozen or so park rangers who live here, the island's only residents are iguanas, lizards, turtles, hermit crabs, and boa constrictors. Amigos de Isla Contoy (Friends of Isla Contoy), a private foundation, jointly administers the park with the Mexican government. ⊕ *www.islacontoy.org* ☎ *998/884–7483 in Cancún.*

TOURS

Captain Tony García

Board the *Guadalupana,* Captain Tony García's tour boat, for a trip to Isla Contoy. While you snorkel around the island, he and his crew will prepare a delicious feast for you. One of the most dependable tour operators, Tony is also an expert on local wildlife. ✉ *Calle Matamoros 7A, Isla Mujeres* ☎ *998/877–0229* ⊕ *isla-mujeres.net* ✉ *MX$1,000.*

Cooperativa Isla Mujeres

Daily boat trips from Isla Mujeres to Isla Contoy for 6–12 people are available through this local cooperative. ✉ *Contoy Pier, Av. Rueda Medina, Isla Contoy* ☎ *998/196–6250* ⊕ *www.islamujeres-tours.com.mx* ✉ *MX$1,021 per person.*

Chapter 5

THE RIVIERA MAYA

Updated by
Luis Domínguez

◉ Sights	🍽 Restaurants	🛏 Hotels	🛍 Shopping	🍸 Nightlife
★★★★★	★★★★★	★★★★★	★★★★☆	★★★★★

WELCOME TO THE RIVIERA MAYA

TOP REASONS TO GO

★ **Tulum:** Only an hour south of Playa del Carmen, the ruins are a dramatic remnant of a sophisticated pre-Columbian people overlooking the Caribbean—one of Mexico's classic views.

★ **Casting for bonefish:** These elusive shallows-dwellers, off the Chinchorro Reef near the Reserva de la Biósfera Sian Ka'an, can match wits with even the most seasoned fly-fisher.

★ **Relaxing at a spa:** The Riviera Maya is flush with luxurious spas, some incorporating native ingredients and ancient rituals into their treatments.

★ **Snorkeling and diving outer reefs and cenotes:** The Mesoamerican Barrier Reef, Banco Chinchorro, and freshwater cenotes (cavernous sinkholes) are teeming with marine life.

★ **Soaking up local culture:** Cradled between mangrove and sea, the quaint fishing village of Puerto Morelos has maintained its authenticity despite neighboring growth.

1 **Bahía Petempich.** The Riviera Maya starts on this wide and beautiful beach.

2 **Puerto Morelos.** Sleepy fishing village.

3 **Punta Brava.** Long and secluded beach at the south end of Puerto Morelos.

4 **Playa del Secreto.** Considered by many as the Riviera Maya's best beach.

5 **Punta Maroma.** Stunning beach with restricted access.

6 **Mayakoba.** Glitzy resort enclave.

7 **Punta Bete (Xcalacoco).** One of Playa del Carmen's most popular beaches.

8 **Playa del Carmen.** One of Latin America's fastest-growing cities, this lively community has a plethora of shops, hotels, restaurants, and beach clubs.

9 **Xcaret.** Combining cultural activities and ecological theme parks, the area around Xcaret offers much more than sun and sand.

10 **Puerto Aventuras.** This Americanized beach community promises good snorkeling plus plenty of hotels and restaurants with all the creature comforts you'd expect back home.

11 **Xpu-Há.** Solitude and tranquility abound on the barren coastlines at Xpu-Há.

12 **Akumal.** Beautiful bay perfect for snorkeling and swimming with turtles.

13 **Tankah.** In this quiet town, the favorite pastime is swinging in a hammock.

14 **Tulum.** Eco-friendly Tulum combines breathtaking ruins with bohemian-chic beach hangouts.

15 **Cobá.** The less-visited (but more impressive) pyramids at Cobá are surrounded by jungle.

16 **Reserva de la Biósfera Sian Ka'an.** Coastal mangrove forests dotted with cenotes give way to dense inland vegetation in Mexico's second-largest wilderness reserve.

17 **Felipe Carrillo Puerto.** Small Maya village away from the beaches and the mass-tourism.

18 **Bacalar.** Spectacular lagoon of seven colors.

19 **Chetumal.** Capital city of the state of Quintana Roo.

20 **Mahahual.** Gorgeous beach town already recognized as "the next Tulum."

21 **Xcalak.** The Riviera Maya ends on this quaint fishing village.

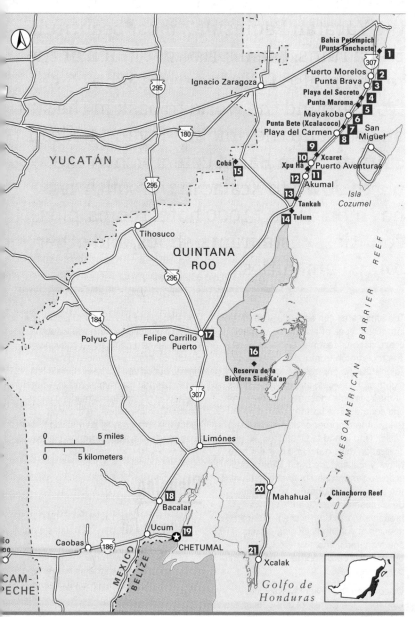

Mexico's Caribbean coast is full of treasures, from spectacular white-sand beaches and offshore reefs to some of the Yucatán Peninsula's most beautiful Maya ruins. Unsurprisingly, much of the region is also full of tourists, who come from around the world to bask in the sun and soak up the unique Mayan-Mexican culture. From Bahía Petempich in the north down to Xcalac in the south, it has more than 23,000 hotel rooms, plus countless restaurants, shops, and other tourist amenities.

The entire area can essentially be divided into three types of terrain: developed coast, national reserve, and wild coast. The top stretch from Bahía Petempich to Tulum has the greatest concentration of sights and services, and includes some of the Yucatán's most memorable ruins and cenotes. The bottom stretch, from the southern border of Sian Ka'an to Xcalak (and inland to Chetumal), is where civilization thins out. Here in the "Costa Maya" you'll find the most alluring landscapes. Sandwiched between the two is the sprawling wilderness of the Reserva de la Biósfera Sian Ka'an: a pristine preserve that is both a shelter for myriad species of wildlife (including jaguars and manatees) and a window to a time before resort development changed this coast forever.

Discovering the Riviera Maya is easy. One road, the Carretera 307, cuts all the way through to the border of Belize and will take you everywhere you want to go. The well-paved conduit is a convenient way to cover long distances between sights, but on your journey there's little to see beyond road signs and the monumental resort entrances marking access roads. Although exploring the region is about the soft sway of palms along sparkling sands, it's also about the highway miles you'll cover to get there.

Planning

When to Go

Peak season is November through April. The coastal weather is heavenly, with temperatures of 27°C (80°F) and near-constant ocean breezes. Hotel rates reflect increased demand from sun-starved northerners, especially in Playa del Carmen. During Christmas week, they often increase by 50% and hoteliers request a minimum five-night stay. If you're planning a Christmas vacation, you'd do well to book six months in advance.

June, September, and October are low season. September and October bring the worst weather, with frequent rain, mosquitoes, and the risk of hurricanes. There's also often rain in June. Breezes disappear, and humidity soars, especially inland. But if you're looking for a spa getaway and don't mind the weather outside, you'll be able to find real deals on accommodations during these months. Just keep in mind that some of the Riviera Maya's best restaurants and boutique hotels shut down during September, while larger resorts undergo renovation.

In May, July, and August, off-season prices and sunny skies make late spring and midsummer a great time to save on airfares and hotels, while having the beach to yourself.

Timing

One week will give you enough time to enjoy the beach and explore many of the best parts of the Riviera Maya. If you use Playa del Carmen as a base, you can easily take day trips to the Xcaret theme park or Tulum's beachfront Mayan ruins. Don't miss swimming in one of the numerous cenotes along Carretera 307. The beaches at Paamul and Xpu-Há are also within driving distance, as is the Mayan village of Pac Chen, the ruins at Cobá, and the Reserva de la Biósfera Sian Ka'an.

Getting Here and Around

BUS

Fifteen first-class ADO buses per day depart from Cancún between 6 am and midnight, stopping incrementally at Puerto Morelos, Playa del Carmen, Tulum, Felipe Carrillo Puerto, Limones, and Chetumal. The full trip from Cancún to Chetumal takes just under six hours and costs between MX$200 and MX$300, depending on the time of day.

BUS CONTACTS ADO. ✉ *Quinta Avenida Nte. LTE 2* ☎ *984/873–0109 in Playa del Carmen, 983/832–5110 in Chetumal* ⊕ *www.ado.com.mx.*

CAR

Discovering the Riviera Maya by car is easy. The entire coast from Cancún to Chetumal is connected by one highway, the Carretera 307. Between Cancún and Tulum it's four divided lanes, and after Tulum it's two, but it's in excellent condition the whole way. (A section of the highway sometimes is not referred to as the 307 but by the towns it connects: Carretera Playa del Carmen–Tulum, Carretera Tulum–Chetumal.) Because this is the only road linking cities, towns, parks, and jungle attractions, expect to spend a lot of time on it to see the region. Addresses along the highway but outside of towns are usually referred to by kilometer markers on small, white, upright signs at the side of the road.

If you want to explore beyond your accommodations, you'll need a rental car. Be aware that some roads off the highway are bumpy or potholed, and the road between Mahahual and Xcalak in the extreme south can be challenging after heavy rain.

Driving: The most dangerous place on the Caribbean coast may be the road. Carretera 307 is in excellent shape, but secondary roads can develop a serious case of the potholes. Combine that with poor lighting, unexpected speed bumps, and the occasional big crab skittering across the road, and you've got ample reason to drive slowly and carefully. Speed bumps, called *topes*, deserve special mention: they range from well-built and-marked tarred hills to a simple but effective thick rope laid across the tarmac. When they're marked, you'll see a yellow or white sign showing bumps or reading "TOPE." Often, however, they're not, so use caution and watch the road.

Obey speed limits: police radar and sudden decreases in speed limits are easy traps for travelers. Should you get pulled over, hand over your license and expect to get it back the next day, when you pay your ticket at the police station. Most police officers are honest, but some will pull you over just to see if you'll pay them a small "tip" to avoid the hassle—don't fall for it. In many cases you'll get off with a warning when you make it clear you're prepared for the official paperwork.

(Check out our Travel Smart chapter for rules of the road and information on rental car agencies if you plan on driving.)

Precautions: Before your trip, purchase travel insurance, monitor the weather, and notify your embassy and credit card company of your whereabouts. Make a copy of your passport and leave your travel itinerary with a friend or family member. To avoid unwanted situations, steer clear of remote locations, travel with a partner, and refrain from driving long distances at night.

COLECTIVOS

These large white vans with the word "Colectivo" displayed prominently on their fronts or sides are how locals get from one town to another along the Riviera. You'll find them running between Cancún and Playa del Carmen and Playa del Carmen and Tulum. If you're going from Cancún to Tulum, you'll need to take the colectivo to Playa and switch to a Tulum colectivo when you get there.

Colectivos are cheaper and faster than buses (a ride from Playa del Carmen to Tulum will run each person about MX$45 and take about 45 minutes), but most drivers won't speak English, so be prepared to speak a little Spanish. Some seats may be without seat belts or there may be standing room only; if you ever feel uncomfortable with the seats that are left, just wait for the next colectivo to pull up (they tend to run every five minutes or so). To take a colectivo, walk out to Carretera 307 and stand on the curb as if you were hitchhiking. When you see a colectivo, wave them down, hop on, say the name of your destination, and take an empty seat. In most cases, you'll pay when you arrive. Keep in mind that colectivos are not a good option if you have a big suitcase. They often don't have trunk areas, so the bus is a better bet if you're not traveling light.

Hotels

There's lodging for every taste and budget here, from giant all-inclusive luxury resorts to small family-run cabanas on the beach. Most are in remote areas off Carretera 307. If your accommodation choice doesn't provide good shuttle service, you may want to rent a car to visit off-site attractions or restaurants. Staying at beach areas in Playa del Carmen, Akumal, or Tulum will allow you to explore on foot from your hotel.

Hotel reviews have been condensed. For full reviews, see Fodors.com.

Restaurants

Restaurants here vary from quirky beachside affairs with outdoor tables and palapas to more elaborate and sophisticated establishments. Dress is casual at most places, so leave your tie and jacket at home. Smaller eateries may not accept credit cards, especially in remote beach villages. Bigger ones and those in hotels normally accept plastic. Many restaurants add *propinas* (tips) to the bill; look for a charge for "*servicio*." If tips aren't included, a 15% gratuity is standard. It's best to order fresh local fish—grouper, dorado, red snapper, and sea bass—rather than shellfish like shrimp, lobster, and oysters, since the latter are often flown in frozen from the Gulf. Playa del Carmen has the largest selection of restaurants.

WHAT IT COSTS in Dollars and Pesos

	$	$$	$$$	$$$$
RESTAURANTS				
	under MX$135	MX$135–MX$200	MX$201–MX$350	over MX$350
HOTELS IN DOLLARS				
	under $100	$100–$200	$201–$300	over $300
HOTELS IN PESOS				
	under MX$2,000	MX$2,001–MX$4,000	MX$4,001–MX$6,000	over MX$6,000

Safety

With its massive resorts and tourist-oriented beach towns, the Riviera Maya is free of most big-city dangers. Though increasingly urban, Playa del Carmen is generally safe in tourist areas, and extensive police patrols keep it that way. Between 2011 and 2013, Playa del Carmen experienced a slight rise in crime outside the major resort areas, most of it associated with criminal groups. Regardless of this, Playa del Carmen is still more secure than most North American cities and remains among the safest areas in Mexico for vacationers. Resorts all have 24-hour security guards, and most have in-room safes. Thanks to advances in water purification, food safety has made great strides in the last decade, but Mexicans drink bottled water and you should, too. However, there's no need to worry about ice—it's made from purified water virtually everywhere.

Look for the barrel-shaped, industrial ice cubes, just to be sure.

Tours

Alltournative

Offering eco-friendly adventures for travelers of all ages and fitness levels, Alltournative will have you feeling like Indiana Jones in no time. You can kayak through a lagoon, snorkel in a cenote, or zipline above a lush jungle. The company also organizes visits to Maya communities on expeditions to Cobá. ⊠ *Carretera 307, Km 287, Playa del Carmen* ☎ *984/803–9999, 877/437–4990 in U.S.* ⊕ *www.alltournative.com* ✉ *From USD$89.*

Maya Sites Travel Services

This outfit uses archaeologists and other experts to lead inexpensive tours of ancient Maya sites. ⊠ *Playa del Carmen* ☎ *505/255–2279 in U.S., 877/620–8715 in U.S.* ⊕ *www.mayasites.com.*

Riviera Adventours

Cycle through the ruins at Cobá, snorkel in a cenote, or get blessed by a Maya Shaman on one of Riviera Adventours's intimate four- to nine-person half- or full-day tours. Hotel pickup anywhere between Playa del Carmen and Tulum is included. ⊠ *Carretera Federal 307, Tulum* ☎ *984/115–9965* ⊕ *riviera-adventours.com* ✉ *From USD$120.*

Visitor Information

Online resources can help you plan your trip. Meaning "white road" in Mayan, Sac-Be.com covers everything from local beaches to environmental issues. TravelYucatan.com has information on transportation, hotels, and attractions, plus travel tips for both novice and veteran travelers. If you're looking for updated info on Playa del Carmen and surrounding areas, visit PlayaMayaNews.com.

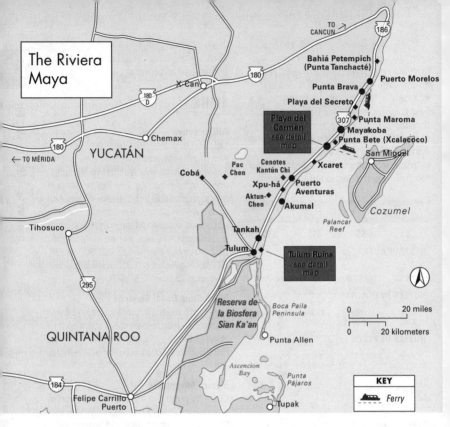

Bahía Petempich (Punta Tanchacté)

44 km (27 miles) north of Playa del Carmen, 23 km (14 miles) south of Cancún.

Riviera Maya's stretch of coastline starts south of Cancún at Bahía Petempich (also known as Punta Tanchacté), where the party atmosphere fades and a feeling of tranquility takes hold. Encountering this area for the first time via monotonous Carretera 307, travelers might ask, "I came all this way for this?" But just wait—beyond those towering security gates, access roads lead to an enviable collection of resorts and, ultimately, to long expanses of white sandy strands lapped by turquoise waters.

Historically a fishing village, this area has recently been overtaken by Puerto Morelos's growth, and now there are new hotels and resorts here as well. Just 20 minutes south of Cancún, Bahía Petempich is quieter than neighboring towns but still close to the action.

It's worth noting that while all beaches in Mexico are open to the public, access is not guaranteed. This means that when a resort snatches a prime beachfront site, it can effectively block access to nonguests.

GETTING HERE AND AROUND

Driving north on Carretera 307, turn right at Km 328. Heading south on Carretera 307, turn left at Km 27.5. The entrance is marked by a large gate reading "Bahía Petempich." This community of resorts does not offer any facilities other than those that are available within the hotels.

Zoëtry Paraíso de la Bonita is unique: a truly luxurious all-inclusive resort.

The nearest shops, restaurants, banks, and clinics are in Cancún and Puerto Morelos.

Hotels

Azul Beach Resort Riviera Cancun

$$$$ | **ALL-INCLUSIVE** | **FAMILY** | Situated on a beautiful beach with a protected reef just offshore, this all-inclusive family-friendly resort has six pools, eight restaurants, and several categories of rooms, including swim-up rooms and family suites that accommodate two adults and three children. **Pros:** excellent service; good food; extremely family friendly. **Cons:** few adult-only spaces; not wheelchair accessible; noisy restaurants. $ *Rooms from: $434* ✉ *Carretera 307, Km 27.5, Punta Tanchacté* ☎ *998/872–8450, 866/527–4762* 🌐 *karismahotels.com* 🛏 *435 suites* 🍴 *All-Inclusive.*

Zoetry Paraíso de la Bonita

$$$$ | **ALL-INCLUSIVE** | A pair of stone dragons guards the entrance to this eclectic resort, where the spacious rooms—all with sweeping sea and jungle views—are elegantly styled after worldwide destinations, Italy, Mexico, and Bali among them. **Pros:** tasteful room design; every room has ocean view; spa included. **Cons:** no kids club; mediocre lunch; sales pitch during the welcome. $ *Rooms from: $549* ✉ *Carretera 307, Km 328, Punta Tanchacté* ✥ *Turn on hwy. at signs for Paraiso de la Bonita; follow rd. about 3 km (2 miles) for gate to Zoëtry* ☎ *998/872–8300, 888/496–3879 in the U.S.* 🌐 *www.zoetryresorts.com/paraiso* 🛏 *100 suites* 🍴 *All-Inclusive.*

Activities

SPAS

★ Thalasso Center & Spa

SPAS | The 22,000-square-foot spa at the Zoëtry Paraiso de la Bonita resort is the first certified thalassotherapy spa in the Riviera Maya, meaning many of its treatments use seawater to wash your cares away. The classic hot-cold treatment cycle will take you from sauna to steam room, cold plunge pool to warm

Jacuzzi, relaxing your muscles so that you can get the maximum benefit from your massage. The extensive menu features body scrubs, saltwater hydrotherapy, and proto-Maya *temezcal* rituals. Although most treatments involve getting wet, you'll also find healing dry remedies like aromatherapy, facials, massages, and acupuncture. Spa products infused with sea kelp and marine mud are said to eliminate toxins. Pilates, wellness cooking classes, and Maya healing practices are available upon request. ⊠ *Zoëtry Paraiso de la Bonita Resort, Carretera 307, Km 328, Punta Tanchacté* ☎ *998/872-8300* ⊕ *www.zoetryresorts.com/paraiso/wellness-spa* ⊠ *Thalasso therapy from USD$69.*

Puerto Morelos

32 km (20 miles) north of Playa del Carmen.

At the edge of a mangrove-tangled jungle pushing up to the shore, Puerto Morelos is one of the few coastal towns on this stretch of the Riviera Maya that's maintained a measure of authenticity. Although it's become a favorite of Canadian and American expat artists, painters, and poets, it's still essentially a salty Mexican seaside village. Nothing here has been prettied up for the gringos, and tourist traps are few and far between. With a wide selection of restaurants, a variety of nearby hotels, and a good road connecting the town with the highway, it makes a great base.

Environmental laws and building restrictions have so far kept growth under tight control. This has prevented Puerto Morelos from becoming the next Cancún or Playa del Carmen—which many locals consider a blessing. The waters here are calm and safe and the beach is relatively quiet.

Where Puerto Morelos shines is out at sea: the superb Mesoamerican Barrier Reef, only 1,800 feet offshore, is an excellent place to explore with a snorkel or scuba tank. The reef is healthy, meaning you'll see plenty of marine life; but it and the surrounding mangrove forests are a protected national park, so you'll need to visit with a licensed guide and purchase a mandatory conservation bracelet (usually included in the price of the guide). Home to many species of birds, the park is also a draw for bird-watchers. (The mangroves are a haven for mosquitoes, too—bring repellent, especially after dusk.)

Architecture fans shouldn't miss the bizarre cartoon castle at the corner of Niños Heroes and Morelos, a carved, curvy, leaning tree-house fantasy that has to be seen to be believed.

GETTING HERE AND AROUND

Puerto Morelos is the first major town on Carretera 307. When the center of the road rises up to an overpass, motorists should stay right and turn left underneath, then just follow the road 2 km (1 mile) east. This will take you directly to the town square and lighthouse. You can also reach Puerto Morelos by turning at the paved road at Croco Cun Zoo off Carretera 307 at Km 31. This paved road dead-ends at the entrance to Excellence Resort, where you will turn right and follow the road along the mangroves to the center of town. ADO (⊕ *www.ado.com.mx*) links Cancún, Puerto Morelos, Playa del Carmen, Tulum, Felipe Carrillo Puerto, Limones, and Chetumal by bus. Colectivos stop along Carretera 307 just outside town.

Downtown, which can be explored by foot, is essentially the sprawling town square, bordered by Avenida Rafael Melgar at the beach, Avenida Rojo Gomez parallel, and Avenidas Tulum and Morelos to the south and north respectively. The square verges on the water, where you'll find a fisherman's shack (for boat tours) next to Pelicanos restaurant. Steps to the left take you down to the beach. The taxi stand is at the northeast corner of the square at Morelos and Rojo Gomez. Avenida Niños Heroes is the next street inland, parallel to Avenida Rojo Gomez.

TAXI CONTACTS Taxi Service. ✉ *Puerto Morelos* ☎ *998/871–0090.*

Sights

Croco Cun Zoo

ZOO | FAMILY | The biologists running the Croco Cun Zoo, an animal farm just north of Puerto Morelos, have collected specimens of many of the reptiles and some of the mammals indigenous to the area. They offer immensely informative tours—you may even get to handle a baby crocodile or feed a monkey. Be sure to wave hello to the 500-pound crocodile secure in his deep pit. ✉ *Carretera 307, Km 31, Puerto Morelos* ☎ *998/850–3719* ⊕ *www.crococunzoo.com* ✉ *USD$32.*

Yaax Che Jardín Botánico del Dr. Alfredo Barrera Marín (*Dr. Alfredo Barrera Marín Botanical Garden*)

GARDEN | This 150-acre botanical garden is the largest in Mexico. Named for a local botanist, it exhibits the peninsula's plants and flowers, which are labeled in English, Spanish, and Latin. The park features a 130-foot suspension bridge, three observation towers, and a library equipped with reading hammocks. There's also a tree nursery, a remarkable orchid and epiphyte garden, an authentic Mayan house, and an archaeological site. A nature walk goes directly through the mangroves for some great birding; more than 220 species have been identified here (be sure to bring bug spray, though). Spider monkeys can usually be spotted in the afternoons, and a tree-house lookout offers a spectacular view—but the climb isn't for those afraid of heights. ✉ *Carretera 307, 1 km (½ mile) south of Puerto*

Beach Safety 🏃 5

Deserted beaches invite thieves—never leave anything visible in your car. Remember that even the calmest-looking waters can have currents and riptides. Take note that waves are most powerful during December, and that hurricane season lasts from June into November. If visiting isolated beaches, bring sunscreen and drinking water to avoid overexposure and dehydration.

Morelos, Puerto Morelos ✛ Entrance is on northbound side of highway. From southbound side, turn around after town ☎ *998/206–9233* ⊕ *facebook.com/ JBPuertoMorelos* ✉ *MX$150* ⊗ *Closed weekends.*

Beaches

Puerto Morelos Main Beach

BEACH | Newcomers to Puerto Morelos might be disappointed by the blankets of seaweed and boats that dock ashore—after all, this place is more about snorkeling on the reef than sunning on the sand. Your best bet is to head for the stretch of beach two blocks north of the square in front of Ojo de Agua Hotel. Park on the town square or adjacent streets. **Amenities:** food and drink; parking (free). **Best for:** snorkeling; walking. ✉ *North of town square, Puerto Morelos.*

🍴 Restaurants

Al Chimichurri

$$$ | SOUTH AMERICAN | FAMILY | The smoky aromas of a South American *parillada* waft down the street from this Uruguayan barbecue joint. The heaping portions of short ribs, flank steak, and chorizo have developed a cult following up and down the Riviera, and locals swear by the empanadas. **Known for:** friendly staff; good steaks; creative empanadas. [$] *Average main: MP300* ✉ *Av. Javier Rojo Gomez, between Avs. Tulum and Isla Mujeres, Puerto Morelos* ☎ *998/252–4666* 🌐 *facebook.com/AlChimichurri* 🕙 *Closed Mon. No breakfast.*

★ John Gray's Kitchen

$$$ | **INTERNATIONAL** | Using only the freshest ingredients—from local fruits and vegetables to seafood right off the pier—the chefs at this jungle-side restaurant work their magic in a comfortable, contemporary setting that feels more Manhattan than Mayan. Ask about the tender roasted duck breast with tequila, chipotle, and honey, or order an addictive, understated bowl of shrimp macaroni and cheese with notes of truffle. **Known for:** duck breast with honey, tequila, and chipotle sauce; tuna tostadas; hamburgers and chicken wings for lunch. [$] *Average main: MP325* ✉ *Av. Niños Heroes, 1 block north of Av. Morelos, on jungle side, Puerto Morelos* ☎ *998/871–0665* 🌐 *facebook.com/johngrayskitchen* 🕙 *Closed Sun. No lunch Mon.*

La Petita en la Playita

$ | **MEXICAN** | Two blocks north of the town square, this "restaurant" is actually made up of plastic tables and chairs shaded by mini palapas and tarps. What it lacks in charm is more than made up for by the food and prices. **Known for:** shrimp tacos; seafood soup; fried fish. [$] *Average main: MP120* ✉ *Av. Rafael Melgar, Sm 02, Puerto Morelos* ☎ *998/871-0737.*

★ La Sirena

$$$ | **INTERNATIONAL** | Overlooking the town square, La Sirena serves an eclectic mix of dishes ranging from mini sliders and grilled grouper to hearty plates of barbecue pulled pork with shoestring fries. If you like Mediterranean food, opt for Greek specialties prepared by chef Anthony Chalas, who credits his skills to his years spent in Greece. **Known for:** the dip sampler with homemade hummus and tzatziki; Greek meatballs; Greek salad. [$] *Average main: MP300* ✉ *Jose Maria Morelos, Puerto Morelos* ☎ *998/117–1082* 🌐 *www.lasirenapm.com* 🕙 *Closed Sun.*

Le Café D'Amancia

$ | **CAFÉ** | **FAMILY** | This colorful hangout on the corner of the main plaza is the best place in town to watch the world go by (or take advantage of free Wi-Fi) while lingering over coffee and a pastry. Most items are organic, and the fruit smoothies are delicious. **Known for:** tasty Mexican breakfasts; organic fruit smoothies; good coffee. [$] *Average main: MP95* ✉ *Av. Tulum at Av. Rojo Gomez, Puerto Morelos* ☎ *998/206–9242* 🌐 *facebook.com/CafeDeAmancia* 🕙 *Closed Mon.*

Pangea Food and Music

$$ | **ECLECTIC** | Abutting the plaza at the beach, Pangea has it all: breakfast, lunch, and dinner served on an umbrella-shaded terrace overlooking the sea, plus live music and entertainment until late. Daily menus—all prepared with organic ingredients and without preservatives—may include grilled fresh tuna, vegetarian lasagna, or shrimp kebabs, and there's fresh ginger-lemongrass tea and pancakes for breakfast. **Known for:** ginger-lemongrass tea; fresh fish; themed menus. [$] *Average main: MP180* ✉ *Av. Morelos at the water, Puerto Morelos* ☎ *998/256–6346* 🌐 *facebook.com/pangeafoodandmusic* 🕙 *Closed Sun.*

★ Pelicanos Restaurant & Marina

$$$ | **SEAFOOD** | **FAMILY** | Enjoy fresh seafood on the shaded patio of this family-owned restaurant in the heart of town. Try fish prepared *al ajo* (in a garlicky butter sauce), breaded, grilled, or *tikin–xic* style (marinated with *adobo de achiote* and sour oranges). Pelicanos also offers a variety of four-hour excursions that include fishing, snorkeling, then cooking

the daily catch at the restaurant. **Known for:** massive margaritas; catch and cook (and eat) options; fish al ajo (in garlicky butter sauce). [$] *Average main: MP244* ✉ *Av. Rafael Melgar at Av. Tulum, Puerto Morelos* ☎ *998/871–0014* 🌐 *pelicanos.com.mx.*

Hotels

★ Casa Caribe & Cabañas

$$ | B&B/INN | Five minutes from the town square and opposite the main beach, this charming hacienda-style B&B has five rooms with firm, comfortable king-size beds plus private terraces, some with partial ocean views, and six larger cabañas all with kitchen included. **Pros:** free beach chairs and umbrellas provided; cabañas have their own kitchen; lovely staff. **Cons:** some nighttime street noise; no pool; five-night minimum stay in high season. [$] *Rooms from: $120* ✉ *Av. Rojo Gómez 768, Puerto Morelos* ☎ *998/251–8060* 🌐 *www.casacaribepuertomorelos.com* 🛏 *11 rooms* 🍴 *No Meals.*

Dreams Riviera Cancún

$$$$ | ALL-INCLUSIVE | FAMILY | This sprawling resort is built around a lofty lobby with views across the grounds and to the sea. **Pros:** family-friendly; children under 12 years stay free; plenty of activities. **Cons:** only 60% of rooms have ocean views; some visible wear and tear in guest rooms and common areas; sea grass on the beach. [$] *Rooms from: MP472* ✉ *Carretera Federal 307,* ☎ *998/872–9200, 866/237–3267 in the U.S.* 🌐 *dreamsresorts.com* 🛏 *486 suites* 🍴 *All-Inclusive.*

★ Excellence Riviera Cancún

$$$$ | ALL-INCLUSIVE | Just 15 minutes from Cancún Airport, this sprawling adults-only resort is centered on an indulgent spa and six meandering pools. **Pros:** rooms have private hot tubs for two; caters to honeymooners; spacious beach. **Cons:** adults only (18-plus); thin walls; some visible wear and tear in guest rooms and common areas. [$] *Rooms from: $358* ✉ *Carretera Federal 307, north of Puerto Morelos, Puerto Morelos* ☎ *998/872–8500, 866/211–6223 in U.S.* 🌐 *excellenceresorts.com* 🛏 *440 rooms* 🍴 *All-Inclusive.*

Shopping

BOOKS

Alma Libre Bookstore

BOOKS | There are more than 20,000 titles in stock at Alma Libre. You can buy outright or trade in your own books for a discount and replenish your holiday reading list. ✉ *Av. Tulum 4, Puerto Morelos* 🌐 *almalibrebookstore.com* 🕒 *Closed May–Sept.*

CRAFTS AND FOLK ART

Colectivo de Artesanos de Puerto Morelos

CRAFTS | The Puerto Morelos Artists' Cooperative is a series of interconnected buildings where local artisans sell their jewelry, hand-embroidered clothing, hammocks, and other items. You can sometimes find real bargains. ✉ *Av. Javier Rojo Gómez between Av. Isla Mujeres and Av. Tulum, Puerto Morelos.*

Ixchel Jungle Market & Spa

MARKET | This nonprofit organization generates income for Maya women and their families. From December through April, a Sunday market features traditional dances, regional foods, and handmade crafts sold by Maya women wearing embroidered dresses. Year-round, the spa offers traditional Maya treatments such as deep-tissue massage and body wraps with aloe vera or chocolate fresh from the cacao; it's open by appointment only, with bookings at 10, noon, 2, and, when full, 4. ✉ *Villa Morelos 1, Puerto Morelos* ☎ *998/180–5424* 🌐 *www.mayaccho.com* 🕒 *Closed Sun.–Mon. and May–Nov.*

🏃 Activities

ADVENTURE TOURS

Selvática

ZIP LINING | FAMILY | Just outside Puerto Morelos, Selvática offers tours over the jungle on more than 10 zip lines and a bungee swing. The highest zip is more than 12 stories above the jungle floor. The full trip—including zip lines, aerial bridges, dirt buggies, a bungee swing, a cenote swim, lunch, and transfers—takes a full day, but half-day zip line adventures are also available. Advance reservations are required. ⊠ *Ruta de los cenotes Km 18, 19 km (12 miles) from turnoff on Carretera 307, Puerto Morelos* ☎ *998/881–3034* ⊕ *www.selvatica.com. mx* 🎫 *USD$97.*

Xenotes Oasis Maya

DIVING & SNORKELING | FAMILY | Operated by Experiencias Xcaret, Xenotes Oasis Maya includes a trip to four cenotes where you can kayak, zipline, rappel, and snorkel. Tours begin between 8 and 10 am and take about nine hours, including transfers. Transportation, lunch, and equipment are included. Tickets for kids age 6 through 11 are half off. Only biodegradable sunscreen, makeup, and mosquito repellent are allowed during the tour. ⊠ *Carretera Puerto Morelos–Leona Vicario km 22, Puerto Morelos* ☎ *998/883–3143, 855/326–0682 in the U.S.* ⊕ *www.xenotes.com* 🎫 *USD$116* 🕐 *Closed Sun.*

SCUBA DIVING AND SNORKELING

Aquanauts Dive Adventures

SCUBA DIVING | The oldest family-run dive shop in Puerto Morelos is located in the back of the Hacienda Morelos hotel, overlooking the ocean. It offers both scuba and snorkeling adventures in over 40 different dive sites that range from easy reef dives to shipwreck explorations. Van service from your hotel is available for an extra fee. ⊠ *Marina El Cid, Puerto Morelos* ☎ *998/206–9365*

⊕ *aquanautsdiveadventures.com* 🎫 *2-tank dive from MX$2260.*

Punta Brava

24 km (15 miles) north of Playa del Carmen.

Punta Brava is a long, winding sweep of sand strewn with seashells. The only direct access to this beach area is through the security gate at the Grand Velas or El Dorado Royale resort. Past the entrance is a tropical jungle and more than 1½ km (1 mile) of coastline at Punta Brava Beach. In an effort to calm the powerful waves, artificial sandbars have been built along the shore. Not only are these burlap sacks an eyesore, but also they have eliminated one of the few spots in the area where bodysurfing was once possible.

GETTING HERE AND AROUND

If you're heading north from Playa del Carmen, turn right into El Dorado Royale gate at Km 45. Currency exchange is available within El Dorado Royale Resort. Otherwise, the nearest banks, medical facilities, and police stations are 8 km (5 miles) north in Puerto Morelos.

🛏 Hotels

El Dorado Royale

$$$$ | ALL-INCLUSIVE | Although this beachfront property has been over-shadowed by its newer neighbors, the location—amid 500 acres of lush jungle—is as alluring as ever. **Pros:** sprawling property; on-site health bar and ATM; green practices. **Cons:** rocky beach with sea grass; slow room service; no kids under 18. 🏷 *Rooms from: $580* ⊠ *Carretera 307, Km 45, Punta Brava* ☎ *998/872–8030, 844/887–9488 in U.S.* ⊕ *eldoradosparesorts.com/royale* 🛏 *478 rooms* 🍽 *All-Inclusive.*

Playa del Secreto

23 km (14½ miles) north of Playa del Carmen.

The secret is out—the ½-km (1/3-mile) stretch of white sand at Playa del Secreto is one of the most beautiful in the Riviera Maya. Surrounded by jungle and Caribbean waters, the protected shores are a favorite nesting ground for giant leatherback sea turtles, weighing up to 300 pounds. From May through October, early risers can watch baby turtles struggle from their shells and skitter down to the sea. The bordering jungle is home to foxes, deer, crocodiles, wild boars, and coatimundis. Bird-watching is excellent here, with species ranging from wild parrots and hawks to kingfishers and black-necked stilts. This coastal community is midway between Cancún and Playa del Carmen, meaning that nightclubs, shopping, and restaurants are less than 20 minutes away.

GETTING HERE AND AROUND

From Playa del Carmen, drive approximately 20 minutes north on Carretera 307 and turn right at Km 312. The entrance for Playa del Secreto is just past the Cirque du Soleil Theater. From Cancún, take Carretera 307 south. Approximately 10 km (6 miles) past Puerto Morelos, turn left at Km 312 onto the Playa del Secreto road that leads to the beach. For those staying at the Valentin resort, there's a designated entrance off Carretera 307 at Km 311. Because only private villas and a resort make up this beach community, there are no restaurants, shops, or services available. The nearest are north in Puerto Morelos.

Beaches

Playa del Secreto

BEACH | Free of rocks, sea grass, and drop-offs, Playa del Secreto is perfect for swimming, kayaking, or snorkeling. On windy days, the waves are large enough for boogie boarding or bodysurfing. At the nearby reef, divers can get down with lobster, octopus, crabs, and turtles. The powdery white sand makes it great for long walks. The stretch near Valentin Imperial Maya is especially clean, with clear warm water where fish come to eat out of your hand. Dotting the shore are vacation rentals and a private community of homeowners, meaning that there is no public access to this beach other than through the private roads off Carretera 307. Despite the fact this is a public beach, non-hotel guests will be turned away at security gates. That also means that there are no public facilities other than those offered exclusively to guests. **Amenities:** none. **Best for:** snorkeling; swimming; walking. ✉ *Carretera 307, Km 311, 15 mins south of Cancún Airport, Playa del Secreto.*

Hotels

Valentin Imperial Maya

$$$$ | **ALL-INCLUSIVE** | Nestled in thriving mangrove forests, this adults-only all-inclusive is one of the few in the region that still embraces Mexican tradition. **Pros:** enormous pools; authentic Mexican coffee; pillow menu. **Cons:** no kids under 18; slippery hallways during rainy season; evening entertainment disappointing. [$] *Rooms from: $500* ✉ *Carretera 307, Km 311.5, Playa del Secreto* ☎ *984/206–3660, 800/232-8316 in U.S.* 🌐 *www.valentinmaya.com* 🛏 *540 rooms* 🍴 *All-Inclusive.*

Nightlife

JOYÀ by Cirque du Soleil

THEATER | From the creators of Cirque du Soleil, this whimsical show follows the adventures of a rebellious teenage girl swept away to a mysterious jungle. Several ticket packages are available. ✉ *Carretera 307, Km 48, near Mayan Palace Resort, Playa del Secreto*

☎ 800/247–7837 ⊕ cirquedusoleil.com/joya ✉ From USD$77 ⊘ Closed Sun., Mon., and Wed..

Punta Maroma

23 km (14 miles) north of Playa del Carmen.

The waters of this protected bay stay calm even on blustery days, and the enchanting beach ranks among Mexico's finest. A string of resorts has taken advantage of its enviable position—including the Belmond Maroma Resort & Spa, the Blue Diamond Resort, and Secrets Maroma. Unfortunately, nonguests will not be able to access the beach since the only entry point is through the security gate.

GETTING HERE AND AROUND

Driving north from Playa del Carmen, turn right into the Punta Maroma gate at Km 51. Heading south from Cancún, take Carretera 307 to the east (left) turnoff at Km 306.5. Signs (and a security guard) will point you to your resort. Blue Diamond Resort is accessed by way of a private entrance at Km 298.8 off Carretera 307. Because Punta Maroma is a gated community, the only available facilities are within the resorts themselves. The closest shops, restaurants, banks, and emergency facilities are 10 minutes south in Playa del Carmen.

🏖 Beaches

Punta Maroma

BEACH | One of Mexico's most beautiful beaches has deep white sand that feels like powdered sugar and crystalline water that's free of rocks. The small waves crashing onshore make it great for bodysurfing; 10 minutes off the coast of the Blue Diamond Resort, you'll find terrific diving, too. Hotels supply lounge chairs and offer activities like volleyball, yoga, and even remote-control boat racing for guests. Unfortunately, this beach can only be accessed by way of the security gate on Carretera 307 that leads to Secrets Maroma, Catalonia Playa Maroma, and Belmond Maroma Resort & Spa. Unless you plan to visit by boat or stay at one of these resorts, you're probably out of luck. **Amenities:** food and drink; toilets (for resort guests only). **Best for:** walking. ✉ *Carretera 307, Km 306, Punta Maroma.*

🛏 Hotels

Blue Diamond Luxury Boutique Hotel

$$$$ | **ALL-INCLUSIVE** | Midway between Punta Bete and Punta Maroma, this all-inclusive resort is on the south end of Maroma Beach. **Pros:** golf carts and bikes available; huge rooms; excellent service. **Cons:** strict dress code at some restaurants; lots of mosquitoes; no children under 18. $ *Rooms from: $402* ✉ *Carretera 307, Km 298, Punta Maroma* ☎ *984/206–4100* ⊕ *bluediamondluxuryboutiquehotel.com* ➲ *128 rooms* ⦿ *All-Inclusive.*

★ Secrets Maroma Beach Riviera Cancún

$$$$ | **ALL-INCLUSIVE** | Strip away the gourmet restaurants, elegant rooms, and 18 swimming pools, and you're still basking on Mexico's best beach. **Pros:** romantic property; unlimited luxury; swim-up rooms. **Cons:** no children under 18; dress code at all restaurants; huge property means walking long distances. $ *Rooms from: $684* ✉ *Carretera 307, Km 306.5, Punta Maroma* ☎ *984/877–3600, 866/467–3273 in U.S.* ⊕ *www.secretsresorts.com* ➲ *412 rooms* ⦿ *All-Inclusive.*

🏃 Activities

SPAS
Blue Diamond Spa

SPAS | Exclusively for guests of the Blue Diamond resort, this 25,000-square-foot spa merges ancient Maya philosophy with Asian healing rituals. Both the design and philosophy are inspired by the Maya healing elements of water, air, fire, and earth. Signature treatments include Four Hand Harmony (a four-hands massage), Temazcal Ceremony (a ritual guided by a Maya shaman), and Peace Stone Ritual (a stone massage to balance energy levels). Scrubs and wraps made with chocolate and coffee are also popular. Body treatments, ranging from one to six hours, take place in jungle palapas, Thai suites, or garden villas. Travelers who've spent too long basking in the sun can try the sunburn remedy wrap and hydrating facial. ✉ *Blue Diamond Riviera Maya, Carretera 307, Km 298, Punta Bete* ☎ *984/206–4100* ⊕ *bluediamondluxury-boutiquehotel.com.*

Mayakoba

10 km (6 miles) north of Playa del Carmen.

Mayakoba (meaning "village of water") is home to four of the world's most exclusive resorts—the Banyan Tree Mayakoba, Fairmont Mayakoba, Rosewood Mayakoba, and the newly added Andaz Mayakoba. They are connected by a network of canals that inspire the property's tag line, "the Venice of the Caribbean." Aside from luxury lodgings, this 1,600-acre enclave supports mangrove forests, freshwater lagoons, beach dunes, and sunken cenotes; the resident wildlife includes monkeys, turtles, crocodiles, and 160 species of birds. Here, spas are perched amid jungle treetops, and thatch-roof boats drift between limestone waterways.

GETTING HERE AND AROUND
The only way to reach this resort community is by car. From Playa del Carmen, head north on Carretera 307 for approximately 15 minutes; after passing the entrance for Grand Velas, turn right at Km 298 into Mayakoba. From

Cancún, take Carretera 307 south to the east turnoff at Km 298. The entrance is marked by a large metal gate with silver lettering. Security guards will direct you to the property of your choice. Access to hotels, restaurants, spas, and the golf course are permitted by reservation only. Cars are banned, but guests can explore the jungle habitat by golf cart or bike (a paved trail connects the four properties); there's also a complimentary eco-boat that cruises through 11 km (7 miles) of waterways.

🍴 Restaurants

Agave Azul
$$$ | ASIAN FUSION | There's more to Agave Azul than those sweeping lagoon and mangrove views. The glass-walled restaurant at the elegant Rosewood Mayakoba is hands down the best place to go for fresh sushi and premium tequila. **Known for:** romantic setting; more than 100 varieties of tequila; fresh fish. $ *Average main: MP368* ✉ *Rosewood Mayakoba, Carretera 307, Km 298, Mayakoba* ☎ *984/875–8000* ⊕ *www.rosewoodhotels.com* ☉ *No lunch.*

🛏 Hotels

Andaz Mayakoba Resort
$$$$ | RESORT | FAMILY | The most recent addition to the Mayakoba ultra-luxury universe at the heart of the Riviera Maya, this sleek resort keeps with the tradition that says that Mayakoba hotels are among the best in the country. **Pros:** PGA golf club next-door; all-inclusive package available; walk-in rain showers. **Cons:** lagoon-front rooms get a lot of mosquitoes; transportation inside the resort takes its time; not all rooms are beach-front. $ *Rooms from: $400* ✉ *Carretera 307 Km 298, Mayakoba* ☎ *984/149–1234* ⊕ *hyatt.com* ⬩ *214 rooms* 🍴 *No Meals.*

The Rosewood Mayakoba is one of the Riviera Maya's most elegant resorts.

Banyan Tree Mayakoba

$$$$ | **RESORT** | This Thai chain has brought its own traditions to Mexico's Riviera with stunning results: in addition to vaulted ceilings, lounge areas, dining rooms, private gardens, and Talavera earthenware sinks, all rooms have outdoor bathtubs and private 376-foot swimming pools—a unique perk. **Pros:** top-notch spa; world-class service; excellent food. **Cons:** not many activities; fee to use bicycles on property; small kids club. [$] *Rooms from: $1029* ✉ *Carretera 307, Km 298, Mayakoba* ☎ *984/877–3688* 🌐 *www.banyantree.com* 🛏 *118 rooms* 🍴 *No Meals.*

Fairmont Mayakoba

$$$$ | **RESORT** | Set under a mangrove canopy, this sprawling luxury resort sets new standards in the Riviera Maya for sustainability and comfort. **Pros:** free shuttle to neighboring properties; all-inclusive plan available Oct.–May; bird-watching tours. **Cons:** limited free hours at kids club; some rooms lack water views; 20-minute walk from lobby to ocean. [$] *Rooms from: $470* ✉ *Carretera 307, Km 298, Mayakoba* ☎ *984/206–3000, 800/540–6088 in U.S.* 🌐 *www.fairmont.com/mayakoba* 🛏 *401 rooms* 🍴 *No Meals.*

★ Rosewood Mayakoba

$$$$ | **RESORT** | **FAMILY** | From the moment you set foot on the palapa-roofed boat that brings you to your room's private dock, the Rosewood transports you to an exotic world. **Pros:** free kids' club; check-in takes place on the boat; extraordinary spa. **Cons:** narrow beach; no meals included; limited food options. [$] *Rooms from: $1,100* ✉ *Carretera 307, Km 298, Mayakoba* ☎ *984/875–8000, 877/737–7538 in U.S.* 🌐 *www.rosewoodmayakoba.com* 🛏 *130 suites* 🍴 *No Meals.*

Activities

GOLF

El Camaleón Mayakoba

GOLF | Designed by the legendary Greg Norman, El Camaleón's 18-hole course is back-dropped by jungle, mangrove, and sea. It is home to Mexico's only

PGA tour event—the OHL Classic at Mayakoba, held in November. The layout is exceptional, from the first hole with a cenote in the middle of the fairway to the par 3s on the back with ocean views. Throughout the perfectly manicured course, each hole has a minimum of five tee blocks, so there is distance for every skill level. Holes 7 and 15 skirt the ocean; Hole 17 plays directly between a limestone canal and the Fairmont Mayakoba Resort. ⊠ *Carretera 307, Km 298, Mayakoba* ☎ *984/206–4653* ⊕ *www. mayakobagolf.com* ⊰ *$239 for 18 holes* ⅃. *18 holes. 7024 yards. Par 72.*

SPAS
Banyan Tree Spa
SPAS | Built over freshwater lagoons, the Banyan Tree Spa draws on centuries-old Asian traditions. The therapists (most of whom are from Thailand) begin with a heavenly footbath, followed by your choice of Asian-flavored healing treatments, including scrubs with turmeric, lemongrass, or green tea. Treatments take place in private pavilions, each with its own steam room, shower, and outdoor Jacuzzi enclosed by bamboo walls. Unique to Banyan Tree are its signature Rainmist Steam Bath and the romantic couples' Rainforest Experience, which combines hydrotherapy with infrared light to release tension and revitalize the body. ⊠ *Banyan Tree Resort, Carretera 307, Km 298, Mayakoba* ☎ *984/877–3688* ⊕ *www.banyantree.com.*

★ Sense A Rosewood Spa
SPAS | Rosewood's 17,000-square-foot spa is on its very own jungle-covered island. Wooden walkways lead to a swimming pool and limestone cenote, which is fed by subterranean springs. Many treatments, such as the *temazcal* ritual and the Mayakoba ancient massage, incorporate the Mayan tradition of aligning the energies of the body in rhythmic harmony. The *chaya*-mojito body scrub and antiaging facial are both heavenly. Nonguest visitors can book a

treatment, then enjoy the spa facilities, including the gym, sauna, Jacuzzi, plunge pool, and the eucalyptus steam room for free. ⊠ *Rosewood Mayakoba, Carretera 307, Km 298, Mayakoba* ☎ *984/875–8000* ⊕ *www.rosewoodhotels.com.*

Willow Stream Spa
SPAS | It's easy to lose yourself (literally) within the 20,000-square-foot spa at the Fairmont Mayakoba. Signature treatments include the Mexican stone massage, the Mayan clay massage, and the Cha Chac Rain ritual (a massage that takes place on a seven-jet Vichy table). Weary travelers will want to try the Deep Sleep treatment, a massage that purports to reverse the negative effects of flying and time zone changes. After a gym workout, ease your muscles at the rooftop vitality pool. ⊠ *Fairmont Mayakoba, Carretera 307, Km 298* ☎ *984/206–3000* ⊕ *fairmont.com.*

Punta Bete (Xcalacoco)

6 km (4 miles) north of Playa del Carmen.

Beyond Punta Maroma, a river spills into the sea, dividing the coastline. South of the split, Playa Xcalacoco *(scala-coco)* is a 7-km-long (5½-mile-long) beach dotted with bungalows; small, exclusive resort hotels; and thatch-roof restaurants, backing into dense jungle. The beach is beautiful, a more natural extension of Playa del Carmen, but the shore can be rocky. Some hotels here supply water shoes for swimming, and the Viceroy has a dock to enter deeper water.

GETTING HERE AND AROUND
Driving north from Playa del Carmen, turn right at the Coca-Cola factory and follow the road east. Heading south from Cancún on Carretera 307, turn at the huge sign for the Princess Resort at Km 296 to reach Petit Lafitte, Cocos Cabanas, the Viceroy, and the beach. (To reach Le Rêve, you'll have to take the

road about 100 yards south, marked with a blue sign for Azul Fives condos.) Punta Bete has few shops, bars, or restaurants outside of the hotels; however, there is a convenience store and a pizzeria on the way to Le Rêve.

🏖 Beaches

If long walks on the beach are your thing, you'll love the 6-km (4-mile) stretch from Playa Xcalacoco to Playa del Carmen. Although delightfully deserted, the beach itself is not the area's best; the sand is somewhat coarse and often draped in sea grass. There's decent snorkeling, however, and the isolation is unbeatable. Plus, it's a way to explore Playa from Xcalacoco without bumping over the jungle road.

🏨 Hotels

Coco's Cabañas

$ | **B&B/INN** | **FAMILY** | Tranquility and seclusion are the name of the game in these bright, cozy bungalows located a stone's throw from the beach. **Pros:** good pizza; friendly staff; suites include kitchenette. **Cons:** not directly on the beach; tons of mosquitoes; tiny pool. ⓢ *Rooms from: $95 ⊠ Carretera 307, Km 296, Playa del Carmen ⊹ Take the paved road at Princess Resort and follow signs. Turn left onto the dirt road. Cocos Cabanas will be on your right. ☎ 998/874–7056 ⊕ www. cocoscabanas.com ⇆ 6 rooms* ⃝⃝| *Free Breakfast.*

Grand Velas Riviera Maya

$$$$ | **ALL-INCLUSIVE** | **FAMILY** | This all-inclusive resort offers Mexican luxury at its best with everything you may have in mind: top-notch gastronomy, stylish rooms, certified Blue Flag beach, outstanding spa, and lots of activities for all ages. **Pros:** stunning spa with hydrotherapy circuit; infinity pools with volcanic stones; kids and teens clubs. **Cons:** huge property means long walks; common

---

Antojería Night 🍴

Viceroy Riviera Maya (☎ 800/578–0281, ⊕ www.viceroyhotelsandresorts.com) offers a wide array of traditional Mexican street food every Tuesday at 6:30 pm. The resort's chef will reveal his own modern interpretation of the famous Mexican *antojitos*. By reservation only.

---

areas can get too crowded at times; away from downtown Playa. ⓢ *Rooms from: $1300 ⊠ Carretera 307 Km 62, Punta Bete ☎ 322/226–8689 ⊕ rivieramaya.grandvelas.com ⇆ 506 rooms* ⃝⃝| *All-Inclusive.*

Le Rêve Boutique Beachfront Hotel

$ | **HOTEL** | At the end of a short, bumpy dirt road, this secluded little resort seems tailor-made for a romantic getaway. **Pros:** all rooms have balcony or garden; free use of kayaks, iPad, and snorkel gear; all-inclusive meal plan available. **Cons:** time-share sales pitch; small resort means few amenities; dirt access road full of potholes. ⓢ *Rooms from: $69 ⊠ Carretera 307, Km 295, Playa del Carmen ⊹ From Carretera 307, turn at Azul Fives highway sign and follow signs ☎ 984/206–3295 ⊕ www.hotellereve. com ⇆ 23 rooms* ⃝⃝| *No Meals.*

Petit Lafitte

$$$ | **HOTEL** | **FAMILY** | Named after the famous pirate, this warm and family-friendly resort has multi-unit cabanas plus freestanding bungalows on the beach's north end that are more private and charming. **Pros:** kids love the small animal refuge; breakfast and dinner included; peaceful atmosphere. **Cons:** no TVs in bungalows; mosquitoes; rocky beach. ⓢ *Rooms from: $215 ⊠ Carretera 307, Km 296, Punta Bete ⊹ From*

Carretera 307, turn onto the paved road for the Princess Resort and follow the signs to Petit Lafitte ☎ 984/877–4000 🌐 www.petitlafitte.com 🛏 55 rooms 🍴 Free Breakfast.

★ The Viceroy Riviera Maya

$$$$ | RESORT | Punta Bete's most luxurious jungle-beach resort is as romantic and exotic as ever. **Pros:** several meal plans available; romantic and private; luxurious villas. **Cons:** rocky beach; bugs in jungle setting; no children under 14. *[$] Rooms from: $595 ✉ Playa Xcalacoco, Carretera 307, Km 296, Punta Bete ✥ From Carretera 307, turn onto the paved road for Princess Resort and follow the signs to the Viceroy ☎ 984/877–3000 🌐 www.viceroyrivieramaya.com 🛏 41 villas 🍴 Free Breakfast.*

Activities

SPAS

Wayak Spa

SPAS | Although not as grandiose as most spas in the Riviera Maya, this small spot (meaning "the dreamer") utilizes natural surroundings to create a unique pampering experience. From the shaman who greets you with a purifying waft of cobal smoke to the treatment rooms oriented toward sun, moon, and stars, the Wayak Spa makes a point of reminding you that you're in the land of the Maya. Opt for massages in jungle palapa huts surrounded by waterfalls (and mosquito curtains) or a purifying steam bath with a heavenly oculus. Client favorites include the honey-citrus scrub and seaweed body wrap. The black lava treatment infuses minerals in a three-step process including a body scrub, hydration, and a heated wrap. *✉ Viceroy Riviera Maya Resort, Carretera 307, Km 296, Playa del Carmen ✥ From Carretera 307, turn onto the paved road at Princess Resort and follow the signs to the Viceroy. ☎ 984/877–3000 🌐 www.viceroyhotelsandresorts.com.*

Playa del Carmen

68 km (42 miles) south of Cancún.

Welcome to the party! "Playa," currently Latin America's fastest-growing community, has a population of more than 150,000 and an international flavor lent by the *estadounidenses* (United States citizens), Canadians, and Europeans who have been moving here since the early 1990s. Full of lively bars, restaurants, beach clubs, shops, and hotels, its eminently walkable downtown is one of the few places on the Riviera Maya where you can have a car-free vacation.

Sunbathe and swim at trendy beach clubs by day, then drink and dance at nightclubs until the sun comes up and start all over again. In between, there's an enjoyable array of diversions along Avenida 5, a pedestrian-only cobbled street that is the town's main drag. Its southern section, from about Calle 4 to Constituyentes, is busy, noisy, and sometimes rowdy—the place to go for nightlife, tequila shots, and souvenir shopping. Its quieter, more upscale northern end, north of Constituyentes up to about Calle 38, is the place for chic cafés and stylish boutiques. Rapid development means a decline in Mexican culture, with chain stores and cheap souvenirs emerging on every corner (Starbucks junkies can easily get their fix). It also means businesses open and close monthly, surviving on the hope they can offer a better service than their neighbors.

Although building-height restrictions have helped to keep Playa from turning into the next Cancún, you'll have to leave town to get off the beaten path. Much of the area is developed, most recently by a slew of all-inclusive resorts opening up on the city's outskirts. If you plan on leaving the town center, be aware of your surroundings.

GETTING HERE AND AROUND

Driving from Cancún airport, follow the signs on Carretera 307. Shortly before town, take the overpass up and descend at the Avenida Constituyentes exit. Turn left under the overpass and follow Constituyentes into town. The trip takes about an hour. Note that there are several rather intimidating police checkpoints as you approach Playa del Carmen from the highway. Officers occasionally check vehicles at random, especially at night.

If you are coming from Cancún by taxi, expect to pay MX$813–MX$1,220. Shared vans from the airport generally cost MX$338 per person; if you're traveling with a group or even find some other Playa-bound travelers at the airport, a van can be a good way to go.

Buses traveling south from Cancún stop at Playa del Carmen's bus terminal at Avenida 20 and Calle 12, a short walk from downtown and the main drag, Avenida 5 (known as "la Quinta"). Buses headed to Cancún from Playa del Carmen use the main bus terminal at Avenida Juárez and Avenida 5. ADO (⊕ www. ado.com.mx) runs express, first-class, and second-class buses to major destinations.

Colectivos stop on Calle 2 a few blocks (and an easy walk) from Avenida 5.

The town is set up on a grid system that's easy to navigate, if you know the rules. North–south avenidas are numbered in multiples of five, with Avenida 1 along the beach, and then moving westward through Avenidas 5, 10, 15, 20, and so on. East–west calles are even numbers only, starting with Calle 2 and progressing northward through 4, 6, 8, and so on. The Playacar resort development is south of the numbered calles, starting at Avenida Juárez. To get there from Cancún, stay on the highway past the Constituyentes exit and turn left after the overpass at the Playacar sign.

In Playa del Carmen, parking is prohibited at yellow curbs. If you're ticketed, your license plate will be taken to a nearby police station and returned only after the fine has been paid.

⭐ Beaches

Playa del Carmen is famous for its pristine beaches, which have various access points staggered between the hotels on Avenida 5. Of course, it is equally famous for its thriving nightlife, and the trendy beach clubs here—all located in central Playa del Carmen—offer the best of both. The combination of DJ music, cocktails, and twentysomethings makes these open-air bars a can't-miss for young singles. Outside resorts, they're also the only places you'll find beach amenities.

There are beach clubs all the way from Calle 8 to Calle 46, the hottest being at Mamita's and Kool beach between Calles 26 and 30. (In between, you can also find little ad hoc massage places for about MX$542 per hour.) Coco Beach, where Calle 46 meets the ocean, is popular with snorkelers drawn to the outer Chunzubul Reef. For deserted strands, head even farther north, where the waves are small and the water is shallow.

The southern beaches of Playacar extending to the ferry dock at Avenida Benito Juárez are shored up against erosion with buried sandbags, but there's still a sharp drop-off from the beach level to the water; beaches north of the ferry dock are more level. Although all local strands are technically open to the public, those in Playacar are difficult to access since they are dominated by all-inclusive resorts. You also won't find any beach clubs in Playacar.

Although Playa's beaches lack protective outer reefs, the strong wind and waves make these areas great for water sports. For an underwater adventure, organize a

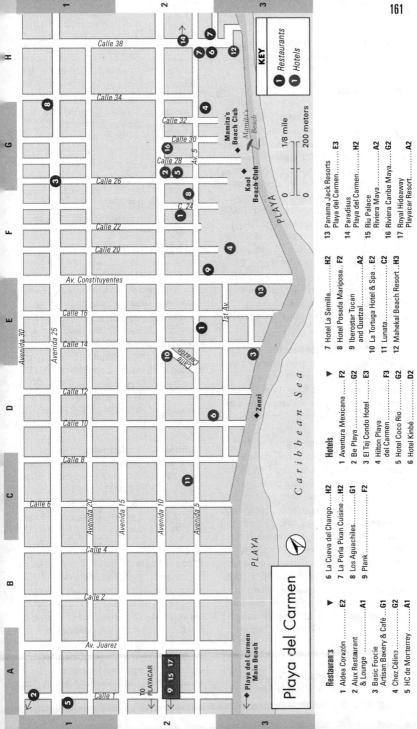

Playa del Carmen

Restaurants ▶

1 Aldea Corazón........**E2**
2 Alux Restaurant
 & Lounge **A1**
3 Basic Foocie
 Artisan Bakery & Café...**G1**
4 Chez Céline............**G2**
5 HC de Morterrey **A1**
6 La Cueva del Chango.....**H2**
7 La Perla Pixan Cuisine ...**H2**
8 Los Aguachiles............**G1**
9 Plank.........................**F2**

Hotels ▶

1 Aventura Mexicana **F2**
2 Be Playa **G2**
3 El Taj Condo Hotel........**E3**
4 Hilton Playa
 del Carmen................**F3**
5 Hotel Coco Rio............**G2**
6 Hotel Kinbé **D2**
7 Hotel La Semilla.........**H2**
8 Hotel Posada Mariposa...**F2**
9 Iberostar Tucan
 and Quetzal...............**A2**
10 La Tortuga Hotel & Spa ..**E2**
11 Lunata.......................**C2**
12 Mahekal Beach Resort ...**H3**
13 Panama Jack Resorts
 Playa del Carmen........**E3**
14 Paradisus
 Playa del Carmen........**H2**
15 Riu Palace
 Riviera Maya **A2**
16 Riviera Caribe Maya......**G2**
17 Royal Hideaway
 Playacar Resort...........**A2**

KEY

① Restaurants
① Hotels

Caribbean Sea

PLAYA

161

tour with one of the local dive companies that will take you to outer reefs and cenotes.

Mamita's Beach

BEACH | This stretch of beach north of the ferry dock, from Constituyentes to Calle 38, is known to locals as Mamita's, although it also encompasses Kool beach club and the Royal and Mahekal hotels. Independent of the main beach's drop-off (and the sandbags that are sometimes visible there), it's a lovely straight stretch of flat sand and clear water, which you'll share with lots of other visitors. The trade-off is that Wave Runners, which are largely absent from the main beach, are very present here. It's a good spot for fun in the sun, not seclusion. **Amenities:** food and drink; toilets; lifeguards; water sports. **Best for:** partiers; swimming. ⊠ *Between Constituyentes and Calle 38, Playa del Carmen.*

Playa del Carmen Main Beach

BEACH | **FAMILY** | The community's most central section of beach stretches from the ferry docks up to Calle 14 at Panama Jack Resort, a swath of deep white sand licked by turquoise water. The beach and water are clean, but there is some boat traffic that makes swimming less idyllic. Snorkelers aren't likely to see much here, but you can't beat the beach for convenience: countless bars and restaurants are a short walk away on 5th Avenue, masseurs compete (discreetly) to knead out your kinks, and it's easy to find a dive shop ready to take you out to sea. The closer you get to the docks, the more people you'll find. If you're looking for seclusion, head farther north outside Playa del Carmen. **Amenities:** food and drink; water sports; lifeguards. **Best for:** swimming; walking. ⊠ *Between ferry docks and Calle 14, Playa del Carmen*

BEACH CLUBS

Kool Beach

BEACH | A giant sparkling KOOL sign marks the entrance to this hip, glitzy beach club across from Mamita's. Playa's party crowd loves Kool for its vast ocean-view terrace, two bars, international restaurant, massage palapa, and access to a catamaran just steps from the sun beds. A lounger by the pool runs MX$350 and MX$725 will get you a front-row spot on the beach. Both amounts are fully refundable as long as you spend that much on food and drinks. **Amenities:** food and drink; showers; toilets. **Best for:** partiers. ⊠ *Calle 28 at the beach, Playa del Carmen* ☎ *984/873–1255* ⊕ *www. koolbeachclub.com.mx* ⊠ *Starting at MX$350.*

Mamita's Beach Club

BEACH | Accessible by way of Calle 28, this is Playa's hottest spot to catch some rays. You can rent an umbrella and two chairs (the smallest beachfront package) for MX$600; MX$3,500 will get you a plush, shady couch in the sand (and a refund of up to MX$3,000 if you purchase that much in drinks). Expect to pay around MX$165 for a cocktail and MX$60 for a beer. Guests can relax in the VIP area while a DJ spins trance and techno beside the freshwater pool. Facilities include three restaurants, four bars, two swimming pools, and a second-floor Champagne bar. **Amenities:** food and drink; toilets; water sports. **Best for:** partiers. ⊠ *Calle 28 at the beachfront, Playa del Carmen* ☎ *984/803–2867* ⊕ *facebook. com/MamitasBeachClub* ⊠ *Starting at MX$600, with partial refunds with food or drink purchase.*

★ Zenzi

BEACH | This beach club and restaurant is one of the few open every day from morning (8:30 am) to late (2 am). Take a dip in the ocean and then catch some rays on one of the sun beds or chaise longues. When the sun goes down, there is live music, shows, and salsa lessons on the beach. **Amenities:** food and drink; toilets. **Best for:** partiers; swimming. ⊠ *Calle 10 at the beach, Playa*

del Carmen ☎ 984/803–5738 ⊕ *www.
zenzi-playa.com* 🍴 *Free with purchase of
food or drink.*

🍴 Restaurants

Aldea Corazón

$$$ | MEXICAN | Playa's most dramatically
sited restaurant sits atop a small cenote
in a vast jungly garden full of strangler
vines and Mayan ruins—right in the mid-
dle of Avenida 5. Designed in accordance
with Maya building practices, it's a feast
for the eyes, with living "green walls"
covered with plants, a bar built on a
stone wall, and a park in back that makes
for a romantic setting at night (bring bug
spray). **Known for:** jicama tacos; bottled
water filtered from the cenote; exotic
jungle setting. $ *Average main: MP345*
☒ *Av. 5 between Calles 14 and 16, Playa
del Carmen* ☎ 984/803–1942 ⊕ *facebook.
com/aldeacorazon.*

Alux Restaurant & Lounge

$$$$ | ECLECTIC | Although this restaurant
is a 10-minute drive from downtown, its
location in an underground cavern makes
it extremely popular. A candlelit rock
stairway leads to a setting that's part
Carlsbad Caverns, part *The Flintstones.*
Some of the "cavernous" rooms are for
lounging, some for drinking, some for
eating, some for dancing. **Known for:**
cenote duck; a unique location inside
a cave; chile Mexico lindo. $ *Average
main: MP500* ☒ *Av. Juárez between
Calles 65 and 70, Playa del Carmen*
☎ 984/206–1401 ⊕ *www.aluxrestaurant.
com/en/* ⊗ *No lunch.*

★ Basic Foodie Artisan Bakery & Café

$ | BAKERY | FAMILY | Basic Foodie is that
cool bakery we all wish we had in our
neighborhood, as its artisan bakery has
no equal in town, and the rest of its
menu caters to organic-minded, vegan,
and gluten-free customers. A modern
design and laidback atmosphere (plus
a reliable Wi-Fi connection), mean the

place has become a magnet for hipsters,
digital nomads, and the like. **Known
for:** organic smoothies; wide variety of
handmade bread; vegetarian molletes
(baguette w/beans Mexican style). $ *Av-
erage main: MP120* ☒ *Avenida 25, entre
calle 26 y calle 28, Fracc. La Toscana*
☎ 984/182–5772 ⊕ *facebook.com/basic-
foodie* ⊗ *No dinner.*

★ Chez Céline

$$ | FRENCH | Céline's fresh-baked breads
and pastries bring honor to France, espe-
cially exquisite desserts like the classic
lemon tart and bold passion-fruit crème
brûlée. Classic bistro fare—including
quiche Lorraine and flavorful croque mad-
ames—make for a light lunch *comme il
faut.* **Known for:** pastries and sweets to
eat in or take away; French bistro-style
croques; quiche Lorraine. $ *Average
main: MP140* ☒ *Av. 5 at Calle 34, Playa
del Carmen* ☎ 984/803–3480 ⊕ *www.
chezceline.com.mx.*

HC de Monterrey

$ | MEXICAN | Follow your nose to this
Mexican grill house, where locals gather
for some of the best-tasting steak in
town. Far from romantic, the open-air
restaurant is filled with the sounds of
mariachi music blaring from the radio;
a mounted bull's head hangs above the
plastic tables and chairs. **Known for:** tasty
arrachera; the best-tasting steak in town;
ample portions. $ *Average main: MP95*
☒ *Calle 1, between Avs. 20 and 25, Playa
del Carmen* ☎ 984/169–1347 ⊗ *Closed
Mon.*

★ La Cueva del Chango

$$$ | MEXICAN | This Playa institution, in
a funky jungle garden with fountains,
palmettos, and a rambling koi pond, is
a favorite breakfast spot. The well-pre-
pared, authentic Mexican selections
include multiple styles of *chilaquiles,* a
tart mix of meat, sauce, and egg on a
bed of tortillas that will have you skipping
lunch. **Known for:** enchiladas with mole;
chilaquiles, served spicy or mild; good

coffee. $ *Average main: MP224* ✉ *Calle 38, between Av. 5 and the beach, Playa del Carmen* ☎ *984/147–0271* ⊕ *www. lacuevadelchango.com* ⊗ *No dinner Sun.*

La Perla Pixan Cuisine

$$$ | **MEXICAN** | **FAMILY** | If you want to try authentic Mexican and pre-Hispanic cuisine, La Perla Pixan is the place for you with its wide variety of tradition-al specialties such as *pozole* (and its vegetarian option), *barbacoa, enchiladas, tlayudas*, and more. Look for the week-end brunch buffet, and the extraordinary variety of mezcal cocktails. **Known for:** vegetarian pozole (traditional Mexican stew); pre-Hispanic cuisine; mezcal cock-tails. $ *Average main: MP220* ✉ *Calle 38, entre Av. 5 and the beach, Fracc. La Toscana* ☎ *984/120–2616* ⊕ *facebook. com/Laperlapixan* ⊗ *Closed Mon.*

Los Aguachiles

$$ | **MEXICAN** | This upscale taquería is an anchor of Playa's alternative culinary scene, reimagining tacos sautéed in olive oil and topped with cucumber or straw-berry-habanero salsa. Local favorites include shrimp tacos with "black gold" (beans), fish ceviche with green salsa, and fish tacos wrapped in your choice of corn tortilla, flour tortilla, or a giant leaf of Bibb lettuce. **Known for:** shrimp tacos with black gold (beans); unusual salsas; a new, modern take on tacos. $ *Average main: MP150* ✉ *Calle 34 at Av. 25, Playa del Carmen* ☎ *984/859–1442, 984/803–1583* ⊕ *facebook.com/LosAguachilesRM.*

★ Plank

$$$ | **STEAKHOUSE** | The name says it all at this New York–inspired restaurant where entrées are grilled on wooden planks or Himalayan salt blocks. The smoky flavors of cedar, maple, hickory, and oak come through in signature dishes like grilled salmon or beef Wellington encased in braided dough. **Known for:** grilled salmon; entrées grilled on wooden planks; beef Wellington in braided dough. $ *Average main: MP340* ✉ *Calle 16, between Avs. 5*

and 1, Playa del Carmen ☎ *984/135–1648* ⊕ *www.plank.mx* ⊗ *No lunch.*

🛏 Hotels

PLAYA DEL CARMEN

Aventura Mexicana

$ | **HOTEL** | This small, colorful inn three blocks from the beach is split in two, with a family-friendly side and a separate adults-only area, both with pools. **Pros:** good restaurant; discounts at Kool Beach Club; friendly staff. **Cons:** no ocean views; open shower layout in some rooms; patchy Wi-Fi. $ *Rooms from: $90* ✉ *Calle 24, between Avs. 5 and 10, Playa del Carmen* ☎ *800/537–4197 in the U.S., 984/873–1876 in Mexico* ⊕ *www.aven-turamexicana.com* ⤳ *49 rooms* ⦿ *Free Breakfast.*

Be Playa

$$ | **HOTEL** | This funky boutique hotel melds retro vintage with a touch of modern, from the red vinyl couches in the lobby all the way up to the exceed-ingly cool rooftop pool bar, where tables and chairs wade in the water. **Pros:** free use of bikes; creative design; good views from rooftop bar. **Cons:** rooms don't have ocean views; four blocks from beach; bland breakfast. $ *Rooms from: $140* ✉ *Calle 26, between Avs. 5 and 10, Playa del Carmen* ☎ *877/265–4139* ⊕ *www. beplaya.com* ⤳ *23 rooms* ⦿ *Free Breakfast.*

★ El Taj Condo Hotel

$$$ | **APARTMENT** | This pair of curvaceous buildings contains stylish condo rentals—each complete with a fully equipped kitchen and washer-dryer—with Balinese furnishings. **Pros:** free access to neigh-boring fitness club, including fitness classes; the property is right on the beach; private kitchens. **Cons:** stale smell in some units; units are mostly two- and three-bedroom; three-night minimum stay in high season (though they're flexible if not fully booked). $ *Rooms from: $277* ✉ *1 Norte Esquina Calle*

La Tortuga Hotel & Spa

14, Playa del Carmen ☎ *984/141–3874, 866/479–2738* 🌐 *www.eltaj.com* 🛏 *57 units* 🍴 *Free Breakfast.*

Hilton Playa del Carmen
$$$$ | **ALL-INCLUSIVE** | If you are looking for the royal treatment, this massive, colonial-style resort has everything from laundry service and a 24-hour on-site doctor to in-room Jacuzzi tubs and fully stocked minibars. **Pros:** live-entertainment evenings; hydrotherapy at the spa included; on Playa's best beach. **Cons:** pool area can get too crowded; adults only (18-plus); most rooms face the garden. [$] *Rooms from: $383* ✉ *Av. Constituyentes 2, Playa del Carmen* ☎ *984/877–2900, 833/844–5866 in U.S.* 🌐 *hiltonbyplaya.com* 🛏 *524 rooms* 🍴 *All-Inclusive.*

Hotel Coco Rio
$ | **HOTEL** | A tropical garden beckons near the entry to this small, quiet hotel on a tree-lined street in Playa's north end. **Pros:** pleasant staff; great value; comfortable beds. **Cons:** patchy Wi-Fi in rooms; no breakfast; no ocean views. [$] *Rooms from: $80* ✉ *Calle 26, between Avs. 5 and 10, Playa del Carmen* ☎ *984/879–3361* 🌐 *www.hotelcocorio.com* 🛏 *18 rooms* 🍴 *No Meals.*

Hotel Kinbé
$ | **HOTEL** | An interesting fusion of Mayan and contemporary decor, budget-friendly Kinbé (which means "path to the sun") is steps from the beach. **Pros:** in the heart of Playa; discounts at nearby beach clubs; great value. **Cons:** some street noise; lots of stairs; small rooms. [$] *Rooms from: $65* ✉ *Calle 10 Norte, between Avs. 1 and 5, Playa del Carmen* ☎ *984/873–0441, 984/873–0443* 🌐 *www.kinbe.com* 🛏 *29 rooms* 🍴 *No Meals.*

Hotel La Semilla
$$ | **B&B/INN** | From the lush jungle courtyard to the airy, stone-walled rooms to the sunny, plush rooftop deck with distant ocean views, this boutique hotel is designed to charm at every turn. **Pros:** beautiful design; free use of bikes; laundry included. **Cons:** no phones or TVs; adults only (18-plus); no pool. [$] *Rooms from: $160* ✉ *Calle 38 North, between*

Av. 5 and the beach, Playa del Carmen ☎ 984/147–3234 🌐 www.hotellasemilla.com 🛏 9 rooms 🍴 Free Breakfast.

Hotel Posada Mariposa

$$ | **HOTEL** | Although it has few facilities, this hotel is still a great value, with impeccable rooms set around an open-air garden courtyard where trees grow past the third floor. **Pros:** beach club discounts; elevator building; cozy setting. **Cons:** no pool or gym; few guest common areas; no breakfast included. [$] *Rooms from: $150 ✉ Av. 5 No. 314, between Calles 24 and 26, Playa del Carmen ☎ 984/878–1016 🛏 30 rooms 🍴 No Meals.*

★ La Tortuga Hotel & Spa

$ | **B&B/INN** | Mosaic stone paths wind through lovely gardens, and colonial-style hardwood furnishings gleam throughout at this inn on a side street. **Pros:** some rooms have rooftop terraces; lovely grounds; intimate atmosphere. **Cons:** spa is a bit kitschy; no kids under 16; not on the beach. [$] *Rooms from: $80 ✉ Av. 10, at the corner of Calle 14, Playa del Carmen ☎ 984/873–1484 🌐 facebook.com/hotellatortuga 🛏 51 rooms 🍴 Free Breakfast.*

Lunata

$$ | **B&B/INN** | An elegant entrance, Spanish-tile floors, a quiet back garden, and hand-tooled furniture from Guadalajara greet you at this classy inn. **Pros:** prime location; intimate setting; warm, welcoming staff. **Cons:** no pool; mediocre breakfast; some nighttime noise from nearby clubs. [$] *Rooms from: $110 ✉ Av. 5, between Calles 6 and 8, Playa del Carmen ☎ 984/873–0884 🌐 www.lunata.com 🛏 10 rooms 🍴 Free Breakfast.*

Mahekal Beach Resort

$$$$ | **RESORT** | With three blocks of beach and grounds that sprawl through sandy beachfront and cool jungle garden, this 196-room resort offers a taste of everything the Riviera geography has to offer. **Pros:** three blocks of beachfront property; free movie nights on the beach; excellent service. **Cons:** large property may feel impersonal to some; no TVs in rooms; lack of privacy on beachfront rooms. [$] *Rooms from: $389 ✉ Calle 38, at the beach, Playa del Carmen ☎ 984/873–0611, 877/235–4452 🌐 www.mahekalbeachresort.com 🛏 196 rooms 🍴 Free Breakfast.*

Panama Jack Resorts Playa del Carmen

$$$ | **RESORT** | **FAMILY** | The family-friendly hotel features a rooftop pool and sky Jacuzzi for the grown-ups and pirate-ship playgrounds, minigolf, and puppet shows for the kids. **Pros:** lots of amenities for kids; complimentary Wi-Fi; central location. **Cons:** laundry costs extra; beach erosion; gaudy style. [$] *Rooms from: $250 ✉ Av. Constituyentes 1, at the beach, ☎ 984/873–4000, 833/266–5757 in the U.S. 🌐 panamajackresorts.com 🛏 287 rooms 🍴 All-Inclusive.*

Paradisus Playa del Carmen

$$$$ | **RESORT** | **FAMILY** | This all-inclusive offers flash and class in a Vegas-meets-cruise-ship environment with 14 restaurants, 11 bars, and nearly 1,000 rooms scattered between two buildings. **Pros:** plenty of children's activities; beautiful swim-up rooms; spa with hydrotherapy circuit. **Cons:** 10-minute drive from downtown Playa; rocky beach; not all restaurants are open to children. [$] *Rooms from: $399 ✉ Av. 5 and Calle 112, Playa del Carmen ☎ 984/877–3900, 929/207–1078 in U.S. 🌐 www.melia.com 🛏 906 rooms 🍴 All-Inclusive.*

Riviera Caribe Maya

$ | **HOTEL** | It may not have the bells and whistles of other Playa hotels, but this small property, on a quiet street two blocks from the beach, is very pleasant. **Pros:** outstanding pool area; huge bathrooms; breezy rooms. **Cons:** minimal street noise; Wi-Fi in common areas only; hard mattresses. [$] *Rooms from: $80 ✉ Av. 10 and Calle 30, Playa del Carmen ☎ 984/873–1193 🌐 www.hotelrivieramaya.com 🛏 25 rooms 🍴 Free Breakfast.*

PLAYACAR

South of downtown Playa del Carmen, the upscale gated community of Playacar is home to a string of all-inclusive resorts, beachfront condos, and rental properties. It also features an 18-hole golf course and the small open-air mall (Plaza Playacar) but is of little interest otherwise. A paved bike path skirts the tree-lined streets of the development, past private neighborhoods, all the way north to downtown Playa and south to the adventure parks Xplor and Xcaret.

Iberostar Tucan and Quetzal

$$$$ | RESORT | FAMILY | This unique all-inclusive resort has preserved its natural surroundings—among the resident animals are flamingos, turtles, toucans, peacocks, and monkeys. **Pros:** tropical setting; great facilities for kids; bicycles for guests. **Cons:** food lacks variety; water at swim-up bar can be chilly; no elevators. [$] *Rooms from: $305* ✉ *Av. Xamanha, Playacar* ☎ *984/877–2000* 🌐 *www.iberostar.com* 🛏 *730 rooms* 🍴 *All-Inclusive.*

Riu Palace Riviera Maya

$$$$ | RESORT | FAMILY | This enormous all-inclusive serves its luxury with an extra helping of glitz, but its breathtaking beach and exceptional service are what really shine. **Pros:** sports bar open nonstop; friendly staff; lots of scheduled activities. **Cons:** no poolside service; reservations needed for certain restaurants; hallways echo at night. [$] *Rooms from: $339* ✉ *Av. Xaman-Ha, Lote 9 and 10, Playacar* ☎ *984/877–2280* 🌐 *www.riu.com* 🛏 *460 rooms* 🍴 *All-Inclusive.*

★ Royal Hideaway Playacar Resort

$$$$ | ALL-INCLUSIVE | Art and antiques from around the world fill the lobby, and streams, waterfalls, and fountains fill the grounds of this 13-acre resort on a stretch of pristine beach. **Pros:** romantic setting; attentive service; taxes and gratuities included. **Cons:** adults only; pool service can be slow; restaurants require reservations. [$] *Rooms from: $376* ✉ *Av Xaman-Ha, Lote 6, Playacar* ☎ *984/873–4500, 800/858–2258* 🌐 *barcelo.com* 🛏 *201 rooms,* 🍴 *All-Inclusive.*

🍸 Nightlife

The club scene is a major draw in the South Beach of Mexico. The action is on Calle 12, lined with nightclubs and lively young things ready to set the night afire. Most clubs are open-air, so this part of town gets very noisy until very late—something to keep in mind if you're planning to stay downtown and actually want to sleep. By day, Playa's lively beach clubs are packed with travelers lounging in the sun or dancing to the sounds of a live DJ. The Riviera Maya Jazz Festival (🌐 *www.rivieramayajazzfestival.com*) splashes cool on Playa's music scene every year during the last week of November.

Alux

DANCE CLUBS | Inside a cavern, Alux has a bar, disco, wine cellar, and restaurant. There's a MX$100 drink minimum. ✉ *Av. Juárez, Playa del Carmen* ☎ *984/206–1401* 🌐 *www.aluxrestaurant.com.*

Bar Ranita

BARS | Attached to the Rana Cansada Hotel, Bar Ranita is a favorite among rowdy expats. The prices are unbeatable, and the margaritas pack a powerful punch. ✉ *Rana Cansada Hotel, Calle 10, between Avs. 5 and 10, Playa del Carmen* ☎ *984/873–0389* 🌐 *www.ranacansada.com.*

CoCo Bongo

DANCE CLUBS | Following the success of its sister property in Cancún, CoCo Bongo has flying acrobats, bar-top conga lines, live bands, and DJs mixing everything from rock to hip-hop. The cover charge includes unlimited drinks. ✉ *Calle 10 at Av. 10, Playa del Carmen* ☎ *984/803–5939* 🌐 *cocobongo.com.*

La Bodeguita del Medio

LIVE MUSIC | Graffiti-styled La Bodeguita del Medio, a franchise of the famous Havana outpost, features live Cuban music Tuesday to Sunday. ⊠ *Av. 5 and Calle 34, Playa del Carmen* ☎ *984/803-3951* ⊕ *www.labodeguitadelmedio.com.mx.*

Mandala

DANCE CLUBS | The biggest, loudest and most expensive party spot on Calle 12, trendy Mandala is divided into a street-level bar, a rooftop terrace, and a dance club; each has its own DJ spinning anything from house and hip-hop to disco and techno. ⊠ *Calle 12, between Avs. 1 and 5, Playa del Carmen* ☎ *998/883-3333* ⊕ *grupomandala.com.mx.*

🛍 Shopping

Avenida 5 between Calles 4 and 38 has the Riviera Maya's best shopping. Small galleries sell original folk art from around Mexico, clothing boutiques offer everything from chic bikinis to tacky tees, and there are stores dedicated to Mexican specialties as varied as silver, chocolate, and tequila. Mexico's upscale Liverpool department store puts in an appearance at Calle 14, and you'll find international brand names like Diesel and Havaianas scattered up and down the avenue.

BOOKS

Librería Mundo

BOOKS | This spot has an extensive selection of books on Mayan culture, along with used English-language books. Profits from all English-language tomes are donated to Mexican schools to buy textbooks. ⊠ *Plaza las Américas, Calle 58 Norte, Playa del Carmen* ☎ *984/109-1566* ⊕ *facebook.com/americaslibreriamundo.*

CRAFTS

Candle Boutique

CRAFTS | The outsized, handmade candles that you see lighting the night so elegantly in Playa's restaurants and hotels are sold at Candle Boutique. ⊠ *Calle 6 Nte, between 55 and 60, Playa del Carmen* ☎ *984/114-9602* ⊕ *candleboutique.mx* ⊘ *Closed Sat.–Sun.*

La Hierbabuena Artesanía

CRAFTS | Owner Melinda Burns offers a collection of fine Mexican clothing and crafts at Hierbabuena. ⊠ *Av. 5 between Calles 8 and 10, Playa del Carmen* ☎ *984/745-0635* ⊕ *facebook.com/tiendalahierbabuena.*

FOOD & DRINKS

Ah Cacao

OTHER FOOD & DRINK | This modish chocolate shop sells Mexico's finest, in bars, tablets, soaps, massage oils, and brownies. Locals swear by the coffee. There are other four branches around Playa del Carmen and Cancún. ⊠ *Avs. 5 and Constituyentes, Playa del Carmen* ☎ *984/803-5748* ⊕ *www.ahcacao.com.*

Bio-Orgánicos Playa del Carmen

OTHER SPECIALTY STORE | From snacks to groceries to organic soaps, lotions, and shampoos, this little shop has a little something for every health-conscious traveler. There's also an organic restaurant attached and another branch at avenida 25 and calle 30. ⊠ *Calle 26 Nte #128, between Avs. 5 and 10, Playa del Carmen* ☎ *984/803-2881.*

Hacienda Tequila

CRAFTS | Over 600 different types of tequila plus an assortment of kitschy Mexican crafts and souvenirs are sold at Hacienda Tequila. Free tastings are available, and the staff would love to share their deep knowledge of tequila making with you. ⊠ *Av. 5 and Calle 14, Playa del Carmen* ☎ *984/128-2195.*

JEWELRY

Ambar Mexicano

JEWELRY & WATCHES | Come here for jewelry crafted of Chiapan amber by a local designer. ⊠ *Av. 5, between Calles 4 and 6, Playa del Carmen* ☎ *984/873-2357.*

MALLS
Paseo del Carmen
SHOPPING CENTER | Upscale, open-air Paseo del Carmen has numerous boutiques—including Zara, Ultrafemme, and Old Navy. Seattle-coffee lovers can get their fix at the Starbucks that dominates the center of the mall. A cobblestone path makes this one of the area's most popular and pleasant shopping destinations. ⊠ *Av 5 Nte 10, Playa del Carmen* ☎ *984/803–3789.*

Plaza Las Américas
MALL | **FAMILY** | This family-friendly mall features restaurants, shops, and cinemas. ⊠ *Av Chemuyil y CTM, Playa del Carmen* ☎ *984/109–2161.*

Plaza Playacar
SHOPPING CENTER | **FAMILY** | This Mexican-colonial-style outdoor mall in Playacar sells handcrafts, clothes, jewelry, and specialty items like tequila and cigars. There is also a Starbucks. ⊠ *Paseo Xaman-Ha, Playacar* ☎ *984/873–0006* ⊕ *www. plazaplayacar.com.*

Quinta Alegría
SHOPPING CENTER | **FAMILY** | This three-story plaza on Playa's main drag houses Sanborn's department store, Victoria's Secret, Forever 21, Nike, Desigual, Levi's, and much more. There's even a Häagen-Dazs where you can cool off with an ice cream before more shopping. ⊠ *Av. 5 at Av. Constituyentes, Playa del Carmen* ☎ *984/211–1573* ⊕ *www.quintaalegria.com.mx.*

Activities

GOLF
Gran Coyote Golf
GOLF | This 18-hole championship course was designed by Nick Price. Not as busy (or expensive) as neighboring courses at Mayakoba or Playacar, Gran Coyote is challenging without being overly intimidating. You'll face a good amount of bunkers and water on the holes. The greens are slow, but the course is well maintained. If you can swing it, opt for the all-inclusive package that covers food and drink. Otherwise greens fees cover only the cart, bottled water, and golf tees. ⊠ *Gran Coyote Golf, Carretera 307, Km 294, Playa del Carmen* ☎ *984/109–6025* ⊕ *grancoyotegolf.com* 🏌 *$210 for 18 holes* 🏌. *18 holes. 7043 yards. Par 71.*

Hard Rock Golf Club Riviera Maya
GOLF | The 18-hole course at the Hard Rock Golf Club Riviera Maya is considered to be one of the most challenging in the region. There's not a ton of water here, but watch out for sand traps and tricky Hole 14. Signature holes are Hole 13 (342 yards, par 4) and Hole 18 (530 yards, par 5). Included in the greens fee is food and drink, which is delivered cart-side every few shots. Plan to lose a few balls during your game as the greens are tight and narrow. The fairways are well manicured and full of wildlife. If it gets too challenging, swing on over to the practice area complete with a driving range and putting green with its own chipping, pitching, and green-side bunker areas. Come after 1 pm for the twilight fee. ⊠ *Paseo Xaman-Ha, near Riu Palace, Playacar* ☎ *998/881–3699* ⊕ *hardrockhotels.com* 🏌 *$250 for 18 holes* 🏌. *18 holes. 7144 yards. Par 72.*

SCUBA DIVING AND SNORKELING
The Abyss
SCUBA DIVING | PADI and SSI affiliated, the Abyss offers introductory courses and dive trips. It also runs dives in Tulum through the cenotes. ⊠ *Av. 1 between Calles 10 and 12,* ☎ *984/876–3285* ⊕ *www.abyssdivecenter.com* 🏊 *2-Tank dive from USD$79.*

Dune Mexico Blue Dream
SCUBA DIVING | Custom snorkel tours in Playa, Laguna Yal-Ku, Akumal, and nearby cenotes are available through Dune Mexico Blue Dream; dive trips to Cozumel are also arranged. ⊠ *Calle 28, Between Av. 1 and Mamitas Beach, Playa del Carmen* ☎ *984/143–7400* ⊕ *www. mexicobluedream.com* 🏊 *From USD$79.*

Tank-Ha Dive Center

SCUBA DIVING | Playa's original dive outfit has PADI-certified teachers and runs diving and snorkeling excursions to the reefs and caverns. Dive packages and Cozumel trips are available, too. ✉ *Av. 1 between Calles 20 and 22, Playa del Carmen* ☎ *984/873–0302* ⊕ *www.tankha.com* ✉ *From USD$89.*

Yucatek Divers

SCUBA DIVING | PADI-affiliated Yucatek Divers offers cenote dives, dive packages, and instruction. A one-tank introductory course costs USD$110; the open water diver training course with 4 dives included costs USD$430. ✉ *Av. 15, between Calles 2 and 4, Playa del Carmen* ☎ *984/803–1363* ⊕ *www.yucatek-divers.com* ✉ *2-tank dives from USD$85.*

SKYDIVING

Skydive Playa

SKYDIVING | Adrenaline junkies can take the plunge high above Playa in a tandem sky dive (where you're hooked up to an instructor the whole time). Jumps take place every hour; reserve at least one day in advance. For an extra MX$2,155, SkyDive Playa will shoot video of your free fall. ✉ *Avenida 15 Sur 131, Playa del Carmen* ☎ *984/187–4868* ⊕ *www.skydive.com.mx* ✉ *USD$269.*

Xcaret

6 km (4 miles) south of Playa del Carmen.

Once a sacred Maya city and port, Xcaret (pronounced *ish*-cah-ret) is now home to two popular parks on a gorgeous stretch of coastline. The 250-acre ecological theme park, simply known as "Xcaret," is the Riviera Maya's most heavily advertised attraction. Billed as "nature's sacred paradise," it has its own published magazines plus a collection of stores. Just 2 km (1 mile) away is Xplor; half the size of Xcaret, this sister property is targeted at extreme-adventure seekers.

Navigating Xcaret ◉

You can easily spend at least a full day at Xcaret. This place is big, so it's a good idea to check the daily activities against a map of the park to organize your time. Plan to be in the general area of an activity before it's scheduled to begin—you'll beat the crowds and avoid having to sprint across the property.

GETTING HERE AND AROUND

If you're driving, the entrance for both parks and the Occidental Grand Xcaret Resort is at Km 282 on Carretera 307. Organized day trips from Cancún will also take you to Xcaret; a cab ride from nearby Playa del Carmen will cost about MX$220.

◉ Sights

★ Xcaret

THEME PARK | FAMILY | Take a small collection of Maya ruins and build a mammoth theme park around them and you have Xcaret, one of the Yucatán Peninsula's most popular destinations. Among its most-visited attractions are the Paradise River raft tour that takes you on a winding, watery journey through the jungle; the Butterfly Pavilion, where thousands of butterflies float dreamily through a botanical garden while New Age music plays in the background; and an ocean-fed aquarium, where you can see local sea life drifting through coral heads and sea fans. The park also has a wild bird breeding aviary, nurseries for abandoned flamingo eggs and sea turtles, and a series of underwater caverns that you can explore by snorkeling or Snuba (a hybrid of snorkeling and scuba). A replica

There's plenty to do and see in Xcaret.

Maya village includes a colorful cemetery with catacomb-like caverns underneath; traditional music and dance ceremonies (including performances by the famed Voladores de Papantla, or Flying Birdmen of Papantla) are performed here at night. But the star performance is the evening "Spectacular Mexico Night Show," which tells the history of Mexico through song and dance. The list of Xcaret's attractions goes on and on: you can visit a dolphinarium, a bee farm, a manatee lagoon, a bat cave, an orchid and bromeliad greenhouse, an edible-mushroom farm, and a small zoo. You can also visit a scenic tower that takes you 240 feet up in the air for a spectacular view of the park. The entrance fee covers only access to the grounds and the exhibits; some other activities and equipment—from sea treks and dolphin tours to lockers and swim gear—are extra. The Plus Pass includes park entrance, lockers, snorkel equipment, food, and drinks. You can buy tickets from any travel agency or major hotel along the coast. You can also book slightly discounted tickets through Xcaret's website. ✉ *Carretera 307, Km 282, Xcaret* ☎ *984/206–0038, 855/326–0682 in U.S.* ⊕ *www.xcaret.com* 🎟 *Basic Pass USD$98; Plus Pass USD$125; Night Pass USD$80.*

Museo de Arte Popular Mexicano

ART MUSEUM | FAMILY | This entrancing folk-art museum is a must for anyone interested in Mexican culture and handicrafts. It's brimming with original works by the country's finest artisans, which are arranged in fascinating tableaux. The collection represents different regions of Mexico—from nativity scenes sculpted out of Oaxaca's clays to the intricate *arbol de la vida* (tree of life) sculptures crafted in Metepec. Children will love the toy room, which includes an impressive display of *alebrijes* (fantastical wood carvings). Since this is one of the many attractions inside Xcaret, the only way to visit the museum is by purchasing a day pass to the theme park. ✉ *Carretera 307, Km 282, at Xcaret, attraction No. 41,*

Xcaret ☎ *998/883–3143* 🌐 *www.xcaret.com* 🎫 *Free with admission to Xcaret.*

Xplor

THEME PARK | FAMILY | Designed for thrill seekers, this 125-acre park features underground rafting in stalactite-studded water caves and cenotes. Swim in a stalactite river, ride in an amphibious vehicle, or soar across the park on 14 of the longest ziplines in Mexico. Daytime admission (valid 9 am to 5 pm) includes all food, drink, and equipment. A separate evening admission from 5:30 to 10:30 pm includes "Xplor Fuego" activities, which includes similar things but with a nighttime theme. Mix-and-match packages can be purchased online to include both day and evening admission and entry to Xcaret next door. ✉ *Carretera 307, Km 282* ☎ *998/883–3143, 855/326–0682 in U.S.* 🌐 *www.xplor.travel* 🎫 *Xplor USD$116; Xplor Fuego USD$98* 🕒 *Closed Sun.*

Hotels

Occidental at Xcaret Destination

$$$$ | ALL-INCLUSIVE | FAMILY | In such an enormous all-inclusive, it's surprising to find the excellent service that you get here. **Pros:** free scuba course; pleasant lagoon; minimum three-night stay includes free entrance to Xcaret. **Cons:** small beach; time-share sales reps give you the hard sell; squawking parrots in the lobby. [$] *Rooms from: $309* ✉ *Carretera 307, Km 282, Xcaret* ☎ *984/871–5400* 🌐 *barcelo.com* 🛏 *765 rooms* 🍴 *All-Inclusive.*

Puerto Aventuras

26 km (16 miles) south of Playa del Carmen.

The most Americanized of all the Riviera Maya's resorts is a 900-acre gated community and golf course more reminiscent of coastal Florida than Mexico. This has its advantages if you want to speak English exclusively and have the option to eat American food. Fatima Bay (the beach in front of the Omni hotel) is glorious, but the town itself is not particularly scenic. The main marina is closed off to boat traffic and is instead home to Dolphin Discovery's dolphins and sea lions, which are fun to watch from the waterside restaurants and benches.

GETTING HERE AND AROUND

Puerto Aventuras is a 20-minute drive south of Playa del Carmen along Carretera 307. Its orientation around a small marina makes it very walkable—it's the sort of place where you can let older kids go off by themselves for the afternoon. Taxis are stationed at the small parking area near the marina outside the Omni hotel. You can also find them outside all major hotels. Taxis from Playa del Carmen cost about MX$338.

Sights

Cenotes Kantún Chi

BODY OF WATER | FAMILY | This Maya-owned and-operated eco-park has cenotes and a few beautiful underground caverns that are great for snorkeling and diving, as well as some small Maya ruins. The place is low-key—a nice break from the crowds. Bring natural mosquito repellent. ✉ *Carretera 307, Km 266, in front of Barceló Hotel, Puerto Aventuras* ☎ *984/803–0143* 🌐 *www.kantunchi.com* 🎫 *USD$71.*

Beaches

Fatima Bay (*Omni Beach*)

BEACH | FAMILY | Although the marina is the main focus here, Puerto Aventuras's beaches are naturally stunning and seldom crowded. The main one, Fatima Bay, commonly referred to as Omni Beach, stretches nearly 3 km (2 miles) south between Chac Hal Al condominiums

Continued on page 178

ANCIENT ARCHITECTS
THE MAYA

Visiting the Yucatán Peninsula and not touring any Mayan sites is like going to Greece and not seeing the Acropolis or the Parthenon. One look at the monumental architecture of the Maya and you might feel transported to another world. The breathtaking structures are even more impressive when you consider that they were built 1,000 to 2,000 years ago or more without iron tools, wheels, pulleys, or beasts of burden—and in terrible heat and difficult terrain.

El Castillo, Tulum,

THE ARCHITECTURAL PERIODS

Calakmul

PRECLASSIC PERIOD: Petén

Between approximately 2000 BC and AD 100, the Maya were centered around the lowlands in the south-central region of Guatemala. Their communities were family-based, and governed by hereditary chiefs; their worship of agricultural gods (such as Chaac, the rain god), who they believed controlled the seasons, led them to chart the movement of heavenly bodies. Their religious beliefs also led them to build enormous temples and pyramids—such as El Mirador, in the Guatemalan lowlands—where sacrifices were made and ceremonies performed to please the gods.

The structures at El Mirador, as well as at the neighboring ruin site of Tikal, were built in what is known today as the Petén style; pyramids were steeply pitched, built on stepped terraces, and decorated with large stucco masks and ornamental (but sometimes "false" or unclimbable) stairways. Petén-style structures were also often roofed with corbeled archways. The Maya began to move northward into the Yucatán during the late part of this period, which is why Petén-style buildings can also be found at Calakmul, just north of the Guatemalan border.

EARLY CLASSIC PERIOD: Río Usumacinta

The Classic Period, often referred to as the "golden age," spanned from about AD 100 to AD 1000. Maya civilization expanded northward and became much more complex. A distinct ruling class emerged and hereditary kings ruled over densely populated jungle cities, filled with increasingly impressive-looking palaces and temples.

During the early part of the Classic Period, Maya architecture began to take on some distinctive characteristics. Build-ers placed their structures on hillsides or crests, and the principal buildings were covered with bas-reliefs carved in stone. The pyramid-top temples had vestibules and rooms with vaulted ceilings; many chamber walls were carved with scenes recounting important events during the reign of the ruler who built the pyramid. Some of the most stunning examples of this style are at the ruins of Palenque, near Chiapas.

Palenque

Chicanná

MID-CLASSIC PERIOD: Río Bec and Chenes

It was during the middle part of the Classic Period (roughly between AD 600 and AD 800) that the Maya presence exploded into the Yucatán Peninsula. Several Maya settlements were estab-lished in what is now Campeche state, including Chicanná and Xpujil, near the southwest corner of the state. The archi-tecture at these sites was built in what is now known as the Río Bec style. As in the earlier Petén style, Río Bec pyramids had steeply pitched sides and ornately decorated foundations. Other Río Bec-style buildings, however, were long, one-story affairs incorporating two or sometimes three tall towers. These tow-ers were typically capped by large roof combs that resembled mini-temples.

During the same part of the Classic Period, a different architectural style, known as Chenes, developed in some of the more northerly Maya cities, such as Hochob. While some Chenes-style structures share the same long, single-story con-struction as Río Bec buildings, others have strikingly different characteristics —like doorways carved in the shape of huge Chaac faces with gaping open mouths.

LATE CLASSIC PERIOD: Puuc and Northeast Yucatán

Chichén Itzá

The fusion of two distinct Maya groups—the Chichén Maya and the Itzás—produced another striking architectural style. This style, known as Northeast Yucatán, is exemplified by the ruins at Chichén Itzá. Here, columns and grand colonnades were introduced. Palaces with row upon row of columns carved in the shape of serpents looked over grand patios, platforms were dedicated to the planet Venus, and pyramids were raised to honor Kukulcán (the plumed serpent god borrowed from the Toltecs, who called him Quetzalcoátl). Northeast Yucatán structures also incorporated carved stone Chacmool figures—reclining statues with offering trays carved in their midsections for sacrificial offerings.

Some of the Yucatán's most spectacular Mayan architecture was built between about AD 800 and AD 1000. By this time, the Maya had spread into territory that is now Yucatán state, and established lavish cities at Labná, Kabah, Sayil, and Uxmal—all fine examples of the Puuc architectural style. Puuc buildings were beautifully proportioned, often designed in a low-slung quadrangle shape that allowed for many rooms inside. Exterior walls were kept plain to show off the friezes above—which were embellished with stone-mosaic gods, geometric designs, and serpentine motifs. Corners were edged with gargoyle-like, curved-nose Chaac figures.

Uxmal

▼
Between 2000 BC and AD 100, the Maya are based in lowlands of south-central Guatemala, and governed by hereditary chiefs.

2000 BC   1000

PETÉN

PRECLASSIC

POSTCLASSIC PERIOD: Quintana Roo Coast

Although Maya culture continued to flourish between ad 1000 and the early 1500s, signs of decline also began to take form. Wars broke out between neighboring city-states, leaving the region vulnerable when the Spaniards began invading in 1521. By 1600, the Spanish had dominated the Maya empire.

Mayan architecture enjoyed its last hurrah during this period, mostly in the region along the Yucatán's Caribbean coast. Known as Quintana Roo Coast architecture, this style can be seen today at the ruins of Tulum. Although the structures here aren't as visually arresting as those at earlier, inland sites, Tulum's location is breathtaking: it's the only major Maya city overlooking the sea.

Tulum

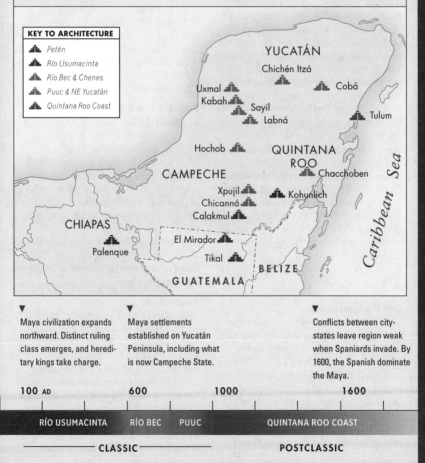

KEY TO ARCHITECTURE
- Petén
- Río Usumacinta
- Río Bec & Chenes
- Puuc & NE Yucatán
- Quintana Roo Coast

YUCATÁN

Chichén Itzá

Uxmal   Cobá
Kabah
Sayil
Labná   Tulum

Hochob   QUINTANA
ROO
CAMPECHE   Chacchoben

Xpujil   Kohunlich
Chicanná
Calakmul

CHIAPAS
El Mirador
Palenque   Tikal   BELIZE

GUATEMALA   Caribbean Sea

Maya civilization expands northward. Distinct ruling class emerges, and hereditary kings take charge.

Maya settlements established on Yucatán Peninsula, including what is now Campeche State.

Conflicts between city-states leave region weak when Spaniards invade. By 1600, the Spanish dominate the Maya.

100 AD   600   1000   1600

RÍO USUMACINTA   RÍO BEC   PUUC   QUINTANA ROO COAST

CLASSIC   POSTCLASSIC

and the Grand Peninsula residence. Its shallow, calm waters are kid-friendly, especially inside the breakwater. Farther out the temperature drops, making for a refreshing swim. To the north is a smaller bay, known as Chan Yu Yum, used by guests of the Catalonia Resort; better beaches lie just south of Puerto Aventuras in the community of Xpu-Há. **Amenities:** food and drink. **Best for:** snorkeling; swimming. ✉ *Behind the Omni Hotel, Puerto Aventuras.*

Paamul Beach

BEACH | FAMILY | Beachcombers, campers, and snorkeling snowbirds love Paamul (pronounced pah- *mool*), a crescent-shaped lagoon 21 km (13 miles) south of Playa del Carmen with clear, placid waters sheltered by a coral reef. Shells, sand dollars, and even glass beads—some from the sunken, 18th-century Spanish galleon *Mantanceros,* which lies off nearby Akumal—wash up onto the sandy parts of the beach. (There's a sandy path into deeper water in front of the restaurant—on the rocks, watch out for sea urchins.) Sea turtles hatch here June to November. If you'd like to stay on this piece of paradise, Hotel and Cabanas Paamul is a laid-back option. **Amenities:** food and drink; toilets; showers; parking (free); water sports. **Best for:** snorkeling; swimming; walking. ✉ *Paamul Bay, Carretera 307 Cancún–Chetumal, Km 85, between Xcaret and Puerto Aventuras* 🎫 *Free.*

🍴 Restaurants

Café Olé International

$$$ | INTERNATIONAL | FAMILY | The laid-back hub of Puerto Aventuras is a terrace café with a varied menu, including coconut shrimp and chicken with a chimichurri sauce made from red wine, garlic, onion, and fine herbs. If you and local fisherman get lucky, the nightly specials might include fresh-caught fish in garlic sauce. There's live music on Sunday, Wednesday, and Friday in high season. **Known for:** live music; fresh-caught fish in garlic sauce; all you can eat BBQ ribs. [$] *Average main: MP220* ✉ *Centro Comercial Marina,* ☎ *984/873–5125* 🌐 *facebook.com/cafeoleinpuertoaventuras* 🕒 *Closed Mon.*

🛏 Hotels

Hard Rock Hotel Riviera Maya

$$$$ | ALL-INCLUSIVE | FAMILY | Focused on music, this 85-acre all-inclusive resort lets you live out your rock-star fantasies while getting pampered by Hard Rock hospitality. **Pros:** outstanding spa; access to neighboring golf course; great aquapark. **Cons:** theme isn't for everyone; artificial beach; time-share sales pitch. [$] *Rooms from: $700* ✉ *Carretera 307, Km 72, 3 km (2 miles) north of Puerto Aventuras, Puerto Aventuras* ☎ *984/875–1100, 817/567–7516 in U.S.* 🌐 *www.hrhrivieramaya.com* 🛏 *1,264 rooms* 🍽 *All-Inclusive.*

PA Beach Club & Hotel

$$ | RESORT | Atop the main beach and in the center of the action, this property formerly known as "the Omni" is the focal point of Puerto Aventuras, but its low-key luxury is a cut above the town's other resorts. **Pros:** pretty beach; nearby marina with dolphins; decent golf course. **Cons:** food choices could be better; no elevator; extra charge for beach amenities. [$] *Rooms from: $180* ✉ *Calle Punta Celis, Puerto Aventuras* ☎ *984/875–1950* 🌐 *puertoaventurashotel.com* 🛏 *30 rooms* 🍽 *Free Breakfast.*

Paamul Hotel

$$$ | HOTEL | FAMILY | Located in Paamul, south of Playa del Carmen, this rustic resort sits on a perfect white-sand beach. **Pros:** in-room Wi-Fi; some lovely views; rooms have spacious balconies. **Cons:** somewhat pricey restaurant with mediocre food; need car to get around; lots of mosquitoes at night. [$] *Rooms from: $210* ✉ *Paamul, Carretera Cancún-Tulum, Km 85, 19 km (12 miles) south of*

Playa del Carmen, Puerto Aventuras ☎ *984/239–9484, 612/442–9577 in the U.S.* ⊕ *paamul.com* ⤳ *13 rooms* ⏹ *Free Breakfast.*

🏃 Activities

DOLPHIN SWIMS
Dolphin Discovery

WILDLIFE-WATCHING | FAMILY | You can swim with dolphins in the closed-off waters of the marina—or get up close and personal with manatees, stingrays, and sea lions—at Dolphin Discovery. Programs are available daily from 9 to 3:30. ⊠ *On the marina, Calle Bahia Xca-cel, Puerto Aventuras* ☎ *998/193–3360, 866/393–5158 in U.S.* ⊕ *www.dolphindis-covery.com* ⤳ *From USD$69.*

SCUBA DIVING AND SNORKELING
Aquanauts Dive Shop

SCUBA DIVING | The reef here invites exploration. Aquanauts, a full-service dive shop, specializes in open-water dives, cenote dives, multitank dives, and certification courses. ⊠ *Calle Punta Celis, by the marina, Puerto Aventuras* ☎ *984/873–5041, 877/623–2491 in U.S.* ⊕ *aquanautsdiveshop.com* ⤳ *2-tank dives from USD$118.*

SPAS
Rock Spa

SPAS | With 75 treatment rooms, steam baths, and hydrotherapy pools, the Rock Spa is one of the largest in the Caribbean. In keeping with Hard Rock's music theme, massage therapists synchronize movements with an expertly curated playlist. From facials to wraps, each treatment connects the healing power of music with the power of touch and relaxation. There's also a yoga temple, beauty salon, and fitness center, but the Maya temazcal is the big draw; only resort guests have access to the spa. ⊠ *Hard Rock Hotel Riviera Maya, Carretera 307, Km 72, 3 km (2 miles) north of Puerto Aventuras, Puerto Aventuras* ☎ *984/875–1100* ⊕ *www.hrhrivieramaya.com.*

Xpu-Há

31 km (19 miles) south of Playa del Carmen.

Located 20 minutes south of Playa del Carmen and 20 minutes north of Tulum, Xpu-Há is the perfect base to relax and get away from the crowds. The beach is startling white, with soft clean sand that is raked by the few boutique hotels and villas that dot the shores. Other than the Catalonia Royal Tulum, you won't find sprawling resorts taking over the area. But this stellar stretch has recently brought in several beach clubs and restaurants, which means this hush-hush haven is now officially on the map.

GETTING HERE AND AROUND

The Xpu-Há entrance is just south of Puerto Aventuras at Km 265, after the Barceló Resort. If you're coming from the south, make a U-turn at the *retorno* across from the Pemex gas station; if you're coming from the north, individual signs for Al Cielo, Esencia, and Catalonia Royal mark the three entrances on the east side of the highway. Bumpy dirt roads will drop you in paradise. Since Xpu-Há is simply a beach community comprising hotels and villas, the closest services are in Puerto Aventuras to the north and Akumal to the south.

🏖 Beaches

Chan Yu Yum

BEACH | North of Tulum is a smaller bay, known as Chan Yu Yum, edging the Catalonia Royal Tulum. While it's marginally less protected than Fatima Bay, it's also delightfully calm, with flat white sands melting into shallow waters great for snorkeling. Divers are likely to spot turtles, stingrays, toadfish, and perhaps even a nurse shark; however, underwater currents can make diving a challenge. **Amenities:** none. **Best for:** snorkeling; swimming. ⊠ *Bahia Xcacel,* *near Catalonia Royal Tulum, off Carretera 307 at Km 264.5, Xpu-Há.*

La Playa Xpu-Ha Beach Club

BEACH | FAMILY | Located at Playa Xpu-Há, this beach club is open year-round from 11 to 6. Guests of nearby villas are often lured here by the plethora of amenities—including showers, lockers, hammocks, umbrellas, chaise longues, and a rental shop that has snorkeling gear, Wave Runners, boogie boards, and kayaks. In full beach club tradition, there's a restaurant and a bar with swings instead of stools. You can burn off your lunch with a game of volleyball, or opt for hair braids and henna tattoos. **Amenities:** food and drink; showers; toilets; water sports. **Best for:** partiers; swimming; walking. ✉ *Carretera 307, Km 265, Xpu-Há* ☎ *984/133–6701* 🌐 *www.laplayaxpuha.com* 🎟 *MX$40 entry and MX$120 drink minimum.*

★ Xpu–Há Beach

BEACH | FAMILY | Other than the occasional villa and resort, including Royal Catalonia Tulum smack-dab in the center, this stretch of white sand is fairly isolated. South of here are a few spots where you can grab a midday snack, like La Playa Beach Club. There are no hidden rocks in shallow areas, so many people come to swim or snorkel, especially when the winds are calm; the sugary sand is raked, making it a good place for an unobstructed stroll, too. Unlike many beaches, this one isn't blocked by resort security. You can access it through La Playa or by having lunch at one of the nearby restaurants and beach clubs. **Amenities:** lifeguards; parking (fee); food and drink; showers; toilets; water sports. **Best for:** partiers; snorkeling; swimming; walking. ✉ *Carretera 307, Km 265, Xpu-Há.*

Hotels

Catalonia Royal Tulum

$$$ | RESORT | This lavish, adults-only resort was designed around the surrounding jungle and has a great beach and terrific food for a resort in its price range; however, it may not be the place for you if you don't want a nonstop environment. **Pros:** excellent beach; great diving classes; enthusiastic staff. **Cons:** no kids under 18; no elevator; no pool bar. [$] *Rooms from: $289* ✉ *Carretera 307, Km 264.5, Xpu-Há* ☎ *984/875–1800* 🌐 *www.hoteles-catalonia.com* 🛏 *288 rooms* 🍴 *All-Inclusive.*

★ Hotel Esencia

$$$$ | HOTEL | Situated on 50 acres of jungle, this sprawling estate—once the home of an Italian duchess—has been converted into one of the Riviera Maya's most luxurious hotels. **Pros:** stunning beach; daily yoga; remarkable food. **Cons:** small section of the beach is rocky; not all rooms have ocean views; no gym. [$] *Rooms from: $1005* ✉ *Carretera 307, Km 265, Predio Rústico Xpu-Há, Llotes 18 and 19,* ☎ *984/873–4830* 🌐 *www.hotelesencia.com* 🛏 *29 rooms* 🍴 *Free Breakfast.*

Activities

KITEBOARDING

Morph Kiteboarding

WINDSURFING | These certified IKO (International Kiteboarding Organization) instructors offer three-hour lessons that can be tailored for all levels. Based in Xpu-Há, they'll pick you up at your hotel and take you to the nearest kite-friendly location. ✉ *Carretera 307, Km 265, Xpu-Há* ☎ *984/114–9524* 🌐 *www.morphkiteboarding.com* 🎟 *From MX$3,050.*

SCUBA DIVING AND SNORKELING

Zero Gravity Dive Center

DIVING & SNORKELING | This dive shop rents equipment and has a staff of experienced instructors that specialize in cave diving. ✉ *Carretera 307, Km 265, in front of Hotel Maeva,* ☎ *1984/840–9030* 🌐 *www.zerogravity.com.mx* 🕒 *Closed Sat.*

Akumal

37 km (23 miles) south of Playa del Carmen.

In Mayan, Akumal (pronounced ah-koo-maal) means "place of the turtle," and this portion of coast is a storied nesting ground, especially at Half Moon Bay. Akumal first attracted international attention in 1926, when explorers discovered the *Mantanceros,* a Spanish galleon that sank there in 1741; then, in the 1960s, diver Pablo Bush Romero established the Hotel Akumal Caribe. The rest is history.

Today Akumal is an Americanized beach community, home to divers, fishermen, and laid-back expats from the United States and Canada. It's essentially a long string of upscale homes and condos along three bays. Akumal Bay is the best base for visits, with a good selection of hotels and restaurants plus the best all-around beach for swimming and snorkeling. Half Moon Bay, just beyond, has decent snorkeling and more condos for rent, but the beach is narrow and rocky. Laguna Yal-kú is a protected snorkeling lagoon.

Bypass the vendors at Akumal's entrance offering snorkel gear for rent. Although their rates are slightly less than you'll pay elsewhere, once you tack on conservation fees, parking, and a guide, you're better off going through an official dive shop.

GETTING HERE AND AROUND

The entrance to town is on the east side of the highway, so coming from the north you'll have to make a U-turn at the well-marked retorno; coming from the south, exit at Km 264 off Carretera 307. From either direction, follow the signs to "Akumal Playa." Getting around is easy as there's only one road. It runs from the highway through the Arch—the town's gateway, at Hotel Akumal Caribe—and along Akumal Bay past Half Moon Bay to Laguna Yalku, a distance of about

10 minutes by car. Unlike many beach communities, this one can be entered even when a guard is stationed. Simply explain that you're heading to the beach. Akumal's tourist office is a small booth on the main road before the Arch as you enter town.

◉ Sights

★ Aktun-Chen (*Indiana Joe's*)

CAVE | FAMILY | The name is Mayan for "the cave with cenotes inside," and these amazing underground caverns—estimated to be about 5 million years old—are the area's largest. You walk through the underground passages, past stalactites and stalagmites, until you reach the cenote with its various shades of deep green. There's also an on-site canopy tour and one cenote where you can take a swim. This top family attraction isn't as crowded or touristy as Xplor, Xel-Há, and Xcaret. ✉ *Carretera 307, Km 107, opposite Bahia Principe resort, between Akumal and Xel-Ha, Akumal* ☎ *984/806–4962* ⊕ *www.aktun-chen.com* ✆ *Cave tour USD$29; cenote tour USD$33; canopy tour USD$44.*

Laguna Yal-kú (*Yal-kú Lagoon*)

BODY OF WATER | FAMILY | Devoted snorkelers may want to follow the unmarked dirt road to Laguna Yal-kú, about 3 km (2 miles) north of Akumal town center. A series of small mangrove-edged lagoons that gradually reach the ocean, Yal-kú is an eco-park that's home to schools of parrot fish in clear water with visibility to 160 feet in winter and spring. Snorkeling equipment can be rented in the parking lot; the site also has toilets, lockers, changing rooms, outdoor showers, and a snack bar. Sunscreen is not allowed, so bring a T-shirt to keep from getting burned. ✉ *End of main road, Akumal* ☎ *084/875 0065* ⊕ *facebook.com/yalku* ✆ *USD$15.*

Did You Know?

At Aktun-Chen, you can snorkel in a cenote and see 5-million-year-old stalactites and stalagmites. Need a bit of fresh air? Try a zip line tour.

★ Xel-Há

WATER PARK | **FAMILY** | Part of the Xcaret nature-adventure park group, Xel-Há (pronounced shel- *hah*) is a natural aquarium made of coves, inlets, and lagoons cut from the limestone shoreline. The name means "where the water is born," and a natural spring here flows out to meet the salt water, creating a unique habitat for tropical marine life. There's enough to impress novice snorkelers, though there seem to be fewer fish each year, and the mixture of fresh and salt water can cloud visibility. Low wooden bridges over the lagoons allow for leisurely walks around the park, and there are spots to rest, swim, cliff–jump, zip-line, or swing from ropes over the water. Xel-Há gets overwhelmingly crowded, so come early. The grounds are well equipped with bathrooms and restaurants. At the entrance you'll receive specially prepared sunscreen that won't kill the fish; other sunscreens are prohibited. The entrance fee includes a meal, towel, locker, inner tubes, and snorkel equipment; other activities, like scuba diving, zip-lining, swimming with the dolphins, and spa treatments, are available at additional cost. Discounts are offered when you book online. ⊠ *Carretera 307, Km 240, Xel-Ha* ☎ *998/883–3143, 855/326–0682 in U.S.* ⊕ *www.xelha.com* ⊠ *USD$89.*

🏖 Beaches

Akumal Bay

BEACH | **FAMILY** | Known for the sea turtles that swim in its waters, Akumal Bay is sheltered by an offshore reef—though, sadly only about 30% of it is alive. It's best to explore the waters with a certified guide available through dive shops in town. Do not wear sunscreen in the water as it can harm the reef, and, above all, do not touch the wildlife or coral. Be careful to stay clear of the red "fire reef," which stings on contact. When you drag yourself away from the snorkeling, there are plenty of palm trees for shade, as well as a variety of waterfront shops, restaurants, and cafés. If you continue on the main road, you'll reach Half Moon Bay and Laguna Yal-kú, also good snorkeling spots. **Amenities:** food and drink; parking (fee); showers; toilets; lifeguards; water sports. **Best for:** snorkeling; swimming; walking. ⊠ *Enter at Hotel Akumal Caribe, Akumal.*

Half Moon Bay

BEACH | **FAMILY** | The crescent bay on the north end of Akumal has shallow water and almost no current, making it a safe swimming spot for children; the snorkeling is also good here (you might even see the occasional sea turtle). Beach chairs and hammocks line the narrow, rocky shore at La Buena Vida restaurant, which has a pool, restrooms, and limited street parking for patrons. The area near Casa Maya is protected by an outer reef; however, the entry point is rocky, so bring water shoes. Bring an umbrella, too—Half Moon Bay is known for its white sand and clear waters, but the lack of trees means you'll have trouble finding shade. **Amenities:** food and drink; toilets. **Best for:** snorkeling; swimming. ⊠ *Beach Rd., Lote 35, North Akumal, Akumal.*

X'cacel Beach

BEACH | About 10 km (6 miles) south of Akumal, this beach (also written Xca-Cel), has white powdery sand and a nearby cenote that can be accessed through a jungle path to your right. Snorkeling is best on the beach's north end. To reach it from Carretera 307, turn at the dirt road that runs between Chemuyil and Xel-Há. The route is blocked by a guard who will charge you MX$30 to enter; after paying, simply continue on to the beach itself. From May through November, this area is reserved for turtle nesting. Avoid stepping on any raised mounds of sand as they could be turtle nests. Note that the beach road is open daily 9–5. **Amenities:** parking (free); toilets. **Best for:** snorkeling; solitude. ⊠ *Carretera 307, Km 248, Akumal.*

🍴 Restaurants

La Buena Vida

$$$ | **MEXICAN** | **FAMILY** | With driftwood tables overlooking Half Moon Bay, swings at the lively bar, and salsa music keeping things moving, this might be the perfect beach restaurant. The usual Mexican fare—quesadillas, empanadas, burritos, and fish tacos with handmade tortillas—is perfectly fine, but the food isn't the point. **Known for:** a two-seater tower table above the sand; sweeping waterfront views; incredible beachfront location. [$] *Average main: MP250* ✉ *North Akumal, Half Moon Bay, Lote 35, Akumal* ☎ *984/875–9061* 🌐 *www.labuenavidarestaurant.com.*

La Cueva del Pescador

$$$ | **SEAFOOD** | **FAMILY** | Dig your toes in the sand floor and enjoy the catch of the day at La Cueva del Pescador. A crowd of easygoing expats hunkers down for the afternoon to feast on octopus, shrimp, or conch ceviche prepared with lime juice and flavored with cilantro—usually with a generous helping of beer on the side. **Known for:** ceviche with octopus, shrimp, or conch; good beer; grilled garlic shrimp. [$] *Average main: MP250* ✉ *Plaza Ukana, Main rd., Akumal Bay* ☎ *984/875–9002* 🌐 *lacuevadelpescador.mx.*

Turtle Bay Café & Bakery

$$$ | **CAFÉ** | **FAMILY** | This funky café, where expats and locals congregate, serves up smoothies, baked goods, tacos, homemade ice cream, and everything in between. The breakfast menu spans acai bowls, eggs Benedict, pancakes, and fruit plates. **Known for:** Quintana Roo vodka; homemade ice cream; sticky buns. [$] *Average main: MP300* ✉ *Plaza Ukana, Main rd., Akumal Bay, Akumal* ☎ *984/875–9138* 🌐 *www.turtlebaycafe.com.*

🛏 Hotels

Bahía Princípe Riviera Maya Resort (*Grand Bahia Principe*)

$$ | **ALL-INCLUSIVE** | **FAMILY** | This all-inclusive megacomplex consists of four upscale hotels (Akumal, Cobá, Tulum, and Sian Ka'an) with extensive shared facilities reachable by shuttle from 7:30 am to midnight. **Pros:** good food; on the beach; attentive staff. **Cons:** Wi-Fi only available in the lobby at Tulum and Cobá; you'll need a car to get to town; most restaurants require advance booking. [$] *Rooms from: MP150* ✉ *Carretera 307, Km 250, Akumal* ✥ *Access the property through the resort gate off Carretera 307 rather than the main entrance into Akumal town* ☎ *984/875–5000, 800/607–0179* 🌐 *bahia-principe.com* 🛏 *Akumal 758 rooms, Cobá 1080 rooms, Tulum 976 rooms, Sian Ka'an 420 rooms* 🍽 *All-Inclusive* ☞ *3-night stay minimum.*

Del Sol Beachfront

$$ | **HOTEL** | **FAMILY** | Each small room in the main building of this bright, colorful seaside hotel has an ocean view and a private terrace; next door are more expensive condos with Spanish colonial touches. **Pros:** on beach; well-kept grounds; all rooms have ocean views. **Cons:** no meals; beds aren't very comfortable; beach is a little rocky. [$] *Rooms from: $140* ✉ *Calle Caleta Yalku Lt 41G, Akumal* ✥ *Next to La Buena Vida* ☎ *984/875–9060, 888/425–8625 in U.S.* 🌐 *delsolbeachfront.com* 🛏 *28 rooms* 🍽 *No Meals.*

Hotel Akumal Caribe

$$ | **HOTEL** | Back in the 1960s, Pablo Bush Romero established this resort as a place for his diving buddies to crash, and it still offers pleasant accommodations and a congenial staff. **Pros:** easy snorkeling; comfortable beds; on the beach. **Cons:** no elevator; most rooms lack ocean views; basic decor. [$] *Rooms from: $170* ✉ *At Akumal Arch, Main rd., Akumal* ☎ *984/875–9012, 915/533–8392 in U.S.*

⊕ *www.hotelakumalcaribe.com* ⌇ *55 rooms* ⫮ *No Meals.*

🛍 Shopping

CRAFTS AND FOLK ART
Galería Lamanai
ART GALLERIES | A laid-back spot under a palapa roof, Galería Lamanai carries a mix of folk and fine art from over 200 Mexican artists. ⊠ *Yodzonot, Akumal Bay, Akumal* ☎ *984/875–9055* ⊕ *galerialamanai.com.*

Mexicarte
CRAFTS | This colorful little shop sells high-quality crafts from around the country. ⊠ *Main rd., Akumal Bay, next to Hotel Akumal Caribe, Akumal* ☎ *984/875–9115* ⊕ *mexicarte.shop.*

🏃 Activities

BIKING
Akumal Guide
BIKING | The small booth inside Hotel Akumal Caribe rents bikes for $8 per day, as well as golf carts for $40 per day. Golf carts are a very popular way to get around Akumal. Tours can also be purchased here for popular spots like Cobá, Sian Ka'an, and Chichén Itzá. ⊠ *Hotel Akumal Caribe, Akumal Bay, Akumal* ☎ *984/875–9115* ⊕ *www.akumalguide.com.*

SCUBA DIVING AND SNORKELING
Akumal Dive Center
DIVING & SNORKELING | The area's oldest dive operation offers reef or cenote diving as well as one-hour snorkeling tours; the latter includes gear, lockers, showers, guides, and conservation wristbands for $50 per person. Three-hour fishing trips for up to four people can also be arranged. Take a sharp right at the Akumal Arch and you'll see the dive shop on the beach. ⊠ *Hotel Akumal Caribe, Akumal Bay* ☎ *984/875–9025* ⊕ *www.akumaldivecenter.com* ⟐ *Dives from USD$48.*

★ Akumal Dive Shop
DIVING & SNORKELING | **FAMILY** | You can go snorkeling with turtles or diving at cenotes with the Akumal Dive Shop. Certification courses are also available. If boating is more your thing, it runs daytime and sunset catamaran cruises, too. ⊠ *, Akumal* ☎ *984/875–9030, 984/875–9031* ⊕ *www.akumaldiveshop.com* ⟐ *Snorkeling tour $50; diving trip $75; cruises $110.*

Centro Ecológico Akumal
ECOTOURISM | From May through October, the ecological center in Akumal offers guided walks through sea turtle nesting sites. Learn about conservation efforts and participate in nighttime nest visits for a suggested $15 donation. Proceeds go to turtle conservation. ⊠ *Carretera Puerto Juarez Tulum Km 104, Akumal* ☎ *999/297–1127* ⊕ *ceakumal.org* ⟐ *Suggested donation $15.*

SPAS
Budha Garden Spa
SPAS | This small day spa in Akumal offers Swedish massage, reflexology, facials, body scrubs, wraps, manicures, and pedicures. After a day in the sun, try the popular Maya clay mask, said to firm the skin and draw out impurities. Body scrub options range from mango-ginger to bamboo-walnut, while the cooling body wraps incorporate local ingredients like cucumber and lavender to rehydrate the skin. Each wrap and scrub is accompanied by a mini facial and head massage. ⊠ *Past Akumal Arch on main rd., next to Hotel Akumal Caribe, Akumal* ☎ *984/745–4942* ⊕ *budhagardenspa.com.*

Tankah

56 km (35 miles) south of Playa del Carmen.

If you plan on staying in the Cobá area, nearby Tankah is a good option—especially if you want to avoid the Tulum crowds. In ancient times Tankah was an important

Maya trading city. A number of small, reasonably priced hotels have cropped up here over the past few years, and several expats who own villas in the area rent them out year-round. Often overlooked by travelers, this spectacular stretch of coastline offers great snorkeling, diving, and best of all, isolation. A cenote that tunnels under the beach road and spills into the sea makes the area even more unique.

GETTING HERE AND AROUND

To reach the coastal road in Tankah, turn east off Carretera 307 at Km 237 (a sign for Nuh Hotel and a peacock mural mark the turn). At the end of the long, pitted road, turn left (north) where a string of villas and small hotels parallel the beach. The closest medical clinics, grocery stores, and emergency services are 4 km (2½ miles) south in Tulum.

Beaches

Tankah Bay

BEACH | Nestled in a protected cove, this wide stretch of beach is popular with divers and snorkelers due to the outer reef that keeps waters calm. The fine sand is perfect for a barefoot stroll, but the shallow waters have sharp rocks just below the surface. Across the road from Casa Cenote Restaurant is Manatee Cenote, an underwater cave that spills from the mangroves into the sea. This freshwater pool, coupled with the outer reef, make Tankah a snorkeler's paradise. The main draw is that the area is relatively isolated since most sun worshipers tend to bask on the shores of Playa del Carmen. **Amenities:** food and drink; toilets. **Best for:** solitude; snorkeling; walking. ⊠ *Tulum.*

 Restaurants

Casa Cenote

$$$ | MEXICAN | FAMILY | The cheapest restaurant along Tankah's beachfront serves up fresh, simple, satisfying Mexican food from 8 am to 9 pm every day. Grab a table at the waterfront and order up beef fajitas or fish tacos, topped with a healthy helping of fresh-made salsa and fresh-squeezed lime juice. **Known for:** beef and chicken fajitas; powerful margaritas; fish tacos. Ⓢ *Average main: MP250 ⊠ Interior Fracc. Tankah, Mza 3, Lote 32, across from Cenote Manatee, Tulum ☎ 984/115–6996, 646/634–7206 in U.S. ⊕ casacenote.com.*

★ **Restaurante Oscar y Lalo**

$$ | SEAFOOD | FAMILY | Enter through the massive gate and wind your way up a garden pathway through the main dining area and into the back garden where intimate four- or five-table palapas are surrounded by jungle and hung with bright white hammocks and twinkling lights. Many ingredients, as well as medicinal plants, are grown on property and the owners would be happy to cut you a piece of fresh aloe for your sunburn or brew you up some anti-food-poisoning tea. **Known for:** organic chicken and pork; intimate jungle garden seating; Mayan dishes. Ⓢ *Average main: MP200 ⊠ Carretera 307, Km 241, Tulum ☎ 984/127–1587, 984/115–9965 ⊕ www.oscarandlalo.com.*

🛏 Hotels

★ **Jashita**

$$$$ | HOTEL | FAMILY | This sophisticated little hotel at the northern end of Soliman Bay has style in spades. **Pros:** kid-friendly; very private; clear, calm bay. **Cons:** not all rooms have ocean views; bay too shallow for swimming in some places; not much to do in the nearby area. Ⓢ *Rooms from: $650 ⊠ Bahia de Soliman, Tankah Rd. IV, across Carretera 307 from Restaurante Oscar y Lalo, ☎ 984/179-1659 ⊕ www.jashitahotel.com ⇄ 31 rooms ⏍ Free Breakfast.*

Mereva Tulum

$$$ | HOTEL | Formerly Blue Sky Tulum, this boutique beach property—complete with

oceanfront pool and exquisite accommodations just steps from the secluded white sand—is one of the area's best. **Pros:** stunning rooms; sublime beachfront setting; excellent mixologist (mixing up both juices and cocktails that will transport you to paradise). **Cons:** some rooms lack full ocean view; need car to get around; restaurant is nothing special. [$] *Rooms from: $295* ⊠ *Bahía Tankah, past Casa Cenote,* ☎ *984/147-6571* ⊕ *mereva.mx* ⤳ *25 rooms* ⦿ *No Meals.*

🎿 Activities

Due to the outer reef, calm bay, and connecting cenote, Tankah has become a popular dive spot. The closest dive shop is Maya Dive Center; however, most dive shops along Riviera Maya can organize trips to Tankah.

KITEBOARDING
Extreme Control Kite School

WINDSURFING | All levels of kitesurfing lessons and the latest equipment are available through Extreme Control Kite School. Led by IKO (International Kiteboarding Organization) instructor Marco Cristofanelli, courses take place at Caleta Tankah Beach Club, about five minutes from Tulum. The outfit operates on the beach from 9 am to sunset every day unless there is absolutely no wind (call ahead to check conditions). Paddleboarding, diving, and snorkeling are also offered. ⊠ *Caleta Tankah Beach Club, Carretera 307, Km 230, Tulum* ☎ *984/130–1596, 984/745–4555* ⊕ *www. extremecontrol.net* ⦿ *1-hour lessons from USD$90.*

SCUBA DIVING AND SNORKELING
Cenote Manatee (*Casa Cenote*)

DIVING & SNORKELING | **FAMILY** | Directly across from Casa Cenote Hotel, this open lagoon (often referred to as Casa Cenote) is popular with experienced cave divers since a freshwater tunnel—dropping below the main road—connects directly to the ocean. Here two ecosystems collide with both fresh and salt water, offering a maximum diving depth of 26 feet. The constant currents draw in a variety of marine life including parrot fish, swimming crabs, moray eels, juvenile barracuda, and tarpon. Only skilled divers should enter the underwater cave since the distance between the cenote and ocean is dangerously long. There is a small parking lot, and a shack renting snorkeling equipment, but no facilities other than those at neighboring hotels and restaurants. ⊠ *Interior Fracc. Tankah, Mza 3, Lote 32, Tulum* ⦿ *MX$40.*

Tulum

61 km (38 miles) south of Playa del Carmen.

It used to be that Tulum was simply known as dusty little town with a stellar archaeological site and a few palapa huts. No longer. Discovered by the international eco-set, it now has whitewashed, solar-powered bungalow hotels that line the spectacular beach 2 km (1 mile) east of town. Locals speak of a battle for Tulum's bohemian soul, and although first-time visitors may not notice the changes, it's indisputable that the free-spirited hippie days are over.

Tulum is divided into three main areas: the downtown pueblo, south from the shore along Carretera 307 (here known as Avenida Tulum); the Mayan ruins to the north on the coast; and the beach (Zona Hotelera), which extends down from the ruins.

Those ancient structures were the town's original draw, and Tulum (meaning "wall" in Mayan) now lures more than 2 million people annually. Even if you couldn't care less about history, the site's waterfront location elevates it to the sublime. The pueblo, conversely, is a jumble of food stalls, souvenir shops, budget hostels, and cheap eateries, some catering to tourists, some to locals, and some to both. Although it's more appealing to stay at the beach, the town offers an authentic slice of Mexico.

Tulum's irresistible beach begins just east on the Boca Paila road. (Technically there's beach all the way from the ruins down to Sian Ka'an, but the coast by the ruins, and south to Zamas restaurant, is a series of rocky coves. The endless powdery sand you came for is south of the bridge and police checkpoint after Zamas.) Miles of magnificent white sand sparkle before the aquamarine waves, backed by eco-hotels on one side of the narrow road, and tropical hipster restaurants, yoga centers, and the odd spa on the other.

Tulum's ongoing transformation has brought new services, including a 24-hour hospital, four gas stations, and a Chedraui supermarket. But there's still no community power supply at the beach, so eco-resorts—both rustic and chic—rely on wind turbines, solar energy, recycled water, and generators and candlelight. Rooms are usually void of TVs and phones, and they seldom have Wi-Fi or 24-hour air-conditioning (although this is slowly changing); it's also worth noting that some hotels draw water from cenotes, which might result in a salty shower and low water pressure.

GETTING HERE AND AROUND

Tulum is a 20-minute drive from Akumal and a 45-minute drive from Playa del Carmen. You can hire a taxi from Cancún for approximately MX$1,355. Tucan Kin has a direct (shared) shuttle service from Cancún airport for MX$596 per person one way. Buses operated by ADO (⊕ www.ado.com.mx) link Cancún, Puerto Morelos, Playa del Carmen, Tulum, Felipe Carrillo Puerto, Limones, and Chetumal. Colectivos travel from Cancún to Playa and Playa to Tulum and should cost you less than MX$100.

From the pueblo, you can walk the 2 km (1 mile) to the archaeological site

entrance, rent a bike, or catch one of the shuttles that pass every few minutes. Within the hotel zone, travelers must rely on taxis, cars, or bikes to get around. If you plan on driving, watch carefully for the large beach crabs that cross the roads after dark. To reach the beachfront Zona Hotelera, head south on Carretera 307 and turn left (east) at the second stoplight in Tulum. Shortly after passing the fire station, you'll come to a "T" in the road. There you'll find dozens of signs directing travelers to hotels; the best beach is to the right, and the ruins are to the left. A taxi from the pueblo to the Zona costs MX$120–MX$150, depending on how far down the coast you plan to go.

TAXI CONTACTS Tucan Kin. ☎ 984/871–3538 ⊕ www.tucankin.com.

◉ Sights

★ Rivera Kitchen Tulum

OTHER ATTRACTION | Join a vibrant Mexican mama from the foodie-beloved region of Oaxaca for an excellent four-hour cooking adventure in her jungle kitchen, starting at either 10:30 am or 5:30 pm. The four-plus courses you'll make vary by season, but often include authentic mole and ceviche. Classes stay small, with a maximum of 10 people. Once you're done prepping, stirring, and learning about the cuisine, you'll sit down to enjoy the lunch you prepared. Transportation is provided from Villas Tulum to the jungle house where you'll cook up your authentic local meal. ✉ Carretera Tulum-Cobá, Km 9.9, Tulum ☎ 984/129–2690 ⊕ riverakitchentulum.com ⎙ From USD$77 per person.

★ Tulum

RUINS | Tulum is one of the few Maya cities known to have been inhabited when the conquistadores arrived in 1518. In the 16th century it was a trade center, a safe harbor for goods from rival Maya factions who considered the city neutral territory. Tulum reached its height when its merchants, made wealthy through

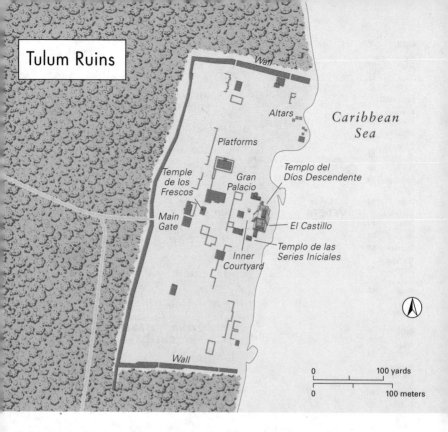

Tulum Ruins

Wall

Altars

Caribbean
Sea

Platforms

Temple
de los
Frescos

Gran
Palacio

Templo del
Díos Descendente

Main
Gate

El Castillo

Templo de las
Series Iniciales

Inner
Courtyard

Wall

| 0 | | 100 yards |
| 0 | | 100 meters |

trading, for the first time outranked Maya priests in authority and power. But when the Spaniards arrived, they forbade the Maya traders to sail the seas, and commerce among the Maya died. Tulum has long held special significance for the Maya as a symbol of resistance and independence. A key city in the League of Mayapán (AD 987–1194), it was never conquered by the Spaniards, although it was abandoned by the Maya about 75 years after the conquest of the rest of Mexico. For 300 years thereafter it symbolized the defiance of an otherwise subjugated people, and it was one of the last outposts of the Maya during their insurrection against Mexican rule in the Caste Wars, which began in 1847. Uprisings continued intermittently until 1935, when the Maya ceded Tulum to the Mexican government. At the entrance to the ruins you can hire a guide for

MX$500, but keep in mind that some of their information is more entertaining than historically accurate. (Disregard that stuff about virgin sacrifices.) Although you can see the ruins thoroughly in two hours, you might want to allow extra time for a swim or a stroll on the beach. The first significant structure is the two-story **Templo de los Frescos**, to the left of the entryway. The temple's vault roof and corbel arch are examples of classic Maya architecture. Faint traces of blue-green frescoes outlined in black on the inner and outer walls depict the three worlds of the Maya and their major deities, and are decorated with stellar and serpentine patterns, rosettes, and ears of maize and other offerings to the gods. One scene portrays the rain god seated on a four-legged animal—probably a reference to the Spaniards on their horses. Unfortunately, the frescoes are difficult to see from the

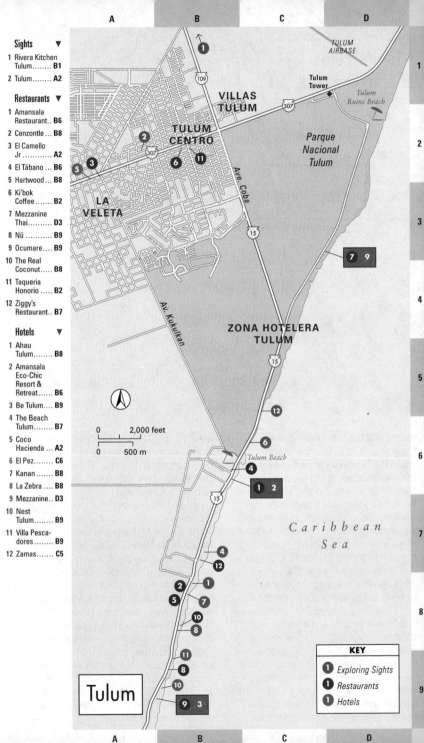

path to which visitors are restricted. The largest and most photographed structure, the **Castillo** (Castle), looms at the edge of a 40-foot limestone cliff just past the Temple of the Frescoes. Atop it, at the end of a broad stairway, is a temple with stucco ornamentation on the outside and traces of fine frescoes inside the two chambers. (The stairway has been roped off, so the top temple is inaccessible.) The front wall of the Castillo has faint carvings of the Descending God and columns depicting the plumed serpent god, Kukulcán, who was introduced to the Maya by the Toltecs. To the left of the Castillo, facing the sea, is the **Templo del Dios Descendente**—so called for the carving over the doorway of a winged god plummeting to Earth. A few small altars sit atop a hill at the north side of the cove, with a good view of the Castillo and the sea. To avoid the longest lines, be sure to arrive before 11 am. Outside the entrance are dozens of vendors selling Mexican crafts, so bring some extra cash for souvenirs. ✉ *Carretera 307, Km 133* ☎ *983/837–2411* 🎟 *MX$65 entrance; MX$54 parking; MX$67 video fee; MX$27 shuttle from parking to ruins.*

Beaches

Tulum Beach

BEACH | Extending 11 km (7 miles), Tulum's main beach is a tropical paradise comprised of glassy water and powdery sand, set off from the jungle by hip restaurants and low-slung bungalow hotels where the yoga set take their virtuous rest. It's divided by a rocky promontory into two main sections, similar to each other, although the farther south you go on the Carretera Tulum–Boca Paila beach road, the more secluded and lovelier it gets. The beach is bordered on the south by the Sian Ka'an biosphere reserve, whose coast is even more deserted. To the north, you'll find the Tulum ruins. Beach access can be tricky; even though the beach is public, the hotels and restaurants along the shore often limit access to guests only, and public access points are few and far between. If you're not staying on the beachfront, make sure to ask your hotel where the closest access point is. **Amenities:** food and drink; toilets; water sports. **Best for:** swimming; walking. ✉ *Carretera Tulum-Boca Paila, Tulum.*

Tulum Ruins Beach

BEACH | Talk about a beach with a view! At Tulum's archaeological site, the Caribbean's signature white sand and turquoise waters are framed by a backdrop of Maya pyramids. The small cove can get crowded, especially during peak season when travelers flock to the ruins for a day of sightseeing. The south end by the rocks tends to have more breathing room. Only those who purchase a ticket to the ruins can access this beach, unless you approach the shores by boat. **Amenities:** none. **Best for:** swimming. ✉ *Carretera 307, Km 130, Tulum* 🎟 *MX$65 for entrance via ruins.*

Restaurants

Amansala Restaurant

$$$ | **INTERNATIONAL** | In the back of the Amansala Resort & Retreat, this shady beachfront restaurant is the place to be for sweeping ocean views and light, healthy lunches. Smoothies are served fruity and not overly sweet, guacamole is fresh and flavorful, and the salsa selection is excellent. **Known for:** vegan and vegetarian options; meals with a view; health-conscious cuisine. [$] *Average main: MP280* ✉ *Carretera Tulum-Boca Paila, Km 5.5,* ☎ *984/239–7639* 🌐 *www.amansala.com.*

★ Cenzontle

$$$ | **MEXICAN FUSION** | This hidden jungle garden with hardwood tables and twinkling candlelight is hard to spot from the road, but once you're here, you won't want to leave. Start your meal with stuffed piquillo peppers or a *relleno* *negro* shrimp tostada, and don't miss the sweet-savory pork ribs with organic vanilla, sweet potato, and an apple-cinnamon topper. **Known for:** duck carnitas; vegetarian options; beers brewed in house. $ *Average main: MP350* ✉ *Carretera Tulum-Boca Paila, Km 7.3, Tulum* ☎ *984/204-8628* ⊕ *facebook.com/CenzontleTulum* ☾ *No lunch.*

El Camello Jr.

$$$ | SEAFOOD | FAMILY | Called "Camellito" by locals, this restaurant is famed for having Tulum's freshest seafood—and the jammed parking lot is testament to its enduring popularity. Fish or shrimp tacos are light and fresh, but the full splendor of the place is expressed by its whole grilled or fried fish, served with generous mounds of rice, beans, and *plátanos*. Come hungry. **Known for:** whole grilled or fried fish; fresh seafood; fish or shrimp tacos. $ *Average main: MP230* ✉ *Avs. Tulum and Luna, at back end of town,* ☎ *984/871-2036* ⊕ *facebook.com/RestauranteElCamelloJr* ☾ *Closed Wed.*

El Tábano

$$$ | MEXICAN | This jungle-side hangout is laid-back, casual, and comfortable, with an open kitchen and airy layout in a large, traditional palapa. Standout dishes include organic-chicken-stuffed jalapeños and organic chicken in red sauce (so tender that it practically falls off the bone). **Known for:** traditional Mexican dishes; Mexican wines; spicy margaritas. $ *Average main: MP350* ✉ *Carretera Tulum-Boca Paila, Km 5.7, Tulum* ☎ *984/134-2706* ⊕ *facebook.com/eltabanotulum* ☾ *Closed Sun. in Apr.–Sept.*

Hartwood

$$$$ | ECLECTIC | New York chefs cooking New York food for New York prices—in a wood-fired jungle lot, open to the night sky—that's Hartwood. Try slow-roasted pork ribs marinated in agave honey or a light, fresh ceviche and finish up with homemade ice cream in flavors like peanut brittle, sweet corn, and cream cheese. **Known for:** long waits in high season; marinated pork ribs; locally farmed rabbit. $ *Average main: MP420* ✉ *Carretera Tulum–Boca Paila, Km 7.6, Tulum* ⊕ *www.hartwoodtulum.com* ☾ *Closed Mon., Tues., Sept., and Oct. No lunch.*

Ki'bok Coffee

$ | CAFÉ | Rub shoulders with cab drivers, local government officials, and expat regulars over coffee at Tulum's favorite family-owned and-run coffee shop, where espresso drinks are made with 100% Mexican-grown coffee from places like Oaxaca and Veracruz. Upstairs you'll find a small bakery, out back a quiet jungle garden, and up front a relaxed beachy bar space, all serving up coffee, baked goods, and Mexican dishes like *mollete*—spiced toast over black-bean puree with pico de gallo (pro tip: add a fried egg for something special). **Known for:** homemade baked goods; espresso drinks made with Mexican coffee; carrot cake muffins. $ *Average main: MP90* ✉ *Centauro Sur MZ05 LT11, Tulum* ☎ *984/135-9509* ⊕ *kibokcoffee.com.*

Mezzanine Thai

$$$ | THAI | People come from up and down the Riviera for the zingy flavors of this southern Thai restaurant. Popular dishes include pad Thai, drunken noodles, and money bags (crispy fried wonton wrappers filled with a Thai shrimp mix). **Known for:** pad Thai with chicken or shrimp; Thai whole fish with mango salad; fresh fruit and salads. $ *Average main: MP250* ✉ *Carretera Tulum–Boca Paila, Km 1.5, Zona Hotelera* ☎ *984/131-1596* ⊕ *mezzaninetulum.com.*

★ Nü

$$$$ | MEXICAN FUSION | The mystical jungle atmosphere of this sophisticated restaurant is only beaten by its exquisite blend of Mexican and Mayan traditional cuisines. Dine to the tune of indigenous drums and the tenuous shapes formed by candlelight, while enjoying delicious cocktails prepared with local and organic ingredients. **Known for:** eco-conscious

Did You Know?

Tulum is the only ancient Maya city overlooking the sea, and while the architecture may not be as striking as inland sites, the location is breathtaking.

restaurant; Mexican-Mayan fusion cuisine; romantic jungle setting. $ *Average main: MP440* ✉ *Carretera Tulum Boca Paila Km 8.7, Zona Hotelera* ⊕ *nutulum. com* ⊙ *Closed Tues. and Wed.*

★ Ocumare

$$$ | ECLECTIC | This jungle-chic restaurant serves up creative fine-dining fare unlike anything else you'll find in the region. Standout dishes include deconstructed sushi (where the rice comes in foam form and the soy sauce is a cream), burning grouper with Thai veggies (lightly smoked right at your table), and a rich pork belly dish in a tangy Asian-inspired sauce. **Known for:** molecular gastronomy; inventive flavor combinations; decadent desserts. $ *Average main: MP350* ✉ *Carretera Tulum-Boca Paila, Km 10, Tulum* ☎ *984/146–9722* ⊕ *ocumaretulum.com* ⊙ *No lunch.*

The Real Coconut

$$$$ | CARIBBEAN | FAMILY | Health-conscious travelers rejoice: the menu at The Real Coconut features as much organic produce and free-range meat as possible and is entirely dairy-, gluten-, and refined-sugar-free. Stop by for lunch in the bright, modern beachfront dining room and order up some tacos with shrimp *al pastor* (served on tortillas made with coconut flour), a nacho bowl with organic chile, free-range chicken, or a light soup with a healthy bone-broth base. **Known for:** gluten-free cookies; organic, fresh ingredients; thick, rich smoothies. $ *Average main: MP600* ✉ *Sanara Tulum, Carretera Cobá-Boca Paila, Km 8.2, Tulum* ☎ *998/820–5559* ⊕ *realcoconutkitchen. com.*

Taquería Honorio

$ | MEXICAN | This collection of plastic tables under a tarp may not look like much from the outside, but it's where the locals go for some of the best (and cheapest) tacos in town. Grab a seat and order up some pork or vegetarian tacos, priced at just MX$15 to MX$17 each, and a bottle of *agua fresca* (water mixed with fruit and sugar). **Known for:** aguas frescas; cheap, flavorful tacos; excellent salsas. $ *Average main: MP15* ✉ *Av. Satélite Sur, Tulum* ✛ *Between Calle Sol Oriente and Calle Andromeda Oriente* ☎ *984/802–5778* ⊕ *facebook.com/taqueriahonorio* ⊙ *No dinner.*

Ziggy's Restaurant

$$$$ | MEXICAN | With tables under a palapa roof and on the beach, this restaurant is a perfect place to sink your toes in the sand while dining. Chef Hidalgo offers understated appetizers like tuna nachos (tuna tartare and avocado with tortilla strips) or guacamole on a bed of fried cheese. **Known for:** excellent beachfront location; live local music; tuna nachos. $ *Average main: MP560* ✉ *The Beach Tulum, Carretera Tulum-Boca Paila, Km 7.5, Zona Hotelera* ☎ *984/871–1132* ⊕ *ziggybeachtulum.com.*

🏨 Hotels

★ Ahau Tulum

$$$ | HOTEL | Named after the Mayan sun god, Kin Ahau, this beachfront property has rooms ranging from simple Balinese huts to palapa suites with 20-foot vaulted ceilings, enormous decks, and two-person hammocks that make you forget the day of the week. **Pros:** all furnishings built on-site by locals; good restaurant; sprawling beachfront. **Cons:** meals not included; yoga, aerial dance, and water sports cost extra; lots of mosquitoes. $ *Rooms from: $310* ✉ *Carretera Tulum–Boca Paila, Km 7.5, Zona Hotelera* ☎ *984/147–5225* ⊕ *www.ahautulum.com* ⇄ *24 rooms* ⊙ *No Meals.*

★ Amansala Eco-Chic Resort & Retreat

$$$ | HOTEL | This small eco-friendly resort hotel caters to the yoga and meditation set, with three spacious, second-floor yoga studios—one with sweeping beachfront views. **Pros:** beautiful beach and ocean views; excellent, healthy food; intimate atmosphere. **Cons:** small pool; air-conditioning only available in some rooms and only between 10 pm and 7 am; no door locks (though you can ask the staff to provide one). [$] *Rooms from: $295* ✉ *Carretera Tulum-Boca Paila, Km 5.5, Tulum* ☎ *984/239–7639* 🌐 *www.amansala.com* 🛏 *25 rooms* 🍴 *Free Breakfast.*

Be Tulum

$$$$ | **HOTEL** | Designed by owner-architect Sebastian Sas, this chic beachfront hotel is like stepping onto a beautifully executed canvas—each room is a pure work of art, with exteriors made from the wood of reclaimed train tracks, Brazilian wood floors, cowhide rugs, wicker couches, and peaceful outdoor terraces and balconies on nearly every room. **Pros:** two restaurants on property; free use of bikes and Wi-Fi; every room has its own unique (though cohesive) design. **Cons:** no elevators; no kids under 13; few rooms have ocean views. [$] *Rooms from: $640* ✉ *Carretera Tulum-Boca Paila, Km 10.5, Zona Hotelera* ☎ *984/803–2243, 877/265–4139 in U.S.* 🌐 *betulum.com* 🛏 *64 suites* 🍴 *No Meals.*

★ The Beach Tulum

$$$$ | **HOTEL** | This upscale, adults-only boutique hotel raised the bar on beachfront luxury when it opened in 2013, with a luxury price tag to match. **Pros:** private rooftop decks; excellent breakfast; all rooms are oceanfront. **Cons:** slow Internet; some nighttime noise in rooms closest to Ziggy's (though live music ends before 10); adults only (18-plus). [$] *Rooms from: $693* ✉ *Carretera Tulum–Boca Paila, Km 7.5, Zona Hotelera* ☎ *984/871–1130, 855/246–5575 in U.S.* 🌐 *www.thebeach-tulum.com* 🛏 *28 rooms* 🍴 *Free Breakfast.*

Coco Hacienda

$ | **HOTEL** | **FAMILY** | Slip through the nondescript entrance at Coco Hacienda and you'll find a charming property with a lush, sprawling garden interwoven with partly tiled pathways, lights strung up from palm trees, two inviting pools, and a spacious central palapa with whirring ceiling fans. **Pros:** beautiful grounds; excellent value; great restaurant. **Cons:** 15-minute drive or cab ride from the beach; location on the main road may mean traffic noise on parts of the property; plenty of mosquitoes. [$] *Rooms from: $90* ✉ *Av. Tulum Mz. 39 Lt. 1, Tulum* ☎ *984/130–9318* 🌐 *cocohacienda.com* 🛏 *19 rooms* 🍴 *Free Breakfast.*

★ El Pez

$$$$ | **HOTEL** | Perched on the shores of Turtle Cove, this chic boutique hotel has elevated rooms with private balconies that catch the ocean breeze. **Pros:** saltwater pool; unlimited bottled water; gourmet breakfast included. **Cons:** several open-plan bathrooms don't have doors; some rooms get street noise; beach not great for swimming. [$] *Rooms from: $483* ✉ *Carretera Tulum–Boca Paila, Km 5.5, at Turtle Cove, Zona Hotelera* ☎ *984/116–3357, 303/952–0595 in U.S.* 🌐 *www.tulumhotelpez.com* 🛏 *12 rooms* 🍴 *No Meals.*

Kanan

$$$$ | **HOTEL** | A perfect spot for a romantic getaway is this lavish adults-only hotel located at the heart of Tulum's world-famous hotel zone. **Pros:** exotic sunset dinner in nest-like setting; great beach; stunning handmade wood bathtub. **Cons:** no meals included; some rooms don't have ocean views; no kids allowed. [$] *Rooms from: $480* ✉ *Carretera Tulum a Boca Paila Km 7.5, Zona Hotelera* ☎ *984/280–5556* 🌐 *ahaucollection.com* 🛏 *23 rooms* 🍴 *No Meals.*

La Zebra

$$$$ | **RESORT** | This jungle-chic, environmentally conscious hotel on a pristine beach is all about the details: colorful, traditional cotton robes made on a loom, handblown glasses from Jalisco, and plunge pools that can be cool or heated. **Pros:** plunge pool in your private cabana; on-site beach bar with a mix-your-own-drink menu; good restaurant that uses sustainable practices. **Cons:** high prices; usually booked months in advance; no

TVs in rooms. [$] *Rooms from: $744* ✉ *Carretera Tulum–Boca Paila, Km 8.2, Zona Hotelera* ☎ *303/952–0595 in the U.S.,* *984/115–4728* ⊕ *www.lazebratulum. com* ⌁ *29 suites* ⦿ *No Meals.*

Mezzanine

$$$ | **HOTEL** | On the quieter side of Tulum's beachfront, this small, hip hotel is a 25-minute walk from the ruins along a powdery stretch of white sand. **Pros:** yoga mats, beach baskets, earplugs, sleeping masks, and sun hats provided; popular Thai restaurant on-site; fresh morning coffee basket delivered to your door. **Cons:** some rooms lack view; small pool area gets crowded; no kids under 16. [$] *Rooms from: $383* ✉ *Carretera Tulum–Boca Paila, Km 1.5, Tulum* ☎ *984/115–4728, 303/952–0595 in U.S.* ⊕ *www.mezzaninetulum.com* ⌁ *9 rooms* ⦿ *No Meals.*

Nest Tulum

$$$$ | **HOTEL** | When you think in Tulum, you have in mind something like this chic beachfront boutique hotel of minimalist design and luxury comfort throughout its 12 rooms and 1 private villa. **Pros:** shared bikes; intimate atmosphere; complimentary welcome cocktail. **Cons:** no swimming pool; some rooms don't have ocean views; no kids. [$] *Rooms from: $438* ✉ *Carretera Tulum Boca Paila Km 9.5, Zona Hotelera* ☎ *984/141–5433, 970/433–2019 in U.S.* ⊕ *nesttulum.com* ⌁ *13 rooms* ⦿ *Free Breakfast.*

Villa Pescadores

$$$$ | **HOTEL** | What used to be a fishermen's village is now a hip, upscale hotel consisting of 18 rustic-like but quite classy bungalows, with an eclectic design doing great use of local woods and thatched roofs. **Pros:** great restaurant; outdoor balconies with hammocks; non-motorized water sports available. **Cons:** no TV; no swimming pool; no meals included. [$] *Rooms from: $400* ✉ *Carretera Tulum - Boca Paila Km 0.5, Zona*

Hotelera ☎ *984/214–3457* ⊕ *ahaucollection.com* ⌁ *18 rooms* ⦿ *No Meals.*

Zamas

$$$$ | **HOTEL** | On wild Punta Piedra (Rock Point), Zamas has small, rustic cabanas with palapa roofs and ocean views as far as the eye can see, as well as jungle-side rooms overlooking a garden, palapas facing a coconut grove strung with colorful hammocks, and two spacious private houses that sleep up to 11. **Pros:** good restaurant; one of the least dense properties in Tulum; unspoiled views. **Cons:** parts of beach are rocky; some traffic noise; four-night minimum stay in houses (no minimum for rooms). [$] *Rooms from: $410* ✉ *Carretera Tulum–Boca Paila, Km 5, Zona Hotelera* ☎ *984/145–2602* ⊕ *www.zamas.com* ⌁ *22 cabanas* ⦿ *No Meals.*

🍸 Nightlife

Gitano

GATHERING PLACES | This atmospheric jungle bar—with bulbs hanging from the trees and flickering candles at every table blinking like fireflies in the night— is known for its handcrafted mezcal cocktails. Cool beats come compliments of a DJ Friday nights and live bands on Wednesday and Sunday in high season. Mezcal tastings are also available. Bring a loaded wallet as drinks are pricey but powerful. Night owls take note, this place shuts down around 11. ✉ *Boca Paila Rd., Km 7.5, jungle side, next to Hartwood, Zona Hotelera* ☎ *984/745–9068* ⊕ *www. gitanotulum.com.*

La Zebra

COCKTAIL LOUNGES | Enjoy the sophistication of New York city's Mulberry Project at this beachfront hot spot, where you can hear live music and enjoy cocktails made with their own sugarcane. Every Tuesday, cocktails are 2 for 1 and La Zebra becomes the place to be. ✉ *Carretera Tulum–Boca Paila, Km 8.2,*

Zona Hotelera ☎ 303/952–0595 in U.S., 984/115–4726 ⊕ www.lazebratulum.com.

Papaya Playa Project

DANCE CLUBS | Party people gather at this beachfront nightclub where DJs spin electronic and house music on Saturday nights. It's especially renowned for its monthly full-moon parties. Papaya Playa Project doubles as a hotel, but most people come here to simply kick off their flip-flops and dance among the trees. ✉ *Carretera Tulum-Boca Paila, Km 4.5, Zona Hotelera ☎ 984/116–3774 ⊕ www.papayaplayaproject.com.*

🏃 Activities

BICYCLING
Punta Piedra Bike Rental

BIKING | Daily bike rentals are the focus at this small shop—but don't be fooled by the name. It rents boogie boards (MX$67), scooters (MX$542), and snorkel gear (MX$135), too. The owner, Felix, can also organize two-hour snorkeling tours for MX$406. Cash only. ✉ *Carretera Tulum–Boca Paila, Km 4, Zona Hotelera ☎ 984/157–4248 ⊕ facebook.com/PuntapiedraTulum ⚑ Bikes MX$135 per day.*

KITEBOARDING
Mexican Caribbean Kitesurf & Paddlesurf

WINDSURFING | Located in front of the Ahau Tulum, this school gives lessons in kitesurfing and paddleboarding. Its popular stand-up paddleboard tours take you to a cenote, a reef, or a gorgeous lagoon in the Sian Ka'an Biosphere. ✉ *Carretera Tulum–Boca Paila, Km 7.5, Tulum ☎ 984/168–1023 ⊕ www.mexicancaribbeankitesurf.com ⚑ Paddleboard lessons from USD$70; kitesurf lessons from USD$80; tours from USD$100.*

SPAS
Sanara Tulum Spa & Wellness Center

SPAS | This small, quiet spa in the center of the Sanara boutique hotel property, decorated with dreamcatchers, bamboo ladders, and whitewashed furnishings,

is home to four treatment rooms and a rooftop relaxation area with 360-degree views over the jungle and beach. Head-to-toe relaxing massage is the specialty here, though special Maya wellness treatments—including a Maya astrology reading and meditating at a cenote—are also available both on- and off-site. ✉ *Sanara Hotel, Carretera Cobá–Boca Paila, Km 8.2, Tulum ☎ 984/185–5059 ⊕ sanaratulum.com/wellness-spa ⚑ Massage starting at USD$135 for 60 mins.*

Cobá

42 km (26 miles) northwest of Tulum.

Near five lakes and between coastal watchtowers and inland cities, Cobá (pronounced ko- *bah*) once exercised economic control over the region through a network of at least 16 *sacbeob* (white-stone roads)—one, measuring 100 km (62 miles), is the longest in the Maya world. The city covered 70 square km (27 square miles), making it a noteworthy sister to Tikal in northern Guatemala, with which it had close cultural and commercial ties. Cobá is noted for its massive temple-pyramids, including the largest and highest one in northern Yucatán (it stands 138 feet tall). Although often overlooked by visitors who opt for better-known Tulum, Cobá is less crowded, giving you a chance to immerse yourself in ancient culture.

GETTING HERE AND AROUND
Cobá is a 35-minute drive northwest of Tulum, along a road that leads straight through the jungle. Taxis from Tulum cost about MX$338. ADO (⊕ www.ado.com.mx) runs buses here from Playa del Carmen and Tulum at least three times a day: expect to pay about MX$95 between Cobá and Playa, MX$85 between Cobá and Tulum

The ruins of Cobá are best explored by bike.

⊙ Sights

★ Cobá Ruins

RUINS | Mayan for "water stirred by the wind," Cobá flourished from AD 800 to 1100, with a population of as many as 55,000. Now it stands in solitude, and the jungle has overgrown many of its buildings—the silence is broken only by the occasional shriek of a spider monkey or the call of a bird. Most of the trails here are pleasantly shaded; processions of huge army ants cross the footpaths as the sun slips through openings between the tall hardwood trees, ferns, and giant palms. Cobá's ruins are spread out and best explored on a bike, which you can rent for MX$40 a day. Taxi-bike tours are available for MX$120 for an hour and 20 minutes or MX$190 for two hours. If you plan on walking instead, expect to cover 5 to 6 km (3 to 4 miles). The main groupings of ruins are separated by several miles of dense vegetation, but you can scale one of the pyramids to get a sense of the city's immensity. Don't be tempted by the narrow paths that lead into the jungle unless you have a qualified guide with you. It's easy to get lost here, so stay on the main road, wear comfortable shoes, and bring insect repellent, sunscreen, and drinking water. Inside the site, there are no restrooms and only one small hut selling water (cash only). The first major cluster of structures, to your right as you enter the ruins, is the **Cobá Group**, whose pyramids are around a sunken patio. At the near end of the group, facing a large plaza, is the 79-foot-high temple, which was dedicated to the rain god, Chaac. Some Maya still place offerings and light candles here in hopes of improving their harvests. Around the rear, to the left, is a restored ball court, where a sacred game was once played to petition the gods for rain, fertility, and other blessings. Farther along the main path to your left is the **Chumuc Mul Group**, little of which has been excavated. The principal pyramid here is covered with the remains of vibrantly painted stucco motifs (*chumuc mul* means "stucco pyramid"). A kilometer (½ mile) past this site is the **Nohoch Mul Group** (Large Hill

Caste Wars 👁

When Mexico won independence from Spain in 1821, there wasn't much for the Maya to celebrate. They continued to be treated as second-class, "lower-caste" citizens, just as they had under centuries of Spanish rule, and the new government refused to return confiscated lands. In Valladolid in 1847, the Maya rose up in a coordinated rebellion. Within a year, hundreds of Mexicans were dead, and the Caste War of the Yucatán was on.

Help for the embattled Mexicans arrived with a vengeance from Mexico City, Cuba, and the United States. By 1850 the tables had turned, and as many as 200,000 Maya—nearly half the population—were killed. Survivors fled to the jungles and held out for decades, until government troops finally withdrew in 1915. The Maya controlled Quintana Roo from Tulum, their headquarters, but were finally forced to accept Mexican rule in 1935.

Group), the highlight of which is the pyramid of the same name, the tallest at Cobá. It has 120 steps—equivalent to 12 stories—and shares a plaza with Temple 10. The Descending God (also seen at Tulum) is depicted on a facade of the temple atop Nohoch Mul, which you can climb for an excellent view. Beyond the Nohoch Mul Group is the **Castillo**, with nine chambers that are reached by a stairway. To the south are the remains of a ball court, including the stone ring through which the ball was hurled. From the main route, follow the sign to **Las Pinturas Group**, named for the still-discernible polychrome friezes on the inner and outer walls of its large, patioed pyramid. An enormous stela here depicts a man standing with his feet on two prone captives. Take the minor path for 1 km (½ mile) to the **Macanxoc Group**, not far from the lake of the same name. The main pyramid at Macanxoc is accessible by a stairway. ✉ ⊕ *42 km (26 miles) northwest of Tulum* 🎫 *MX$55.*

Pac Chen

TOWN | This Maya jungle settlement is home to about 200 people who still live in round thatch huts and pray to the gods for good crops. You can only visit on trips organized by Alltournative, an ecotour company based in Playa del Carmen.

The "Cobá Maya Encounter" includes transportation, entrance to Cobá ruins, lunch, and Maya guides within Pac Chen, which accepts no more than 120 visitors on any given day. Alltournative pays the villagers a monthly stipend to protect the land; this money has made the village self-sustaining, and has given the inhabitants an alternative to logging and hunting, which were their main means of livelihood before. The half-day tour starts with a trek through the jungle to a cenote where you grab onto a harness and zipline to the other side. Next is the Jaguar cenote, set deeper into the forest, where you must rappel down the cave-like sides into a cool underground lagoon. You'll eat lunch under an open-air palapa overlooking another lagoon, where canoes await. The food includes such Maya dishes as grilled achiote (annatto seed) chicken, fresh tortillas, beans, and watermelon. ✉ *Cobá* ☎ *877/437–4990, 984/803–9999* ⊕ *www.alltournative.com* 🎫 *USD$139.*

🍽 Restaurants

Ki-Hanal

$$ | **MEXICAN** | You can't get any closer to the ruins than this two-story restaurant in a palapa setting with Mexican blankets draped over wooden tables. Some of the more traditional selections include fish prepared Yucatán style, chicken in banana leaves, and *cochinita pibil*. **Known for:** cochinita pibil; fresh salads; Yucatán-style fish. [$] *Average main: MP160* ✉ *To the right of the Cobá ruins entrance, Cobá* ☎ *984/173–5661* ⏲ *No dinner.*

Hotels

La Selva Mariposa

$ | **HOTEL** | Halfway between Tulum's beaches and Cobá's ruins, this jungle sanctuary provides the perfect escape for travelers wanting the best of both worlds. **Pros:** bikes for exploring; peaceful retreat; delightful breakfast. **Cons:** advance reservations required; 20 minutes from beach; not all rooms allow children. [$] *Rooms from: $1000* ✉ *Carretera Tulum–Coba, Km 20, Cobá* ✥ *On road to Cobá, turn right at Km 20 after first speed bump, just past the small store with "SOL" sign. Follow signs to hotel* ☎ *553/204–7042* 🌐 *facebook.com/laselvamariposa* 🛏 *4 rooms* 🍴 *Free Breakfast.*

Reserva de la Biósfera Sian Ka'an

15 km (9 miles) south of Tulum to Punta Allen turnoff, 252 km (156 miles) north of Chetumal.

Wildlife has understandably been affected by the development of coastal resorts; however, thanks to the federal government's foresight, 1.3 million acres of coastline and jungle have been set aside for protection as the Reserva de la Biósfera Sian Ka'an. Whatever may happen elsewhere along the coast, this pristine wilderness preserve (Mexico's second largest after the Reserva de la Biósfera Calakmul) remains a haven both for thousands of species of wildlife and for travelers who seek the Yucatán of old.

GETTING HERE AND AROUND

To explore on your own, follow the beach road past Boca Paila to the secluded 35-km (22-mile) coastal strip of land that's part of the reserve. You'll be limited to swimming, snorkeling, and camping on the beaches, as there are no trails into the surrounding jungle. The narrow, rough dirt roads down the peninsula are filled with monstrous potholes, completely impassable after a rainfall. In rainy season, don't attempt it without a four-wheel-drive vehicle.

The archaeological ruins at Muyil sit on the northwestern edge of Sian Ka'an, about 16 km (10 miles) south of Tulum on Carretera 307.

TOURS

Visit Sian Ka'an. ✉ *Coastal rd. Tulum-Boca Paila-Punta Allen, Km 15.8, Sian Ka'an* ☎ *984/141–4245, 984/108–8853* 🌐 *www.visitsiankaan.com.*

VISITOR INFORMATION

CONTACTS Sian Ka'an Visitor Center. ☎ *998/887–1969, 984/141–4245.*

Sights

Muyil (*Chunyaxché*)

RUINS | This photogenic archaeological site at the northern end of the Sian Ka'an biosphere reserve is underrated. Once known as Chunyaxché, it's now called by its ancient name, Muyil (pronounced *moo-HILL*). It dates from the late preclassic era, when it was connected by road to the sea and served as a port between Cobá and the Maya centers in Belize and Guatemala. A 15-foot-wide *sacbé*, built during the postclassic period, extended from the city to the mangrove swamp and was still in use when the Spaniards arrived. Structures were erected at 400-foot intervals along the white limestone road, almost all of them facing west, but there are only three still standing. At the beginning of the 20th century the ancient stones

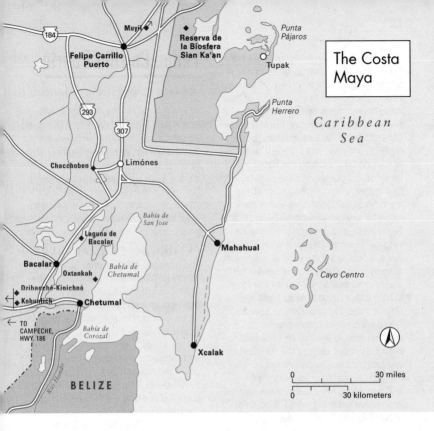

The Costa Maya

Punta Pájaros

Muyil

Reserva de
la Biosfera
Sian Ka'an

Tupak

Felipe Carrillo
Puerto

Punta
Herrero

*Caribbean
Sea*

Chacchoben   Limónes

*Bahía de
San José*

Laguna de
Bacalar

Mahahual

Bacalar

Oxtankah

*Bahía de
Chetumal*

Cayo Centro

Dzibanché-Kinichná

Kohunlich   Chetumal

TO
CAMPECHE,
HWY. 186

*Bahía de
Corozal*

Xcalak

BELIZE

Río Hondo

| 0 | | 30 miles |
| 0 | | 30 kilometers |

were used to build a chicle (natural gum) plantation, which was managed by one of the leaders of the Caste Wars. The most notable site at Muyil today is the remains of the 56-foot Castillo—one of the tallest on the Quintana Roo coast—at the center of a large acropolis. During excavations of the Castillo, jade figurines representing the goddess Ixchel were found. Recent excavations at Muyil have uncovered some smaller structures. The ruins stand near the edge of a deep-blue lagoon and are surrounded by almost impenetrable jungle, so be sure to bring insect repellent. You can drive down a dirt road on the side of the ruins to swim or fish in the lagoon. The bird-watching is also exceptional here; come at dawn, before the site officially opens (there's no gate) to make the most of it. ⊠ *Carretera 307, 16 km (10 miles) south of Tulum,* ⊕ *www.inah.gob.mx* ⊠ *MX$40.*

★ Sian Ka'an

NATURE PRESERVE | FAMILY | One of the last undeveloped stretches of coastline in North America, Sian Ka'an was declared a wildlife preserve in 1986, and a UNESCO World Heritage Site in 1987. The 1.3-million acre reserve accounts for 10% of the land in the state of Quintana Roo and covers 100 km (62 miles) of coastline. It's amazingly diverse, encompassing freshwater and coastal lagoons, mangrove swamps, cayes, savannas, tropical forests, and a barrier reef. Hundreds of species of local and migratory birds, fish, animals, and plants share the land with fewer than 1,000 Maya residents. The area was first settled by the Maya in the 5th century AD—the name Sian Ka'an translates to "where the sky is born." There are approximately 32 ruins (none excavated) linked by a unique canal system—one of the few of its kind in Mayan Mexico. There's a MX$29 entrance charge for the park, but to see much of anything, you should take a guided tour.Many species of the once-flourishing wildlife have fallen into the endangered category, but the waters here still teem with roosterfish, bonefish, mojarra, snapper, shad, permit, sea bass, and crocodiles. Fishing the flats for wily bonefish is popular, and the peninsula's few lodges also run deep-sea fishing trips. Most fishing lodges along the way close for the rainy season in August and September, and accommodations are hard to come by. The road ends at Punta Allen, a fishing village whose main catch is spiny lobster, which was becoming scarce until ecologists taught the local fishing cooperative how to build and lay special traps to conserve the species. There are several small, expensive guesthouses. If you haven't booked ahead, start out early in the morning so you can get back to civilization before dark. ✉ *Coastal rd. Tulum-Boca Paila-Punta Allen, Km 15.8, just beyond the Arco Maya (arch entrance), Sian Ka'an* ☎ *998/887–1969.*

🛏 Hotels

Casa Blanca Lodge

$$$$ | **ALL-INCLUSIVE** | This fishing lodge is on a rocky outcrop on remote Punta Pájaros Island, reputed to be one of the best places in the world for light-tackle saltwater fly-fishing. **Pros:** remote location; Mayan ruins on the island; comfortable rooms. **Cons:** one-week minimum stay; far from anywhere else; all-inclusive package doesn't cover drinks. 💲 *Rooms from: $659* ✉ *Punta Pájaros, Sian Ka'an* ☎ *877/261–8867 in U.S.* ⊕ *www. casablancafishing.com* ➪ *10 rooms* ⏐◎⏐ *All-Inclusive.*

Felipe Carrillo Puerto

156 km (97 miles) north of Chetumal.

Felipe Carrillo Puerto, the Costa Maya's first major town, is named for the governor of Yucatán in 1920, who was hailed as a hero after instituting a series of reforms to help the impoverished *campesinos* (peasants). Midway between Tulum and the beaches of the Costa Maya, the town itself has very little to offer visitors; however, Chacchoben, a little-explored archaeological site, isn't·far.

GETTING HERE AND AROUND

You guessed it—Carretera 307, known locally as Avenida Benito Juárez, runs right through the center of town. Just drive straight and you can't miss it. ADO (⊕ *www.ado.com.mx*) links Cancún, Puerto Morelos, Playa del Carmen, Tulum, Felipe Carrillo Puerto, Limones, and Chetumal by bus. Taxis drive up and down the street if you arrive without your own wheels. The tourist office is at the corner of Avenida Juárez and Avenida Santiago Pacheco Cruz. As you enter town, there's an HSBC bank with an ATM and a Pemex gas station (it's one of the few places to fuel up between here and Chetumal).

👁 Sights

Chacchoben

RUINS | Excavated in 2005, Chacchoben (pronounced *CHA-cho-ben*) is an ancient city that was a contemporary of Kohunlich and the most important trading partner with Guatemala north of the Bacalar Lagoon area. Several newly unearthed buildings are still in good condition. The lofty Templo Uno, the site's main temple, was dedicated to the Maya sun god, Itzamná, and once held a royal tomb. (When archaeologists found it, though, it had already been looted.) Most of the site was built around AD 200, in the Petén style of the early classic period, although the city could have been inhabited as early as 200 BC. It's thought that inhabitants made their living growing cotton and extracting chewing gum and copal resin from the trees. ✉ *Felipe Carrillo Puerto* ✣ *From Carretera 307, turn right on Carretera 293 south of Cafetal, continue 9 km (5½ miles) passing Lázaro Cardenas town* 🌐 *www.inah.gob.mx* 🎫 *MX$55.*

Hotels

El Faisán y El Venado

$ | **HOTEL** | If you absolutely need a place to stay in the area, then this simple three-story hotel is really your only remotely acceptable option. **Pros:** best place to stay in town; strong air-conditioning; central location. **Cons:** Wi-Fi in common areas only; staff speaks little English; no-frills rooms. [$] *Rooms from: $44* ✉ *Av. Benito Juárez, Lote 781,* ☎ *983/834–0702, 983/834–0043* 🛏 *37 rooms* 🍴 *No Meals.*

Bacalar

40 km (25 miles) northwest of Chetumal.

Founded in AD 435, Bacalar (pronounced *baa*-ka-lar) is one of Quintana Roo's oldest settlements. The town's most notable feature is a cenote-fed lake of the same name—Laguna de Bacalar. The mix of freshwater and salt water that intensifies its color has earned this long, narrow body of water the nickname "Lago de los Siete Colores" (Lake of the Seven Colors). Marking the entrance to Bacalar is Cenote Azul, a crystalline cenote that's 300 feet deep and 600 feet across. The water is clean and the diving is excellent here.

GETTING HERE AND AROUND

Bacalar is 30 minutes north of Chetumal, just off Carretera 307. If you're coming from Cancún, follow the well-marked signs. Upon entering the town, you'll cross over two huge speed bumps. Pass the Catholic church on your right, take a left at the first corner, and continue straight to the town square (Bacalar has no bank, but there is an ATM on this square); to your left will be the Fort of San Felipe. Northbound drivers should take Carretera 106 to 307 and enter at Km 34, marked by a sign for "Cenote Azul." Just past the cenote is a paved road that parallels Laguna de Bacalar and eventually leads to the town center.

Sights

Fuerte de San Felipe Bacalar (*San Felipe Fort*)

MILITARY SIGHT | This 17th-century stone fort was built by the Spaniards using stones from the nearby Mayan pyramids. It was originally constructed as a haven against pirates and marauding bandits, then was transformed into a Maya stronghold during the Caste Wars. Today the monolithic structure, which overlooks the enormous Laguna de Bacalar, houses government offices and a museum with exhibits on local history (ask for someone to bring a key if museum doors are locked). ✉ *Av 3, Centro, Bacalar* ☎ *983/832–6838* 🕒 *Closed Mon.* 🎫 *MX$67.*

★ **Laguna de Bacalar** (*Lago de los Siete Colores*)

BODY OF WATER | Some 42 km (26 miles) long but no more than 2 km (1 mile) wide, Laguna de Bacalar is the town's focal point. The lake is renowned for both its vibrant green-and-blue waters and for the age-old limestone formations (stromatolites) that line its shores. Fed by underground cenotes, the mix of freshwater and salt water here creates ideal conditions for a refreshing swim. Most hotels along Laguna de Bacalar rent kayaks and paddleboats; however, there are no beaches or amenities other than those found in rental properties or hotels. English-speaking guide Victor Rosales (☎ *983/733–6712*), who organizes

The Laguna de Bacalar is known for its giant stromatolites—limestone formations that are estimated to be 3½ billion years old.

custom excursions throughout the Costa Maya, offers a particularly fascinating tour of the lake's 3.5-billion-year-old stromatolites. ✉ *Bacalar coastal rd., Bacalar.*

🍴 Restaurants

Jaguara Cocina Mexicana

$$$ | **MEXICAN** | This lagoon shore restaurant serves gourmet Mexican dishes and exotic cocktails to enjoy with the best view in town and live music most days. Go for the al pastor seared tuna as the main course, and don't leave without trying the tribute to cacao as dessert. **Known for:** outstanding location; organic cocktails; live music. [$] *Average main: MP295* ✉ *Boulevard Costero Norte 1255, Bacalar* ☎ *983/112–1311* 🌐 *facebook.com/jaguara.mx* ⏲ *Closed Mon. and Tues.*

Restaurant Cenote Azul

$$$ | **SEAFOOD** | Perched on the rim of the 300-foot-deep cenote, this palapa restaurant charges a MX$10 entrance fee to access the site. Busloads of tourists come to dine on chicken, pork, and fish dishes, as well as house specialties like the seafood platter and shrimp kebab. **Known for:** shrimp kebab; seafood platter; a lovely setting. [$] *Average main: MP203* ✉ *Carretera 307, Km 34, Bacalar* ☎ *983/834–2460.*

🛏 Hotels

Akalki (*Centro Holistico Akalki*)

$$$ | **B&B/INN** | Considered the most upscale property on Laguna de Bacalar, Akalki offers nine luxurious cabanas built over the water, each with a private dock and direct access to the enchanting turquoise waters. **Pros:** overwater bungalow experience; romantic setting; immaculate rooms. **Cons:** tons of mosquitoes; Wi-Fi in common areas only; no outlets in the rooms. [$] *Rooms from: $258* ✉ *Carretera 307, Km 12.5, Bacalar* ☎ *983/106–1751* 🌐 *www.akalki.com* 🛏 *11 rooms* 🍴 *No Meals.*

Carolina Lake Front Hotel

$$$ | HOTEL | FAMILY | This chic little hotel set right in front of the lagoon provides its guests with comfort without exuberance, an excellent restaurant, and the tranquility one craves when visiting Bacalar. **Pros:** complimentary use of kayaks; private dock; balconies with hammocks. **Cons:** spotty WI-FI; some rooms have no lagoon views; lots of mosquitoes. $ *Rooms from: $220* ⊠ *Boulevard Costero de Bacalar Sur No.625, Bacalar* ☎ *983/154–1810* ⊕ *carolinabacalar.mx* ⇌ *16 rooms* ⦿ *Free Breakfast.*

Makaabá Hotel Eco Boutique

$$ | HOTEL | This eco-friendly hotel is located just a block away from the lagoon shore and offers a laidback attitude with personalized service. **Pros:** eco-friendly practices; spectacular swimming pool; great restaurant. **Cons:** small rooms; not in the lagoon shore; lack of privacy. $ *Rooms from: $125* ⊠ *Blvd. Costera de Bacalar Sur No. 506, Bacalar* ☎ *555/215–1511* ⊕ *hotelmakaaba.com* ⇌ *11 rooms* ⦿ *Free Breakfast.*

★ Rancho Encantado

$$ | HOTEL | On the shores of Laguna Bacalar, Rancho Encantado's property is dotted with freestanding Mayan-themed casitas; each is uniquely decorated with murals and hammocks and can comfortably sleep four people. **Pros:** huge Jacuzzi; friendly staff; Wi-Fi in restaurant. **Cons:** mosquitoes; need car to get around; low water pressure. $ *Rooms from: $110* ⊠ *Carretera 307, Km 24, look for turnoff sign, Bacalar* ☎ *998/884–1181, 998/884–2071* ⊕ *www.encantado.com* ⇌ *16 rooms* ⦿ *Free Breakfast.*

Chetumal

328 km (283 miles) southeast of Playa del Carmen.

At times, Chetumal—the capital city of Quintana Roo—feels more Caribbean than Mexican; this isn't surprising, given its proximity to Belize. A population that includes Afro-Caribbean and Middle Eastern immigrants creates a melting pot of music (reggae, salsa, calypso) and cuisines (Yucatecan, Mexican, Lebanese). Because this is the closest major community to Bacalar, Mahahual, and Xcalak, many residents from neighboring towns come here to do banking and stock up on supplies. Traffic can get very congested, but you will see very few tourists. Nevertheless, this small city has a number of parks on a waterfront that's as pleasant as it is long: the Bay of Chetumal surrounds the city on three sides. Tours can take you to the fascinating nearby ruins of Kohunlich, Dzibanché, and Kinichná, a trio dubbed the "Valley of the Masks."

GETTING HERE AND AROUND

Aeropuerto Internacional Chetumal (CTM), on the city's southwestern edge, has daily Interjet flights to and from Mexico City. Chetumal's main bus terminal, at Avenida Salvador Novo 179, is served mainly by ADO (⊕ *www.ado. com.mx*). The bus trip from Cancún takes five hours and 45 minutes, with stops along the way in Puerto Morelos, Playa del Carmen, Tulum, Felipe Carrillo Puerto, and Limones; tickets costs MX$354. There's an ATM at the bus station. On Avenida Insurgentes, there's a bank and ATM in the center of the shopping mall. If you're driving here, be sure to fill up at the Pemex station in Felipe Carrillo Puerto, one of the few stations along this stretch of Carretera 307.

VISITOR INFORMATION

CONTACTS Chetumal Tourist Information.
✉ *Calles 28 de Enero and Reforma, Chetumal* ☎ *983/832–6647.*

👁 Sights

Dzibanché-Kinichná

RUINS | The alliance between sister cities Dzibanché and Kinichná was thought to have made them the most powerful cities in southern Quintana Roo during the Mayan classic period (AD 100–1000). The fertile farmlands surrounding the ruins are still used today as they were hundreds of years ago, and the winding drive deep into the fields makes you feel as if you're coming upon something undiscovered. Archaeologists have been making progress in excavating more and more ruins, albeit slowly. At Dzibanché ("place where they write on wood," pronounced *zee-ban-CHE*), several carved wooden lintels have been found; the most perfectly preserved sample is in a supporting arch at the **Plaza de Xibalba**. Also at the plaza is the **Templo del Búho** (Temple of the Owl), atop which a recessed tomb was discovered—only the second of its kind in Mexico (the first was at Palenque in Chiapas). In the tomb were magnificent clay vessels painted with white owls, messengers of the underworld gods. More buildings and three plazas have been restored as excavation continues. Several other plazas are surrounded by temples, palaces, and pyramids, all in the Petén style. The carved stone steps at **Edificio 13** and **Edificio 2** (Buildings 13 and 2) still bear traces of stone masks. A copy of the famed lintel of **Templo IV** (Temple IV), with eight glyphs dating from AD 618, is housed in the Museo de la Cultura Maya in Chetumal. (The original was replaced in 2003 because of deterioration.) Four more tombs were discovered at **Templo I** (Temple I). ✉ *Carretera 186 (Chetumal–Escárcega), 80 km (50 miles) west of Chetumal, Chetumal* ✚ *Following Carretera 186 (Chetumal–Escárcega), turn north at Km 58 and pass through town of Morocoy; continue 2 km (1 mile) farther, and turn right at sign for Dzibanché. The entrance is 7 km (4½ miles) away* ⊕ *www.inah.gob.mx* 🎫 *MX$55.*

Kinichná

RUINS | After you see Dzibanché, make your way back to the fork in the road and head to Kinichná ("House of the Sun," pronounced kin-itch-*na*). At the fork, you'll see the restored **Complejo Lamai** (Lamai Complex), the administrative buildings of Dzibanché. Kinichná consists of a two-level pyramidal mound split into Acropolis B and Acropolis C, apparently dedicated to the sun god. Two mounds at the foot of the pyramid suggest that the temple was a ceremonial site. Here a giant Olmec-style jade figure was found. At its summit, Kinichná affords one of the finest views of any archaeological site in the area. ✉ *Carretera 186 Chetumal–Escárcega, 80 km (50 miles) west of Chetumal, Chetumal* ✚ *Following Carretera 186 Chetumal–Escárcega, turn north at Km 58 and pass through town of Morocoy; continue 2 km (1 mile) farther, and turn right at the sign for Dzibanché. The entrance for both ruins is 7 km (4½ miles) away. Pass Dzibanché, and veer left toward the hill where Kinichná is located* ☎ 🎫 *MX$48 (includes Dzibanché).*

Kohunlich

RUINS | Kohunlich (pronounced *KO-hoon-lich*) is renowned for the giant stucco masks on its principal pyramid, the **Edificio de los Mascarones** (Mask Building). It also has one of Quintana Roo's oldest ball courts and the remains of a great drainage system at the **Plaza de las Estelas** (Plaza of the Stelae). Masks that are about 6 feet tall are set vertically into the wide staircases at the main pyramid, called **Edificio de las Estelas** (Building of the Stelae). First thought to represent the Maya sun god, they're now considered to be composites of Kohunlich's rulers and important warriors. Another giant mask was discovered in 2001 in the building's upper staircase. Kohunlich was built and occupied during the classic period by various Maya groups. This explains the eclectic architecture, which includes the Petén and Río Bec styles. Although there are 14 buildings to visit, it's thought that there are at least 500 mounds on the site waiting to be excavated. Digs have turned up 29 individual and multiple burial sites inside a residence building called **Temple de Los Viente-Siete Escalones** (Temple of the Twenty-Seven Steps). This site doesn't have a great deal of tourist traffic, so it's surrounded by thriving flora and fauna. ✉ *Off Carretera 186 (Chetumal–Escárcega), 65 km (46 miles) west of Chetumal, Chetumal* ✣ *Follow Carretera 186 west of Chetumal for 65 km (40 miles); continue another 9 km (5½ miles) south on side road to ruins* 🌐 *www.inah.gob.mx* 🎫 *MX$65.*

Museo de la Cultura Maya

HISTORY MUSEUM | FAMILY | Dedicated to the complex world of the Maya, this interactive museum is outstanding. Exhibits in Spanish and English trace Maya architecture, social classes, politics, and customs. The most impressive display is the three-story Sacred Ceiba Tree, a symbol used by the Maya to explain the relationship between the cosmos and Earth. The first floor represents the tree's roots and the Maya underworld, called Xibalba; the middle floor is the tree trunk, known as Middle World, home to humans and all their trappings; on the top floor, leaves and branches evoke the 13 heavens of the cosmic otherworld. ✉ *Av. Héroes and Calle Mahatma Gandhi,* ☎ *983/832–6838* 🎫 *MX$62* ⏲ *Closed Mon.*

Oxtankah

RUINS | The small ruins at Oxtankah are worth a visit if you're in the Chetumal area. Named for the Ramon trees ("ox" in Mayan) that populate the grounds, they're in a parklike setting and take about an hour to explore. The ruins include a Spanish mission, a pyramid, and several other structures. Archaeologists believe this city's prosperity peaked between AD 200 and 600. Maya groups returned to the area during the 15th and 16th centuries, using old stone to build new structures. There are toilets, free parking, and a tiny museum on-site but no food or drink available, so come prepared. ✉ *Calderitas, 16 km (10 miles) north of Chetumal, Chetumal* ✣ *Take Carretera Chetumal-Calderitas (Av. Heroes) north of town and continue on the paved road bordering the bay; 4½ km (3 miles) to the north is the sign that marks access to the archaeological zone* 🎫 *MX$43.*

Beaches

Chetumal Bay

BEACH | Several grassy beach parks, including Punta Estrella and Dos Mulas, surround the bay. The latter is not recommended due to cleanliness issues. But Punta Estrella has parking, toilets, volleyball courts, and a small boat marina. The water here is calm, if cloudy, and there's plenty of shade from trees and little palapa-topped picnic tables. Popular with fishermen, the bay itself is shallow and the flats go on for miles. **Amenities:** food and drink; parking (no fee); toilets. **Best for:** walking. ✉ *Chetumal.*

Restaurants

Sergio's Restaurant & Pizzas

$$$ | PIZZA | FAMILY | Locals rave about the grilled steaks and garlic shrimp at Sergio's—one of the nicest restaurants in Chetumal. The barbecued chicken (made with the owner's special sauce) and smoked-oyster or seafood pizzas are equally tasty. **Known for:** grilled steak; garlic shrimp; barbecued chicken. [$] *Average main: MP203* ✉ *Av. Alvaro Obregón 182, at Av. 5 de Mayo, Chetumal* ☎ *983/832–0882* 🌐 *sergiospizzas.com.mx.*

El Patio del 30

$$$ | **INTERNATIONAL** | Very few places in Chetumal offer the kind of dining experience available at this cozy restaurant. Come for the pizza, stay for the cocktails and the live music. **Known for:** original cocktail menu; specialty pizzas; live music. [$] *Average main: MP300* ✉ *Álvaro Obregón 165, Bacalar* ☎ *983/285–3898* 🌐 *facebook.com/ElPatioDel30.*

Hotels

★ The Explorean Kohunlich

$$$ | **RESORT** | About 40 minutes outside Chetumal, at the edge of the Kohunlich ceremonial grounds, this ecological luxury resort lets you feel adventurous without really roughing it. **Pros:** tours, meals, and transportation included; attentive staff; excellent food. **Cons:** no Internet; expensive; no children under 14. [$] *Rooms from: $250* ✉ *Carretera Chetumal–Escarega, Km 5.6, on rd. to ruins, Chetumal* ☎ *983/689–0042* 🌐 *explorean.com* 🛏 *40 suites* 🍴 *All-Inclusive.*

Hotel Los Cocos

$ | **HOTEL** | Large and modern by Chetumal's standards, Hotel Los Cocos has a pool framed by a pleasant garden (a boon on sweltering days) plus rooms that are clean, if not especially stylish; some have balconies or outside sitting areas. **Pros:** strong water pressure; good location; free Wi-Fi in rooms. **Cons:** loud air-conditioning; staff speaks minimal English; uncomfortable beds. [$] *Rooms from: $76* ✉ *Av. Héroes 134, at Calle Chapultepec, Chetumal* ☎ *983/835–0430* 🌐 *www.hotelloscocos.com.mx* 🛏 *140 rooms* 🍴 *No Meals.*

Hotel Villanueva

$ | **HOTEL** | **FAMILY** | This functional hotel serves as a good launching base for your explorations around the region, just don't expect more than what its basic rates can offer. **Pros:** pet-friendly hotel; centric location; nice indoor swimming pool. **Cons:** mediocre restaurant; uninspired design; limited services at on-site spa. [$] *Rooms from: $60* ✉ *Carmen Ochoa de Merino No. 166, Chetumal* ☎ *983/267–3370* 🌐 *hotelvillanueva.com.mx* 🛏 *72 rooms* 🍴 *No Meals.*

Mahahual

143 km (89 miles) northwest of Chetumal via Carreteras 186 and 307.

Tiny Mahahual (also spelled Majahual) has something of a split personality. With a population of only 600, it's a quiet beachfront outpost with clear, calm waters, good snorkeling and diving, and not a whole lot to do. That's just the way its Mexican and expat U.S. and Canadian residents like it. When the cruise ships are in port, however, this sleepy spot gets a locally unwelcome shot in the arm. Passengers flood its waterside palapa restaurants, beach clubs, and the boardwalk fronting the town's few blocks; it's lively but can be overwhelming. That's when locals and savvy overnight visitors retreat to the handful of delightfully remote beachfront hotels and inns on Mahahual's outskirts, waiting out the crowds in a hammock, beach book in hand.

GETTING HERE AND AROUND

If you're coming by car, take Carretera 307 to Carretera 10, approximately 2½ km (1½ miles) past dusty little Limones (you can't miss the road; it's marked "Mahahual"). Continue for 50 km (30 miles) until you reach the coast; then turn right at the lighthouse and follow the road into town, where a string of hotels and restaurants line the beach. If you're staying at the Almaplena Beach Resort (halfway between Mahahual and Xcalak), turn right at the paved road toward Xcalak and continue for 16 km (10 miles) until you see a sign for Punta Herradura; turn left on this bumpy road and follow the signs to the resort. To reach the port

A stay at the luxurious Almaplena Resort may be just what the doctor ordered if you are looking for a prescription for relaxation.

area of New Mahahual, turn left at Km 55, just past the mayor's office.

Be advised that the beach road south of town is rough and potholed. After it rains driving here can be an adventure. If you're planning to drive south, check with locals for road conditions, and plan plenty of time.

There's a taxi stand at the corner of Avenida Mahahual and Calle Rubic. A full day of transportation with a private driver can be arranged for around MX$1,355. Otherwise, you can expect to pay around MX$10 per km (½ mile). Additional taxis are parked on the west side of the soccer field. Always ask to see a rate card before agreeing to a price.

🔼 Beaches

The three cruise ships that stop here daily have made Mahahual's beach the liveliest place in town. Seaside restaurants dish out cerveza and ceviche, and several vendors offer boat tours

and rental equipment like glass-bottom kayaks. The main beach in the center of town has fine sand and calm waters, great for swimming and snorkeling. Some hotel owners have opened beach clubs to cater to cruise passengers looking for a day (and a drink) in the sun.

BEACH CLUBS
Nacional Beach Club

BEACH | This colorful beach club, exclusively for overnight guests and cruise-ship passengers who purchase a VIP beach club package, is the only one on the Mahahual strip with a pool. Bungalows start at $85 a night and VIP Beach Breaks for cruise passengers are $110 per adult. Both will get you access to the club's pool, restaurant, beach chairs, umbrellas, showers, and changing facilities; VIP guests can also expect a free 20-minute massage (upgrade to an hour for $25), all-you-can-drink cocktails, all-you-can-eat food, and transportation from the port. Margaritas can be delivered to you beachside, or you can escape the heat by grabbing a bite in the enclosed

Mayan Beach Garden Inn

patio. Free Wi-Fi is also included. There's decent snorkeling right out front, and equipment is available next door at Gypsea Divers. Even if you don't get in the water, the four shades of turquoise are breathtaking. Cash only. **Amenities:** food and drink; showers; toilets. **Best for:** partiers; snorkeling; swimming. ⊠ *Av. Mahahual, Mahahual* ☎ *983/834–5719* ⊕ *www.nacionalbeachclub.com.*

Nohoch Kay Beach Club

BEACH | This beachfront restaurant on the boardwalk doubles as a beach club, offering a bar, lunch, beach chairs, umbrellas, and kayaks. There's no fee for using the beach chairs and equipment, but you'll need to consume at least MX$500 worth of food and drink per person. There are restrooms, showers, and an on-site massage therapist ready to work her magic for an extra fee. The restaurant cooks up ceviche, tacos, sandwiches, and nachos, but most people opt for the fresh fish served with tortillas and homemade tartar sauce. Between tanning sessions, you can head to the outer reef on a

private catamaran for a snorkeling tour. Cruise passengers flock to this simple beachfront hot spot, so reserve ahead if you want to be part of the action. **Amenities:** food and drink; showers; toilets; water sports. **Best for:** partiers; snorkeling. ⊠ *Malecón, between Calles Liza and Cazón,* ☎ *983/834-5981* ⊕ *elgrannohoch-kaybigfish.com* ⊠ *MX$500.*

🛏 Hotels

★ Almaplena Resort

$$ | HOTEL | One of only two fully green eco-hotels in the area, Almaplena Resort also happens to be the most luxurious, with rustic-chic rooms featuring textiles from Chiapas, rugs from Michoacan, wood from Yucatán, and iron from Jalisco. **Pros:** spotless rooms; great snorkeling out front; stunning views from rooftop terrace. **Cons:** no TV; low water pressure; bland breakfast. 💲 *Rooms from: $110* ⊠ *Carretera Costera, Mahahual–Xcalak, Km 12.5, Mahahual* ☎ *983/137–5070* ⊕ *www.almaplenabeachresort.com* 🛏 *9 rooms* ❏ *All-Inclusive.*

Balamku Inn on the Beach

$ | **HOTEL** | Ecologically sensitive Balamku, located 5 km (3 miles) south of town, sits on a stretch of pristine private beach where you can lose all track of time. **Pros:** spacious beachfront location; friendly owner; perfect for a quiet getaway outside town, outside the reach of the cruise ship crowds. **Cons:** no TVs; no air-conditioning; a 45-minute walk from town. $ *Rooms from: $85* ⊠ *Carretera Majahual-Xcalak, Km 5.7, Mahahual* ☎ *983/732–1004* ⊕ *www.balamku.com* ⊷ *10 rooms* ⭑◉⭑ *Free Breakfast.*

El Caballo Blanco

$ | **HOTEL** | Since El Caballo Blanco can be accessed only by walking along the beach, there isn't much standing in the way of you and the ocean. **Pros:** great views; great location; rooftop bar and pool. **Cons:** small bathrooms; not all rooms have ocean views; meals not included. $ *Rooms from: MP75* ⊠ *Av. Mahahual, Mza 12, Lote 1, Mahahual* ☎ *983/126–0319* ⊕ *www.hotelelcaballo-blanco.com* ⊷ *7 rooms* ⭑◉⭑ *No Meals.*

★ Kalma 40 Cañones

$$ | **HOTEL** | Ocean breezes sweep through this pretty little hotel adorned with wicker-basket pendant lamps and mosquito-net-draped queen-size beds that swing from ropes. **Pros:** reasonably priced; charming design; comfortable beds. **Cons:** mediocre restaurant; no breakfast included; no pool. $ *Rooms from: MP107* ⊠ *Calle Huachinango,* ☎ *983/123–8591* ⊕ *40-canones.com* ⊷ *26 rooms* ⭑◉⭑ *No Meals.*

Maya Luna

$ | **B&B/INN** | Far from the boardwalk, this small inn on the beach is a quiet, relaxing place. **Pros:** nice restaurant open to the public; relaxed atmosphere; quiet, spacious beachfront location. **Cons:** garbage often washes up on the beach; 10-minute walk to town; no air-conditioning, TVs, or refrigerators in rooms. $ *Rooms from: MP85* ⊠ *Carretera Mahahual-Xcalak, Km 5.2, Mahahual* ☎ *983/836–0905* ⊕ *www.*

hotelmayaluna.com ⊷ *5 bungalows* ⭑◉⭑ *Free Breakfast.*

★ Mayan Beach Garden

$$ | **B&B/INN** | There isn't another hotel for miles, so this solar-powered B&B offers blessed isolation. **Pros:** custom tours available; huge movie and book library; free use of bikes, kayaks, paddleboards, and snorkels. **Cons:** bumpy dirt road means 30-minute drive to town; extra fee to use air-conditioning; no kids under 12 during high season (Christmas to April). $ *Rooms from: $60* ⊠ *N. Carretera Costera Majahual–Punta Herrera, 20 km (12½ miles) north of Mahahual town, Mahahual* ☎ *983/130–8568, 206/905–9665 in the U.S.* ⊕ *www.mayan-beachgarden.com* ⊷ *8 rooms* ⭑◉⭑ *Free Breakfast.*

🏃 Activities

ADVENTURE TOURS

Native Choice

ADVENTURE TOURS | Ivan and David know all there is to know about Cosa Maya sites like Chacchoben, Kohunlich, and Dzibanché. Aside from archaeology-themed outings, their company has tours that focus on adventure and contemporary Maya culture, too. ⊠ *Paseo del Puerto 1239, corner of Chinchorro, Nuevo Mahahual* ☎ *983/103–5955, 998/869–4000* ⊕ *www.thenativechoice.com* 🎫 *From USD$75.*

FISHING

Western Caribbean Fly Fishing School

FISHING | This fly-fishing school offers trips to Sian Ka'an Biosphere, Xcalak, Chetumal Bay, or local cenotes in search of tarpon and snook. Fly-fishing instructor Nick Denbow leads beginners and experts through the fine arts of fly-tying and casting; he also customizes trips for individuals and groups. ⊠ *Calle Bacalar 39, Malecón between calles Liza and Cazón, Mahahual* ☎ *983/732–3144* ⊕ *catchafish.net* 🎫 *From USD$99.*

SCUBA DIVING AND SNORKELING

Dreamtime Dive Resort

DIVING & SNORKELING | This PADI resort has snorkeling tours plus an assortment of one- to three-tank dive trips managed by some of the most experienced divers in the area. It's one of the few operators licensed to organize trips to Banco Chinchorro. Rental gear is available. ✉ *Av. Mahahual, Km 2.5, south of town, Mahahual* ☎ *983/124–0235* ⊕ *www.dreamtimediving.com* ✉ *Snorkeling tours from USD$40; 2-tank dives from USD$85.*

Gypsea Divers

DIVING & SNORKELING | Owners Catherine and Abel offer both dive trips and snorkeling tours. Group discounts are available. ✉ *Av. Mahahual, next to Nacional Beach Club, Mahahual* ☎ *983/130–3714, 983/111–2563* ⊕ *www.gypseadivers.com* ✉ *2-tank dives from $95; snorkeling tours $30.*

Xcalak

180 km (111 miles) southwest of Chetumal.

The southernmost town in Quintana Roo, Xcalak (pronounced *ish*-ka-lack) is only 11 km (7 miles) from the Belize border by water, and a little of both places is evident in local life. Spanish is still the primary language, although most people speak English, and you'll sometimes hear a Caribbean patois. Getting here is an adventure, but it's worth the effort. After all, this remote area offers excellent saltwater fly-fishing; flowers, birds, and butterflies are abundant; and the terrain is marked by savannas, marshes, streams, and island-dotted lagoons. You'll also find fabulously deserted beaches and a small town center comprised of bars, restaurants, and a few food shops.

The entire coast in this area is a designated National Marine Park, and all construction near Xcalak is bound by stringent environmental laws, which protect the natural beauty. By extension, electricity isn't very dependable and tourist amenities are few; the community has no nightlife, and hotels (the majority of which close down during hurricane season) cater mostly to rugged outdoorsy types.

Since there are no standard phones here and cell service is very limited, visitors should plan on being out of touch, or doing as the locals do and keep connected via email or WhatsApp. The lack of phone lines means most hotels don't accept credit cards (or only do so through PayPal) either; moreover, there are no banks or ATMs in or near Xcalak—the closest ATMs are 64 km (40 miles) north in Mahahual—so bring plenty of cash for your entire stay.

GETTING HERE AND AROUND

Following Carretera 10, turn right at the intersection 2 km (1 mile) before Mahahual and continue along the rough and tricky road until you reach Xcalak, about 61 km (37 miles) away. Pass the soccer field and turn left onto the bumpy beach road, now heading north toward "Zona Hotelera," a 14-km (9-mile) stretch of properties lining the beach. Your hotel will probably be within this main area. If you arrive in Xcalak without a car, don't rely on taxi service or local transportation. Consider staying close to town or in a hotel that offers bicycles. Note that this is a great launching point for day trips to Belize and for diving trips to Banco Chinchorro, a coral atoll and national park some two hours northeast by boat.

On a map, the 55 km (34 miles) of bay separating Chetumal from Xcalak looks like an easy boat trip. Unfortunately, shallow sections of the bay make it impassable.

SAFETY
Make sure you have a full tank before you drive south. Although there is a Pemex gas station in Mahahual, it is sometimes closed for no apparent reason. Unlike the trafficked roads along Riviera Maya, the two-lane stretch near Belize is seldom visited by tourists. It's always best to travel with a partner and to drive during daylight hours. Drive with caution and be careful of wild animals and potholes. Once you leave the paved road and enter Xcalak, the road goes from bad to worse. Be sure to rent a car that can handle pitted dirt roads.

Xcalak's growing expat community includes several nurses, who are always willing to help if health issues arise. There's a small clinic in the center of town; however, the "medic" (not always a doctor) is seldom around. Usually, a local can point you in the right direction for rudimentary first aid until you can reach the nearest staffed clinic in Bacalar. The closest small hospital (Carranza Clinic) is in Chetumal.

Beaches

Playa Xcalak
BEACH | Snorkelers and divers love this stretch of coastline, but beachgoers might be a little disappointed. The beach alongside Xcalak town is narrow—eaten away by past hurricanes—and often covered in seaweed and piles of garbage washed in on the tide. The hotels and B&Bs north of town do their best to keep their beaches clean and comfortable, making them the area's best spots for swimming or kayaking. Sections of the beach connect to a network of protected mangroves frequented by manatees. Moreover, the offshore reef of nearby Banco Chinchorro is great for snorkeling, diving, and fishing. **Amenities:** none. **Best for:** snorkeling; swimming. ✉ *Xcalak.*

Restaurants

★ The Leaky Palapa
$$$ | **MEXICAN FUSION** | Nobody expected the kind of sophisticated flavors that the Leaky Palapa brought to town, but this little eight-table palapa restaurant with its upscale-hacienda-meets-secret-garden decor has quickly become *the* place to meet, enjoy a beer, and eat like kings. Feast on lobster bites with cilantro-rice noodles and a ginger sauce that'll keep you coming back for more, squid-ink risotto, tangy pork osso buco, or seared shrimp on bean cakes with tamarind salsa. **Known for:** grilled octopus; shrimp on bean cakes; pork osso buco. [$] *Average main: MP280* ✉ *Calle Pedro Moreno, just past the lighthouse, in the big red house on the left, Xcalak* ☎ *983/210–6559* 🌐 *www.leakypalaparestaurant.com* 🕓 *Closed Sun.–Wed. Nov.–Christmas; Mon.–Wed. Christmas–late Apr.; and May–Oct. No lunch.*

Toby's
$$ | **MEXICAN** | Near the entrance to Xcalak, this modest Mexican restaurant is made up of a few plastic tables and chairs. Locals stop by for fajitas, fried fish, coconut shrimp, and chicken quesadillas. **Known for:** fried fish; chicken quesadillas; coconut shrimp. [$] *Average main: MP135* ✉ *Leona Vicario s/n, across from parking lot and volleyball court, Xcalak* ☎ *983/107–5426* 🕓 *Closed Sun.*

Hotels

Casa Paraiso
$ | **B&B/INN** | This small hotel is a wonderful place to stay if you want to dive, snorkel, kayak, fly-fish, or just relax in one of the hammocks. **Pros:** kayaks, bikes, paddleboards, and fishing and snorkeling equipment provided; on a nice beach; private fishing dock. **Cons:** no air-conditioning; no restaurant; seaweed on beach. [$] *Rooms from: $80* ✉ *Carretera Majahual–Xcalak, Km 48,* ✣ *Beach road*

"Calle Costero," 2 km (1 mile) north of Xcalak town ☎ *477/275–4931* ⊕ *casaparaisoresort.com* ⚲ *4 rooms* ⦿ *Free Breakfast.*

Sin Duda Villas

\$\$ | B&B/INN | Poised on a lovely beach, this property has several types of accommodations, all adorned with Mexican pottery and other collectibles. **Pros:** solar powered; credit cards accepted via PayPal; world-class snorkeling. **Cons:** lots of bugs; getting here on the rough, potholed road isn't easy; no restaurant. Ⓢ *Rooms from: \$115* ⊠ *Xcalak Peninsula, Xcalak* ✛ *60 km (37 miles) south of Mahahual, 5½ km (3½ miles) north of Costa de Cocos* ☎ *306/500–3240 in U.S.* ⊕ *www.sindudavillas.com* ⚲ *7 rooms* ⦿ *No Meals.*

 Activities

FISHING

Costa de Cocos

DIVING & SNORKELING | Xcalak's only full-service fishing resort offers half- and full-day fly-fishing trips plus all-inclusive, multinight packages at its 16-room wind- and solar-powered resort. Scuba diving and snorkeling are also available, and locals recommend the pizza at the on-site restaurant. ✛ *Head north on beach rd., through Xcalak town, past the lighthouse and pier; turn left at 2-story white building (Captain's Office) and then right at next street. Cocos is less than 1 km (½ mile) north of the bridge* ⊕ *www.costadecocos.com* ✉ *Fly-fishing from USD\$175.*

SCUBA DIVING AND SNORKELING

XTC Dive Center

SCUBA DIVING | This is the town's sole full-service dive shop and one of the few outfits licensed to take passengers to Chinchorro. In addition to recreational diving, it provides DAN and PADI instruction; fly-fishing and snorkeling can also be arranged. Serious divers might be interested in renting one of the three basic rooms attached to the property. ⊠ *Camino Costero Mahahual–Xcalak, Km 54, Xcalak* ☎ *984/179–5692* ⊕ *www.xtcdivecenter.com* ✉ *2-tank dives from USD\$125; snorkeling from USD\$50.*

Chapter 6

COZUMEL

Updated by
Luis Domínguez

👁 Sights	🍴 Restaurants	🛏 Hotels	🛍 Shopping	🍸 Nightlife
★★★★☆	★★★★☆	★★★★☆	★★★★☆	★★★★☆

WELCOME TO COZUMEL

TOP REASONS TO GO

★ **Diving the Great Mayan Reef:** Tropical fish, coral, and other marine creatures enliven the 1,000-km-long (621-mile-long) Mesoamerican Barrier Reef, which stretches from Cozumel to Central America.

★ **Slowing down:** Stroll along a white-sand beach, then explore the gardens above and below the waters at Chankanaab. Or just grab a table at a sidewalk café and watch the world go by.

★ **Savoring local life:** San Miguel's Plaza Central is a Sunday evening hot spot for locals who gather for music and dancing. On any major holiday, you'll see parades, processions, and food stands with seasonal treats.

★ **Visiting Maya sites:** Take a refresher course on Maya culture past and present at the Museo de la Isla de Cozumel, then explore the temples dedicated to Ixchel, the Maya goddess of childbirth, fertility, and healing, at San Gervasio.

A 490-square-km (189-square-mile) island lying just 19 km (12 miles) east of the Yucatán Peninsula, Cozumel is mostly flat, with an interior covered by low scrub jungle and marshy lagoons. White beaches with calm waters line the island's leeward (western) side, which is fringed by a spectacular reef system; the windward (eastern) side, facing the Caribbean Sea, has rocky strands and powerful surf.

1 The Northwest Coast. Broad beaches and the island's only golf course occupy the quiet northwest tip of Cozumel. The sand sometimes gives way to limestone shelves jutting over the water. Dive operations regularly visit this area to coincide with the annual eagle ray migrations.

2 San Miguel. Though cruise ships loom over the piers during the day and souvenir shops line the streets, Cozumel's only town still retains some of the flavor of a Mexican village. On weekend nights, musicians and food vendors gather in the main square and attract lively crowds.

3 The Southwestern Beaches. Proximity to Cozumel's best reefs makes the beaches south of San Miguel a prime destination for divers and snorkelers. An inviting string of hotels, beach clubs, commercial piers, and dive shops line the shore here.

4 The Southern Nature Parks. Cozumel's natural treasures are protected both above and below the sea. At Punta Sur, mangrove lagoons and beaches shelter nesting sea turtles. Chankanaab, one of Mexico's first marine parks, is superb for snorkeling.

5 The Windward Coast. The rough surf of the Caribbean pounds against the limestone shore here, creating pocket-size beaches that seem tailor-made for solitary sunbathing. The water can be rough, though, so pay attention to tides, currents, and sudden drop-offs in the ocean floor.

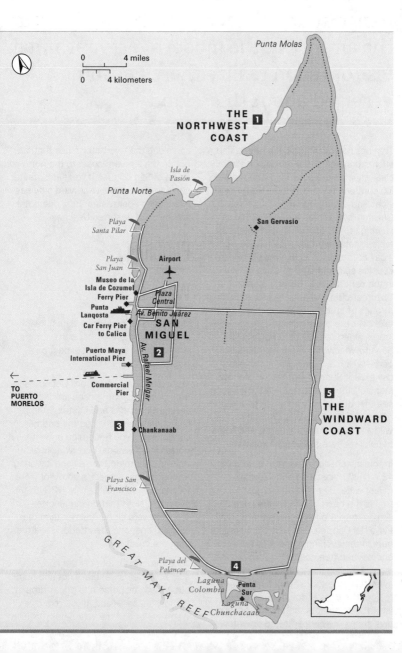

Punta Molas

0   4 miles
0   4 kilometers

THE
NORTHWEST
COAST **1**

Isla de
Pasión

Punta Norte

San Gervasio

Playa
Santa Pilar

Playa
San Juan

Airport

Museo de la
Isla de Cozumel
Ferry Pier

Punta
Lanqosta

Car Ferry Pier
to Calica

Plaza
Central

Av. Benito Juárez

S A N
M I G U E L

Av. Rafael Melgar

Puerto Maya
International Pier

2

←

TO
PUERTO
MORELOS

Commercial
Pier

5

THE
WINDWARD
COAST

3 ◆ **Chankanaab**

Playa San
Francisco

G R E A T
M A Y A
R E E F

Playa del
Palancar

Laguna
Colombia

Punta
Sur

4

Laguna
Chunchacaab

It's not another Cancún yet, but Cozumel's days as a rustic divers' hangout are history. Whether arriving at the airport or the modern ferry terminal, visitors soon realize there's nothing deserted about this island.

That has its advantages. It's rare to find such stunning natural beauty, crystal clear aquamarine seas, and vast marine life combined with top-flight visitor services and accommodations. As a result, Cozumel's devotees are legion. Divers sharing stories of lionfish and sharks sit table to table with families tanned from a day at the beach club, while Mexican couples spin and step to salsa music in the central plaza. But the elephant in Cozumel's big and bountiful room is the throngs of cruise-ship passengers who take over the countless craft and jewelry stores along the seaward boulevard downtown any day there are ships in port—which is to say, just about every day except Sunday. But take just a few steps off the beaten path and you'll soon see that the country's third-largest island offers big rewards. Windswept beaches, wild and vibrant natural parks, and miles of coral reef are still yours to discover.

Irregularly shaped, Cozumel is, at most, 48 km (30 miles) long and 15 km (9 miles) wide. Plaza Central, or just "El Centro," is the heart of San Miguel, directly across from the ferry docks that serve Playa del Carmen. Residents congregate here in the evening, especially on weekends, when free concerts begin around 8 pm. Heading inland (east) takes you away from the tourist zone and toward residential areas of town. Most of the island's restaurants, hotels, stores, and dive shops are concentrated downtown and along the two hotel zones that fan out on the leeward coast to the north and south of San Miguel. If you seek greater solitude, Cozumel's windward side has a few beach-bar restaurants, one hotel, and miles of deserted beaches.

Planning

When to Go

When choosing vacation dates, keep in mind that the weather here is more extreme than you might expect on a tropical island.

High season extends from December until mid-April, with prices spiking around Christmas and Easter. Spring, being warm and dry, has the optimal conditions. If you're coming in winter, *nortes* (north winds) occasionally blow through, churning the sea and lowering temperatures, so pack a shawl or jacket for the comparatively chilly 18°C (65°F) evenings. Note that during a norte, the windward side is calmer than the leeward one, and the interior is warmer than the coast.

June through October is the rainy season. Summer is generally hot and humid, but crowds disperse and prices drop in the low season—and, if you're a diver, warm water and the year's-best visibility might be enough to induce you to brave the heat. Mid-April through May is the sweet spot. With a lull in tourism and the fine weather that precedes the rainy season, late spring might be your all-around best bet. November is another good option, provided you avoid Thanksgiving weekend.

Getting Here and Around

AIR

National and international flights land at the Aeropuerto Internacional de Cozumel (CZM), 3 km (2 miles) north of San Miguel, but flights to Cancún are usually less expensive. A small airline called Mayair offers comfortable twin turbo-prop service between Cancún and Cozumel; one-way flights start at about MX$997, and luggage is limited to 20 kg (44 pounds) per passenger. A budget alternative is to take an ADO bus from the Cancún airport to Playa del Carmen and then the ferry to Cozumel. If everything runs on schedule, the trip should cost less than MX$350 and take about three hours.

The Cozumel airport is less than 10 minutes from downtown. On arrival, take the shared shuttle to your hotel; fares range from MX$57 to MX$462 per person depending on where you're going. Tickets are available just outside customs, and there is no need to prepurchase.

CONTACTS Mayair. ⊠ *Cozumel Airport, Blvd. Aeropuerto at Av. 65, Cozumel* ☎ *998/870–0010* ⊕ *www.mayair.com.mx.*

BOAT AND FERRY

Passenger-only ferries bound for Cozumel leave Playa del Carmen's dock about every other hour on the hour, from 6 am to 11 pm. On the return trip, they leave Cozumel's main pier approximately every other hour from 5 am to 10 pm. The crossing takes 45 minutes and costs about MX$250 each way. The number of trips per day varies by season, so be sure

to check ferry websites for times. The lone car ferry leaves from Calica; it charges from MX$700 per vehicle and MX$80 for each person after the driver.

CONTACTS Barco Caribe. ⊠ *Av. 15 Norte, Cozumel* ⊹ *Directly across from the square* ☎ *987/869–2079* ⊕ *www.barcoscaribe.com.* **Car Ferry from Calica.** ⊠ *Av. Melgar, Cozumel* ⊹ *2⅓ km (1½ miles) south of El Centro* ☎ *987/141–4031* ⊕ *transcaribe.net.* **Ultramar.** ⊠ *Terminal Maritima San Miguel, Av. Rafael Melgar, Cozumel* ⊹ *Directly across from El Centro* ☎ *998/881–5890* ⊕ *www.ultramarferry.com.*

BUS TRAVEL

Bus service on Cozumel is basically limited to San Miguel's residential areas and mostly used by locals, so you'll need a rental car or taxi to explore.

CAR

If you want to explore Cozumel (particularly the eastern side) at your own pace, you can rent a car. Fuel is available at any of the four government-owned Pemex stations around the island. Though it's tempting to drive on Cozumel's dirt roads (which lead to the least crowded beaches), most car-rental companies have a policy that voids your insurance once you leave the paved roadway.

(Check out our Travel Smart chapter for rules of the road and information on rental car agencies if you plan on driving.)

MOPED

Mopeds are popular, but heavy traffic, potholes, and hidden stop signs make them a risky option. Mexican law requires all riders to wear helmets (it's a MX$350 fine if you don't). If you do decide to rent a moped, drive slowly, check for oncoming traffic, and don't ride when it's raining or you've been drinking. Mopeds rent for about MX$600 per day or MX$400 for a half day, including insurance.

TAXI

Cabs wait at all the major hotels, and you can hail them on the street. The fixed rates run about MX$45–MX$70 within town; MX$70–MX$125 between town and the north hotel zone; MX$115–MX$350 between town and the south hotel zone; MX$200–MX$425 from most hotels to the airport; and MX$210–MX$350 from the northern hotels or town to Parque Chankanaab or Playa San Francisco. The cost from the Puerta Maya cruise-ship terminal by El Cid La Ceiba to San Miguel is about MX$140.

Hotels

Small, one-of-a-kind hotels have long been the norm in Cozumel. Most of the island's accommodations are on the leeward (western) and south sides of the island, but there's one peaceful hideaway on the windward (eastern) side. The larger resorts are north and south of San Miguel, while the less expensive places are found in town. Cozumel also has a growing condo rental market; rates are competitive, and condos are easily found via any of the numerous vacation rental websites.

Hotel reviews have been condensed, for full reviews, see Fodors.com.

Restaurants

Dining options on Cozumel reflect the island's laid-back attitude: breezy and relaxed, with casual dress and no reservations the rule at most places. Generally, restaurants emphasize fresh ingredients, simple presentation, and amiable service. As befits an island, there's lots of just-caught seafood on the menu. Yucatecan cuisine is harder to come by; you're more likely to find standard Mexican fare like tacos, enchiladas, and huevos rancheros. For budget meals, head into the untouristed part of downtown and look for the places that are filled with locals. Although some restaurants are turning out creative cuisine to suit the most demanding of palates, most visitors say their best dining experiences are in little family-owned spots that seem to have been here forever. While many restaurants accept credit cards, casual cafés generally don't.

Cab drivers are often paid to shill for restaurants, so take their dining suggestions with a grain (or two) of salt.

WHAT IT COSTS in Dollars and Pesos			
$	$$	$$$	$$$$
RESTAURANTS			
under MX$135	MX$135–MX$200	MX$201–MX$350	over MX$350
HOTELS IN DOLLARS			
under $100	$100–$200	$201–$300	over $300
HOTELS IN PESOS			
under MX$1,450	MX$1,450–MX$2,900	MX$2,901–MX$4,400	over MX$4,400

Banks and Currency Exchange

San Miguel is dotted with bank offices, and ATMs are abundant—including a few that dispense U.S. dollars; some major hotels and resorts along the northern and southern hotel zones also have ATMs on site. However, it's best to stick with bank-affiliated machines and withdraw only pesos, since independent ones offering U.S. dollars charge exorbitant fees. If you'd prefer to pay by credit card, ask first, as not all businesses accept them.

Safety

Cozumel is very safe; the most trouble you're likely to get in has four wheels and a motor (drive carefully). Some petty theft does exist on the island, so keep an eye on your belongings at the beach and don't leave valuables in plain sight in your car. Carry a photocopy of your passport and driver's license and keep the original tucked away at the hotel. If you plan to try water sports, make sure that your health or travel insurance has a sports rider.

Tours

Tours of the island's sights, including the San Gervasio ruins, El Cedral, Parque Chankanaab, and the Museo de la Isla de Cozumel, cost about MX$710 per person and can be arranged through travel agencies; most larger hotels have an on-site agency or tour operator. Another option is to take a private tour of the island via taxi, which costs about MX$1,130 for a half day.

Visitor Information

The website ⊕ *www.thisiscozumel.com* has up-to-date news items and info on all things Cozumel. The Facebook page Cozumel4You is edited by full-time island residents with insider tips on activities, sights, and places to stay and eat. You can also post questions, but use the search function first, as many of your questions may have already been asked.

CONTACTS Cozumel Tourist Information Office. ⊠ *Plaza del Sol, Calle 2 Norte No. 299-B, Cozumel* ☎ *987/872–7585* ⊕ *www.cozumel.travel.*

◉ Sights

Unless you want to stick around your hotel or downtown San Miguel for your whole stay, you'll do well to rent a car. Most worthwhile sites, such as the island's Mayan ruins and pristine windward beaches, are readily accessible only with wheels. Taxi fares can be astronomical, and after just a few trips a rental car is clearly a better deal.

San Miguel is Cozumel's only town. Wait until the cruise ships sail toward the horizon before strolling the *malecón,* or boardwalk. The waterfront has been taken over by large shops selling jewelry, imported rugs, leather boots, and souvenirs to cruise-ship passengers, but the northern end of the malecón, past Calle 10 Norte, is a pleasant area lined with sculptures of Mayan gods and goddesses that draws more locals than tourists. The town feels increasingly traditional as you head inland to the pedestrian streets around the plaza, where family-owned restaurants and shops cater to residents and savvy travelers.

San Miguel's heart is the plaza, where families gather Sunday nights to stroll, snack, enjoy the lighted fountains, and dance to live music around the central *kiosk.* There are plenty of benches for watching the action. Facing the square is an artisans' market, a good stop for souvenirs. Renovated in late 2014, the plaza has lost some of its rustic charm but remains a place to see and be seen.

Chankanaab Beach Adventure Park
THEME PARK | FAMILY | *Chankanaab,* translated as "small sea," consists of a saltwater lagoon, an archaeological park, and a botanical garden, with reproductions of a Maya village and Olmec, Toltec, Aztec, and Maya stone carvings scattered throughout. You can swim at the beach, and there's plenty for snorkelers and divers to see beneath the surface—picture underwater caverns, a sunken ship, crusty old cannons and anchors, and a sculpture of the Virgen del Mar (Virgin of the Sea), all populated by parrotfish and sergeant majors galore. The seal show is included in your admission. To preserve the ecosystem, rules forbid touching the reef or feeding the fish. You'll find dive shops, restaurants, gift shops, a snack stand, and dressing rooms with lockers and showers right on the sand. Chankanaab also has a Dolphin Discovery facility where visitors can

swim with the much-loved marine mammals. ⊠ *Carretera Sur, Km 9, Cozumel* ☎ *987/872–0093* ⊕ *www.cozumelparks. com* ⊡ *USD$26* ⊘ *Closed Sun.*

Discover Mexico

MUSEUM VILLAGE | FAMILY | Want to see all of Mexico while staying on the island? This theme park purports to show you the country's archaeological sites, important architectural landmarks, and cultures, without leaving Cozumel. The scale models of temples, pyramids, monasteries, and more have kitsch value, but a slickly produced film about the country and high-quality folk art exhibits begin to touch on the real thing. An outdoor café serves tasty fruit sorbets and light meals; you can also reserve in advance for the daily tequila tasting. The gift shop has an array of beautiful Mexican folk art for sale. ⊠ *Carretera Sur, Km 5.5, Cozumel* ☎ *987/875–2820* ⊘ *Closed Sun.* ⊡ *USD$26.*

El Cedral

RUINS | Spanish explorers discovered this site—once the hub of Mayan life on Cozumel—in 1518, and in 1847 it became the island's first official city. Today it's a residential community with small, well-tended houses and gardens. Conquistadores tore down much of the Mayan temple, so there's little in the way of actual ruins apart from one small stone arch; if you're in the market for souvenirs, however, vendors around the main plaza display embroidered blouses and hammocks. Kun Che Park, just past the village, offers an interactive tour of the Mayan lifestyle. ⊠ *Off Carretera Sur, Cozumel* ⊹ *Turn at Km 17.5 off Carretera Sur or Av. Rafael E. Melgar, then drive 3 km (2 miles) inland to site* ⊡ *MX$40.*

Museo de la Isla de Cozumel

HISTORY MUSEUM | FAMILY | Filling two floors of a former hotel, Cozumel's museum has displays on natural history—the island's origins, endangered species, topography, and coral-reef ecology—as well as human history during the pre-Columbian and colonial periods. The photos of the island's transformation over the 20th and 21st centuries are especially fascinating, as is the exhibit of a typical Maya home. Guided tours are available. ⊠ *Av. Rafael E. Melgar, between Calles 4 and 6 Norte, Cozumel* ☎ *987/872–0093* ⊕ *www.cozumelparks. com* ⊡ *USD$11* ⊘ *Closed Sun.*

Punta Molas Faro (*Molas Point Lighthouse*)

LIGHTHOUSE | The lighthouse at Cozumel's northernmost point is a solitary, beautiful sight. The rutted road to Punta Molas is accessible by four-wheel-drive vehicles, dirt bikes, and ATVs only, but the scenery is awe-inspiring no matter how far you're able to go. Some tour operators travel out this way when the oceans are calm, providing a photo op from the top of the lighthouse. If making the trip, the small military garrison based there always appreciates a few snacks and soft drinks if you have some to spare. ⊡ *Free.*

Punta Sur

NATURE PRESERVE | FAMILY | This 247-acre national preserve is a protected habitat for numerous birds and animals, including crocodiles, flamingos, egrets, and herons. At the park's (and Cozumel's) southernmost point stands the Faro de Celarain, a lighthouse that's now a museum of navigation. Climb the 134 steps to the top for the best view of the island. Spot birds from observation towers near Laguna Colombia or Laguna Chunchacab, or visit the ancient Mayan lighthouse El Caracol, which was designed to whistle when the wind blows in a certain direction. Beaches here are wide and deserted, and there's great snorkeling offshore; snorkeling equipment is available for rent, as are kayaks. Leave your car at the Faro and take a park shuttle or rental bike to either of the two beach bars. Admission price includes a pontoon-boat ride in the crocodile-infested lagoon. If you're coming by cab, expect to pay about MX$400 for a round-trip ride from San Miguel.

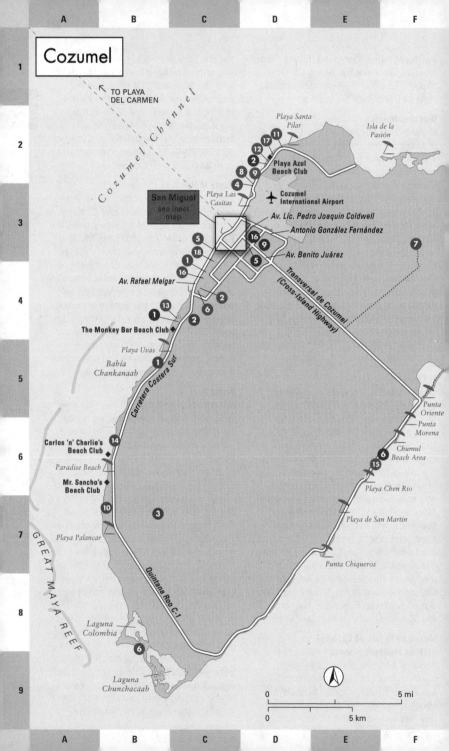

Laguna
Xlapak

Caribbean Sea

KEY

- ❶ *Exploring Sights*
- ❶ *Restaurants*
- ❶ *Quick Bites*
- ❶ *Hotels*

Sights ▼

1. Chankanaab Beach Adventure Park **B5**
2. Discover Mexico......... **C4**
3. El Cedral **B7**
4. Museo de la Isla de Cozumel **H7**
5. Punta Molas Faro........ **I1**
6. Punta Sur **B8**
7. San Gervasio............ **F3**

Restaurants ▼

1. Alfredo Di Roma **B4**
2. Buccanos at Night...... **D2**
3. Burritos Gorditos **I8**
4. Casa Denis **H8**
5. Casa Mission........... **D3**
6. Coconuts Bar & Grill **F6**
7. Dick's Dive............... **H8**
8. El Foco **H8**
9. El Moro.................. **D3**
10. Guido's Restaurant **I7**
11. Kinta...................... **H7**
12. Kondesa **H8**
13. La Choza Cozumel **H8**
14. La Cocay.................. **I8**
15. Le Chef Gastropub...... **H7**
16. Mr. Taco.................. **D3**
17. Pancho's Backyard........ **I7**
18. Pepe's Grill............... **H8**
19. Rock 'n Java Caribbean Bar & Grill **G8**

Quick Bites ▼

1. Novena Ola.............. **H7**

Hotels ▼

1. Blue Angel Resort **C4**
2. Casa del Mar **C4**
3. Casa Mexicana **H8**
4. Coral Princess Golf and Dive Resort **D2**
5. Cozumel Palace.......... **C3**
6. El Cid la Ceiba **C4**
7. Hacienda San Miguel **I7**
8. Hotel B Cozumel **D2**
9. Hotel B Unique Cozumel................. **D2**
10. Iberostar Cozumel **B7**
11. Meliá Cozumel **D2**
12. Playa Azul Cozumel Hotel..................... **D2**
13. Presidente InterContinental Cozumel Resort and Spa **B4**
14. Secrets Aura Cozumel.................. **B6**
15. Ventanas al Mar **E6**
16. Villablanca Garden Beach Hotel.............. **C4**
17. The Westin Cozumel **D2**
18. Wyndham Cozumel Hotel & Resort **C3**

San Miguel

Playa del Carmen-Cozumel Ferry Dock

Cruise Ship Terminal

The streets of Cozumel's main town, San Miguel, lead to sun-soaked beaches and resorts.

⊠ *Carretera Costera Sur, Km 30, Cozumel* ☎ *987/872–0093* ⊕ *cozumelparks. com* ⊠ *USD$18* ⊘ *Closed Sun.*

San Gervasio

RUINS | Rising from the jungle, these temples make up Cozumel's largest remaining Maya and Toltec site. San Gervasio was the island's capital and ceremonial center, dedicated to the fertility goddess Ixchel. The classic- and postclassic-style buildings and temples were continuously occupied from AD 300 to 1500. Typical architectural features include limestone plazas and arches atop stepped platforms, as well as stelae and bas-reliefs. Don't miss the temple Las Manitas, with red handprints all over its altar. Water and light snacks are available to purchase, and bug spray is recommended—and be sure to wear your walking shoes for this adventure. Plaques in Mayan, Spanish, and English clearly describe each structure, but it's worth hiring a guide to fully appreciate the site. ⊠ *Benito Juárez Transversal Rd., Km 7.5, Cozumel* ✦ *From San Miguel, take cross-island road east to San Gervasio access road; turn left and follow road 7 km (4½ miles)* ☎ *987/872–0093* ⊕ *www.cozumelparks. com* ⊠ *USD$10.50.*

🏖 Beaches

Cozumel's beaches range from broad strands and secluded coves to pockets of sand collected between parts of ancient, exposed reefs. The best of the bunch lie at northern end of the island's leeward side, and the numerous private beach clubs and public beaches extending the full length of this coast all promise a day of sun and sea. The windward coast has stretches of spectacular isolated beaches, some rocky, some sandy. Prevailing winds create rip currents that make swimming dangerous when the surf is up, so stay close to shore if you feel inclined to enter the water.

LEEWARD BEACHES

Wide, sandy beaches washed with shallow waters are typical at the far north and south ends of Cozumel's west coast.

Cozumel's History

Cozumel's name is believed to have come from the Mayan "Ah-Cuzamil-Peten" ("Land of the Swallows"). For the Maya, who lived here intermittently between about AD 600 and 1200, the island was not only a center for trade and navigation but also a sacred place. Pilgrims from all over Mesoamerica came to honor Ixchel, the goddess of fertility, childbirth, and healing. The mother of all other gods, Ixchel (also known as Lady Rainbow) was often depicted with swallows at her feet. Maya women, who were expected to visit her site at least once in their lives, made the dangerous journey from the mainland by canoe. Cozumel's main exports were salt and honey, both of which at the time were considered more valuable than gold.

In 1518 Spanish explorer Juan de Grijalva arrived on the island in search of slaves. His tales of treasure inspired Hernán Cortés, Mexico's most famous Spanish explorer, to visit the following year. There he met Gerónimo de Aguilar and Gonzalo Guerrero, Spaniards who had been shipwrecked years earlier. Initially enslaved by the Maya, the two were later accepted into the community. Aguilar joined forces with Cortés, helping set up a military base on the island and using his knowledge of the Maya to defeat them. Guerrero, in contrast, died defending his adopted people, and the Maya still consider him a hero. By 1570 most Maya islanders had been massacred by the Spanish or killed by disease, and by 1600 the island was abandoned.

In the 17th and 18th centuries, pirates found Cozumel to be the perfect hideout. The notorious buccaneers Jean Lafitte and Henry Morgan favored the island's safe harbors and hid their treasures in Mayan catacombs and tunnels. By 1843 Cozumel had again been abandoned. Five years later, 20 families fleeing Mexico's brutal Caste War of the Yucatán resettled the island, and their descendants still live there today.

By the early 20th century the island began capitalizing on its abundant supply of *zapote* (sapodilla) trees, which produce *chicle*, a chewy substance prized by the chewing-gum industry. (Now you know how Chiclets got its name.) Shipping routes began to include Cozumel, whose natural harbors made it a perfect stop for large vessels. Jungle forays in search of chicle led to the discovery of ruins, and soon archaeologists began visiting the island as well. Meanwhile, Cozumel's importance as a seaport diminished as air travel grew, and the demand for chicle dropped off with the invention of synthetic chewing gum.

For decades Cozumel was another backwater where locals fished, hunted alligators and iguanas, and worked on coconut plantations to produce *copra*, the dried kernels from which coconut oil is extracted. Cozumeleños subsisted largely on seafood, still a staple of the local economy. During World War II, the U.S. Army paid to have an airstrip built to hunt the German U-boats that were sinking Mexican ships. Then, in the 1960s, the underwater explorer Jacques Cousteau helped make Cozumel famous by featuring its reefs on his television show. Today, Cozumel is among the world's most popular diving destinations.

Cozumel's best beaches and reefs are on the leeward side.

The topography changes between the two, with small sandy coves interspersed with limestone outcroppings.

Generally, the best snorkeling from shore is wherever piers or rocky shorelines provide a haven for sergeant majors and angelfish.

Isla de la Pasión

BEACH | Off Punta Norte on the northwest coast, private Isla de Pasión has one of Cozumel's loveliest beaches. Most guests arrive on organized excursions (from MX$1,300), but you can also get to the Isla dock independently (it's at the end of the bumpy dirt road to Punta Norte) and come over for MX$150 per person. If coming as part of an organized excursion, your visit includes the short round-trip boat ride, a buffet lunch, soft drinks, some alcoholic drinks, and use of the extensive facilities. You can easily spend a whole day here strolling the strand, floating in the shallow water, swinging in a hammock, playing volleyball, indulging in a massage (for an extra fee), or even getting married in the island's chapel. This is a favorite stop for hordes of cruise-shippers, but the beach stretches for 4 km (2½ miles), so you can still escape the crowds. **Amenities:** food and drink; showers; toilets. **Best for:** swimming; walking; snorkeling. ⊠ *Bahia Ciega Lagoon, Cozumel* ⛴ *Round trip from MX$150.*

Playa Las Casitas

BEACH | FAMILY | Hugely popular with locals, Playa Las Casitas has several large palapa-style restaurant-bars, small palapas and palm trees for shade, calm waters, and a long stretch of beach. Swim out 150 yards from the north end to enjoy the fish-filled artificial reefs. Windsurfers and stand-up paddleboards are also available for rent. The beach is fairly deserted on weekdays but completely packed on Sunday, the traditional day for family outings. **Amenities:** food and drink; parking (free); toilets; water sports. **Best for:** snorkeling; sunsets; swimming. ⊠ *Carretera Norte at Blvd. Aeropuerto, Cozumel* ⛴ *Free.*

The Quieter Side of Cozumel

Blazing-white cruise ships parade in and out of Cozumel like a regatta of floating apartment buildings. Sundays aside, there's at least one on the horizon every day of the year; some days the island gets six or more. The day-trippers they carry pack the tourist-trap souvenir shops and bars on San Miguel's waterfront every afternoon, making the place feel more like a suburban shopping mall than a small Mexican town.

Luckily, there's plenty of Cozumel to go around. If you're fortunate enough to overnight on the island, try these tricks to avoid the crowds.

1. **Keep a low profile.** Stick close to the beach and pool when more than two ships are in port.

2. **Time your excursions.** Go into San Miguel for early breakfast and errands, then stay out of town for the rest of the day. Wander back after you hear the ships blast their departure warnings around 5 or 6 pm.

3. **Dive in.** Hide from the hordes by slipping underwater. But be sure to choose a small dive operation that travels to less popular reefs.

4. **Drive on the wild side.** Rent a car and cruise the windward coast, still free of rampant construction. You can picnic and sunbathe on private beaches hidden by limestone outcroppings, and watch the waves roll in. Use caution when swimming, though, since the surf can be rough and there can be rip currents.

5. **Frequent the "other" downtown.** Most of Cozumel's residents live and shop far from San Miguel's waterfront. Avenidas 15, 20, and 25 are packed with taco stands, *papelerías* (stationery stores), and neighborhood markets. While driving here can be messy, park on a quieter side street and explore the shops and neighborhoods to see a whole different side of Cozumel.

Playa Palancar

BEACH | **FAMILY** | South of the resorts, down a dirt road and way off the beaten path, lies serene Playa Palancar—a long, walkable beach with hammocks hanging under coconut palms. The on-site dive shop can outfit scuba enthusiasts for trips to the famous Palancar and Columbia reefs, just offshore; boats will take snorkelers out every two hours from 9 to 5. There's also a nice open-air restaurant-bar here if you'd rather just relax. **Amenities:** food and drink; parking (free); showers; toilets; water sports. **Best for:** snorkeling; swimming; walking. ✉ *Carretera Sur, Km 19.5, Cozumel* ☎ *987/117–5863* ⊕ *facebook.com/palancarczm* ✑ *Free.*

Playa Santa Pilar

BEACH | Running along the northern hotel strip where the Melia and El Cozumeleño hotels are located, you'll find long stretches of sand and shallow water that encourage leisurely swims. Beach hotels have all the facilities you would need, but most are all-inclusive and don't allow nonguests on the premises. If you're not staying at one, bring your own shade and slip onto the beach between properties. Kiteboarders gather in this area when the winds are good, offering hours of entertaining acrobatics; equipment can be rented nearby from De Lille Sports. **Amenities:** food and drink (for guests only); parking (free). **Best for:** swimming; snorkeling; walking. ✉ *Carretera San*

Juan, just south of Punta Norte, Cozumel
📧 *Free.*

BEACH CLUBS
Carlos 'n' Charlie's Beach Club
BEACH | Easily accessible by cab from downtown or the cruise piers, this spot at Playa San Francisco is a rowdy affair with a restaurant and bar where waiters break into song and draw customers into line dances. The food is typical of the chain—burgers, barbecued ribs, tacos—and the alcohol flows generously. While there's a wide array of water sports offered, the water is shallow, not always clear, and congested with Jet Skis and water toys. **Amenities:** food and drink; parking (free); showers; toilets; water sports. **Best for:** partiers. ✉ *Carretera Costera Sur, Km 14, Cozumel* 📞 *987/564–0960 mobile* ⊕ *www.carlos-ncharliesbeachclub.com* 📧 *Entry free with food or drink purchase.*

The Money Bar Beach Club
BEACH | **FAMILY** | Situated on Dzul-Ha reef, the island's most upscale beach club has a small sandy beach, sunset views, and great food. Entry is free; once inside, you can pay for individual activities or choose an all-inclusive package that might cover anything from meals and massages to guided snorkel tours. (If you snorkel the fish-filled reef on your own, watch out for sea urchins on the rocks.) A water-sports center rents snorkel gear, kayaks, and small sailboats. Mingle with locals and sip frothy cocktails during the two-for-one sunset happy hour. There's live music and dancing on weekend nights. **Amenities:** food and drink; parking (free); showers; toilets; water sports. **Best for:** snorkeling; sunset; swimming. ✉ *Carretera Sur, Km 6.5, Cozumel* 📞 *987/869–5140* ⊕ *www.moneybarbeachclub.com* 📧 *Free.*

Mr. Sancho's Beach Club
BEACH | **FAMILY** | There's always something going on at Mr. Sancho's. Scores of vacationers come here to swim, snorkel, drink, parasail, and ride around on Jet Skis. The restaurant, which offers a number of meal options, holds a lively, informative tequila seminar at lunchtime. Grab a swing seat under the palapa and sip a mango margarita, or opt for a massage. Lockers are available and souvenirs are for sale. This is one of the few bars on the west side that is free to enter and also offers an all-inclusive package. **Amenities:** food and drink; parking (free); showers; toilets; water sports. **Best for:** partiers; swimming. ✉ *Carretera Sur, Km 15, Cozumel* 📞 *987/871–9174 cell* ⊕ *www.mrsanchos.com* 📧 *Free; all-inclusive from USD$60.*

Paradise Beach
BEACH | **FAMILY** | Home to one of the largest heated pools on the island, this club charges USD$3 for lounge chairs; a Fun Pass (USD$64) gives you all-day use of kayaks, stand-up paddleboards, and snorkel gear, plus numerous large floats in the water. Parasailing equipment and Jet Skis are available for rent. Food at the club's three restaurant-bars is expensive, and there's a minimum per-person consumption cost (USD$6) that's easily reached. **Amenities:** food and drink; parking (free); showers; toilets; water sports. **Best for:** swimming. ✉ *Carretera Sur, Km 14.5, Cozumel* 📞 *987/689–0010* ⊕ *paradisebeachcozumel.com* 📧 *USD$64.*

Playa Azul Beach Club
BEACH | **FAMILY** | This club sits just north of the hotel of the same name. The beach is actually pockets of soft sand between limestone shelves; there's also a pool at the hotel that is open to club guests. The restaurant beneath a large palapa serves delicious ceviche and bountiful club sandwiches with a side of fries, and there's free Wi-Fi to boot. Live music on Sunday afternoon draws a crowd of fun-loving people. There's good snorkeling along the reef wall. **Amenities:** food and drink; parking (free); showers; toilets. **Best for:** snorkeling; sunsets; swimming. ✉ *Carretera Norte, Km 4, Cozumel*

Cozumel's main town, San Miguel, is full of casual, local restaurants.

☎ 987/869–5160 ⊕ playa-azul.com/beach-club ✉ Free.

Playa Uvas

BEACH | FAMILY | Sitting on a narrow sandy beach, Uvas caters to small cruise-ship groups and independent tourists. On-site amenities include a dive shop, kayaks, massages, and more. The basic entrance fee gets you one beverage and the use of beach umbrellas, lounge chairs, and a guided snorkel tour, but additional food and drink purchases can quickly run up your tab; all-inclusive packages are also available. Phone or online reservations are required since the club limits the number of guests. **Amenities:** food and drink; parking (free); showers; toilets; water sports. **Best for:** swimming. ✉ Carretera Sur, Km 8.5, Cozumel ☎ 987/120–1420 ✉ USD$15.

WINDWARD BEACHES

The east coast of Cozumel presents a splendid succession of deserted rocky coves and narrow powdery beaches

poised dramatically against the turquoise Caribbean.

Swimming can be treacherous here if you go out too far—in some places the strong undertow can sweep you out to sea in minutes.

These beaches are perfect for solitary sunbathing. Several casual restaurants dot the coastline; they all close around sunset as there is no electricity on this side of the island.

Beyond Punta Oriente, the sandy road beside Mezcalitos leading to the wild northeast coast is sometimes open and sometimes gated—a shame, because the beaches there are superb. Other than ATV outings there are no tours to this part of the coast, and the road is too rutted for rental cars. Rumors abound as to this area's future—some say there will be a small-scale resort here someday, while others hope it will become an ecological reserve. A small navy bivouac at the Punta Molas lighthouse is the only settlement on the road for now, though some of the scrub jungle is divided into housing lots.

Chumul Beach Area

BEACH | About 3 km (2 miles) to the north of Playa San Martín the island road turns hilly and offers panoramic ocean views. Coconuts, a hilltop palapa restaurant, is a prime lookout spot that also serves decent food. One hundred yards away, Ventanas al Mar (the only hotel on the windward coast) attracts travelers who value solitude. Locals picnic on the long beach directly north of the hotel. When the water is calm, there's good snorkeling around the rocks beneath Ventanas al Mar, but steer clear if it's rough. **Amenities:** food and drink; parking (free); toilets. **Best for:** solitude; snorkeling; surfing. ⊠ *Carretera C-1, Km 43.5, Cozumel* 🔧 *Free.*

Playa Chen Rio

BEACH | FAMILY | This long and wide white sand beach has natural rock formations that serve as protection from the waves providing calm waters that are perfect for swimming with kids. There are several palapas scattered here and there to relax under. Visit the nearby "Mirador Chen Rio" for some of the best views on this side of the island. **Amenities:** food and drinks; lifeguards; parking (free); showers; toilets; water sports. **Best for:** snorkeling; swimming; walking; sunrise. ⊠ *Carr. Costera Oriente, San Miguel* 🔧 *Free.*

Playa de San Martín

BEACH | Not quite 3 km (2 miles) north of Punta Chiqueros, a long stretch of beach begins along the Chen Río Reef. Turtles come to lay their eggs on the section known as Playa de San Martín. Soldiers or ecologists sometimes guard the beach during full moons from May to September to prevent poaching. This is a particularly good spot for swimming when the water is calm. However, if red flags are displayed, it means there is a dangerous rip current—be cautious. When the wind is blowing from the south though, the water is best for kiteboarders and

windsurfers. When you're ready to kick back, La Palapa de St. Martin serves cold drinks and seafood. **Amenities:** lifeguards (part-time); parking (free). **Best for:** solitude; swimming; surfing. ⊠ *Carretera C-1, Km 41, Cozumel* 🔧 *Free.*

Punta Chiqueros

BEACH | Sheltered by an offshore reef, this secluded half-moon cove is Mexico's furthest eastern spot. Part of a longer beach that some locals call "Playa Bonita," it has fine sand, clear water, turtle nests, and moderate waves. There used to be a popular restaurant and beach club here, but it's now abandoned. The road to get here has been neglected in the last few years, so not many people frequent this beautiful beach these days. **Amenities:** parking (free). **Best for:** sunrise; swimming; walking. ⊠ *Carretera C-1, Km 38, Cozumel* 🔧 *Free.*

Punta Morena

BEACH | Surfers, kiteboarders, and boogie boarders have made Punta Morena beach and the restaurant of the same name one of their official hangouts—and for good reason: it has great waves and a restaurant serving surfer-friendly burgers, fries, and Mexican fare. If you are away from the main palapa, ask the waiter for a beverage-service flag, and settle your bill in pesos to avoid conversion costs. **Amenities:** food and drink; lifeguards; parking (free); showers; toilets; water sports. **Best for:** surfing; swimming; sunrise; walking. ⊠ *Carretera C-1, Km 46, Cozumel* 🔧 *Free.*

Punta Oriente

BEACH | This typical east-side beach is great for beachcombing but unsuitable for swimming due to the currents. It's nicknamed Playa Mezcalitos after the much-loved Mezcalito Café, which serves seafood and beer and has beachfront hammocks for an afternoon siesta. Senor Iguana's is the other restaurant option here. For privacy, walk north along the beach. **Amenities:** food and drink; toilets; parking (free). **Best for:** partiers; nudists (to the north); walking. ✉ *Carretera C-1, Km 49, Cozumel* 🎟 *Free.*

🍴 Restaurants

SAN MIGUEL

★ Burritos Gorditos

$ | **MEXICAN** | If you've got a hankering for a hole-in-the-wall place that serves cheap, delicious meals, Burritos Gorditos fits the bill for breakfast and lunch. The made-to-order shrimp burritos are excellent and big enough to split; a solid assortment of tacos and salads is also available, but no alcohol is served. **Known for:** fast service; shrimp burritos; steak quesadillas. [$] *Average main: MP100* ✉ *Av. Norte 5A, between Calles 2 and 4, San Miguel* ☎ *987/116–7214* 🌐 *www.burritosgorditos.wixsite.com/burritos-gorditos* ⏲ *Closed Sun. No dinner.*

Casa Denis

$$$ | **MEXICAN** | **FAMILY** | This little yellow house near the plaza has been satisfying cravings for Yucatecan favorites like *cochinita pibil* (spiced pork baked in banana leaves) since 1945. Locals tend to stop in between 8:30 and 1 for cheap breakfast and lunch menus that highlight tacos and empanadas; *tortas* (sandwiches) are also a real bargain. **Known for:** grilled seafood; Yucatán-style cooked fish; beef fajitas. [$] *Average main: MP300* ✉ *Calle 1 Sur 132, between Avs. 5 and 10, San Miguel* ☎ *987/872–0067* 🌐 *www.casadenis.com.*

Casa Mission

$ | **MEXICAN** | **FAMILY** | Part private home, part restaurant (and owned by the same family since the 1980s), this place evokes a country hacienda in mainland Mexico. The setting, with tables lining the veranda, outshines the food, which caters to the tourist palate. **Known for:** grilled lobster; relaxed "in-home" dining; Veracruz fish fillet. [$] *Average main: MP100* ✉ *Av. 55, between Avs. Juárez and Calle 1 Sur, San Miguel* ☎ *987/138–0666* 🌐 *facebook.com/CASAMISSIONCZM.*

Dick's Dive

$$ | **AMERICAN** | Hardly a dive bar, this bar's name refers to Cozumel's great diving experience. Rub elbows with friendly expats and locals alike while you dine on burritos, shrimp bruschetta, and burgers. **Known for:** nachos; Sunday BBQ; pub fare. [$] *Average main: MP180* ✉ *Av. 5 between Calles 2 and Juárez, Cozumel* ☎ *987/872–4279* 🌐 *www.dicksdive.com.*

El Foco

$$ | **MEXICAN** | Popular among locals, this *taquería* captures some of the charm of the barrios and remains open late (until 1 am daily). The soft tacos stuffed with pork, chorizo, cheese, or beef aren't the cheapest tacos on the island, but they're tasty and filling. **Known for:** good fast food; chorizo tacos; late-night atmosphere. [$] *Average main: MP160* ✉ *Av. 5 Sur No. 433, between Calles 5 and 7 Sur, San Miguel* ☎ *987/107–4108* 🌐 *facebook.com/ElFocoCozumel.*

★ El Moro

$$$ | **MEXICAN** | **FAMILY** | You'll have to work hard to find El Moro, but your perseverance will be rewarded with one the better meals in Cozumel with a wide range of seafood and beef dishes. After dinner, try a taste of *Xtabentun*, a traditional Yucatecan liqueur made of fermented honey and anise seeds.This family-owned, open-air restaurant has been feeding hungry locals and tourists for years. **Known for:** seafood; Yucatán-style food; excellent service. [$] *Average main: MP230* ✉ *75 Bis Norte 124, between Calles 2 and 4, San Miguel* ✥ *Head east on Calle 4 from Av. 65; take 4th right turn onto 75 Bis (no street signs). It's in the middle of the block on the right* ☎ *987/120–2907* 🌐 *facebook.com/RestauranteElMoroCozumel* ⏲ *Closed Thurs.*

★ Guido's Restaurant

$$$ | **ITALIAN** | Chef Yvonne Villiger works wonders with fresh fish—if the wahoo with capers and black olives is on the menu, don't miss it. But Guido's is best known for pizzas that are baked in a

Island Dining 🍴

There's no shortage of dining choices on Cozumel, where restaurateurs from Mexico, the United States, and Europe bring every visitor a taste of home. The narrow streets of San Miguel are filled with the aromas of grilling steaks and smoking shrimp, as waiters deliver platters of enchiladas and pizza to sidewalk tables and passersby eye the tables full of food, trying to choose where to eat. At rooftop restaurants, groups gather over Italian feasts; along the shoreline, lobster and fresh fish are the catch of the day. All over the island, there is a bias toward tourist taste buds. Yucatecan dishes such as cochinita pibil, *queso relleno* (Gouda cheese stuffed with ground meat), and *sopa de lima* (lime soup) rarely appear on menus aimed at foreign visitors; however, you will still find authentic regional cuisine at San Miguel's small family-owned eateries, which are often simply a cluster of wobbly tables in a tiny café.

Although there are a growing number of restaurants that serve fine cuisine, even the island's top chefs tend to emphasize natural flavors and simple preparations. The same spirit holds for the dining room, where casual clothes are the rule and a shirt with buttons qualifies as dressed up. (There are a few places here where you can let your sartorial excellence shine.)

wood-fired oven and served by an incredibly attentive staff. **Known for:** puffy garlic bread; sangria; fresh seafood. [$] *Average main: MP350* ✉ *Av. Rafael E. Melgar 23, between Calles 6 and 8 Norte, San Miguel* ☎ *987/869–2589* 🌐 *www.guidoscozumel.com.*

Kinta

$$$$ | MEXICAN FUSION | Kinta delivers sophisticated interpretations of classic Mexican fare in an open kitchen. The menu is updated seasonally, but favorites dishes include savory black bean soup, pork in a smoky *pasilla* chile sauce, and filet mignon with *huitlaoche* (a corn truffle) and cheese. **Known for:** artisanal cocktails; upscale dining; romantic setting. [$] *Average main: MP400* ✉ *Av. 5 No. 148B, between Calles 2 and 4, San Miguel* ☎ *987/869–0544* 🌐 *facebook.com/KintaCozumel* 🕒 *Closed Mon.*

Kondesa

$$$ | MEXICAN FUSION | FAMILY | You can't miss the hot-pink-and-turquoise exterior of this restaurant—it features a palapa-covered bar that opens onto a dimly lit garden dining area. Kondessa puts modern spins on classic flavors, and this menu centers on fresh-caught fish, with favorite dishes like the Kondesa *kake* (an interpretation of crab cakes made with lionfish) and enchiladas filled with seafood. **Known for:** lionfish "crab" cake; artisanal cocktails; fresh seafood. [$] *Average main: MP300* ✉ *Av. 5 No. 456, between Calles 5 and 7, San Miguel* ☎ *987/869–1086* 🌐 *www.kondesacozumel.com* 🕒 *Closed Mon. No lunch.*

La Choza Cozumel

$$$ | MEXICAN | FAMILY | Locals and expats gather here for breakfasts of *migas* (scrambled eggs with bits of bacon and tortilla) and the daily lunchtime *comida corrida* (a set-priced meal with a choice of appetizers and entrées); the latter is a great deal. Favorite dishes include *pollo con mole poblano* (chicken in a smooth, earthy chile sauce), chile relleno *de camarón* (chile stuffed with shrimp), and pork with pumpkin seed sauce. **Known for:** mole poblano; Mexican-style breakfasts; chilled avocado pie. [$] *Average main: MP240* ✉ *Av. 10, San Miguel*

☎ *987/872–0958* ⊕ *facebook.com/ lachozaczm.*

★ La Cocay

$$$ | MEDITERRANEAN | This casually sophisticated dining room and garden is a local favorite. Although the menu changes frequently, you can expect to find salads with fruits, pastas dishes, steaks, and seafood entrées like seared sashimi-grade tuna or the sweet-mango-topped mahimahi. **Known for:** great service; fresh-prepared meals; beautiful garden dining. $ *Average main: MP350* ✉ *Calle 8 Norte 208, between Avs. 10 and 15, San Miguel* ☎ *987/872–5533* ⊕ *www.lacocay.com.*

Le Chef Gastropub

$$$ | MEDITERRANEAN | Dining is a relaxed affair at this intimate café and restaurant. For lunch, you can have a full meal for less than MX$250; the must-have lobster BLT sandwich, assorted soups, salads, or special pizzas all make a great lunch choice. **Known for:** creative meal presentations; fresh salads; BLT lobster sandwich. $ *Average main: MP265* ✉ *Rafael E. Melgar 201-4, between Calles 3 and 5, San Miguel* ☎ *987/878–4391* ⊕ *www. facebook.com/lechefcozumel/* ⊗ *Closed Mon. No breakfast.*

Mr. Taco

$ | MEXICAN | FAMILY | If you are looking for an authentic taco joint where the locals go, this is the place. The tacos *al pastor*, carved from a vertical spit, are big, juicy, and inexpensive. **Known for:** tacos al pastor; cheap eats; fast service. $ *Average main: MP18* ✉ *Av. Juárez between Avs. 55 and 60, Cozumel* ⊕ *mistertaco.restaurantwebexperts.com.*

★ Pancho's Backyard

$$$ | MEXICAN | FAMILY | Marimbas play beside a bubbling fountain in the charming courtyard behind one of Cozumel's best folk art shops. The English menu is geared toward tourists and priced in pesos, but regional ingredients like smoky chipotle chile make even the standard steak stand out for a true Mexican-inspired meal. **Known for:** strong margaritas; open-air courtyard dining; vegan and vegetarian options. $ *Average main: MP320* ✉ *Av. Rafael E. Melgar 27, between Calles 8 and 10 Norte, San Miguel* ☎ *987/872–2141* ⊕ *facebook. com/PanchosBackyard.*

Pepe's Grill

$$$$ | STEAKHOUSE | This popular second-story restaurant has a casual steak-house feel. The air-conditioned dining room's tall windows allow for fantastic sunset and ocean views. **Known for:** delicious seafood; sunset and ocean views; fresh salads. $ *Average main: MP500* ✉ *Av. Rafael E. Melgar and Calle Adolfo Rosado Salas, San Miguel* ☎ *987/872–0213.*

Rock 'n Java Caribbean Bar & Grill

$$ | ECLECTIC | FAMILY | A favorite of expats and locals, the extensive breakfast menu here includes whole-wheat French toast and cheese crepes. For lunch or dinner try the vegetarian tacos, linguine with clams, or choose from more than a dozen salads. **Known for:** oceanfront views; leisurely breakfasts; fresh ingredients. $ *Average main: MP185* ✉ *Av. Rafael E. Melgar No. 602-6, San Miguel* ☎ *987/872–4405* ⊕ *www.rocknjavacozumel.com.*

ZONA HOTELERA SUR
Alfredo di Roma

$$$$ | ITALIAN | The opportunity to dine graciously amid crystal and candlelight (and blessedly cool air-conditioning) is just one reason to book a special dinner at Alfredo's. The pastas are made fresh daily, and cheeses are flown in from Italy so that the chef can prepare the house special—authentic fettuccine Alfredo—at your table. **Known for:** ocean views; fresh-made pasta dishes; impressive wine selection. $ *Average main: MP450* ✉ *Presidente InterContinental Cozumel, Carretera Chankanaab, Km 6.5, Cozumel*

The Presidente InterContinental Cozumel Resort & Spa

☎ *987/872–9500* 🌐 *ihg.com/intercontinental* ⏲ *No lunch.*

★ Buccanos at Night

$$$$ | **MODERN MEXICAN** | Sunset views and an incredible meal await you at this oceanfront restaurant on the island's North Shore. Buccanos offers fresh seafood and meats as well as seasonal salads, all presented beautifully. **Known for:** artisanal cocktails; seasonal fresh seafood; delicious desserts. [$] *Average main: MP21* ✉ *Playa San Juan Km 4.5 Norte, Cozumel* ☎ *987/114–5607* 🌐 *buccanos.com* ⏲ *Closed Mon. and Tues.*

WINDWARD COAST

Coconuts Bar & Grill

$$ | **INTERNATIONAL** | Located at the highest point on the island, the T-shirts and bras hanging from the palapa of this hilly, windward-side hangout are good indicators of its party-time atmosphere. Classic rock and reggae tunes play in the background while crowds down cervezas, fish, fajitas, and garlic shrimp. **Known for:** variety of cocktails; adults-only party; fantastic hilltop views. [$] *Average main: MP180* ✉ *Carretera C-1, Km 43, Cozumel* ☎ *987/107–7622* 🌐 *coconutscozumel.com* 💳 *No credit cards.*

☕ Coffee and Quick Bites

Novena Ola

$$$ | **SEAFOOD** | On the terrace off the second floor of the Museo de la Isla de Cozumel, *Novena Ola* serves breakfast, lunch, and dinner from 8 am to 11 pm. The menu is large and varied, but specialties are mostly fine seafood dishes. **Known for:** open-air terrace; gourmet seafood; vegan and vegetarian options. [$] *Average main: MP300* ✉ *Museo de la Isla de Cozumel, Av. Rafael E. Melgar, between Calles 4 and 6 Norte, Cozumel* ☎ *999/271–1109* 🌐 *en.novenaola.com.*

🛏 Hotels

ZONA HOTELERA NORTE

Coral Princess Golf and Dive Resort

$$ | **RESORT** | **FAMILY** | Good snorkeling off the rocky shoreline and a relaxed family

feel makes this resort, which offers both hotel rooms and apartmentlike units, a north-coast favorite. **Pros:** snorkeling right off beach; decent, well-priced meals; family-friendly. **Cons:** some rooms lack bathtubs; can be noisy at pool; time-share pitches. $ *Rooms from: $145 ⊠ Carretera Costera Norte, Km 2.5, Cozumel ☎ 987/564–5889 ⊕ www. coralprincess.com ⇨ 148 rooms ⊙ Free Breakfast.*

Hotel B Cozumel

$$ | HOTEL | This sleek boutique property has quickly become the preferred lodging choice for a discerning, young crowd. **Pros:** intimate atmosphere; great snorkeling; close to town and marina. **Cons:** pool service is slow; small sandy beach; some rooms don't have ocean views. $ *Rooms from: MP150 ⊠ Carretera Costa Norte, Km 2.5, Cozumel ☎ 987/872–0300 ⊕ www.hotelbcozumel.com ⇨ 45 rooms ⊙ Free Breakfast.*

Hotel B Unique Cozumel

$$$ | HOTEL | This hip adults-only design hotel has a wellness, holistic, and bo-ho style overall attitude. **Pros:** quality spa; chic Mexican design; adults-only. **Cons:** no bathtub in rooms; some rooms have no ocean views; rocky beach. $ *Rooms from: MP300 ⊠ Carretera playa San Juan Km 2.5, Puerto Abrigo ☎ 987/872–0194 ⊕ en.hotelbunique.com ⇨ 27 rooms ⊙ Free Breakfast.*

Meliá Cozumel

$$$ | ALL-INCLUSIVE | FAMILY | One of the very first hotels in Cozumel, Meliá continues to satisfy guests by offering a bit of everything at a grand scale; guests can choose from a wide variety of restaurants, activities, motorized and non-motorized water sports. An 18-hole mini-golf, plus well-equipped kids' club and gameroom, mean that children and teenagers will be busy and happy; while a top-notch spa is available for parents to unwind and disconnect. **Pros:** great beach; 40+ activities available every day; kids' club. **Cons:** some rooms have no

Spring Festival 🎟

If you're here in April, tap your toes to some traditional dance during the **Fería del Cedral**, a fair held in the settlement of El Cedral around the last weekend of the month. Park in dirt lots nearby or take one of many available buses. To get here, turn at Km 17.5 off Carretera Sur or Avenida Rafael E. Melgar, then drive 3 km (2 miles) inland to the site.

ocean views; extra charge for room service; massive property. $ *Rooms from: MP250 ⊠ Carretera Costera Norte, Km 5.8, Zona Hotelera Nte., Puerto Abrigo ☎ 987/872–9870 ⊕ melia.com ⇨ 210 rooms ⊙ All-Inclusive.*

Playa Azul Cozumel Hotel

$$$ | HOTEL | FAMILY | Playa Azul feels like a charming, understated Mexican hacienda—there's elegance in its simplicity. **Pros:** good snorkeling; excellent spa; intimate. **Cons:** far from downtown; rocky beach entry in areas; adjacent beach club is shared with cruisers. $ *Rooms from: MP214 ⊠ Carretera Costera Norte, Km 4, Cozumel ☎ 987/869–5160 ⊕ www.playa-azul.com ⇨ 50 rooms ⊙ All-Inclusive.*

The Westin Cozumel

$$$ | HOTEL | FAMILY | This sophisticated white tower in Cozumel's exclusive North Shore area is one of the islands most luxurious hotels, with ultramodern decor and incredible ocean views. **Pros:** modern, chic design; pet-friendly up to 40 pounds; good snorkeling just offshore. **Cons:** beach beverage service can be spotty; rooftop pool bar is not always open; beach is small. $ *Rooms from: MP263 ⊠ Carretera Costera Norte Km 4.8, Cozumel ☎ 987/872–9200 ⊕ www. westincozumel.com ⇨ 152 rooms ⊙ Free Breakfast.*

ZONA HOTELERA SUR
Blue Angel Resort
$$ | HOTEL | FAMILY | Locally owned, this diver-friendly hangout is a big favorite among hard-core divers; the guest rooms are casual, clean, and bright, and all have balconies or terraces with hammocks and racks for drying dive gear. **Pros:** incredible sunsets; close to town; on-site PADI outfit. **Cons:** busy street behind the hotel; small pool; street parking only. $ *Rooms from: MP125* ✉ *Carretera Sur, Km 2.2, Cozumel* ☎ *987/872–0819* ⊕ *www.blueangelresort.com* ⬐ *22 rooms* ⦿ *Free Breakfast.*

Casa del Mar
$ | HOTEL | All rooms at this diver-oriented hotel are enlivened by simple Mexican artwork, but those with sea-facing balconies are lighter, airier, and don't cost that much more. **Pros:** close to other dining options; good dive base location; optional, reasonably priced all-inclusive plan. **Cons:** beach is across the street; food choices and serving times are limited; weak Wi-Fi. $ *Rooms from: MP65* ✉ *Carretera Sur, Km 4, Cozumel* ☎ *987/872–1900* ⊕ *www.casadelmarcozumel.com* ⬐ *106 rooms* ⦿ *All-Inclusive.*

Cozumel Palace
$$$$ | RESORT | FAMILY | Gleaming white in the afternoon sun, the Cozumel Palace seems more like a cruise ship than an upscale all-inclusive hotel; the tight confines of the pool deck area, when combined with music and flowing drinks, can create a lively outdoor atmosphere. **Pros:** walking distance to downtown; on-site spa and dive shop; extremely attentive staff. **Cons:** pool and lobby get noisy at happy hour; time-share reps; lack of premium liquors. $ *Rooms from: MP340* ✉ *Av. Rafael E. Melgar, Km 1.5 Sur, Cozumel* ☎ *987/872–9430, 305/374–4752 in U.S.* ⊕ *cozumel.palaceresorts.com* ⬐ *175 rooms* ⦿ *All-Inclusive* ☞ *Day passes available for a fee.*

El Cid la Ceiba
$$$ | ALL-INCLUSIVE | FAMILY | Next door to the Puerta Maya cruise pier and shopping center, this smallish resort is a comfortable choice, with some condo-style rooms that come equipped with kitchenettes. **Pros:** close to town and other restaurants; comfy accommodations; reasonably priced all-inclusive option available. **Cons:** heavy boat traffic in snorkel areas; pool area is small and the scene can be boisterous; time-share reps. $ *Rooms from: MP200* ✉ *Carretera Chankanaab, Km 4.5, Cozumel* ☎ *987/872–0844, 866/306–6113 in U.S.* ⊕ *www.elcid.com* ⬐ *76 rooms* ⦿ *All-Inclusive.*

Iberostar Cozumel
$$$ | RESORT | FAMILY | Jungle greenery surrounds this all-inclusive resort at Cozumel's southernmost point. **Pros:** friendly, personal service; short trip to most dive sites; large pool area with plenty of lounge chairs. **Cons:** rocky beach entry; so-so food and reservations required; expensive cab ride to town. $ *Rooms from: MP225* ✉ *Carretera Chankanaab, Km 17, past El Cedral turnoff, Cozumel* ☎ *987/872–9900, 888/923–2722* ⊕ *www.iberostar.com* ⬐ *306 rooms* ⦿ *All-Inclusive.*

★ Presidente InterContinental Cozumel Resort and Spa
$$$ | RESORT | FAMILY | The luxurious InterContinental has top-notch service, expansive lawns, pristine beaches, and spacious, modern rooms. **Pros:** four restaurants; modern, luxurious rooms; impeccable service. **Cons:** some rooms without ocean views; pricey food; marina traffic can create waves for snorkelers. $ *Rooms from: MP265* ✉ *Carretera Chankanaab, Km 6.5, Cozumel* ☎ *800/502–0500, 987/872–9500* ⊕ *presidenteiccozumel.com* ⬐ *218 rooms* ⦿ *Free Breakfast.*

Secrets Aura Cozumel
$$$$ | RESORT | Part of the Secrets brand, the elegant adults-only Aura raises the

A Ceremonial Dance

Women regally dressed in embroidered, lace-trimmed dresses and men in their best guayabera shirts carry festooned trays on their heads during the Baile de las Cabezas de Cochino (Dance of the Pig's Head) at the Fería del Cedral, held in El Cedral. The trays are festooned with trailing ribbons, *papeles picados* (paper cutouts), piles of bread and, in some cases, the head of a barbecued you-know-what.

The pig is a sacrificial offering to God, who is said to have saved the founders of this tiny Cozumel settlement during the 19th-century Caste War, when Yucatán's Maya rose up against their oppressors. The enslaved Maya killed most of the *mestizos* (those of mixed European and indigenous heritage) in the mainland village of Sabán. Casimiro Cárdenas, a wealthy young mestizo, survived while clutching a small wooden cross, and later promised he would establish an annual religious festival once he found a new home.

Today the original religious vigils and novenas blend into the more secular fair, which usually runs through the last weekend in April. Festivities vary by year, but have included horse races, bullfights, and carnival rides, and food stands sell hot dogs, corn on the cob, and cold beer. Celebrations peak with the ritual dance, usually held on the final day.

The music begins with a solemn cadence as families enter the stage, surrounding one member bearing a multitiered tray. The circular procession proceeds, with participants showing off their costumes and offerings. Gradually the beat quickens and the dancing begins. Grabbing the ends of ribbons trailing from the trays, children, parents, and grandparents twirl in ever-faster circles until the scene becomes a whirl of laughing faces and bright colors.

bar for the south coast's string of all-inclusive beach properties. **Pros:** intimate, sophisticated ambience; high-tech; luxurious amenities (rare on Cozumel). **Cons:** offshore snorkeling not very good; far from town; some rooms need updating. Ⓢ *Rooms from: MP400* ⊠ *Carretera Costera Sur, Km 12.9, Cozumel* ☎ *866/467–3273* ⊕ *secretsresorts.com* ↘ *238 suites* ⦿ *All-Inclusive.*

Villablanca Garden Beach Hotel

$ | HOTEL | FAMILY | The landscaped grounds here are lovely, as are most rooms; befitting the price, though, there is a certain budget-hotel sparseness to the place. **Pros:** dive packages offered; lush gardens around pool; good value. **Cons:** spotty Wi-Fi; dated and minimal furnishings; busy street out front. Ⓢ *Rooms from: MP88* ⊠ *Carretera Chankanaab, Km 3, Cozumel* ☎ *987/872–0730* ⊕ *www. villablanca.net* ↘ *54 rooms* ⦿ *No Meals.*

Wyndham Cozumel Hotel & Resort

$$ | RESORT | FAMILY | In high season, families and revelers surround the enormous pool at this bright-orange hotel, while activity directors enliven the crowd with games and loud music. **Pros:** breakfast-only option available; near grocery stores and restaurants; 10 fully accessible rooms. **Cons:** poolside entertainment loud and annoying; rocky beach area; outdated facilities. Ⓢ *Rooms from: MP178* ⊠ *Carretera Costera Sur, Km 1.7, Cozumel* ☎ *987/872–9020* ⊕ *cozumelhotel.com. mx* ↘ *181 rooms* ⦿ *All-Inclusive.*

SAN MIGUEL

★ Casa Mexicana

$$ | **HOTEL** | Although not on the beach, this distinctive and inexpensive hotel overlooks the water; oceanfront rooms, with comfortable balconies from which to enjoy the views, are worth the added cost. **Pros:** near restaurants and shops; substantial breakfast; friendly staff. **Cons:** some street noise; tiny pool; no beach. [$] *Rooms from: MP135* ✉ *Av. Rafael E. Melgar 457, between Calles 5 and 7 Sur, San Miguel* ☎ *987/872–9080* 🌐 *www.casamexicanacozumel.com* 🛏 *88 rooms* 🍴 *Free Breakfast.*

Hacienda San Miguel

$$ | **B&B/INN** | Five blocks south of San Miguel's main plaza, this small inn consists of two-story buildings set around a lush courtyard; second-floor rooms get far more air and light than those at ground level, but all have coffeemakers, purified water, and bathrobes. **Pros:** courtyard gardens make it feel like a private home; quiet but central; plenty of great restaurants nearby. **Cons:** air-conditioning can be noisy and rooms musty; no parking or pool; free Wi-Fi in courtyard only. [$] *Rooms from: MP120* ✉ *Calle 10 Norte 1500, at Av. 5, Cozumel* ☎ *987/872–1986, 866/712–6387 in U.S.* 🌐 *www.haciendasanmiguel.com* 🛏 *11 rooms* 🍴 *No Meals.*

WINDWARD COAST

Ventanas al Mar

$$ | **HOTEL** | The lights of San Miguel are a distant glow on the horizon when you look west from the only hotel on the windward coast. **Pros:** adults-only; blissful solitude; long beach for morning walks. **Cons:** limited food and drink options; air-conditioning operates 8 pm–8 am only; rooms have no TV. [$] *Rooms from: MP145* ✉ *Carretera C-1, Km 43.5, Cozumel* ☎ *984/212–9468, 987/107–1008* 🌐 *www.ventanasalmar.com.mx* 🛏 *19 rooms* 🍴 *Free Breakfast.*

🍸 Nightlife

Not so long ago, Cozumel's already low-key nightlife shut down by midnight, perhaps thanks to the many dive excursions leaving at the crack of dawn. The cruise-ship passengers mobbing the bars seemed to drink enough for the whole island, and the rowdiest action sometimes took place in the afternoon, when mojito-slinging revelers pulled out the stops before reboarding. These days, visitors staying up late will be rewarded by a thriving live-music scene at haunts that are frequented by locals and tourists alike. Many remain open to 4 am. Even if you're not a night owl, you'll find excellent salsa, jazz, acoustic, and rock bands playing downtown at places like Wet Wendy's, Woody's, and Viva Mexico. The Money Bar Beach Club has a live band on Friday, Saturday, and Sunday around sunset, with happy-hour specials. As an alternative, do like the locals and head for the *zócalo* (main square) to hear mariachis or special music presentations on Sunday evenings from around 8 to 10. There is a nightly "dancing" fountain music-and-light show almost every evening that draws a big crowd.

BARS

Cerveceria Punta Sur

BREWPUBS | Cozumel's first and only island microbrewery serves up a range of delicious artisanal brews from lighter ales to darker beers. The pub fare pairs well with the brews offered, and the pizzas are cooked in a wood-fired oven with excellent results. ✉ *298-A Av. 10 between AR Salas and Calle 3,* ☎ *987/111–8642* 🌐 *www.cerveceriapuntasur.com.*

Fat Tuesday

BARS | On the northwest corner of the square, this watering hole draws mostly cruise-ship crowds during the day and vacationers staying on the island at night. Expect frozen daiquiris, ice-cold beers, and blaring rock at tourist prices. There

Did You Know?

The most concentrated shopping area runs for about eight very walkable blocks along Avenida Rafael E. Melgar and around the main square; however, you'll find better deals and more one-of-a-kind items if you venture away from the crowds and do a little backstreet exploring.

is a second location at the Puerta Maya cruise terminal. ☒ *Av. Juárez 2, between Av. Rafael E. Melgar and Calle 3 Sur, San Miguel* ☏ *987/872–5130* ⊕ *facebook. com/FatTuesdayCozumel.*

La Internacional Cervecería Cozumel
BREWPUBS | Mexico is home to a growing number of craft beer brewers and this is the place to try craft Mexican beers as well as additional selections from over 33 other countries. The bartenders are knowledgeable. ☒ *Av. Melgar between Calles 7 and 11,* ☏ *987/869–1289* ⊕ *facebook.com/ lainternacionalcerveceriacozumel.*

'Ohana Cafe and Bar
LIVE MUSIC | This reggae bar serves deep-dish pizza that gets rave reviews, and the Mexican-inspired meals provide something for every palate. ☒ *Av. 5, between Calles 6 and 8 Norte, Cozumel* ☏ *987/564–1771* ⊕ *facebook.com/ohana. czm* ◷ *Closed Sun.*

Señor Frog's
BARS | The *Animal House* ambience at Señor Frog's at night includes loud music and a bar-dancing, bead-throwing, balloon-hat-wearing, anything-goes drinking scene. During the day, the pub grub is better than you'd expect, the drinks are flowing, and the waiters are always entertaining. ☒ *Punta Langosta, Av. Rafael E. Melgar, between Calles 7 and 11, Cozumel* ☏ *987/869–1651* ⊕ *www. senorfrogs.com* ◷ *Closed for breakfast.*

★ Wet Wendy's Margarita House
LIVE MUSIC | FAMILY | You'll find the best and largest frozen margaritas in town at Wet Wendy's. Sit at the bar and down one of the potent concoctions, or grab a table in the outdoor garden to dine on remarkably good food and dance to the salsa, rock, and jazz bands that play here several nights a week. Service is friendly, so don't be surprised if the bartender asks you if you want "the usual" on your second visit. ☒ *Av. 5A Norte, San Miguel* ☏ *987/872–4970* ⊕ *www.wetwendys. com.*

DANCE CLUBS
Tiki Tok Bar
DANCE CLUBS | A second-floor restaurant called Trattoria by day, this spot transforms into a salsa dance club called Tiki Tok after dark. On Friday and Saturday, local bands draw salsa aficionados of all stripes from 10 pm to about 3 am; a DJ spins Latin and reggaeton until all hours of the night. ☒ *Av. Rafael E. Melgar 13, between Calles 2 and 4 Norte, San Miguel* ☏ *987/869–8119* ⊕ *facebook.com/ tikitokcozumel* ◷ *Closed Mon.*

FILM
Cinepolis
GATHERING PLACES | FAMILY | On a sweltering hot or rainy afternoon, slip into Cinepolis. The modern, multiscreen theater shows current hit films in Spanish and English at afternoon matinees and nightly shows. When buying your ticket, select your seats on the computer screen and then head over for some reasonably priced food and drinks at the snack bar. ☒ *Av. Rafael E. Melgar 1001, between Calles 15 and 17 Sur, San Miguel* ☏ *552/122–6060* ⊕ *cinepolis.com/ cartelera/cozumel.*

🛍 Shopping

Cozumel's main souvenir-shopping area is downtown on or near the waterfront; tourist-trap malls at the cruise-ship piers sell jewelry, perfume, sportswear, and low-end souvenirs at high-end prices.

Most downtown shops accept U.S. greenbacks, and many goods are priced in dollars. But to get better prices, pay with pesos and stick to cash—some shops tack a hefty surcharge on credit-card purchases. Shops, restaurants, and streets are always crowded between 10 am and 2 pm, but slow down in the

Continued on page 249

COZUMEL DIVING AND SNORKELING

First comes the giant step, a leap from a dry boat into the warm Caribbean Sea. Then the slow descent to white sand framed by rippling brain coral and waving purple sea fans. If you lean back, you can look up toward the sea's surface. The water off Cozumel is so clear you can see puffy white clouds in the sky even when you're submerged 20 feet under.

With more than 30 charted reefs whose depths average 50–80 feet and water temperatures around 24°C–27°C (75°F–80°F) during peak diving season (June–August, when hotel rates are coincidentally at their lowest), Cozumel is far and away the place to dive in Mexico. More than 60,000 divers come here each year.

Because of the diversity of coral formations and the dramatic underwater peaks and valleys, divers consider Cozumel's Palancar Reef (promoters now call it the Maya Reef) to be one of the top five in the world. Sea turtles headed to the beach to lay their eggs swim beside divers in May and June. Fifteen-pound lobsters wave their anten-nae from beneath coral ledges; they've been protected in Cozumel's National Marine Park for so long they've lost all fear of humans. Long, green moray eels still appear rather menacing as they bare their fangs at curious onlookers, and snaggle-toothed barracuda look ominous as they swim by. But all in all, diving off Cozumel is relaxing, rewarding, and so addictive you simply can't do it just once.

Hurricane Wilma damaged the reefs during her 2005 attack and rearranged the underwater landscape. Favorite snorkeling and diving spots close to shore were affected, and the fish may not be as abundant as they were in the past.

The reef is home to brain coral and huge sponges.

DIVE SITES

(left and right) Felipe Xicotencatl (C-53 Wreck)

Cozumel's reefs stretch for 32 km (20 mi), beginning at the international pier and continuing to Punta Celarain at the island's southernmost tip. Following is a rundown of Cozumel's main dive destinations.

Chankanaab Reef. This inviting reef lies south of Parque Chankanaab, about 350 yards offshore. Large underground caves are filled with striped grunt, snapper, sergeant majors, and butterfly fish. At 55 feet, there's another large coral formation that's often filled with crabs, lobster, barrel sponges, and angelfish. If you drift a bit farther south, you can see the Balones de Chankanaab, balloon-shaped coral heads at 70 feet.

Colombia Reef. Several miles off Palancar, the reef reaches 82–98 feet and is best suited for experienced divers. Its underwater structures are as varied as those of Palancar Reef, with large canyons and ravines to explore. Clustered near the overhangs are large groupers, jacks, rays, and an occasional sea turtle.

Felipe Xicotencatl (C-53 Wreck). Sunk in 2000 specifically for scuba divers, this 154-foot-long minesweeper is located on a sandy bottom about 80 feet deep near Tormentos and Chankanaab. Created as an artificial reef to decrease some of the traffic on the natural reefs, the ship is open so divers can explore the interior and is gradually attracting schools of fish.

Maracaibo Reef. Considered one of the most difficult reefs, Maracaibo is a thrilling dive with strong currents and intriguing old coral formations. Although there are shallow areas, only advanced divers who can cope with the current should attempt Maracaibo.

Palancar Reef. About 2 km (1 mi) offshore, Palancar is actually a series of varying coral formations with about 40 dive locations. It's filled with winding canyons, deep ravines, narrow crevices, archways, tunnels, and caves. Black and red coral and huge elephant-ear, and barrel sponges are among the attractions. At the section called Horseshoe, a series of coral heads form a natural horseshoe shape. This is one of the most popular sites for dive boats and can become crowded.

Paraíso Reef. About 330 feet offshore, running parallel to the international cruise-ship pier, this reef averages 30–50 feet. It's a perfect spot to dive before you head for deeper drop-offs. There are impressive formations of star and brain coral as well as sea fans, sponges, sea eels, and yellow rays. It's wonderful for night diving.

Paseo El Cedral. Running parallel to Santa Rosa reef, this flat reef has gardenlike valleys full of fish, including angelfish, grunt, and snapper. At depths of 35–55 feet, you can also spot rays.

San Francisco Reef. Considered Cozumel's shallowest wall dive (35–50 feet), this 1-km (1⁄2-mi) reef runs parallel to Playa San Francisco and has many varieties of reef fish. You'll need to take a dive boat to get here.

Chankanaab Reef

Young yellow sponges, Palancar Reef.

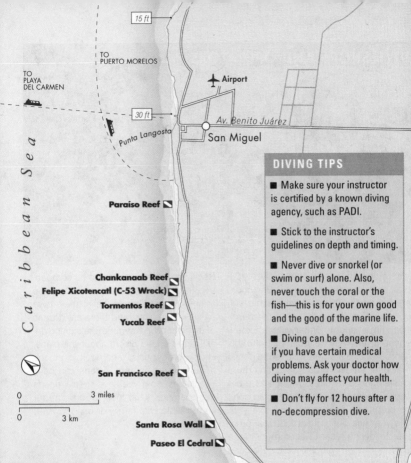

15 ft

TO
PUERTO MORELOS

TO
PLAYA
DEL CARMEN

30 ft

✈ **Airport**

Av. Benito Juárez

Punta Langosta

San Miguel

Caribbean Sea

Paraíso Reef

Chankanaab Reef

Felipe Xicotencatl (C-53 Wreck)

Tormentos Reef

Yucab Reef

San Francisco Reef

0 ——— 3 miles
0 ——— 3 km

Santa Rosa Wall

Paseo El Cedral

*Laguna
Colombia*

*Laguna
Chunchacaab*

Palancar Reef

*Paraje
Punta Sur*

Colombia Reef

Punta Celarain

Maracaibo Reef

30 ft

50 ft

DIVING TIPS

■ Make sure your instructor is certified by a known diving agency, such as PADI.

■ Stick to the instructor's guidelines on depth and timing.

■ Never dive or snorkel (or swim or surf) alone. Also, never touch the coral or the fish—this is for your own good and the good of the marine life.

■ Diving can be dangerous if you have certain medical problems. Ask your doctor how diving may affect your health.

■ Don't fly for 12 hours after a no-decompression dive.

KEY TO DIVE SITES

◣	*Beginner*
◣	*Advanced*

◣Santa Rosa Wall. North of Palancar, Santa Rosa is renowned among experienced divers for deep dives and drift dives; at 50 feet there's an abrupt yet sensational drop-off to enormous coral overhangs. The strong current drags you along the tunnels and caves, where there are huge sponges, angelfish, groupers, and rays—and sometime even a shark or two.

◣Tormentos Reef. The abundance of sea fans, sponges, sea cucumbers, arrow crabs, green eels, groupers, and other marine life—against a terrifically colorful backdrop—makes this a perfect spot for underwater photography. This variegated reef has a maximum depth of around 70 feet.

◣Yucab Reef. South of Tormentos Reef, this relatively shallow reef is close to shore, making it an ideal spot for beginners. About 400 feet long and 55 feet deep, it's teeming with queen angelfish and sea whip swimming around the large coral heads. The one drawback is the strong current, which can reach two or three knots.

DIVE SHOPS AND OPERATORS

It's important to choose a dive shop that suits your expectations. Beginners are best off with the more established, conservative shops that limit the depth and time spent underwater. Experienced divers may be impatient with this approach, and are better suited to shops that offer smaller group dives and more challenging dive sites. More and more shops are merging these days, so don't be surprised if the outfit you dive with one year has been absorbed by another the following year. Recommending a shop is dicey. The ones we recommend are well-established and also recommended by experienced Cozumel divers.

Because dive shops tend to be competitive, it's well worth your while to shop around. Many hotels have their own on-site operations, and there are dozens of dive shops in town. Before signing on, ask experienced divers about the place, check credentials, and look over the boats and equipment. Shops can have specialties, so if you have special needs (for example, kids) look for an outfitter comfortable with family dives.

(top) Felipe Xicotencatl (C-53 Wreck). (bottom) Coral, coral and more coral.

WHAT IT COSTS	
Regulator & BC	$6.30–$25
Underwater camera	$35–$45
Video camera	$75
Pro videos of your dive	$160
Two-tank boat trips	$60–$100
Specialty dives	$70–$150
One-tank afternoon dives	$45–$60
Night dives	$45–$60
Marine park fee	$5

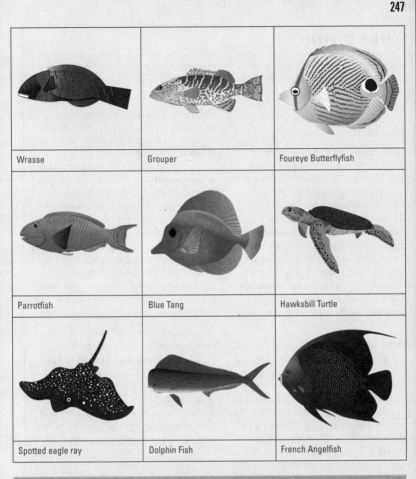

Wrasse	Grouper	Foureye Butterflyfish
Parrotfish	Blue Tang	Hawksbill Turtle
Spotted eagle ray	Dolphin Fish	French Angelfish

SNORKELING TIPS

Snorkeling equipment is available at nearly all hotels and beach clubs as well as at Parque Chankanaab, Playa San Francisco, and Parque Punta Sur. Gear rents for less than $15 a day. Snorkeling tours run about $60 and take in the shallow reefs off Palancar, Chankanaab, Colombia, and Yucab.

■ Never turn your back on the ocean, especially if the waves are big.

■ Ask about rip tides before you go in.

■ Enter and exit from a sandy beach area.

■ Avoid snorkeling at dusk and never go in the water after dark.

■ Wear lots of sunscreen, especially on your back and butt cheeks.

■ Don't snorkel too close to the reef. You could get scratched if a wave pushes you.

■ Be mindful of boats.

SCUBA DIVING

There's no way anyone can do all the deep dives, drift dives, shore dives, wall dives, and night dives in one trip, never mind the theme dives focusing on ecology, archaeology, sunken ships, and photography.

Many hotels and dive shops offer introductory classes in a swimming pool. Most include a beach or boat dive. Resort courses cost about $60–$80. Many dive shops also offer full open-water certification classes, which take at least four days of intensive classroom study and pool practice. Basic certification courses cost about $390, while advanced and specialty courses cost between $270-$1400. You can also do your classroom study at home, then make your training and test dives on Cozumel.

DIVING SAFELY There are more than 100 dive shops in Cozumel, so look for high safety standards and documented credentials. The best places offer small groups and individual attention. Next to your equipment, your dive master is the most important consideration for your adventure. Make sure he or she has PADI or NAUI certification (or FMAS, the Mexican equivalent). Be sure to bring your own certification card; all reputable shops require customers to show them before diving. If you forget, you may be able to call the agency that certified you and have the card number faxed to the shop.

Keep in mind that much of the reef off Cozumel is a protected National Marine Park. Boats aren't allowed to anchor in certain areas, and you shouldn't touch the coral or take any "souvenirs" from the reefs when you dive there. It's best to swim at least three feet above the reef—not just because coral can sting or cut you, but also because it's easily

damaged and grows very slowly; it has taken 2,000 years to reach their present size.

There are two reputable recompression chambers in Cozumel if you need emergency medical attention: **Medicina Hiperbarica Integral** (✉ Calle 5 Sur 37 ☎ 987/872–1430 24-hr hotline); and **Costamed Cozumel** (✉ Calle 1 Sur 101, Adolfo López Mateos ☎ 9400 or 987/872-9400). These chambers, which aim for a 35-minute response time from reef to chamber, treat decompression sickness, commonly known as "the bends," which occurs when you surface too quickly and nitrogen bubbles form in the bloodstream. Recompression chambers are also used to treat nitrogen narcosis, collapsed lungs, and hypothermia.

You may also want to consider buying dive-accident insurance from the U.S.-based **Divers Alert Network (DAN)** (☎ 919/684–9111 emergency hotline ⊕ www.dan.org) before embarking on your dive vacation. DAN insurance covers dive accidents and injuries, and their emergency hotline can help you find the best local doctors, hyperbaric chambers, and medical services. They can also arrange for airlifts.

Diver on the Paradise Reef.

evening. Traditionally, stores are open from 9 to 9, although most do close on Sunday morning.

When you shop for souvenirs, be sure you don't buy anything made with black coral. It's an endangered species, and you'll be barred from bringing it to the United States and other countries.

CLOTHING
Blanc du Nil

MIXED CLOTHING | Be the best-dressed person at your next party wearing one of the many styles of casual, breezy, white clothing for sale here. ⊠ *Av. Melgar and Calle 3, Cozumel* ☎ *987/869–0952* ⊕ *www.blancdunil.com.*

Island Outfitters

OTHER SPECIALTY STORE | FAMILY | Mexican crafts, home decor, sportswear, beach towels, and sarongs are among the offerings at Island Outfitters. ⊠ *Av. Rafael E. Melgar and Calle 4, San Miguel* ☎ *987/872–2741.*

CRAFTS
Balam Art

CRAFTS | Artists here create intricate paintings on feathers from local birds. There's a second location at Plaza Vista Del Mar near Punta Langosta. ⊠ *Av. 5 between Juárez and Calle 2, San Miguel* ☎ *987/869–0548* ⊗ *Closed Sun.*

Galería Azul

ART GALLERIES | At one of Cozumel's best art galleries, Greg Dietrich creates and shows his engraved blown-glass lamps and vases along with paintings, jewelry, photography, and other works by local artists. It's open Monday through Friday from 11 to 7 (others times by appointment). The gallery is three blocks off the waterfront. ⊠ *Av. 15 Norte No. 449, between Calles 8 and 10, San Miguel* ☎ *987/869–0963* ⊕ *www.cozumelglassart.com* ⊗ *Closed weekends.*

★ Los Cinco Soles

CRAFTS | FAMILY | This is the best one-stop shop in Cozumel for Mexican crafts and art. Numerous display rooms, covering almost a block, are filled with clothing, furnishings, home-decor items, quality tequilas, and jewelry. There are smaller branches at Puerta Maya, the international pier (SSA), the Cozumel airport, Punta Langosta, and the gift shops of some hotels. ⊠ *Av. Rafael E. Melgar and Calle 8 Norte, San Miguel* ☎ *987/872–9004* ⊕ *www.loscincosoles.com.*

Viva Mexico

CRAFTS | FAMILY | Downstairs from the bar of the same name, Viva Mexico sells souvenirs and handicrafts from all over Mexico; it's a great place to find vanilla, T-shirts, household goods, art, and assorted trinkets. There are also branches at Puerta Maya and the international pier. ⊠ *Av. Rafael E. Melgar at Calle Adolfo Rosado Salas, San Miguel* ☎ *987/872–0418* ⊕ *facebook.com/cozumelvivamexico.*

GROCERY STORES
Chedraui

SUPERMARKET | Open daily from 7 am to 11 pm, this big, full-service grocery store also carries clothing, kitchenware, appliances, furniture, and a remarkably good selection of wine. For those renting a nearby condo, this is a place to stock up on food and beverages. Brand-name suntan lotions, while expensive, are available. The deli and bakery are excellent places to stock up on picnic provisions; coolers and ice are sold here, too. ⊠ *Av. Rafael E. Melgar, between Calles 15 and 17 Sur, San Miguel* ☎ *987/872–5404* ⊕ *www.chedraui.com.mx.*

Mega Grocery Store

SUPERMARKET | FAMILY | A supermarket, pharmacy, and department store all under one big roof, Mega has a huge covered parking lot and pretty much anything you would need for a short or extended stay on Cozumel. Mega's wine and international beer offerings are second to none. It's open daily from 8 am to 10 pm; alcohol sales on Sunday cease at 3 as they do around the island for carryout. ⊠ *Av. Rafael E. Melgar and Calle 11, San Miguel* ☎ *987/872–2116* ⊕ *soriana.com.*

JEWELRY

Diamonds International

JEWELRY & WATCHES | You can custom design pieces of jewelry from a collection of loose diamonds, emeralds, rubies, sapphires, or tanzanite at Diamonds International. There is also a broad range of watches to choose from. The shop and its affiliates, Tanzanite International and Silver International, have multiple locations along the waterfront, at the cruise piers, and in the shopping malls—in fact, it's hard to avoid them. Repairs and batteries are also available. ⊠ *Av. Rafael E. Melgar 599, Cozumel* ☎ *987/872–5335* ⊕ *www.diamondsinternational.com.*

★ Pama

DUTY-FREE | A trusted longtime business on the island, Pama offers a wide array of imported jewelry, perfumes, watches, and watch repairs while you wait. Sales pitches are definitely low-pressure here, so take your time and enjoy looking around. ⊠ *Av. Rafael E. Melgar Sur 9, San Miguel* ☎ *987/872–0090* ⊕ *www. pamacozumel.com.*

Sergio's Silver

JEWELRY & WATCHES | The renowned artist's wild sculpture and jewelry collections are sold at this gallery. If you have the time, they will make a custom piece for you to take home. ⊠ *Av. Juárez between Avs. 5 and 10, San Miguel* ☎ *987/872–7632* ⊕ *www.sergiosilver. com* ☉ *Closed Sun.*

MARKETS

Crafts Market

MARKET | **FAMILY** | On the east side of the downtown square, a crafts market sells a respectable assortment of Mexican wares. Practice your bartering skills—start low, compromise, smile—while shopping for blankets, T-shirts, hammocks, and pottery. Most shops are cash only. ⊠ *Between Calles 1 and Juarez, San Miguel.*

Mercado Municipal

MARKET | **FAMILY** | For fresh produce, fish, chiles, and a taste of local life, stop by the Mercado Municipal. There are also several inexpensive places to eat serving Mexican and Asian foods. ⊠ *Calle Adolfo Rosado Salas, between Avs. 20 and 25 Sur, San Miguel.*

🏃 Activities

Not surprisingly, water sports—most notably scuba diving, snorkeling, and fishing—are Cozumel's biggest draw. Services and equipment rentals are available throughout the island, especially through major hotels and at the beach clubs.

FISHING

The waters off Cozumel teem with more than 230 species of fish, making this one of the world's best deep-sea fishing destinations. During billfish migration season from late April through June, blue marlin, white marlin, and sailfish are plentiful, and world-record catches aren't uncommon.

The larger sportfishing boats are located in the Puerto Abrigo marina just north of San Miguel. Fishing boats are also located at **Marina Fonatur,** the marina on the south side, near the Presidente InterContinental Resort & Spa. Some sportfishing companies are affiliated with dive shops and offer a full range of water activities. Hotels can help arrange daily charters—some offer special deals, with boats leaving from their own docks.

Albatros Charters

FISHING | **FAMILY** | Half- and full-day outings that include boat and crew, tackle and bait, plus libations and lunch (quesadillas or your own fresh catch) are organized by Albatros Charters. Customized dive trips are also available. ⊠ *Calle 19 Sur Cra.10 Bis, Puerto Abrigo* ☏ *987/872–7904, 888/333–4643 in U.S.* ⊕ *cozumel-fishing. com* ☞ *From half-day USD$500* ☺ *Closed Sun.*

Ocean Tours

DIVING & SNORKELING | FAMILY | All equipment and tackle, lunch with beer, and, of course, the boat and crew are included in Ocean Tours' full-day rates. Deep-sea fishing, scuba diving, and snorkeling tours available. Half-day tours are also offered, and discounts are given for cash payments. ⊠ *Cozumeleno Beach Resort, Playa Santa Pilar, Zona Hotelera Norte, Km 4.5, Cozumel* ☏ *987/872–9530* ⊕ *www.cozumel-diving.net/oceantur* ☞ *From USD$480 for half day.*

Sand Dollar Sports

SCUBA DIVING | FAMILY | Both bottom- and deep-sea fishing trips can be arranged through Sand Dollar; ditto for diving, sailing, Snuba, helmet diving, parasailing, and snorkeling excursions. Charter rates for one to six people include beer, soda, water, and snacks. ⊠ *Carretera Sur, Km 3.2, Cozumel* ☏ *987/876–1452* ⊕ *www. sanddollarsports.com* ☞ *Scuba diving from USD$100.*

★ Spearfishing Today

FISHING | The blue waters of Cozumel are a great place to learn to spearfish. After a short lesson with this outfit's certified instructors, you'll launch out from Puerto Abrigo on a four-hour boat trip. Expect to get shots off at grouper, snapper, or triggerfish. Snacks, water, soft drinks, and all equipment are included. The crew will also clean your catch and provide names of restaurants that will cook it for you. ⊠ *Puerto de Abrigo–Banco Playa, Zona Hotelera Nte., Puerto Abrigo* ☏ *987/876–U862* ⊕ *www.spearfishingtoday.com* ☞ *From USD$250.*

Tres Hermanos

DIVING & SNORKELING | FAMILY | This outfit specializes in deep-sea and fly-fishing trips. It also offers scuba-diving excursions and snorkel trips. Boats are available for group charters, allowing you to move at your own pace. ⊠ *Marina Puerto de Abrigo, Av. Rafael E. Melgar Norte, Puerto Abrigo* ☏ *987/107–2030* ⊕ *cozumelfishing.com* ☞ *From USD$375 half day trip.*

KITEBOARDING AND PADDLEBOARDING

★ De Lille Sports

WATER SPORTS | FAMILY | Cozumel native Raul De Lille—a former world windsurf champion and national kiteboard champion—offers two- to three-hour classes in both stand-up paddleboarding (SUP) and kiteboarding. All tours depart from the De Lille Sports shop at Hotel Barracuda. The equipment is top-of-the-line. The huge, six-person paddleboard is great for a large group. Multiday courses, rental equipment, and sport-oriented tours are available, too. If the winds are calm, inquire about De Lille's private snorkeling tour to the northern tip of the island. ⊠ *Av. Melgar 628, Hotel Barracuda, Cozumel* ☏ *987/103–6711* ⊕ *www.delillesports.com* ☞ *SUP tour from USD$60* ☺ *Closed Sun.*

SNORKELING AND SCUBA DIVING

★ Aldora Divers

SCUBA DIVING | Make the most of your trip by exploring the undersea environment with Aldora Divers. Although it also works with neophytes, this outfit caters to experienced divers. Its all-day, three-tank nitrox trip gets you up close to reef sharks, eagle rays, and huge lionfish. Ask about Aldora's afternoon lionfish hunting trip to the north end of the island. ⊠ *Calle 5 Sur, between Avs. 5 and Rafael E. Melgar, San Miguel* ☏ *987/872–3397, 210/569-1203 in U.S.* ⊕ *www.aldora.com* ☞ *2-tank dives from USD$95.*

Aqua Safari

SCUBA DIVING | FAMILY | One of the island's oldest and most professional shops, Aqua Safari provides beginning and advanced PADI certification and daily introductory scuba courses. The operation uses larger, 12- to 16-passenger boats that are great in rough weather, but they are slow. ⊠ *Av. Rafael E. Melgar 429, between Calles 5 and 7 Sur, San Miguel* ☎ *987/869–0610* ⊕ *www.aquasafari.com* ⊠ *2-tank dives from USD$90.*

Aquatic Sports and Expeditions

SCUBA DIVING | FAMILY | Sergio Sandoval gets rave reviews from his clients, many of whom are repeat customers. In addition to the usual excursions, he'll take you out for wreck dives, underwater photo safaris, or lionfish hunting. He also charters his boat for full- and half-day fishing trips. ⊠ *Carretera Sur, Km 6.5, Cozumel* ☎ *987/112–5002* ⊕ *www.cozumeldivingwithsergio.com* ⊠ *2-tank dives from USD$110.*

Blue Angel Scuba and Scuba School

SCUBA DIVING | FAMILY | The combo dive-and-snorkel excursions arranged by Blue Angel allow family members to have fun together, even if not all are scuba enthusiasts. Dedicated dive trips to local reefs and PADI courses are also offered. Inquire about the snorkel trip to the crystal-blue waters called El Cielo. Dive-and-hotel packages are available at its hotel of the same name. ⊠ *Blue Angel Resort, Carretera Costera Sur, Km 2.2,* ☎ *987/872–0819* ⊕ *www.blueangelresort.com* ⊠ *2-tank dives from USD$100.*

Eagle Ray Divers

SCUBA DIVING | FAMILY | Snorkeling trips and dive instruction are available through Eagle Ray Divers. (The three-reef snorkel trip lets nondivers explore beyond the shore.) As befits its name, the company keeps track of the eagle rays that appear off Cozumel from December to February and runs trips for advanced divers to walls where the rays congregate. Beginners can also see rays around some of the reefs. ⊠ *La Caleta Marina, Cozumel* ☎ *987/107–2315, 866/465–1616 in U.S.* ⊕ *www.eagleraydivers.com* ⊠ *2-tank dives from USD$75.*

Fury Catamarans

SAILING | Vacationers who can't decide between snorkeling and partying can combine the two by boarding one of Fury's 65-foot catamarans. Boats visit the reef en route to a private stretch of beach south of town. Rates include equipment, lunch, soft drinks, beer, and margaritas, plus access to assorted beach toys. A sunset booze cruise is also offered, and there are numerous pickup points at different times along the west coast. ⊠ *Carretera Sur, Km 3.5, beside Casa del Mar Hotel, Cozumel* ☎ *987/872–5145, 305/433–4537 in U.S.* ⊕ *www.furycozumel.com* ⊠ *From USD$79.*

Scuba Du

SCUBA DIVING | FAMILY | Along with the requisite Cozumel reef dives, this diver favorite organizes night dives and an advanced trip to walls off Punta Sur as well as snorkeling and fishing trips. A combination of large and smaller "six pack" boats are available. The Presidente InterContinental Hotel, Casa Mexicana, and Hotel B offer lodging-and-dive packages. A sunset pleasure ride is also offered. ⊠ *Presidente InterContinental hotel, Carretera Sur, Km 6, Cozumel* ☎ *987/872–9505* ⊕ *www.scubadu.com* ⊠ *2-tank dives from USD$109.*

★ ScubaTony

DIVING & SNORKELING | Diving with ScubaTony is like diving with friends you've known for years. The personalized trips include tanks, weights, fresh fruit, and drinks. If you're new to the sport or have a few years between dives, introductory and refresher courses are available; PADI-certified instructors will also work with you to obtain additional certifications (such as nitrox). ⊠ *Puerto Fonatur, Carretera A Chankanaab, Km 5.75 Sur,* ☎ *987/878–2432, 469/361–6573 in U.S.* ⊕ *www.scubatony.com* 🕮 *2-tank dives from USD$90.*

★ Tiger's Adventures

DIVING & SNORKELING | Tiger Aguilar leads one of the island's more enjoyable snorkel-and-party excursions. In the water, you might encounter harmless nurse sharks in addition to turtles, fish, and starfish; aboard the boat, you can indulge in adult beverages, sodas, and fresh snacks. Trips run from around 11 to 4:30, with passengers departing from Marina Fonatur bound for shallow El Cielo lagoon. ⊠ *Carretera Costa Sur, Km 6.2, Cozumel* ✛ *At Marina Fonatur* ☎ *987/871–0897* 🕮 *MX$1,235, cash only, reservations required.*

SUBMARINE TOURS
★ Atlantis Submarine

WILDLIFE-WATCHING | **FAMILY** | If you're curious about what's underneath Cozumel's waters but don't like getting wet, Atlantis Submarine has 1½-hour submarine rides that explore the Chankanaab Reef and surrounding area. Subs descend about 100 feet—deeper than most scuba dives go—but be warned: claustrophobes may not be able to handle the sardine-can conditions. All passengers must be at least 36" tall and over four years old. Three daily trips are offered. ⊠ *Carretera Sur, Km 4, across from Hotel Casa del Mar, Cozumel* ☎ *987/872–5671* ⊕ *www.atlantissubmarines.travel* 🕮 *from USD$105.*

Chapter 7

YUCATÁN STATE

Updated by
John Newton

⊙ Sights	🍴 Restaurants	🛏 Hotels	🛍 Shopping	🍸 Nightlife
★★★★★	★★★★☆	★★★★☆	★★★☆☆	★★★☆☆

WELCOME TO YUCATÁN STATE

TOP REASONS TO GO

★ **Visiting spectacular Maya ruins:** Chichén Itzá and Uxmal are two of the largest, most beautiful sites in the region.

★ **Living like a wealthy hacendado:** You can stay in a restored *henequen* (sisal) hacienda-turned-hotel and delight in its old-world charm.

★ **Browsing at fantastic craft markets:** This region is known for its handmade *hamacas* (hammocks), piñatas, and other local handicrafts.

★ **Swimming in pristine freshwater cenotes:** These sinkholes, like portals to the underworld, are scattered throughout the inland landscape.

★ **Tasting diverse flavors:** Yucatecan specialties served in restaurants here include Mayan-originated dishes like *cochinita pibil* (pork cooked in banana leaves).

1 Mérida. Fully urban, and bustling with foot and car traffic, Mérida was once the main stronghold of Spanish colonialism in the peninsula. Tucked among the restaurants, museums, and markets are grand, old, ornamented mansions and civic buildings that recall the city's heyday as the wealthiest capital in Mexico.

2 Izamal. This town is dominated by the 16th-century Convent of San Antonio while most of its buildings are painted in the same mustard yellow hue, creating a vivid backdrop.

3 The Ruta Puuc. Many smaller archaeological sites—some hardly visited—lie along the Ruta Puuc, an informal designation for the small towns in the slightly hillier, southern part of the state.

4 Uxmal. South of Mérida, beautiful Uxmal is less well known (and typically far less crowded) than Chichén Itzá.

5 Chichén Itzá. Yucatán's spectacular Maya ruins are famous all over the world. The best-known is Chichén Itzá, a magnificent and mysterious site that draws more than a million visitors every year.

6 Valladolid. One of the state's most important colonial towns, Valladolid is a convenient base for day trips.

7 Ek Balam. This long-occupied Maya site not far from Valladolid is best known for the unusually intact façades on El Torre, an enormous pyramid.

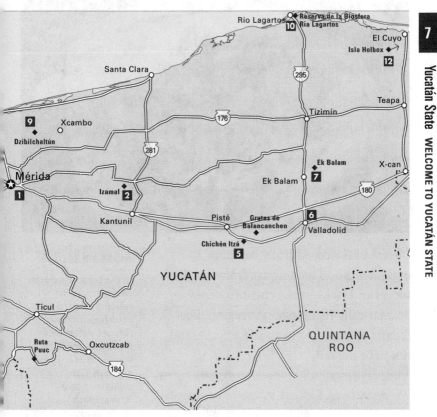

8 Celestún. Bird-watchers and nature lovers flock to Celestún to admire one of the hemisphere's largest colonies of pink flamingos.

9 Dzibilchaltún. An easy stop just off the road between Mérida and Progreso, this Maya site is best known for the building known as the Temple of the Seven Dolls (after sculptures found there) which lines up with the sun on the spring and fall equinoxes.

10 Reserva de la Biósfera Ría Lagartos. Located on Yucatán's northern coast, this biosphere is best known as a destination for birders who come to admire the flamingos—and roughly 400 other species—that are common here.

11 Progreso. Outside the unpretentious town of Progreso, empty beaches stretch for miles in either direction—punctuated only by fishing villages, estuaries, and salt flats.

12 Isla Holbox. This island has a more casual, barefoot feel than the better-known beach towns of the Riviera Maya.

YUCATÁN CUISINE

Chefs in Mexico skillfully combine ingredients and techniques from the New World and Old, but the cuisines here vary dramatically from region to region. The flavors of Yucatán are subtle, unique, and not to be missed.

In terms of culinary traditions, the country can be divided into four regions. Foods from the north tend to be unpretentious; here you'll find dishes that were originally served on ranches and haciendas. On both coasts, seafood takes center stage. The central region includes the area in and around Mexico City, where many of the country's most characteristic plates were invented in convent kitchens during colonial times. Foods from the south, including the Yucatán, are singular within Mexico. This region was once a difficult area to access, so the culinary traditions that developed on the isolated peninsula were quite different from those in other areas of the country. At the same time, centuries of commercial and cultural trade with Cuba, Europe (especially France), and New Orleans have left their mark on Yucatecan cuisine. More recent Middle Eastern influences are also visible.

AGUA FRESCA

In the Yucatán's warm weather, nothing satisfies like a cool *agua fresca* (fruit-infused water). One drink that you won't want to miss is *agua de chaya*. Chaya, sometimes called "tree spinach," is a nutritious leafy green that's used in a wide variety of recipes, including soups, omelets, tamales, and a sweet agua fresca.

Art: (Above) Cochinita pibil can vary from restaurant to restaurant.

Regional Cuisines

Visitors to the Yucatán often discover a wide variety of dishes they've never seen before. This is because Yucatán cuisine is not often served in Mexican restaurants north of the border, or even in other areas of the country. Here are some of the most typical dishes—all of them well worth a try.

Huevos motuleños. This is a popular breakfast dish that originated in Motul, a small town east of Mérida, where the ancient Maya city of Zacmotul once stood. Eggs, sunny-side up, are covered with black beans and cheese and served on a crispy tortilla. Other ingredients like red salsa, ham, and green peas are usually heaped on top. Fried plantains are often served on the side.

Sopa de lima. This soup is traditionally prepared with turkey, indigenous to the Yucatán, and includes pieces of tomatoes, sweet chile or green pepper, and lime juice. It's garnished with strips of lightly fried tortilla.

Queso relleno. Legend has it that in the 19th century a boat from Holland was forced to dock on the peninsula because of bad weather, and the

Huevos motuleños

people in Mérida were delighted with the cargo of Dutch cheese. From this trip, a typical Yucatecan dish made with Gouda or Edam cheese was born. A salty cow's-milk cheese is stuffed with spiced ground meat and served with two sauces: a tomato-caper sauce and a milder creamy sauce.

Cochinita pibil. This is perhaps the most representative dish in the Yucatecan repertoire. The word *pibil* means "roasted in the hole," which describes just how this dish is classically prepared. The Maya used to roast venison in this way, but the Spanish-introduced pork is now the standard. The meat is first marinated in a mixture of bitter orange juice (from the Seville oranges that grow in this region), achiote (an intensely peppery paste that some describe as having a nutmeglike flavor, made from annatto seeds), oregano, salt, and pepper. Next, it's wrapped in banana leaves and placed in a hole lined with stones that have been heated with fire. The meat cooks slowly.

Panuchos and salbutes. These culinary cousins are the Yucatecan version of tostadas—a fried tortilla topped with protein (typically turkey or cochinita pibil), lettuce, tomatoes, and pickled onions. The difference between the two is that the tortillas used with panuchos are stuffed with black beans.

Sopa de lima

In sharp contrast to the resort lifestyle of Cancún and the Riviera Maya, Yucatán caters to a more tranquil traveler who is looking to avoid the spring-break atmosphere. Here you'll find innumerable natural and historic wonders, including mangrove forests, unspoiled beaches, quaint colonial villages, and more than 50% of Mexico's bird species.

Unlike Quintana Roo, Yucatán has many fewer international residents, and there's much less emphasis on beachside activities. With large indigenous populations, these states are defined by Mayan culture and traditions; the area's history, people, and food set it apart from the rest of Mexico.

One of the Yucatán State's biggest draws is its capital, Mérida. It is the handsome regional hub of art and culture, and locals and travelers alike gather in the main square for weekend music and dance performances. Izamal, the oldest town in the Yucatán, will take you back in time with its cobblestone streets, iron lampposts, yellow-painted buildings, and horse-drawn carriages. Near the state's eastern border, the budding cosmopolitan town of Valladolid offers excellent bird-watching and freshwater cenotes where you can explore underwater caves.

More than 2,000 Mayan ruins lie within these two states, but only a handful have been restored for tourism. Nestled amid rampant jungles are the magnificent archaeological sites of Uxmal, Kabah,

Labná, Sayil, Dzibilchaltún, and the world-famous Chichén Itzá, a UNESCO Natural World Heritage Site. Roughly one hour southeast of Uxmal, the Grutas de Loltún show signs of human civilization dating as far back as 800 BC. At these natural caverns, illuminated pathways meander past stalactites, stalagmites, and limestone formations.

The beach town of Celestún offers nature lovers a chance to ogle huge flocks of pink flamingos. To combine wildlife with adventure, head to Río Lagartos where you can kayak through the mangroves. Off the coast of Isla Holbox, diving with whale sharks is possible from June through August. This small island, void of cars, is one of the area's best spots to relax and enjoy beach life. Near Mérida, the sand-rimmed community of Progreso is another coastal favorite.

MAJOR REGIONS
Chichén Itzá and the Maya Interior. Although hordes of buses arrive daily at Chichén Itzá, dropping off groups of tourists only to whisk them away a few hours later, visiting this way is almost criminal.

The area around the celebrated ruins is dotted with stunning cenotes and sleepy little communities, which may make you feel like you've stepped back in time. The pint-size town of Pisté is barely more than an outpost, where visitors to Chichén Itzá can rest at small hotels. But picturesque Valladolid, the second-largest city in the state, is notable for its cenotes and beautiful 16th-century church. Here, perhaps while enjoying a traditional ice cream in the central plaza, you notice that things seem to move at a slower pace.

While some Maya sites like Chichén Itzá are world famous, others are not, The structures may not be as impressive, but they offer instead the opportunity to explore them with fewer tourists. Mayapan, Xcambo, and perhaps the most splendid site in Yucatán after Chichén Itzá, Uxmal, make for fascinating excursions.

Colonial Towns. Many think of Yucatán's Maya sites first, but its Spanish colonial settlements are impressive in their own right. Beyond Mérida and Valladolid, the "yellow town" of Izamal, historic Maní, and countless historic haciendas, many of them now converted into hotels, provide glimpses of a history that dates back almost 500 years. Stop at the central square of many small towns and churches constructed by missionaries that speak to centuries of evangelization.

Progreso and the North Coast. Various routes lead from Mérida to towns along the coast, which are spread across a distance of 380 km (236 miles). Separate roads connect the state capital with the laid-back village of Celestún, which serves as the entrance to an ecological marine reserve that extends south to just beyond the Campeche border. Carretera 261 leads due north from Mérida to the relatively modern but humble port of Progreso, where Meridanos spend their holidays. To get to some of the small beach towns east of Progreso, head east on Carretera 176 out of Mérida, and then

cut north on one of the many access roads. Not as picturesque as the Rivera Maya coastline, beaches here are wide and generally shadeless.

The terrain in this part of the peninsula is absolutely flat. Tall trees are scarce because the region was almost entirely cleared for coconut palms in the early 19th century and again for henequen (better known in English as sisal, after the port of Sisal) in the early 20th century. Locals still tend some of the old fields of henequen, even though there's little profit to be made now from the rope fiber it produces. Other former plantation fields are wildly overgrown with scrub, and are identifiable only by the low, white stone walls that used to mark their boundaries. Many bird species make their home in this area, and butterflies swarm in profusion throughout the dry season.

Planning

When to Go

As with many other places in Mexico, high season begins in late November and continues until early April. The weeks around Christmas and Easter are peak times for visiting; making reservations up to a year in advance is common. Fortunately, Yucatán doesn't get the spring-break crowds like Cancún, but you may see a slight increase in travelers (and prices) during August, when most Europeans take their vacations.

If you're traveling off-season, May is usually the hottest month of the year; rainfall is heaviest between June and October, bringing with it an uncomfortable humidity. Provided you can avoid Thanksgiving weekend, November is one of your best bets for good weather and affordable rates. This time of year, the rainy season is over, the humidity has faded, and temperatures are pleasantly cooler—plus you also won't have to deal with holiday hordes, which means properties and airlines will most likely be offering discounted rates.

Getting Here and Around

AIR

Aeroméxico and Interjet fly from Mexico City to both Aeropuerto Manuel Crescencio Rejón (MID) in Mérida. Volaris also links Mérida to Mexico City, and Mayair, a small regional airline, connects it to Cancún daily. International flights land in Mérida as well. United comes nonstop daily from Houston; American flies from Miami; and Aeroméxico flies from Atlanta.

BUS

ADO runs direct buses to many coastal cities and ruins from Mérida. They depart from the first-class CAME bus station. Regional bus lines to intermediate or more out-of-the-way destinations leave from the second-class terminal just across the street.

CAR

From Mérida, highways radiate in every direction. To the east, Carreteras 180D *cuota* and 180 *libre* are, respectively, the toll and free roads to Cancún; driving the full length of the former costs about MX$450. The toll road has exits for the famous Chichén Itzá ruins and the low-key colonial city of Valladolid; the free road passes through these and many smaller towns. Although it's a dull drive, the toll road is faster, better maintained, and void of detours. Heading south from Mérida on Carretera 261 (Carretera 180 until the town of Umán), you come to Uxmal and the Ruta Puuc, a series of small ruins of relatively uniform style (most have at least one outstanding building). Carretera 261 north from Mérida takes you to the port and beach resort of Progreso. To the west, the laid-back fishing village of Celestún—which

borders protected wetland—can be accessed by a separate highway from Mérida.

If you're independent and adventurous, hiring a rental car is a great way to explore. Daily rental rates are low, but full-coverage car insurance (by Mexican law) will cost you about $45 per day. Be sure to check the lights, windshield wipers, and spare tire before taking off. Carry plenty of bottled water, fill up the gas tank whenever you see a station, and try to avoid driving at night.

Restaurants

Expect a superb variety of cuisines—primarily Yucatecan, of course, but also Lebanese, Italian, French, Chinese, vegetarian, and Mexican—at very reasonable prices. Reservations are advised for the pricier restaurants on weekends and in high season. Beach towns, such as Progreso, Río Lagartos, and Celestún, tend to serve fresh, simply prepared seafood. Specialties include fish and shellfish stews, cream soups, shrimp cocktail, squid and octopus, and *panuchos* (chubby rounds of fried cornmeal covered with refried beans and topped with onion and shredded turkey or chicken).

Mexicans generally eat lunch in the afternoon—certainly not before 2. If you want to eat at noon, call ahead to verify hours. In Mérida the locals make a real event of late dinners, especially in summer. Casual (but neat) dress is acceptable at all restaurants. Avoid wearing shorts or casual sandals in the more expensive places, and anywhere at all—especially in the evening—if you don't want to look like a tourist. Although food servers at most local restaurants are kind and hospitable, they don't always show it like they do in the States. Be patient and realize that, for many, the language barrier may cause them to be more reserved but not necessarily unfriendly.

It's common practice for restaurants to include gratuity and tax in the total bill, so double-check your bill before adding a tip.

Hotels

Yucatán State has around 13,400 hotel rooms—far less than neighboring Quintana Roo but that figure still represents enormous, and continuing, growth in recent years. Mérida's hotels run the gamut from boutique offerings to international brands. Many travelers take advantage of the many houses on Airbnb, VRBO and similar sites. As the historic homes of Centro are renovated, many become available for rental allowing travelers to live like well-heeled locals on their vacation.

If you plan to spend most of your time enjoying downtown Mérida, stay near the main square. If you're a light sleeper, however, opt for one of the high-rises along or near Paseo de Montejo, about a 20-minute stroll (but an easy cab ride) from Plaza Grande.

Inland towns such as Valladolid and Ticul are good options for a look at the slow-paced countryside. There are several charming hotels near the major archaeological sites Chichén Itzá and Uxmal, and a growing number of small hotels in Progreso, Sisal, Celestún, El Cuyo and other seaside towns.

WHAT IT COSTS in Dollars and Pesos

	$	$$	$$$	$$$$
RESTAURANTS				
	under MX$200	MX$200–MX$300	MX$301–MX$500	over MX$500
HOTELS IN DOLLARS				
	under $100	$100–$200	$201–$300	over $300
HOTELS IN PESOS				
	under MX$2,000	MX$2,000–MX$4,000	MX$4,001–MX$6,000	over MX$6,000

Timing

You should plan to spend at least five days in Yucatán. It's best to start your trip with a few days in Mérida. (Weekends, when some streets are closed to traffic and there are lots of free outdoor performances, are a great time to visit.) You should also budget enough time for day trips to the sites of Chichén Itzá and Uxmal; visiting Mérida without traveling to at least one of them is like driving to the beach and not getting out of the car. There are many other Maya sites if you have already seen those two while atmospheric colonial towns like Valladolid and Izamal are also popular stops. Spending a night in a restored hacienda is a highlight for many travelers.

Visitor Information

Oficina de Turismo de Yucatán
✉ *Palacio del Gobierno, Calle 61, between Calles 60 and 62, Centro* ☎ *999/930–3101 main office, 999/954–9290 branch office* ⊕ *www.yucatan.gob.mx.*

Mérida

307 km (184 miles) west of Cancún.

Bustling streets, lively parks, a tropical version of the Champs-Elysées, endless cultural activities, and a varied nightlife: Mérida is the beating urban heart of the state of Yucatán. The hubbub of the city can seem frustrating—especially if you've just spent a peaceful few days on the coast or visiting Maya sites—but as the cultural and intellectual hub of the peninsula, Mérida is rich in art, history, and tradition. A sizable expatriate population serves as testament to its desirability as a place to live, and Mérida consistently appears on lists of best places to retire overseas.

Most streets here are one way and the bus routes are not all that direct, so you're better off parking your car downtown and walking to the local sites and attractions. Most are located around Plaza Grande (the *zócalo,* or main square), bordered by Calles 61 and 63 (on its north and south sides) and Calles 60 and 62 (on its east and west sides). Using the zócalo as your starting point is a great way to get to know the layout of the city. If you need extra help getting oriented, stop by the tourism offices on the square; the friendly, helpful staff have loads of information.

Plaza Grande itself is in the oldest part of town, the Centro Histórico. On Saturday night and Sunday, practically the entire population of the city gathers in the parks and plazas surrounding it to socialize and watch live entertainment. Calle 60 between Parque Santa Lucía and Plaza Grande gets especially lively. Restaurants set out tables in the streets, which quickly fill with patrons enjoying the free tango, salsa, or jazz performances. (Although this is a city of almost 900,000 people, you'll feel reasonably safe here; just take normal travel precautions.) On Sunday mornings, downtown streets are closed for pedestrians and cyclists from Parque de la Ermita through Plaza Grande to Paseo de Montejo.

Most streets in Mérida are numbered, not named, and most run one way. North–south streets have even numbers, which descend from west to east; east–west streets have odd numbers, which ascend from north to south. Street addresses are confusing because they don't progress in even increments by blocks; for example, the 600s may occupy two or more blocks. A particular location is therefore usually identified by indicating the street number and the nearest cross street, as in "Calle 64 and Calle 61," or "Calle 64 between Calles 61 and 63," which is written "Calle 64 x 61 y 63." Take heart: the system does make sense once you see it in action.

GETTING HERE AND AROUND

Mérida's airport, Aeropuerto Manuel Crescencio Rejón, is 7 km (4½ miles) west of the city on Avenida Itzáes. Getting from it to the downtown area usually takes 20 to 30 minutes by taxi, and the fare will be about MX$200. Note that while Uber is a popular service in Mérida, Uber drivers are not allowed to pick up passengers at the airport.

Municipal buses charge about MX$6 for trips around Mérida; having the correct change is helpful but not required. Riding the red, double-decker **Turibus** is a fun and informative alternative. You can buy your ticket (MX$120) on board the open-roof vehicle and get on and off as you please at seven key stops, enjoying recorded commentary along the way. The full route takes an hour and 45 minutes to complete, and buses operate from 9 am until 8:30 pm, daily except Sunday. A smaller bus operator, **Carnavalito,** visits many of the same sites. The upside to this tour is that it's given by real people (in both Spanish and English), so you can ask questions; the downside is that you can't hop on and off at will. Tours cost MX$120 and last around two hours, with a 20-minute break at a small shopping center where you can stretch your legs or buy a drink. The colorful Carnavalito bus takes off from Parque Santa Lucía Monday to Saturday at 10, 1, 4, and 7; Sunday departures are at 1 and 3.

CONTACTS Carnavalito. ☏ *999/927–6119* ⊕ *www.carnavalitocitytour.com.mx.* **Turibus.** ☏ *999/924–7880* ⊕ *www.turibusmerida.com.*

One of the best ways to get a feel for the city is to hire a *calesa,* or horse-drawn carriage. You can hail one of these at Plaza Grande or, during the day, at Palacio Cantón, site of the archaeology museum on Paseo de Montejo. Choose your horse and driver carefully, as some of the animals look dispirited, but others are fairly well cared for. Drivers charge about MX$350 for an hour-long circuit around downtown and up Paseo de Montejo, pointing out notable buildings and providing a little historic background along the route (note the drivers' English-language proficiencies run the gamut from capable to halting); an extended tour costs about MX$600.

Some taxis in Mérida charge beach-resort prices, and most don't use meters. Ones that do have a sign that reads *taxímetro* on the roof; these are recommended because they offer fair rates. Expect to pay MX$20 to MX$35 for a trip around Centro and MX$70 between Centro and Paseo de Montejo. The ride-sharing apps Uber and its local competitor, DiDi, have added some healthy competition, and they make it easier to get a lift—taxis can be difficult to find outside of the busiest areas of Centro.

TOURS

Mérida has more than 50 tour operators, and they generally take you to the same places. Because there are so many reputable, reasonably priced companies, there's no reason to opt for the less predictable *piratas* ("pirates") who sometimes lurk outside tour offices offering to sell you a cheaper trip and don't necessarily have much experience or your best interests at heart.

Amigo Yucatán

This operator offers private and group visits to the major archaeological sites and also to the Celestún, a town known for its massive flamingo colonies living in its river. ⊠ *Av. Colón 508C, Col. García Ginerés* ☎ *999/920–0104* ⊕ *www.amigoyucatan.com.*

EcoTurismo Yucatán

A good mix of day trips, overnight tours, and customized excursions throughout the region is available through this tour operator, based in Mérida. A one-day biking adventure includes cycling plus brief visits to two archaeological sites, a cave, a hacienda, and two cenotes. ⊠ *Calle 3 No. 235, between Calles 32A and 34, Col. Pensiones* ☎ *999/920–2772, 954/242–0007 in the U.S.* ⊕ *www. ecoyuc.com* ⊒ *From MX$875.*

Gray Line Yucatán

This familiar name offers a bit of everything—from a city tour of Mérida to archaeological-themed outings in Chichén Itzá, Uxmal, or Kabah. Other options include bird-watching, cenote swims, and hacienda visits. Airport transfers, private transportation, and overnight packages are available, too. The Yucatán operation is based in Mérida, and most tours leave from there, but they visit the entire region. ☎ *998/887–2495, 01800/719–5465 toll-free in Mexico* ⊕ *www.graylineyucatan.com* ⊒ *Tours from MX$800.*

Mérida English Library

If you enjoy walking and are curious about what's behind the doors of those old homes, the Mérida English Library conducts 2-hour home and garden tours every Tuesday morning from November through April. Meet at the library at 9 am for registration. ⊠ *Calle 53 No. 524, between Calles 66 and 68, Centro* ☎ *999/924–8401* ⊕ *www.meridaenglishlibrary.com* ⊒ *MX$200.*

Municipal Tourist Office Tours

Free 90-minute walking tours are offered year-round by the city's tourist office (Oficina de Turismo de Mérida). These depart from City Hall, on the main plaza, at 9:30 am Monday through Saturday. All tours are conducted in Spanish and English. ⊠ *Palacio Municipal, Calle 62, between Calles 61 and 63, Centro* ☎ *999/942–0000* ⊕ *www.merida.gob.mx.*

VISITOR INFORMATION
CONTACTS Oficina de Turismo de Mérida.
⊠ *Palacio Municipal, Calle 62, between Calles 61 and 63, Centro* ☎ *999/942–0000* ⊕ *www.merida.gob.mx.*

Sights ▼

1 Aké **I7**
2 Casa de Montejo......... **E6**
3 Catedral de Mérida...... **F5**
4 Centro Cultural de Mérida Olimpo **E5**
5 Ermita de Santa Isabel.............. **D9**
6 Gran Museo del Mundo Maya........ **G1**
7 Iglesia de la Tercera Orden de Jesús **F5**
8 Museo de Arte Popular de Yucatán **H5**
9 Museo de Arte Sacro **I1**
10 Museo Fernando García Ponce—MACAY........ **F6**
11 Palacio Cantón........... **G2**
12 Palacio de la Música..... **F5**
13 Palacio del Gobierno..... **F5**
14 Palacio Municipal **E5**
15 Parque Hidalgo **F5**
16 Parque Santa Lucía **F4**
17 Parque Zoológico El Centenario **A4**
18 Paseo de Montejo **G2**
19 Plaza Grande............. **F5**
20 Teatro Peón Contreras **F5**

Restaurants ▼

1 Amaro..................... **F5**
2 Apoala **F4**
3 Casa Chica **G3**
4 Cuna...................... **E1**
5 Dante's................... **F1**
6 Hacienda Teya **I8**
7 K'u'uk.................... **F1**
8 La Negrita **F3**
9 La Poderosa.............. **C8**
10 La Tradición **F1**
11 La Tratto.................. **F4**
12 Los Almendros **H5**
13 Restaurante Bologna.... **F1**
14 Rosas & Xocolate Restaurant.............. **G2**
15 Salón Gallos............. **H6**
16 Trotter's Grill House...... **F1**
17 Wayan'e **F1**

Quick Bites ▼

1 El Colón Sorbetes y Dulces Finos............. **F5**
2 Latte Quatro Sette...... **G3**
3 Pan & Koffee **G2**
4 Pola....................... **E4**

Hotels ▼

1 Casa Azul **F1**
2 Casa del Balam **F4**
3 Casa Lecanda........... **G3**
4 Casa Puuc **B1**
5 Casa San Ángel.......... **G3**
6 Chablé Yucatán **A9**
7 Doralba Inn Mérida..... **G6**
8 Fiesta Americana Mérida **F1**
9 Gran Hotel **E5**
10 Hacienda San José..... **A7**
11 Hacienda Xcanatún by Angsana.............. **F1**
12 Hotel del Peregrino..... **G4**
13 Hotel Hacienda Mérida **F4**
14 Hotel Julamis............ **G4**
15 Hotel Marionetas........ **E3**
16 Hotel Medio Mundo..... **E4**
17 Hyatt Regency Mérida **F1**
18 La Misión de Fray Diego **E5**
19 Maya Yucatán............ **F4**
20 Piedra de Agua **A9**
21 Rosas & Xocolate....... **G2**
22 The Villa Tievoli **G4**
23 Wayam Mundo Imperial **E1**

KEY

1 Exploring Sights
1 Restaurants
1 Quick Bites
1 Hotels
i Tourist Information

👁 Sights

Aké

RUINS | This compact archaeological site east of Mérida offers the unique opportunity to view architecture spanning two millennia in one sweeping vista. Standing atop a ruined Maya temple built more than a thousand years ago, you can see the incongruous sight of workers processing sisal in a rusty-looking factory, which was built in the early 20th century. To the right of this dilapidated building are the ruins of the old Hacienda and Iglesia de San Lorenzo Aké, both constructed of stones taken from Maya buildings. Experts estimate that Aké was populated between AD 250 and 900; today many people in the area have Aké as a surname. The city seems to have been related to the very important and powerful one at present-day Izamal; in fact, the two cities were once connected by a *sacbé* (white road) 43 feet wide and 33 km (20 miles) long. All that has been excavated so far are two pyramids, one with rows of columns (35 total) at the top, reminiscent of the Toltec columns at Tula, north of Mexico City. ⊠ *Near Tixkokob, 32 km (19 miles) east of Mérida, Mérida* ⊕ *www.inah.gob.mx* 🖾 *MX$45.*

Casa de Montejo

NOTABLE BUILDING | Three Franciscos de Montejo—father, son, and nephew—invaded the peninsula and founded Mérida in January of 1542, and they completed construction of this stately home on the south side of the central plaza in 1549. It's the city's oldest and finest example of colonial plateresque architecture, a Spanish architectural style popular in the 16th century and typified by the kind of elaborate ornamentation you'll see here. A bas-relief on the doorway—the facade is all that remains of the original house—depicts Francisco de Montejo the younger, his wife, and daughter, as well as Spanish soldiers standing on the heads of the vanquished Maya. The building has had many owners over the centuries and the museum on the site consists of several rooms that have been restored and furnished as they would have appeared at the end of the 19th century. ⊠ *Calle 63, No. 506, Centro* ☎ *999/253–6732* ⊕ *fomentoculturalbanamex.org* 🖾 *Free* ⊗ *Closed Mon.*

★ Catedral de Mérida

CHURCH | Begun in 1561, Mérida's cathedral is the oldest on the North American mainland (an older one can be found in the Dominican Republic). It took several hundred Maya laborers, working with stones from the pyramids of the ravaged Maya city, 37 years to complete it. Designed in the somber Renaissance style by an architect who had worked on El Escorial in Madrid, its facade is stark and unadorned, with gunnery slits instead of windows and faintly Moorish spires. Inside, the black Cristo de las Ampollas (Christ of the Blisters) occupies a side chapel to the left of the main altar. At 23 feet tall, it's the tallest Christ figure inside a Mexican church. The statue is a replica of the original, which was destroyed during the revolution in 1910 (also when the gold that once adorned the cathedral was carried off). According to one of many legends, the Christ figure burned all night and appeared the next morning unscathed—except for its namesake blisters. You can hear the pipe organ play at the 11 am Sunday Mass. ⊠ *Calles 60 and 61, Centro* ☎ *999/924–7777* ⊕ *catedraldemerida.org.mx* 🖾 *Free.*

Centro Cultural de Mérida Olimpo

PERFORMANCE VENUE | **FAMILY** | Referred to as simply the "Olimpo," this is the best venue in town for free cultural events. The beautiful porticoed cultural center was built adjacent to City Hall in late 1999, occupying what used to be a parking lot. The marble interior is a showcase for top international art exhibits, classical-music concerts, conferences, and theater and dance performances. The adjoining 1950s-style movie house shows classic art films by directors like

Did You Know?

The Catedral de Mérida was built on top of what was once a Maya temple called T'ho.

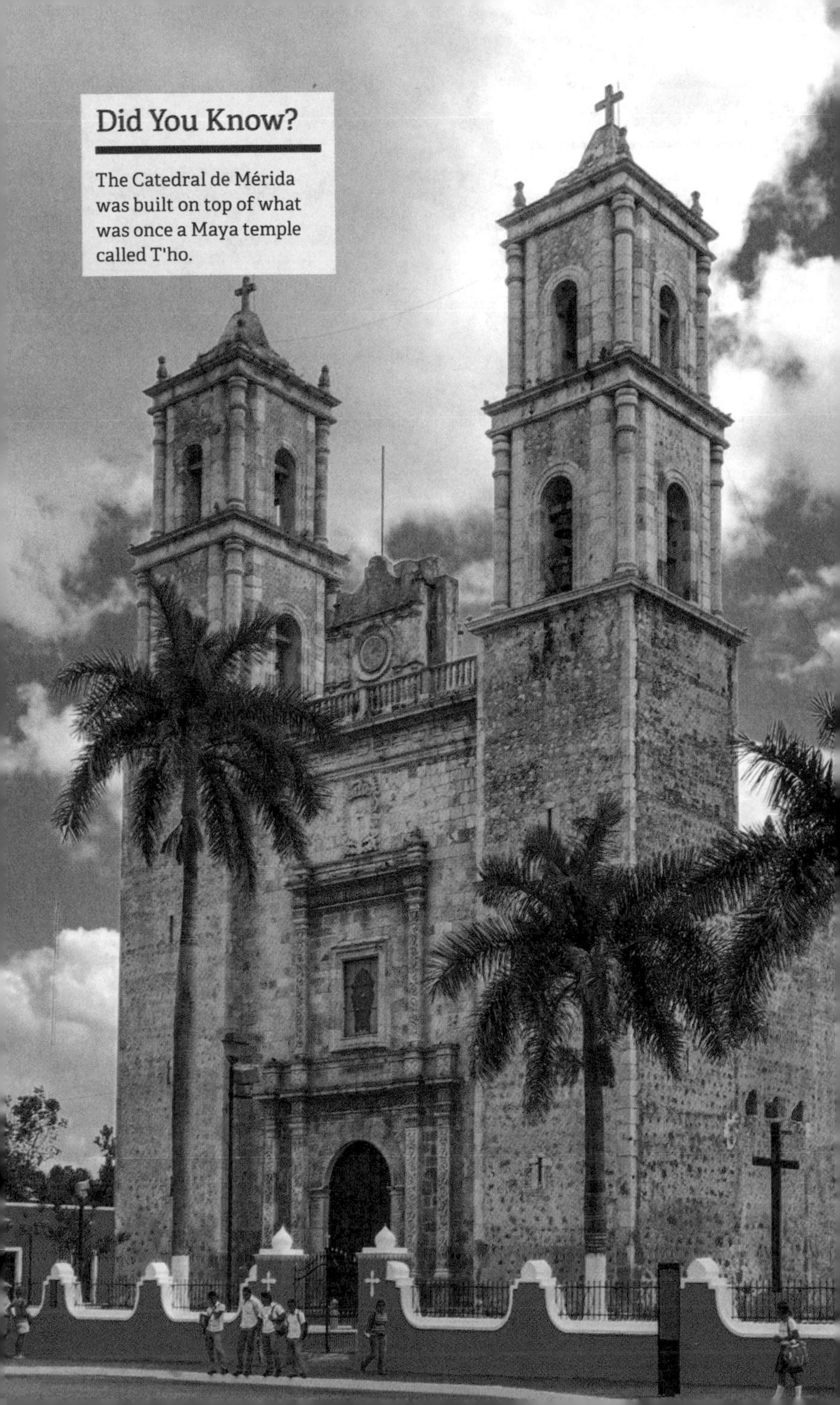

Buñuel, Fellini, and Kazan. The center also houses a planetarium with 60-minute shows explaining the solar system (narration is in Spanish); they run Tuesday through Sunday at 6 pm and Sunday at 10, 11, noon, 6, and 7—be sure to arrive 15 minutes early as nobody is allowed to sneak in once the show has begun. ⊠ *Calle 62, between Calles 61 and 63, Centro* ☎ *999/942–0000* ⊠ *Free; MX$56 for planetarium.*

Ermita de Santa Isabel

CHURCH | Several blocks south of the city center stands the restored Hermitage of St. Isabel, also known as the Hermitage of the Good Trip ("ermita" is the Spanish word for "hermitage"). Completed in 1748 as part of a Jesuit monastery, the beautiful edifice served as a resting place for colonial-era travelers heading to Campeche. It's one of the most peaceful places in the city and a good destination for a ride in a horse-drawn carriage. Behind the hermitage are huge, lush tropical gardens, with a waterfall and footpaths, which are usually unlocked during daylight hours. ⊠ *Calles 66 and 77, La Ermita* ⊠ *Free.*

Gran Museo del Mundo Maya

HISTORY MUSEUM | FAMILY | Whether or not the "Grand Museum of the Mayan World" lives up to its lofty name depends on your tastes and expectations, but the institution certainly makes a big architectural splash. The starkly modern building was designed to resemble a giant ceiba tree, sacred to the Maya, and it looms over the northern outskirts of town on the highway to Progreso. (Plan on a MX$50 Uber or DiDi ride from downtown.) The museum showcases an amazing collection of 1,100 Maya artifacts previously housed at the Palacio Cantón, where there was limited room for displays. Here, exhibitions wind through four themed halls: The Mayab, Nature, and Culture; Ancestral Maya; Yesterday's Maya; and Today's Maya. Much of the exhibit space is given over

to multimedia presentations, and therein lies the problem for some museum purists. The interactive screens *are* enormously popular, especially with younger visitors. (One all-the-rage panel of screens lets you tap in your birth date, convert it to the corresponding date on the Maya calendar, and email yourself your Maya horoscope.) Museum officials have responded to criticisms about the inclusion of modern technology by saying that Maya culture isn't merely an artifact of the past but an evolving way of life that has adapted to modern times. So why not adapt a museum's teaching methods to modernity, too? Everything here—artifact labeling and multimedia narration—is trilingual (Spanish, English, and Mayan). An adjoining theater, named the Mayamax, screens films and there is a concert hall too. ⊠ *Calle 60 Norte, Unidad Revolución* ☎ *999/341–0430* ⊕ *www.granmuseodelmundomaya.com. mx* ⊠ *MX$150* ⊗ *Closed Tues.*

Iglesia de la Tercera Orden de Jesús

CHURCH | Just north of Parque Hidalgo is one of Mérida's oldest buildings and the first Jesuit church in the Yucatán. It was built in 1618 from the limestone blocks of a dismantled Maya temple, and faint outlines of ancient carvings are still visible on the west wall. Although a favorite place for society weddings due to its antiquity, the church interior is not ornate. The former convent rooms in the rear of the building now host the Pinoteca Juan Gamboa Guzmán, a small but interesting art collection. The most engaging pieces here are the striking bronze sculptures of indigenous Maya crafted by celebrated 20th-century sculptor Enrique Gottdiener Soto. On the second floor are about 20 forgettable oil paintings—mostly of past civic officials. ⊠ *Calle 60, between Calles 57 and 59, Centro* ☎ *999/924–9712* ⊕ *www.inah. gob.mx* ⊠ *Free.*

Museo de Arte Popular de Yucatán

ART MUSEUM | FAMILY | This excellent museum at the northwest corner of Parque Mejorada offers a comprehensive introduction to Mexican arts and crafts including ceramics, textiles, stonework, woodwork, and glass. There are six rooms on the second floor that house the permanent collection and an additional gallery on the first floor that's typically used for temporary exhibitions. Leave time to peruse the on-site gift shop, which sells shawls, baskets, dolls, and masks. ⊠ *Calle 50 487, between Calles 57 and 59, Centro* ☎ *999/928–5263* ⊕ *www.facebook.com/artepopularyucatan* ☉ *Closed Mon. and Tues.* ☜ *Free.*

Museo de Arte Sacro

ART MUSEUM | Located in the town of Conkal, about ten kilometers (six miles) to the northeast of Mérida, the Museum of Sacred Art is tucked behind a colonial church in the small town. The museum, which is in one of the peninsula's 20 or so convents that date from the 16th century, is run by the archdiocese of Yucatán. The items on display in its six rooms include sculptures, vestments, paintings, and other objects that shine light on the nearly 500-year-old presence of the Catholic Church in the Yucatán. ⊠ *Calle 20 14, Mérida* ☎ *999/912–4049* ⊕ *museo-de-arte-sacro.negocio.site* ☜ *MX\$50* ☉ *Closed Mon.*

Museo Fernando García Ponce—MACAY

ART MUSEUM | Located next to the cathedral, the building that houses this museum was originally designed as an art school and used until 1915 as a seminary. It now showcases the works of contemporary Yucatecan artists such as Gabriel Ramírez Aznar and Fernando García Ponce, and hosts a variety of temporary exhibits. It's free to visit; just in via sign the guestbook. ⊠ *Plaza Grande, Pasaje de la Revolución 1907, between Calles 58 and 60, Centro* ☎ *999/928–3236* ⊕ *www.macay.org* ☜ *Free* ☉ *Closed Sun.*

Palacio Cantón

HISTORY MUSEUM | FAMILY | The most compelling of the mansions on Paseo de Montejo, this stately palacio was built as the residence for General Francisco Cantón between 1909 and 1911. Designed by Enrique Deserti, who also did the blueprints for the Teatro Peón Contreras, the building has a grandiose air that seems more characteristic of a mausoleum than a home: there's marble everywhere, as well as Doric and Ionic columns and other Italianate Beaux-Arts flourishes. It now houses the Museo Regional de Antropología de Yucatán which focuses mostly on Maya history, art, and culture and sometimes other aspects of Yucatecan life. The exhibitions are generally excellent although signage is often only in Spanish, or Spanish and Mayan, and not translated into English. ⊠ *Paseo de Montejo 485, at Calle 43, Paseo Montejo* ☎ *999/923–0557* ⊕ *www.inah.gob.mx* ☜ *MX\$60* ☉ *Closed Mon.*

Palacio de la Música

OTHER MUSEUM | FAMILY | This museum in the heart of the historic center, designed in a collaboration between four leading architecture firms, made a dramatic statement in Mérida's downtown when in opened in 2019, garnering generally positive reviews. The museum covers the history of Mexican music and its diverse periods of influence—pre-Hispanic, colonial, and contemporary. Dozens of listening stations offer chances to listen to tracks that encompass Mexican music in all its diversity, from traditional rancheras to classical compositions to current pop and rock stars, and more. The museum hosts concerts focused on both contemporary and classical music. ⊠ *Calle 59 497, Centro* ☎ *999/923–0641* ⊕ *palaciomusica.yucatan.gob.mx* ☜ *150 pesos* ☉ *Closed Mon.*

Palacio del Gobierno

GOVERNMENT BUILDING | Visit the seat of state government on the north side of Plaza Grande. You can see Fernando

Castro Pacheco's murals of the bloody history of the conquest of the peninsula, painted in bold colors and influenced by the Mexican muralists José Clemente Orozco and David Alfaro Siqueiros. On the main balcony (visible from outside on the plaza) stands a reproduction of the Bell of Dolores Hidalgo, on which Mexican independence rang out on the night of September 15, 1810, in the town of Dolores Hidalgo in Guanajuato. On the anniversary of the event, the governor rings the bell to commemorate the occasion. There's a branch of the state tourist office on the ground floor. ⊠ *Calle 61, between Calles 60 and 62, Centro* ☎ *999/930–3101* ⊕ *www.yucatan.gob. mx* ⊠ *Free.*

Palacio Municipal

GOVERNMENT BUILDING | The west side of the main square is occupied by Mérida's city hall, or *ayuntamiento*, a handsome building trimmed with white arcades, balustrades, and the national coat of arms. Originally erected on the ruins of the last surviving Maya structure, it was rebuilt in 1735 and then completely reconstructed along colonial lines in 1928. It remains the headquarters of the local government. On the ground floor, you'll find the Oficina de Turismo de Mérida (municipal tourist office). ⊠ *Calle 62, between Calles 61 and 63, Centro* ☎ *999/928–2020* ⊕ *www.merida.gob.mx* ⊠ *Free.*

Parque Hidalgo (*Plaza Cepeda Peraza*)

CITY PARK | FAMILY | A half block north of the main plaza is this small, cozy park, officially known as Plaza Cepeda Peraza. Historic mansions, now reincarnated as hotels and sidewalk cafés (including a Starbucks), line its southern and eastern sides, and at night the area comes alive with marimba bands and street vendors. On Sunday the streets are closed to vehicular traffic, and there's free live music performed throughout the day. ⊠ *Calle 60, between Calles 59 and 61, Centro.*

Parque Santa Lucía

CITY PARK | FAMILY | This park at Calles 60 and 55 is lined with popular, if a bit touristy, restaurants and draws crowds with its Thursday-night music and dance performances (shows start at 9, but come early if you want to sit close to the performers). On Sunday, couples also come to dance to a live band, and enjoy food from carts set up in the plaza and at its restaurants with outdoor seating. The small church opposite the park dates to 1575 and was built as a place of worship for the Maya, who weren't allowed to worship at just any Mérida temple. ⊠ *Calles 60 and 55, Centro.*

Parque Zoológico El Centenario

ZOO | FAMILY | Mérida's top children's attraction is the large Parque Zoológico El Centenario, which features pleasant wooded paths, playgrounds, inexpensive amusement-park rides, an inline skating rink, a small lake you can row on, and a little train that circles the property. It also includes cages that house more than 300 native animals as well as exotic ones like lions and tigers (a modern zoo this is not, and you might not approve of those cages). At the exit, you'll find snack bars and vendors; there are on-site picnic areas, too. The French Renaissance–style arch commemorates the 100th anniversary (in 1910) of Mexican independence. ⊠ *Av. Itzáes, between Calles 59 and 65 (entrances on Calles 59 and 65), Centro* ☎ *999/928–5815* ⊕ *www.merida.gob.mx/ centenario* ⊠ *Entry free, activities extra* ⊘ *Closed Mon. and Tues.*

Paseo de Montejo

PROMENADE | FAMILY | North of downtown, this 10-block-long street was *the* place to reside in the late 19th century, when wealthy hacienda owners sought to outdo each other with the opulence of their elegant city mansions. They typically opted for the decorative styles popular in New Orleans, Cuba, and Paris (imported Carrara marble, European antiques) rather than any style from Mexico. The broad boulevard, lined with breadfruit, tamarind, and laurel trees, has lost much of its former panache—many mansions are now used as office buildings, though three are open to the public (the Palacio Cantón, which houses a museum focused on Maya culture, and Casa Gemela and Quinta Montes Molina, both of which have museums). Though its gilded age peak has passed, the street is still a lovely place to explore on foot or in a horse-drawn carriage. You can also enjoy a drink or meal at one of roughly a dozen restaurants with outdoor seating. ⊠ *Mérida.*

Plaza Grande

PLAZA/SQUARE | FAMILY | Mérida's main square is a Wi-Fi hot spot, but don't be so glued to your smartphone that you fail to take in the parade of activity in one of Mexico's loveliest town centers. Locals refer to it as the Plaza Grande or Plaza de la Independencia, and you'll also hear it called "the *zócalo*" (primarily by foreigners). Whichever name you prefer, it's a good place to start a city tour, watch dance performances, listen to music, or chill in the shade of a laurel tree. You'll find a few vendors here, but they're all low-key. Plaza Grande was laid out in 1542 on the ruins of T'Hó, the Maya city demolished to make way for Mérida, and it's still the focal point around which the most important public buildings cluster. *Confidenciales* (S-shape benches) invite intimate tête-à-têtes, and lampposts keep the park beautifully illuminated at night. ⊠ *Bordered by Calles 60 and 62, 61 and 63, Centro.*

Teatro Peón Contreras

PERFORMANCE VENUE | FAMILY | This 1908 Italianate theater was built along the same lines as grand turn-of-the-20th-century European theaters and opera houses. It is also representative of the final years of the gilded age known in Mexico as the Porfiriato, the 35-year-long dictatorship of Porfirio Diaz (the Mexican Revolution began in 1910). Its

---

Market Snacks 🍴

Parque Santa Ana. The simple market in Parque Santa Ana, just to the west of Paseo Montejo and north of Calle 47, is a popular breakfast spot where you'll find locals happily starting their day with regional dishes and fresh juices at plastic tables. The tamales are good and the *tortas de cochinita*, pork sandwiches flavored with a few drops of sour-orange chile sauce, are heavenly. Most vendors here close around 1:30 in the afternoon, but some reopen to sell snacks between 7 pm until late in the evening. ⊠ *Calle 60, between Calles 45 and 47, Centro.*

---

marble staircase, dome, and frescoes were restored in the early 1980s. It is the home of the excellent Yucatán Symphony Orchestra and tickets to performances are often less than $10 US. In addition to being a performing arts venue, it houses a branch of the tourist information office and a popular café-bar that spills out onto the street facing Parque de la Madre. ⊠ *Calle 60 between Calles 57 and 59, Centro* ☎ *999/924–3954* ⊕ *www.culturayucatan.com.*

🍴 Restaurants

With more than 250 restaurants (not to mention the markets and street-food stands), Mérida has plenty of dining options to choose from. Regional cuisine is the staple, but the flavors and preparations don't stop there. You can find places serving burgers and sandwiches if you're craving something familiar.

★ Amaro

$$ | MEXICAN | The romantic patio of this historic home glows with candlelight in the evening; during the day things look a lot more casual. The emphasis here is on vegetarian dishes like avocado pizza and chaya soup (made from a green plant similar to spinach), and healthful juices. (Meat, fish, and shellfish are served here in moderation.) **Known for:** upscale Yucatecan cuisine; romantic atmosphere; good selection of vegetarian offerings. [$] *Average main: MP220* ✉ *Calle 59 No. 507, between Calles 60 and 62, Centro* ☎ *999/928–2451* 🌐 *www.restauranteamaro.com.*

Apoala

$$ | **MEXICAN** | Apoala is one of the best choices for Mexican food on Parque Santa Lucia, Mérida's lively, restaurant-lined plaza. The menu includes both Oaxacan and Yucatecan dishes—moles and beef dishes from the former, ceviches and cochinita pibil from the latter. **Known for:** elevated approach to Mexican cuisine; outdoor seating; Oaxacan and Yucatecan dishes. [$] *Average main: MP200* ✉ *Calle 60 471, Centro* ✣ *On Parque Santa Lucia* ☎ *999/923–1979* 🌐 *www.apoala.mx.*

Casa Chica

$ | **MEXICAN** | The food is not the primary draw at this restaurant, though it does a good enough rendition of basic pastas, salads, and burgers as well as some Mexican bar-food favorites. Instead, its popularity is due to delicious cocktails, aguas frescas, and a lively atmosphere. **Known for:** good value; outdoor seating on Paseo de Montejo; lively atmosphere. [$] *Average main: MP120* ✉ *Paseo Montejo, 498B, Centro* 🌐 *www.facebook.com/casachicabar.*

★ Cuna

$$$ | **MEXICAN FUSION** | This contemporary restaurant at the Wayam Mundo Imperial hotel in the García Ginerés neighborhood has floor-to-ceiling windows overlooking a lush, plant-filled terrace as well as flavorful Italian and Latin American dishes like ceviches, arroz con pollo, and pastas. Chef Maycoll Calderón's allows the fresh ingredients to take center stage, avoiding anything too fussy. **Known for:** large terrace; stylish decor; innovative dishes. [$] *Average main: MP200* ✉ *Avenida Colón, 508, Col. García Ginerés* 🌐 *www.cuna.mx.*

Dante's

$ | **CAFÉ** | **FAMILY** | Couples, groups of students, and lots of families crowd this bustling coffeehouse at the Centro Cultural Dante, just above Mérida's largest bookshop. The house specialty is crepes: there are 10 varieties with either sweet or savory fillings. **Known for:** quick bites; U.S.-style bookstore café; specialty coffees. [$] *Average main: MP125* ✉ *Calle 17 No. 138B, at Prolongación Paseo de Montejo, Paseo Montejo* ☎ *999/927–7676* 🌐 *www.libreriadante.com.mx.*

★ Hacienda Teya

$$ | **MEXICAN** | A henequen ranch in the 17th century, this beautiful hacienda just outside Mérida serves some of the best regional food around. Start with sopa de lima, then move on to standout mains like *poc chuc* or cochinita pibil (both served with homemade tortillas). **Known for:** elegant atmosphere; country setting with lovely gardens; largest wine selection in town. [$] *Average main: MP210* ✉ *Carretera 180, 12½ km (8 miles) east of Mérida, Kanasín* ☎ *999/988–0800* 🌐 *www.haciendateya.com* 🕓 *Closed Dec. 25–Jan. 1. No dinner.*

K'u'uk

$$$ | **MEXICAN** | K'u'uk, meaning "sprout" in Mayan, offers Mérida's most unique dining experience. Located in a historic mansion facing the Monumento a la Patria on Paseo de Montejo, the restaurant's cutting-edge menu features eight courses, each prepared using molecular gastronomy and fresh ingredients, most of them grown on-site. **Known for:** artistic desserts; pibil-style (Mayan oven) cooking; leisurely—some say "slow"—dining experience. [$] *Average main: MP360* ✉ *Av Rómulo Rozo 488, San Ramon Norte* ☎ *999/944–3377* 🌐 *www.kuukrestaurant.com* 🕓 *Closed Mon. No dinner Sun.*

La Negrita

$ | MEXICAN | This cantina at the corner of Calles 62 and 49 is popular with locals, expats, and visitors to Mérida with its large courtyard as well as large margaritas and other cocktails. You'll be offered free bar snacks as long as you keep ordering drinks, though it is worth ordering some of the delicious (if basically prepared) ceviches, enchiladas, and tacos, too. **Known for:** oversized cocktails; live music; Mexican bar snacks. $ *Average main: MP120* ⊠ *Calle 62 415, at Calle 49, Centro* ☎ *999/121–0411* ⊕ *www.facebook.com/LaNegritaMerida.*

La Poderosa

$ | MEXICAN | Residents of Mérida have strong opinions on who makes the best salbutes and panuchos, two signature Yucatecan dishes, and La Poderosa is at the top of many lists. All the seats at this restaurant in the southern part of Centro—near San Sebastian's square and market—are outdoors, and it's an especially lovely spot on warm evenings. **Known for:** cheap eats; outdoor seating; excellent panuchos and salbutes. $ *Average main: MP100* ⊠ *Calle 70 568D, Centro* ▭ *No credit cards.*

La Tradición

$$ | MEXICAN | FAMILY | This family restaurant is one of the most formal places that serves regional cuisine, but you'll still fit right in wearing jeans. Dishes are prepared with a charcoal stove, portions are huge, and just about everything you'll try is tasty—including the *queso relleno* (hollowed-out cheese, stuffed with a meat-vegetable mixture) and cochinita pibil—but you might not want to pass up the cream of chaya soup, since you won't find it in many other restaurants. **Known for:** huge portions at reasonable prices; queso relleno; cream of chaya soup. $ *Average main: MP220* ⊠ *Calle 60 No. 293, at Calle 25, Col. Alcalá Martin* ☎ *999/925–2526* ⊕ *www.latradicionmerida.com* ⊗ *No dinner Sun.–Wed.*

La Tratto

$$$ | ITALIAN | The open design of this popular family-owned Italian eatery makes it a nice place to enjoy the cool evening weather. The food here is filling and the menu is made up of salads, thin-crust pizzas, and pasta. **Known for:** good pizza selection; huge salads; great wine list. $ *Average main: MP350* ⊠ *Prolongación Paseo de Montejo 479C, Paseo Montejo* ☎ *999/927–0434* ⊕ *www.latrattomerida.com.*

Los Almendros

$$ | MEXICAN | This vintage Yucatecan restaurant with high colonial ceilings and an elegant atmosphere is a longtime local favorite. The *combinado yucateco* (Yucatecan combination plate) is a great way to try different dishes: cochinita pibil, *longaniza asada* (grilled pork sausages), *escabeche de Valladolid* (turkey with chiles, onions, and seasonings in an acidic sauce), and poc chuc (slices of pork in a sour-orange sauce). **Known for:** cheese soup; combination platters; reasonable prices. $ *Average main: MP245* ⊠ *Calle 50A No. 493, between Calles 57 and 59, facing Parque La Mejorada, Centro* ☎ *999/928–5459* ⊕ *www.restaurantelosalmendros.com.mx.*

Restaurante Bologna

$$ | ITALIAN | FAMILY | You can dine alfresco or inside at this beautifully restored old mansion in Itzimná. Most menu items are ordered à la carte; among the favorites are the shrimp pizza and pizza diabola, topped with salami, tomato, and chiles. **Known for:** beef fillet with mushrooms; Sunday brunch; attentive service. $ *Average main: MP220* ⊠ *Calle 21 No. 117A, between Calles 24 and 24A, Col. Itzimná* ☎ *999/926–2505* ⊕ *restaurante-bologna.negocio.site* ⊗ *Closed Mon.*

Rosas & Xocolate Restaurant

$$$ | ECLECTIC | This elegant restaurant at the hotel of the same name is beautifully designed in hues of pink and brown, with long-stem roses on every table.

Chef David Segovia's menu is an haute interpretation of Mexican and Yucatecan cuisines with sauces incorporating local chiles, tamarind, and hibiscus (or jamaica) flowers. **Known for:** six-course tasting menu; rib eye with cardamom-seasoned eggplant; stylish hotel setting. $ *Average main: MP500* ⊠ *Paseo de Montejo No. 480, at Calle 41, Centro* ☎ *999/924–2992* ⊕ *www.rosasandxocolate.com.*

★ Salón Gallos
$$ | MODERN MEXICAN | This innovative cultural complex, bar, and restaurant has brought energy to a part of Mérida that wasn't previously on the map for most visitors and residents. The factory that once stood here now houses a restaurant serving creatively updated Yucatecan dishes, several bars, a gallery, an arthouse cinema, and a pop-up space which typically features the work of a local artisan or collective. **Known for:** movie theater; Innovative Yucatecan and Middle Eastern dishes; art gallery. $ *Average main: MP300* ⊠ *Calle 63 459B, Centro* ☎ *999/189–6564* ⊕ *salongallos.mx.*

Trotter's Grill House
$$$ | STEAKHOUSE | FAMILY | This beautifully designed restaurant is one of Mérida's most upscale eateries, serving house favorites like the tuna steak with black pepper crust or the Angus beef served with a side of rosemary potatoes. A glass wall separates indoor and outdoor dining rooms; although less formal, the outdoor patio is surrounded by lush vegetation, helping you forget that you are on a bustling avenue. **Known for:** foie gras; steaks; contemporary decor. $ *Average main: MP400* ⊠ *Circuito Colonias, between Calles 34 and 36, Paseo Montejo* ☎ *999/927–2320* ⊕ *trottersrestaurants. com* ◷ *No dinner Sun.*

Wayan'e
$ | MEXICAN | This oasis of carnivorous delights serves tortas—Mexico's answer to the sandwich—and tacos at four locations in Mérida. In addition to ham and cheese tortas, you can get pork loin in smoky chipotle-chile sauce, chorizo sausage, turkey strips sautéed with onions and peppers, and several other delicious combos guaranteed to go straight to your arteries. **Known for:** torta-style sandwiches; fun, informal vibe; astounding taco selection. $ *Average main: MP180* ⊠ *Calle 59 408, at Calle 4, Col. Itzimná* ☎ *999/938–0676* ◷ *No dinner. Closed Sun.*

☕ Coffee and Quick Bites

El Colón Sorbetes y Dulces Finos
$ | ICE CREAM | FAMILY | The homemade ice cream and sorbet at El Colón have been keeping locals cool since 1907. Served in a pyramid-shape scoop, the tropical fruit flavors (like *chico zapote*, a brown fruit native to Mexico that tastes a little like cinnamon and comes from a tree used in chewing-gum production) are particularly refreshing. **Known for:** local institution; tropical fruit flavors; sidewalk seating. $ *Average main: MP80* ⊠ *Calle 62 No. 500, at Calle 59 and Calle 61, Centro.*

Latte Quattro Sette
$ | CAFÉ | This bright and sunny café is on Calle 47, which has emerged as a bit of a restaurant row for Mérida (other popular favorites on the street include Catrín, Micaela Mar y Lena, and Oliva Enoteca). Latte Quattro Sette serves only breakfast and lunch, but it is an appealing spot for a cappuccino, latte, or tea, paired with an avocado toast, yogurt and fruit, or a pastry. **Known for:** variety of coffees and teas; cheerful atmosphere; delicious pastries. $ *Average main: MP120* ⊠ *Calle 47 465, between 54 and 56, Centro* ☎ *999/924–8895* ◷ *Closed Sun.*

Pan & Koffee
$ | BAKERY | This bakery just a few blocks north of Parque Santa Ana is a perfect choice when you want to start your day with a light breakfast of a pastry and a coffee rather than a plate of huevos

rancheros. The shop has a small garden and plenty of seating if you want to linger for awhile at your laptop. **Known for:** coffee drinks; garden; delicious pastries, savory and sweet. $ *Average main: MP60* ✉ *Calle 43 No. 485, Centro* ⊕ *panandkoffee.com.*

Pola

$ | **DESSERTS** | **FAMILY** | This little gelato shop in the heart of the historic center has significantly raised the caliber of Mérida's ice-cream offerings. The flavors on any given day vary, but you can typically expect somewhere between five and ten sorbets and the same number of gelato flavors. **Known for:** cheerful store; locally inspired flavors; excellent gelato and sorbets. $ *Average main: MP60* ✉ *Calle 55 467D, Centro* ☎ *999/923–1107* ⊕ *www.polagelato.com* ▤ *No credit cards.*

 # Hotels

Mérida has a wide range of lodgings, from old haciendas and converted colonial homes to big corporate hotels and little B&Bs. Generally, you'll find smaller options in the downtown area, within walking distance of most sights; nights are inevitably a little louder here, especially if your room faces the street. Note that small lodgings usually sport small, easy-to-miss signs; you may need to spin around the block a time or two in your taxi or rental vehicle to find your hotel. A few larger chain hotels around the Paseo de Montejo offer quiet rooms, and are still near major streets, and only a short ride from downtown.

★ Casa Azul

$$$ | **B&B/INN** | Declared a historical monument and a Yucatán Heritage site, the French-style "Blue House" is notable for its extraordinary antiques, luxurious fabrics, rose-filled bouquets, and superior service. **Pros:** filtered tap water; modern comforts in colonial home; flawless

service. **Cons:** no children under 12; small pool; some street noise. $ *Rooms from: $300* ✉ *Calle 60 No. 343, between Calles 35 and 37, Centro* ☎ *999/925–5016* ⊕ *www.casaazulhotel.com* ▧ *8 rooms* ⦿ *Free Breakfast.*

Casa del Balam

$ | **HOTEL** | This pleasant hotel has an excellent location two blocks from the zócalo. **Pros:** spacious rooms; great restaurant service; easy walk to many sights. **Cons:** rooms are due for a refresh; slow elevator; street noise can be a problem. $ *Rooms from: $79* ✉ *Calle 60 No. 488, at Calle 57, Centro* ☎ *999/924–8844, 800/624–8451* ⊕ *www.casadelbalam. com* ▧ *43 rooms* ⦿ *Free Breakfast.*

★ Casa Lecanda

$$$ | **B&B/INN** | From the moment you step off the busy streets into Casa Lecanda's cool lobby, you're wrapped in European grandeur; wrought-iron chandeliers and antique furniture pay tribute to a bygone era in Mérida's most luxurious boutique hotel, while the photographs of the modern-day city bring you back to the present. **Pros:** local flavor; excellent service; elegant atmosphere. **Cons:** street can be busy at night; no children under 12; pool is more of a showpiece than a place to swim. $ *Rooms from: $230* ✉ *Calle 47 No. 471, between Calles 54 and 56, Centro* ☎ *999/928–0112* ⊕ *www.casalecanda. com* ▧ *7 rooms* ⦿ *Free Breakfast.*

★ Casa Puuc

$$ | **HOTEL** | Well-known Mexican artist and boutique owner Claudia Fernández helped convert this 1914 house in García Ginerés into a six-room inn with a flawless sense of style. **Pros:** a quiet retreat; exquisite design; intimate atmosphere. **Cons:** lacks the facilities of a larger property; outside the historic center; small pool. $ *Rooms from: $100* ✉ *Calle 22 No. 199B, Col. García Ginerés* ☎ *55/9195–5646* ⊕ *casapuuc.com* ▧ *6 rooms* ⦿ *Free Breakfast.*

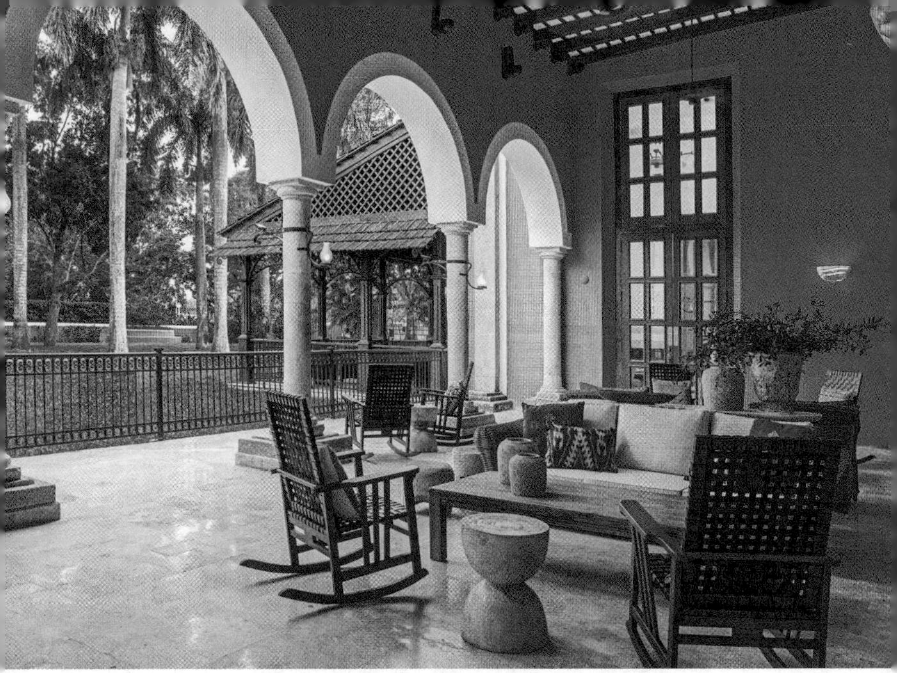

Hacienda Xcanatún by Angsana opens up to three acres of manicured gardens.

Casa San Ángel

$$ | **HOTEL** | The comfortable lobby of this small hotel has an open-air central courtyard with a fountain surrounded by plants. **Pros:** unique setting; fantastic service; comfortable rooms with spacious bathrooms. **Cons:** those with allergies might have issues with two resident cats; no children under 15; small pool. [$] *Rooms from: $184* ✉ *Paseo de Montejo 1, at Calle 49, Centro* ☎ *999/928–0800* 🌐 *www.hotelcasasanangel.com* 🛏 *12 rooms* 🍴 *No Meals.*

★ Chablé Yucatán

$$$$ | **RESORT** | Located about 40 minutes by car to the south of Mérida in the town of Chocholá, Chablé Yucatán is far and away the most expensive resort in the state, but the meticulously restored hacienda with 740 acres of land and 40 freestanding villas, each with their own private pool, justifies the price. **Pros:** all villas come with private pools, elegant design; world-class spa and dining. **Cons:** remote location, 40 miles from central Mérida; very expensive, especially compared to other Yucatán hotels; atmosphere is too quiet for some. [$] *Rooms from: $1,000* ✉ *Tablaje 642, Mérida* ☎ *55/4161–4262* 🌐 *chablehotels.com/yucatan* 🛏 *40 suites* 🍴 *Free Breakfast.*

Doralba Inn Mérida

$ | **HOTEL** | If you can look beyond the plastic flowers, cement bed frames, and vending machines at reception, this cheerful hotel can be quite a bargain—especially the rooms in the newer wing that have powerful air-conditioning, comfy beds, and amenities like large TVs and balconies. **Pros:** nice pool; short walk to Plaza Grande; great prices if you're not too fussy. **Cons:** mediocre breakfast; no bathroom amenities; loud air-conditioning. [$] *Rooms from: $70* ✉ *Calle 63 No. 464, between Calles 52 and 54, Centro* ☎ *999/928–5650* 🌐 *www.doloresalba.com* 🛏 *100 rooms* 🍴 *Free Breakfast.*

Fiesta Americana Mérida

$$ | **HOTEL** | **FAMILY** | This popular choice, a branch of a dependable Mexican chain, attempts to evoke the grandeur of the mansions on Paseo de Montejo with

Hotel Julamis features hand-painted murals that complement the original tile floors.

colonial accents, plush armchairs, and gleaming marble. **Pros:** tasty breakfast buffet; shopping downstairs; comfortable beds. **Cons:** some amenities cost extra; lacks intimacy of other properties; a taxi ride from downtown. $ *Rooms from: $135* ✉ *Paseo de Montejo 451, at Av. Colón, Paseo Montejo* ☎ *999/942–1111, 877/927–7666* ⇨ *350 rooms* ○ *Free Breakfast.*

Gran Hotel

$ | **HOTEL** | Located on leafy Parque Hidalgo, this legendary 1901 hotel has high ceilings, wrought-iron balcony and stair rails, and ornately patterned tile floors. **Pros:** in the middle of downtown shops and services; beautiful antique decorations; great rates. **Cons:** no elevator makes upstairs rooms a hike; downtown noise; parking is sometimes unavailable (check ahead if you are driving). $ *Rooms from: $72* ✉ *Calle 60 No. 496, at Parque Hidalgo, Centro* ☎ *999/924–7622* ⊕ *www.granhoteldemerida.com* ⇨ *28 rooms* ○ *No Meals.*

Hacienda San José

$$$$ | **HOTEL** | One of five haciendas in Marriott's Luxury Collection, this former cattle ranch has fully restored guest rooms on landscaped grounds. **Pros:** authentic hacienda experience; rooms have jungle Jacuzzis; a world-class spa. **Cons:** 45 minutes from Mérida; difficult to find; too remote for some. $ *Rooms from: $333* ✉ *Carretera Tixkobob-Tekanto, Km 30, Tixkokob* ☎ *999/924–1333* ⊕ *www.marriott.com* ⇨ *15 rooms* ○ *No Meals.*

★ Hacienda Xcanatún by Angsana

$$$ | **HOTEL** | Although this restored 18th-century henequen hacienda is only 13 km (8 miles) from Mérida, it feels a world away. **Pros:** stellar service; outstanding restaurant; expansive gardens. **Cons:** not suitable for children; pricey; a drive from the city. $ *Rooms from: $285* ✉ *Carretera 261, Km 12, 13 km (8 miles) north of Mérida, Mérida* ☎ *999/930–2140, 888/883–3633 in the U.S.* ⊕ *www.xcanatun.com* ⇨ *18 rooms* ○ *No Meals.*

Hotel del Peregrino

$ | **B&B/INN** | This restored colonial home with high ceilings and brightly painted walls mixes in modern furnishings to create a comfortable, inexpensive option near the center of Mérida. **Pros:** inexpensive; gracious staff can arrange tours and Spanish tutoring; easy walk to downtown. **Cons:** mediocre breakfast; kitchen and lounge areas can get noisy; spacious but basic rooms. [$] *Rooms from: $40* ✉ *Calle 51 No. 488, between Calles 54 and 56, Centro* ☎ *999/924–3007* 🌐 *www.hoteldelperegrino.com* 🛏 *13 rooms* 🍴 *Free Breakfast.*

Hotel Hacienda Mérida

$$ | **HOTEL** | This urban oasis features a dramatic pool surrounded by pillared archways draped with white curtains. **Pros:** walking distance to city center; unlike some luxury properties, they are very child-friendly; great service. **Cons:** sometimes slow Internet; no restaurant; building showing a bit of wear. [$] *Rooms from: $159* ✉ *Calle 62 No. 439, between Calles 51 and 53, Centro* ☎ *999/924–4363* 🌐 *www.hotelhaciendamerida.com* 🛏 *14 rooms* 🍴 *No Meals.*

★ **Hotel Julamis**

$ | **B&B/INN** | An artist-owned hotel in a 200-year-old building, Hotel Julamis is a Mérida leader when it comes to value and service. **Pros:** remarkable rates; great views from rooftop bar; roughly halfway between Paseo de Montejo and Plaza Grande. **Cons:** no children under 12; note the fine print of their cancellation policy before you book; Wi-Fi can be spotty in some rooms. [$] *Rooms from: $72* ✉ *Calle 53 No. 475B, at Calle 54, Centro* ☎ *999/924–1818* 🌐 *www.hoteljulamis.com* 🛏 *9 rooms* 🍴 *Free Breakfast.*

Hotel Marionetas

$ | **B&B/INN** | Attentive proprietors Daniel and Sofija Bosco have created this lovely B&B on a quiet street seven blocks from the main plaza. **Pros:** intimate feel; personal attention from proprietors and staff; calming courtyard and pool area. **Cons:** restaurant only serves breakfast; no children under 12; off-site parking. [$] *Rooms from: $94* ✉ *Calle 49 No. 516, between Calles 62 and 64, Centro* ☎ *999/928–3377* 🌐 *www.hotelmarionetas.com* 🛏 *8 rooms* 🍴 *Free Breakfast.*

Hotel Medio Mundo

$ | **B&B/INN** | Painted in primary colors, this restored house in a residential part of downtown has Mediterranean accents, thick original walls, and well-preserved tile floors. **Pros:** great location; reasonable rates; friendly staff. **Cons:** no children under eight; off-site parking; some steep stairs. [$] *Rooms from: $30* ✉ *Calle 55 533, between Calles 64 and 66, Centro* ☎ *999/924–5472* 🌐 *www.hotelmediomundo.com* 🛏 *10 rooms* 🍴 *Free Breakfast.*

Hyatt Regency Mérida

$$ | **HOTEL** | The city's first deluxe hotel is still among its most elegant. **Pros:** popular bistro; nice fitness center; reasonable prices. **Cons:** breakfast menu could include more light and healthy options; extra charge for Internet and in-room coffee; far from downtown. [$] *Rooms from: $110* ✉ *Av. Colón s/n, at Calle 60, Paseo Montejo* ☎ *999/942–1234, 800/633–7313 in the U.S.* 🌐 *merida.regency.hyatt.com* 🛏 *285 rooms* 🍴 *No Meals.*

La Misión de Fray Diego

$$ | **HOTEL** | The elegant accommodations in this former convent still retain their colonial charm, and tasteful touches (like crucifixes and statues) ensure they look divine. **Pros:** charming property; courteous staff; great restaurant. **Cons:** stairwell not well lit at night; a bit of a climb to third-floor rooms; no children under 12. [$] *Rooms from: $128* ✉ *Calle 61 No. 524, between Calles 64 and 66, Centro* ☎ *999/924–1111, 866/639–2933* 🌐 *www.lamisiondefraydiego.com* 🛏 *26 rooms* 🍴 *Free Breakfast.*

Maya Yucatán

$ | **HOTEL** | Artwork echoing the style of Mexican muralists graces the public areas of the Maya Yucatán hotel, and a combination of brightly colored textiles and dark hardwood furniture lend the guest rooms a tropical vibe. **Pros:** cool art; terrific rates; business amenities. **Cons:** business-oriented; breakfast buffet isn't included; rooms are ready to be spruced up. [$] *Rooms from: $70* ✉ *Calle 58 No. 483, between Calles 55 and 57, Centro* ☎ *999/923–7070* 🌐 *www.hotelmayayucatan.com.mx* 🛏 *72 rooms* 🍴 *No Meals.*

Piedra de Agua

$ | **HOTEL** | This converted 1842 mansion has been renovated for maximum comfort without compromising its historical charm. **Pros:** centrally located; wonderful old-world decor; decent rates. **Cons:** off-site parking; some street noise; small bathrooms. [$] *Rooms from: $67* ✉ *Calle 60 No. 498, between Calles 59 and 61, Centro* ☎ *999/924–2300* 🌐 *www.facebook.com/HotelPiedradeAgua* 🛏 *20 rooms* 🍴 *No Meals.*

Rosas & Xocolate

$$$ | **B&B/INN** | Designed with romance in mind, this boutique hotel has a roses-and-chocolate theme that carries from the pink exterior to the chocolate soaps in the bathrooms and the Belgian truffles in the gift shop. **Pros:** great breakfasts; beautiful architecture; excellent showers and mattresses. **Cons:** not suitable for children; no elevator; small pool in a very public area. [$] *Rooms from: $245* ✉ *Paseo Montejo 480, at Calle 41, Centro* ☎ *999/924–2992* 🌐 *www.rosasandxocolate.com* 🛏 *17 rooms* 🍴 *Free Breakfast.*

★ **The Villa Tievoli**

$ | **B&B/INN** | The proprietors of this intimate B&B clearly have an eye for detail: for proof, consider the breakfast china—they keep 30 different patterns so that you won't have to see the same plates twice during your stay. **Pros:** creative breakfasts; great rates; gracious, knowledgeable owners. **Cons:** tiny sign makes it difficult to find; step down from bathroom to room; no parking. [$] *Rooms from: $84* ✉ *Calle 54 No. 455, between Calles 51 and 53, Centro* ☎ *1999/242–7474 cell, 407/369–8602 in the U.S.* 🌐 *www.thevillatievoli.com* 🛏 *3 rooms* 🍴 *Free Breakfast.*

Wayam Mundo Imperial

$$$ | **HOTEL** | This 52-suite hotel in García Ginerés blurs the line between indoors and outdoors; after checking into a mid-20th-century house, you'll pass through lush gardens with seating areas, fountains, and contemporary sculptures on the way to your room. **Pros:** quiet neighborhood; excellent restaurant; stylish design. **Cons:** rooftop pool area is small; outside the historic center; on the pricier side. [$] *Rooms from: $200* ✉ *Avenida Colon 508, Col. García Ginerés* ☎ *800/969–2926* 🌐 *www.mundoimperial.com/wayam* 🛏 *52 suites* 🍴 *No Meals.*

Nightlife

Mérida comes into its own once the sun begins to set and the heat of the afternoon gives way to the cool of the evening. The city has an active and diverse cultural life, which includes free government-sponsored music and dance performances many evenings, as well as sidewalk art shows in local parks. On Thursday at 9 pm Meridanos enjoy an evening of outdoor entertainment at the **Serenata Yucateca**, held in **Parque Santa Lucía** (Calles 60 and 55); you'll see trios, the local orchestra, and soloists performing compositions by Yucatecan composers. On Saturday evenings after 7 pm the **Noche Mexicana** (corner of Paseo de Montejo and Calle 47) hosts different musical and cultural events. More free music, dance, comedy, and regional handicrafts can be found at the **Corazón de Mérida,** on Calle 60 between the main plaza and Calle 55. From 8 pm to 1 am, multiple bandstands throughout this area (which is closed to traffic) entertain locals and visitors with an ever-changing playbill, from grunge to classical.

On Sunday, six blocks around Plaza Grande are closed off to traffic, and you can see performances—often mariachi and marimba bands or folkloric dancers—at Plaza Santa Lucía, Parque Hidalgo, and the main plaza. For a schedule of current performances, consult the tourist offices, the local newspapers, or the posters at the Teatro Peón Contreras and Centro Cultural de Mérida Olimpo.

The city center and Paseo de Montejo area are largely safe at night with throngs of people out enjoying themselves. (Standard precautions about watching your things apply, of course.) Restaurants and nightspots are happy to call you a taxi or have a guard hail one for you when you're ready to call it a night.

BARS AND DANCE CLUBS

Mérida has always been a great city to walk in by day and dance in by night. Meridanos love music, and they love to dance, but since they also have to work, many clubs are open only on weekend nights, or Thursday through Sunday.

Be aware that it's becoming common-place for discos and restaurants with live music and "comedy" acts (geared toward young people) to invite custom-ers onstage for some rather shocking "audience participation" acts. Since these are otherwise fine establishments, we can only suggest that you let your sense of outrage be your guide. Locals don't seem to mind.

Café Peón Contreras

LIVE MUSIC | The café-bar at Mérida's landmark 1908 theater is one of the most happening nightspots in town. Tables spill onto the street, where locals gather to hear balladeers singing romantic and politically inspired songs. The drinks are expensive and the food is nothing

special, so only go if you want culture, live music, and an opportunity to splurge. ✉ *Teatro Peón Contreras, Calle 60, between Calles 57 and 59, facing Parque de la Madre, Centro* ☎ *999/924–7003.*

Casa Dominga

LIVE MUSIC | Part food court (15 stands with a variety of food), part bar, part live-music venue in a restored 1906 building, Casa Dominga offers live music many nights, usually Mexican or Cuban. ✉ *Calle 47, between Calles 52 and 54, Mérida* ☎ *999/271–0260.*

Dzalbay Cantina

LIVE MUSIC | One of Mérida's historic traditional cantinas, Dzalbay is experienc-ing a second life in the hands of a group of expat musician-owners. The bar has a crowded calendar of performances by blues and jazz acts, both local musicians and ones passing through Mérida. A large outdoor terrace and menus of signature cocktails, microbrews, and bar snacks also help make Dzalbay a local favorite. If a low-key, welcoming cantina is what you are searching for, it may become your favorite too. ✉ *Calle 64 443, Centro* ⊕ *dzalbaycantina.com.*

La Parrilla

LIVE MUSIC | Location, location, location is the allure of this loud and colorful drink-ing establishment. Right in the heart of the historic center just a block from Plaza Grande—but with branches around the city—the tourist magnet offers live music and drinks served in plastic yard glasses. It's one of the best spots to grab a beer and watch Mérida in action. Check the website for weekly promotions. ✉ *Calle 60 No. 502, between Calles 59 and 61, Centro* ☎ *999/928–1691* ⊕ *www.laparril-lamerida.com.*

Mayan Pub

LIVE MUSIC | A pleasant atmosphere, flowing beer, and live music are what make this bar one of Mérida's best-kept secrets (you might want to pass on the

Hamacas: A Primer

Yucatecan artisans are known for creating some of the finest *hamacas*, or hammocks, in the country. For the most part, the shops of Mérida are the best places in Yucatán to buy these beautiful, practical items—though if you travel to some of the outlying small towns, like Tixkokob, Izamal, and Ek Balam, you may find cheaper prices, and enjoy the experience as well.

One of the first decisions you'll have to make when buying a hamaca is whether to choose one made from cotton or nylon: nylon dries more quickly and is therefore well suited to humid climates, but cotton is softer and more comfortable (though its colors tend to fade faster). You'll also see that hamacas come in both double-thread and single-thread weaves; the double-thread ones are sturdiest because they're more densely woven.

Hamacas come in a variety of sizes, too. A *sencillo* (sen-*see*-yoh) hammock is meant for just one person (although most people find it's a rather tight fit), a *doble* (*doh*-blay), on the other hand, is very comfortable for one but crowded for two. *Matrimonial* or king-size hammocks accommodate two, and *familiares* or *matrimoniales especiales* can theoretically sleep an entire family. (Yucatecans tend to be smaller than Anglos are, and also lie diagonally in hammocks rather than end-to-end.)

For a good-quality king-size nylon or cotton hamaca, prices start at MX$500; sencillos begin at MX$400. Unless you're an expert, it's best to buy a hammock at a specialty shop, where you can climb in to try the size. The proprietors will also give you tips on washing, storing, and hanging your hammock. You'll find lots of hammock stores near Mérida's municipal market on Calle 58, between Calles 69 and 73.

food). Grab a spot in the beer garden where you can listen to live reggae, rock, or jazz. A rather worn billiard table and occasional entertainment—such as belly dancers and fire spinners—draw in a decent crowd. ⊠ *Calle 62 No. 473, between Calles 55 and 57, Centro* ☎ *999/968–7341* ⊗ *Closed Mon. and Tues.*

Parque de Santiago
GATHERING PLACES | If dancing to the likes of romantic trios of the 1940s is your style, don't miss the Tuesday-night ritual at Parque de Santiago, where older folks and the occasional young lovers gather for dancing under the stars at 8:30 pm. ⊠ *Calles 59 and 72, Centro.*

FILM
Teatro Mérida
FILM | International art films are shown most days at Teatro Mérida, also known as the Teatro Armando Manzanero. ⊠ *Calle 62 495, between Calles 59 and 61, Centro* ☎ *999/924–0040.*

FOLKLORIC SHOWS
Universidad Autónoma de Yucatán
THEATER | Pop into the university's main building to check the bulletin boards just inside the entrance for upcoming cultural events. The **Ballet Folklórico de Yucatán** presents a combination of music, dance, and theater here most Fridays at 9 pm (think Mexico City's famous Ballet Folklórico de México, but on a slightly smaller scale); tickets are a bargain

at MX$70. There are no shows from August 1 to September 22 or during the last two weeks of December. ✉ *Calle 60, between Calles 57 and 59, Centro* ☎ *999/924–6729* ⊕ *www.uady.mx.*

● Shopping

When it comes to shopping, Mérida has something for everyone from souvenir enthusiasts to the most discriminating of market trollers. If you're looking for a more standard shopping experience, or need to grab some new tennis shoes or a pair of jeans, there are also a few shopping malls in the northern part of the city.

Crafts at reasonable prices can be found in the markets, parks, and plazas, and local art can be picked up at one of many galleries—the art scene here is burgeoning. While some vendors charge inflated prices, most are honest, but it is still a good idea to shop around to acquaint yourself with the kinds of crafts and the levels of quality that are available.

As is true in much of Mexico, it is common for stores to be open only until 1 or 2 pm on Saturday and to remain closed on Sunday. Also, unlike in the United States, stores are more likely to close on holidays. You may want to confirm a store is open before embarking on a trip to visit it.

MALLS
Plaza Las Américas
MALL | This pleasant mall houses more than 114 stores and eateries plus the Cinépolis movie theater complex. ✉ *Calle 21 No. 327, between Calles 50 and 52, Col. Miguel Hidalgo* ☎ *999/987–3521.*

The Harbor Mérida
MALL | FAMILY | One of the nicest shopping malls in Mérida wraps around an artificial lake—you can even zipline over it. Its main anchor is Gran Chapur, a department store, sitting amid a number of smaller boutiques. The Harbor also has a movie theater as well as a number of restaurants: Maya de Asia has delicious Maya-Asian fusion dishes; Porfirio's is a lively Mexican bar and restaurant; and there are smaller venues including a Starbucks, Mr. Sushi, and Hamburgesia for, yes, burgers. ✉ *Prol. Paseo Montejo, Paseo Montejo* ☎ *999/921–1252* ⊕ *www. theharbormerida.com.*

La Isla
MALL | FAMILY | La Isla inches ahead of The Harbor when it comes to store selection, but either could qualify as the newest and nicest mall in town. The department store Liverpool is the anchor, but Zara and H&M are also big draws. The back of the mall has a row of restaurants overlooking a man-made lake. As with any of Mérida's malls, it may not be on your sightseeing shortlist, but if you have a longer stay in the city, air-conditioned window shopping may be appealing on warm days. ✉ *Calle 24 No. 608, Mérida* ☎ *999/518–3522* ⊕ *www.laislamerida. mx.*

MARKETS
Bazar de Artes Populares
MARKET | As its name implies, "popular art," or handicrafts, are sold at the Parque Santa Lucía beginning at 9 am on Sunday. ✉ *Parque Santa Lucía, at Calles 60 and 55, Centro.*

Mercado de Artesanías García Rejón
MARKET | Although many deal in the same wares, the shops and stalls of the García Rejón Crafts Market sell some quality items, and the shopping experience here can be less of a hassle than at the nearby municipal market. You'll find reasonable prices on palm-fiber hats, hammocks, leather sandals, jewelry, handmade guitars, and locally made liqueurs. Persistent but polite bargaining may get you even better deals. ✉ *Calles 65 and 60, Centro.*

Yucatán's History

The conquest of the Yucatán Peninsula by the three Franciscos de Montejo—father, son, and nephew—took three gruesome wars over a total of 24 years. The resolute Maya, their ancestors long incorrectly portrayed by archaeologists as docile and peace loving, provided the Spaniards and the mainland Mexicans with one of their greatest challenges in the New World. Rebellious pockets of Mayan communities held out against the *dzulo'obs* (dzoo-loh-*obs*)—the upper class, or outsiders—as late as the 1920s and '30s.

Yucatecans are proud of their heritage and culture, and with good reason. Although in a state of decline when the conquistadores clanked into their world with iron swords and fire-belching cannons, the Maya were one of the world's greatest ancient cultures. As mathematicians and astronomers they were perhaps without equal among their contemporaries, and their architecture in places like Uxmal was as graceful as that of the ancient Greeks.

To "facilitate" Catholic conversion among the conquered, the Spaniards superimposed Christian rituals on existing beliefs whenever possible, creating the ethnic Catholicism that's alive and well today. (Those defiant Maya who resisted the new ideology were burned at the stake, drowned, and hanged.) Having procured a huge workforce of free indigenous labor, Spanish agricultural estates prospered like mad. Mérida soon became a thriving administrative and military center, and the gateway to Cuba and to Spain. By the 18th century, huge maize and cattle plantations were making the *hacendados* incredibly rich.

Insurrection came during the Caste War in the mid-1800s, when the enslaved indigenous people rose up with long-repressed furor and massacred thousands of settlers. The United States, Cuba, and Mexico City finally came to the aid of the ruling elite, and between 1847 and 1850 the indigenous population of Yucatán was effectively halved. Those Maya who didn't escape into the remote jungles of neighboring Quintana Roo or Chiapas, or get sold into slavery in Cuba, found themselves even worse off under the dictatorship of Porfirio Díaz (which spanned 31 years at the end of the 19th and beginning of the 20th centuries).

Their hopeless status changed little as the economic base segued from one industry to the next. After the thin limestone soil failed to produce fat cattle or impressive corn, entrepreneurs turned to dyewood and then to henequen, a natural fiber used to make rope. (Henequen is better known in English as sisal, after the Yucatán port of the same name through which much of the fiber was exported.)

After the widespread acceptance of synthetic fibers, the land barons of the peninsula would use the sweat of local labor to convert the resin of *zapote* trees into a latex that is the basis of chewing gum, as well as adhesives and other products. The fruits of the labor of the haciendas' workers can be seen today in the imposing French-style mansions that stretch along Mérida's Paseo de Montejo.

Mercado Lucas de Gálvez

MARKET | FAMILY | Sellers of chiles, herbs, seafood, and produce fill this pungent and labyrinthine municipal market. In the early morning the first floor is jammed with housewives and restaurateurs shopping for the freshest fish and produce. The stairs at Calles 56 and 57 lead to the second-floor Bazar de Artesanías Municipales, where you'll find local pottery, embroidered clothes, guayabera shirts, hammocks, straw bags, sturdy leather huaraches, and piñatas. Note that most initial prices are inflated as vendors expect you'll bargain—one way to begin is to politely request a discount. ⊠ *Calles 56 and 67, Centro.*

BOOKS

Librería Dante

BOOKS | The Mérida-based bookstore chain Dante, with a location on Plaza Grande as well as eight others around the city, has the best selection of Spanish-language books about the peninsula's history, culture, cuisine, and more. It is especially strong on books for kids and works dealing with Yucatecan flora and fauna. ⊠ *Calle 17 138B, at Prolongación Paseo de Montejo, Col. Itzimná* ☎ *999/927–7676* ⊕ *www.libreriadante. com.mx.*

Between the Lines

BOOKS | Mérida's biggest English-language bookstore is relatively small, but it still offers a nicely curated selection of recent popular titles as well as a number that are focused on Mexican culture, cuisine, and history. The store also has bookish gifts including journals, handmade bookmarks, and more. Several stores in the Carmesí complex where the bookstore is located are worth a stop too; they mostly sell local, high-quality handicrafts. There's also Volta Café for a snack and drink. ⊠ *Calle 62 450, Centro* ☎ *000/242 3528* ⊕ *www.betweenthelines.com.mx* ☉ *Closed Mon. and Tues.*

CLOTHING

Camiseria Canul

MIXED CLOTHING | You might not start wearing a guayabera (a traditional and often embroidered cotton or linen dress shirt) to business meetings as is common in much of southern Mexico, but the shirts are cool, comfortable, and attractive. Camiseria Canul has a good selection. Custom shirts take a week to tailor, in sizes 4 to 52. ⊠ *Calle 62 No. 484, between Calles 57 and 59, Centro* ☎ *999/923–0158* ⊕ *www.camiseriacanul. com.mx* ☉ *Closed Sun.*

Guayaberas Jack

MEN'S CLOTHING | This spot has an excellent selection of guayaberas in 18 colors; they also sell typical women's cotton *filipinas* (house dresses), blouses, dresses, classy straw handbags, and lovely rayon *rebozos* (shawls) from San Luis Potosí. Guayaberas can be made to order, even in less than a day, to fit anyone from a year-old baby to a 240-pound person, and anything in the shop can be altered or custom-made. Everything here is of fine quality, and is often quite different from the clothes sold in neighboring shops—the prices reflect this superior quality. You can make purchases on its website as well. ⊠ *Calle 59 No. 507A, between Calles 60 and 62, Centro* ☎ *999/928–6002* ⊕ *guayaberas-jack.negocio.site* ☉ *Closed Sun. and Mon.*

Amerindio Hombre

MEN'S CLOTHING | Once you return home, traditional huaraches, guayaberas, and straw hats might not look as appropriate as they did when you were on vacation. The items from Mexican designers at men's store Amerindio, however, have a cool factor that will be stylish even back at home. ⊠ *Calle 62 469, Centro* ☎ *999/923–0945* ⊕ *www.facebook.com/ AmerindioHombre* ☉ *Closed Sun.*

JEWELRY

Joyería Colonial

JEWELRY & WATCHES | Shop for malachite, turquoise, and other semiprecious stones set in silver at Joyería Colonial. ⊠ *Calle 60 No. 502B, between Calles 61 and 63, Centro* ☎ *999/923–5838.*

LOCAL GOODS AND CRAFTS

El Xiric

OTHER SPECIALTY STORE | You can buy hammocks made to order—choose from standard nylon and cotton, supersoft processed sisal, Brazilian style (six-stringed), or crocheted. You can also purchase xtabentún (a local honey liqueur), as well as jewelry, black pottery, woven goods from Oaxaca, T-shirts, and souvenirs. ⊠ *Calle 57A No. 15, Pasaje Congreso, Centro* ☎ *999/924–9906.*

Hamacas El Aguacate

CRAFTS | A great place to purchase hammocks is Hamacas El Aguacate, a family-run outfit with many sizes and designs. ⊠ *Calle 58 No. 604, at Calle 73, Centro* ☎ *999/947–4641* ⊕ *www.facebook.com/ hamacas.elaguacate.*

La Casa de las Artesanías

CRAFTS | This government-run craft store offers all kinds of items, both from the state of Yucatán but also other parts of Mexico, at fair prices. There's a smaller branch in front of the Palacio Cantón on the Paseo de Montejo, but this main branch offers the best selection. ⊠ *Calle 63, No. 513, between Calles 64 and 66, Centro* ☎ *999/928–6676* ⊗ *Closed Sat. and Sun.*

Miniaturas

CRAFTS | A delightful and diverse assortment of crafts is sold here, but the store specializes in miniatures made of ceramics, tin, and other materials. ⊠ *Calle 59 No. 507A, between Calles 60 and 62, Centro* ☎ *999/928–6503* ⊗ *Closed Sun.*

Izamal

68 km (42 miles) east of Mérida.

Izamal stands out for its carefully cared-for architecture. One of the best examples of a Spanish colonial community in the Yucatán, Izamal is nicknamed "la Ciudad Amarilla" (the Yellow City), because its most important edifices are a golden ocher, which contrasts strikingly with the blue sky. It's also sometimes called "the City of Three Cultures," because of its combined pre-Hispanic, colonial, and contemporary influences. Izamal makes a charming and lower-key alternative to the sometimes frenetic Mérida. Hotels are humble, and the few restaurants here offer basic fare. If you enjoy a quieter, slower-pace vacation, it's worth considering as a base.

GETTING HERE AND AROUND

The drive east from Mérida takes less than an hour on Carretera 180. Calesas (horse-drawn carriages) are stationed at the town's large main square, fronting the lovely cathedral, day and night. Drivers—their English capabilities vary widely—charge about MX$100 an hour for sightseeing, and many will also take you on a shopping tour for whichever items you're interested in buying (for instance, hammocks or jewelry). Pick up a brochure at the visitor center for details.

VISITOR INFORMATION

Oficina de Turismo. ⊠ *Calle 30 No. 323, between Calles 31 and 31A, Centro* ☎ *988/954–1096.*

⊙ Sights

Centro Cultural y Artesanal Izamal

ART MUSEUM | Banamex has set up this small, well-organized art museum right on the main plaza. There are all kinds of high-quality crafts on display, from textiles and ceramics to papier-mâché and woodwork. The center also has a little on-site café and gift shop. ⊠ *Calle*

Izamal's San Antonio de Padua was built from the remains of a Maya pyramid.

31 s/n No. 201, Centro ☎ *9888/954–1012* ✉ *MX$30* 🕑 *Closed Mon.*

Ex-Convento e Iglesia de San Antonio de Padua

CHURCH | Facing the main plaza, the enormous 16th-century former monastery and church of St. Anthony of Padua is perched on—and built from—the remains of a Maya pyramid devoted to Itzámná, god of the heavens. The monastery's ocher-painted church, where Pope John Paul II led prayers in 1993, has a gigantic atrium (supposedly second in size only to the Vatican's) facing a colonnaded facade and rows of 75 white-trimmed arches. The Virgin of the Immaculate Conception, to whom the church is dedicated, is the patron saint of the Yucatán. A statue of Nuestra Señora de Izamal, or Our Lady of Izamal, was brought here from Guatemala in 1562 by Bishop Diego de Landa. Miracles are ascribed to her, and a yearly pilgrimage takes place in her honor. Frescoes of saints at the front of the church, once plastered over, were rediscovered and refurbished in 1996. The monastery

and church are now illuminated in a light-and-sound show of the type common at some archaeological sites. You can catch a Spanish-only narration and the play of lights on the nearly 500-year-old structure at 8 pm Thursday, Friday, and Saturday—buy tickets (MX$110) on-site at 7:30. Diagonally across from the cathedral, the small municipal market is worth a wander. It's the kind of place where if you stop to watch how the merchants prepare food, they may let you in on their cooking secrets. ✉ *Bound by Calles 31, 28, 33, and 30, Izamal.*

Kinich Kakmó

RUINS | FAMILY | The Kinich Kakmó pyramid was the largest pre-Hispanic construction in the Yucatán, and it's all that remains of the royal Maya city that flourished here between AD 250 and 600. Dedicated to Zamná, Maya god of the dew, the massive structure is more remarkable for its size than for any remaining decoration; however, it's nonetheless an impressive monument. ✉ *Calle 39, at Calle 40, Izamal* ✉ *Free.*

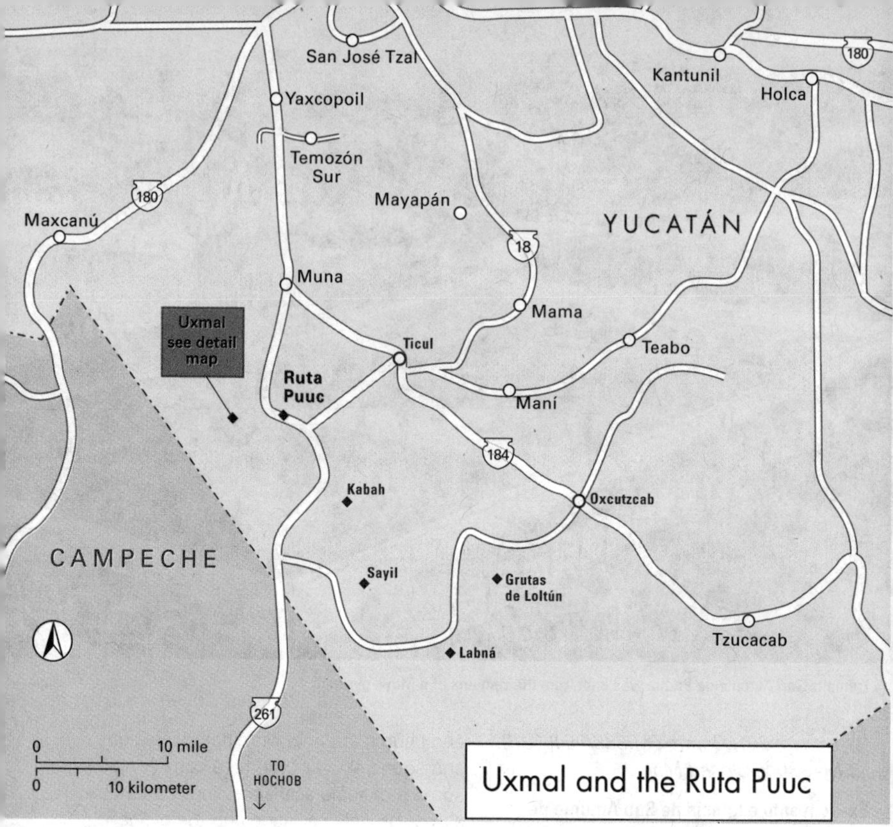

Uxmal and the Ruta Puuc

🍴 Restaurants

Restaurante Kinich

$ | **MEXICAN** | The town's most comfortable eatery comes complete with white tablecloths under a wide palapa, surrounded by plants and with a burbling fountain. In a small hut in the back, the cooks make tortillas by hand and menu highlights include locally made longaniza (a tasty grilled pork sausage) and excellent sopa de lima. **Known for:** traditional atmosphere; longaniza (a local sausage); folk art. [$] *Average main: MP140* ✉ *Calle 27 No. 299, between Calles 28 and 30,* ☎ *988/954–0489* 🌐 *restaurantekinich.com.*

Los Mestizos

$ | **MEXICAN** | This humble restaurant has brightly painted walls; even the ceiling fans are painted a vivid orange. The "Combinado los Mestizos" on the dinner menu offers a taste of several regional specialties including *salbutes* and *panuchos*—both typical appetizers of fried cornmeal, the latter stuffed with beans—as well as chicken and turkey dishes. **Known for:** friendly service; chaya-leaf tamales; combination platter of local specialties. [$] *Average main: MP110* ✉ *Calle 33 No. 301, behind the market, Centro* ☎ *999/364–6905.*

Restaurante Muul

$ | **MEXICAN** | **FAMILY** | Residents of Izamal have strong opinions on which restaurants make the best panuchos, salbutes, papadzules, and other local specialities, but Restaurante Muul is on many short lists. The atmosphere is no-frills, though the location is convenient, right on the main plaza just steps from the ex-convent. **Known for:** good value; location on the main plaza; local specialties. $ Average main: MP100 ✉ Calle 28 300, near Calle 31, Centro ⊕ www.facebook.com/muul.restaurante 🏛 Casual.

🛏 Hotels

Hacienda Sacnicte

$$$$ | B&B/INN | Three miles north of town, this hacienda (whose name refers to a local white flower) dates from 1811, but it's been restored to strike a perfect balance between the old and new with beautifully appointed suites and spacious bathrooms. **Pros:** wonderful staff; thoughtful design; rate includes delicious breakfast. **Cons:** pricey; owners rarely on-site; not centrally located. $ Rooms from: $275 ✉ Carretera a Tekal de Venegas, Km. 5, Izamal ☎ 1988/967–4668 cell ⊕ www.haciendasacnicte.com 🛏 10 suites ❢❶ Free Breakfast.

★ Hacienda Santo Domingo

$ | B&B/INN | Built on a 44-acre property, this hotel has freestanding rooms separated by carefully tended gardens full of exotic plants and fruit trees, as well as sheep and two friendly dogs. **Pros:** cooking lessons available; close to town center; freestanding rooms. **Cons:** not everyone loves animals; Wi-Fi in common areas only; the lush gardens also come with mosquitoes at times. $ Rooms from: $70 ✉ Calle 18, between Calles 33 and 35, Izamal ☎ 988/967–6136 ⊕ www.izamalhotel.com 🛏 10 rooms ❢❶ Free Breakfast.

Hotel Macan Ché

$ | B&B/INN | Each artsy bungalow here has its own themed decor: the Asian room has a Chinese checkers board and origami decorations, while the Safari room has artifacts from Mexico and Africa. **Pros:** great price; private yoga classes available; feels like a hidden village. **Cons:** several blocks from central plaza; some rooms lack air-conditioning; mosquitoes are sometimes an issue. $ Rooms from: $60 ✉ Calle 22 No. 305, between Calles 33 and 35, Izamal ☎ 988/954–0287 ⊕ www.macanche.com 🛏 15 rooms ❢❶ Free Breakfast.

🛍 Shopping

Hecho a Mano

CRAFTS | Just off the main square, Hecho a Mano (at the San Miguel Hotel) is the only place in town to buy folk art from all over Mexico. You'll find something to suit any budget, including a growing collection of textiles. ✉ Calle 31A No. 308, Centro ☎ 988/954–0344 ⊕ www.sanmiguelhotel.com.mx/hotel/handicrafts/.

The Ruta Puuc

The Ruta Puuc, or hilly route, is a highlight of any visit to Yucatán. The series of secondary roads that wind through one of the state's least populated areas not only lead you from one fantastic Maya ruin to the next, but also to an impressive cave system, various restored haciendas, and numerous villages where you can stop for a bite to eat and feel the unique rhythm of the Yucatecan countryside.

Uxmal, meaning thrice-built city, is the largest site along the Ruta Puuc. Several smaller satellite sites—including Kabah, Sayil, and Labná—are all well worth a visit. Another memorable Ruta Puuc attraction is the Grutas de Loltún, Yucatán's most extensive cave system. Here you can still see evidence of ancient Mayan rituals. If you plan on exploring the cave, take along sturdy shoes and a flashlight. If you want to use your video camera at any of the sites, expect to pay a MX$25–MX$35 charge.

It's possible to visit the sites on the Ruta Puuc in one long day or over the course of two days. Almost every Mérida-based tour operator does the former, but the latter is recommended if you have the time and your own transportation; roads are well marked and easy to navigate,

The Grutas de Loltún is an extensive cave system.

since the archaeological attractions line up one right after another. Most of the sites are open from 8 to 5 only, so to devote any less time means either skipping deserving locales or rushing through them. To do Uxmal justice, you'll want to spend anywhere from three to five hours exploring; smaller ruins can easily be seen in 20 to 30 minutes. Plan on spending a couple of hours at the Grutas de Loltún; be aware that guided tours through the cave are mandatory. If you plan on spending the night in Uxmal, you may want to start your trip off at the Grutas de Loltún and work your way toward Uxmal. To reach the caves from Mérida, take Carretera 261 to Muná and turn left on Carretera 184. From there, it's about 65 km (40 miles) to Oxkutzcab. Once in Oxkutzcab, simply follow the signs to the Grutas de Loltún.

Fill up on fuel and cash before entering the area, because both gas stations and ATMs are hard to come by.

Kabah

23 km (14 miles) southeast of Uxmal.

Sights

Kabah

RUINS | FAMILY | The most important buildings at Kabah (meaning "lord of the powerful hand" in Mayan) were built between AD 600 and 900, during the later part of the classic era. A ceremonial center of almost Grecian beauty, it was once linked to Uxmal by a sacbé, or raised paved road, at the end of which looms a great independent arch—now across the highway from the main ruins. The 151-foot-long Palacio de los Mascarones (Palace of the Masks) boasts a three-dimensional mosaic of 250 masks of inlaid stones. On the central plaza, you can see ground-level wells called *chultunes,* which were used to store precious rainwater. The site officially opens at 8 am, but the staff often doesn't show up until 9. ✉ *23 km*

(14 miles) south of Uxmal on Carretera 261 ⊕ www.inah.gob.mx ☜ MX$55.

Sayil

9.5 km (6 miles) south of Kabah. Follow Highway 261 for 5 km and then take a left to Sayil.

 Sights

Sayil

RUINS | FAMILY | Experts believe that Sayil, or "place of the red ants," flourished between AD 800 and 1000. It's best known for its setting in a narrow valley surrounded by rolling hills and its majestic Gran Palacio. Built on one of those hills, the three-story structure is adorned with decorations of animals and other figures, and contains more than 80 rooms. The structure recalls Palenque in its use of multiple planes, columned porticoes, and sober cornices. Also on the grounds is a stela in the shape of a phallus—an obvious symbol of fertility. ⊠ *9 km (5½ miles) south of Kabah on Carretera 31E* ⊕ *www.inah.gob.mx* ☜ *MX$55.*

Labná

8 km (5 miles) east of Sayil on a narrow (though well-maintained) road through the Puuc Biocultural Reserve.

 Sights

Labná

RUINS | FAMILY | This was a small though important settlement in the Puuc region and like many of its neighbors, its peak was roughly between AD 600 and 900. While there is a palace and a small pyramid, the most photographed building at Labná is a striking monumental corbelled arch. (Labná means "old house" or "abandoned house.") With its elaborate latticework and a small chamber on each side; it provided a grand entrance into

a sacred precinct for anyone arriving on the road to and from Uxmal. It is believed that Labná was used mainly by royalty and the military elite. ⊠ *9 km (5½ miles) south of Sayil on Carretera 31E* ☜ *MX$55*

Grutas de Loltún

27 km (17 miles) northeast of Labná, 7½ km (4½ miles) southwest of Oxkutzcab.

 Sights

Grutas de Loltún

CAVE | FAMILY | The Loltún ("stone flower" in Mayan) is one of the largest, most fascinating cave systems on the Yucatán Peninsula. Long ago, Maya ceremonies were routinely held inside these mysterious caverns, and artifacts unearthed in them date as far back as 800 BC. The topography itself is intriguing: there are stalactites, stalagmites, and limestone formations known by such names as Ear of Corn and Cathedral. Illuminated pathways meander a little over a kilometer (½ mile) through the caves, most of which are quite spacious and well ventilated (claustrophobics needn't worry). Nine different openings allow air and some (but not much) light to filter in. Moisture can make these paths somewhat slippery so be sure to wear shoes that grip. You can enter only with a guide. They earn a very small salary and survive on tips—be generous. ⊠ *19 km (12 miles) northeast of Labná on Carretera 31E, down an unmarked road toward Oxkutzcab* ☜ *MX$127; parking MX$35.*

Ticul

27 km (17½ miles) northwest of Grutas de Loltún, 28 km (17 miles) east of Uxmal, 100 km (62 miles) south of Mérida.

One of the larger communities in the Yucatán, Ticul (with a population of around 21,000) is a good base for exploring the Puuc region—provided you don't mind rudimentary hotels and a limited choice of simple restaurants. Many descendants of the Xiu Dynasty, which ruled Uxmal until the conquest, still live here. Industries include the fabrication of shoes and *huipiles* (the traditional white embroidered dresses worn by indigenous women) as well as much of the pottery you see around the Yucatán. Ticul also has a handsome 17th-century church.

GETTING HERE AND AROUND

Ticul is an easy drive south of Mérida, along the Ruta Puuc. Follow Carretera 180 to Umán, where you'll get on the Carretera 261 to Muná; from Muná, simply follow the signs to Ticul by way of Carretera 184.

Sights

Iglesia de San Antonio de Padua

CHURCH | This evocatively faded red church is typical of Yucatán's colonial sanctuaries. It has been ransacked on more than one occasion, but the Cristo Negro ("Black Christ") altarpiece is original. The best view might be from the outside, where you can take in the facade and savor the slow pace of the town as families ride by in carts attached to bicycles and locals mill around in traditional Maya dress. ✉ *Town Sq., Centro, Ticul.*

Mayapán

RUINS | **FAMILY** | Those who are fascinated by Maya sites may want to make a 42-km (26-mile) detour north from Ticul—or a 43-km (27-mile) one south from Mérida—to Mayapán, the last of the major city-states on the peninsula that flourished during the postclassic era. It was destroyed in 1450, presumably by war. It's thought that the city, with an architectural style reminiscent of Uxmal, was as big as Chichén Itzá, and there are more than 4,000 mounds, which might indicate there is truth to the claim. At its height, the population could have been well more than 12,000. A half dozen mounds have been excavated, including the palaces of Maya royalty and the temple of the benign god Kukulcán, where stucco sculptures and murals in vivid reds and oranges have been uncovered. Be sure you head toward the Mayapán ruins (just south of Telchaquillo) and not the town of Mayapán, since they are far apart. ✉ *Off rd. to left before Telchaquillo (follow signs), Ticul* 🌐 *www.inah.gob.mx* 🎫 *MX$45.*

Restaurants

★ El Príncipe Tutul-Xiu

$ | **MEXICAN** | **FAMILY** | This open restaurant under a giant palapa roof is an inviting spot for lunch or an early dinner (it closes at 7 pm). Though you'll find the same Yucatecan dishes here as elsewhere—pollo pibil, lime soup—the preparation is excellent and portions are generous. **Known for:** tasty poc chuc; huge portions at reasonable prices; small-town atmosphere. [$] *Average main: MP140* ✉ *Calle 26 No. 208, between Calles 25 and 27, Mani* ☎ *997/978–4257* 🌐 *elprincipetutulxiu.wixsite.com/website.*

Pizzería La Góndola

$ | **PIZZA** | **FAMILY** | The wonderful smells of fresh-baked bread and pizza waft from this small corner establishment between the market and the main square, where scenes of Old Italy and the Yucatán adorn the bright yellow walls. It's pretty informal here: patrons pull padded folding chairs up to yellow-tile tables, or take their orders to go. **Known for:** the only nighttime dining option in town; fun informal vibe; impressive variety of pizza. [$] *Average main: MP170* ✉ *Calle 23 No. 208, at Calle 26A, Ticul* ☎ *997/972–0112* ⏲ *No lunch.*

Hotels

★ Hacienda Temozón

$$$$ | **HOTEL** | This converted hacienda, roughly 45 minutes by car to the south of

Mérida, sits regally on a hilltop, creating an unforgettable first impression. **Pros:** part of Marriott's Luxury Collection; massages can be arranged in a private cenote; beautiful grounds and rooms. **Cons:** 45 minutes from Mérida; must drive to nearby ruins; expensive meals. $ *Rooms from: $340 ⊠ Carretera 261, Km 182, Ticul* ☎ *999/923–8089, 888/625–5144* ⊕ *www.marriott.com* ⇌ *29 rooms* ○ *No Meals.*

Hotel Plaza

$ | HOTEL | Despite its unimaginative name, this hotel does have a convenient location about a block from Ticul's main plaza. **Pros:** clean rooms; downtown location; very cheap rates. **Cons:** restaurant is merely adequate; no frills; street noise and church bells might keep you up late or wake you early. $ *Rooms from: $32* ⊠ *Calle 23 No. 202, between Calles 26 and 26A, Ticul* ☎ *997/972–0484* ⊕ *www. hotelplazayucatan.com* ⇌ *30 rooms* ○ *No Meals.*

Oxcutzcab

22 km (14 miles) southeast of Ticul, 122 km (76 miles) south of Mérida.

This market town is a good alternative to Ticul for those who want to spend the night in the Puuc area. Strangers will greet you as you walk the streets. Even the teenagers here are friendly and polite. Oxcutzcab (osh-coots-*cob*) supplies much of the state with produce: avocados, mangoes, mameys, papayas, watermelons, peanuts, and citrus fruits are all grown in the surrounding region and sold daily at the cheerful municipal market, directly in front of the town's picturesque Franciscan church. Pedicabs line up on the opposite side of the market, ready to take you on a three-wheeled tour of town for just a few pesos. The town's coat of arms tells the etymology of the name Oxcutzcab. In Mayan, "ox" means *ramon* (twigs cut for cattle

fodder), "*kutz*" is tobacco, also grown in the area, and "*cab*" is honey.

🛏 Hotels

Hotel Puuc

$ | HOTEL | This two-story, motel-style property is the nicest in Oxcutzcab. **Pros:** great rates; close to town center; sprawling pool area. **Cons:** plain rooms; noise can be a problem; restaurant caters to big groups. $ *Rooms from: $40* ⊠ *Calle 55 No. 80, at Calle 44, Oxkutzcab* ☎ *997/975–0103* ⊕ *www.hotelpuuc.com. mx* ⇌ *39 rooms* ○ *No Meals.*

Uxmal

78 km (48 miles) south of Mérida on Carretera 261.

If Chichén Itzá is the most expansive Maya ruin in Yucatán, Uxmal is arguably the most elegant. The architecture here reflects the late classical renaissance of the 7th to 9th century, and is contemporary with that of Palenque and Tikal, among other great Maya cities of the southern highlands. Uxmal is considered the finest and most extensively excavated example of Puuc architecture, which embraces such details as ornate stone mosaics and friezes on the upper walls, intricate cornices, rows of columns, and soaring vaulted arches.

You could easily spend a couple of days exploring the ruins—just keep in mind that the only entertainment offered outside them is provided by hotels and the odd restaurant. The upside is that, unlike some other remote ruin sites, you can buy food, drinks, and souvenirs at the entrance.

GETTING HERE AND AROUND

If you plan to drive, take Carretera 180 south out of Mérida, and then get on Carretera 261 in Umán. This will take you south all the way to Uxmal.

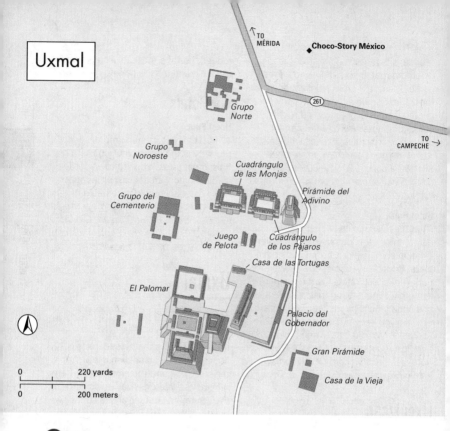

Uxmal

Grupo
Norte

Grupo
Noroeste

Cuadrángulo
de las Monjas

Pirámide del
Adivino

Grupo del
Cementerio

Juego
de Pelota

Cuadrángulo
de los Pájaros

Casa de las Tortugas

El Palomar

Palacio del
Gobernador

Gran Pirámide

Casa de la Vieja

TO
MÉRIDA

Choco-Story México

261

TO
CAMPECHE

0 ——— 220 yards
0 ——— 200 meters

⊙ Sights

Choco-Story México
OTHER MUSEUM | FAMILY | Located on a
cacao plantation near the Uxmal ruins,
this museum highlights the history of
cacao and cocoa (the product derived
from cacao) and their relationship with
Maya culture. Tours take place in traditional homes where you can learn about
the cultivation of cacao and the process
of making chocolate. At the end, you'll
be treated to a traditional Maya drink,
prepared with organic cocoa and local
spices. ✉ Carretera 261, Km 78, near
Hacienda Uxmal, Uxmal ☎ 1999/289–
9914 ⊕ www.choco-storymexico.com
⊠ MX$140.

★ Uxmal
RUINS | FAMILY | Uxmal rivals Chichén Itzá,
Coba, and other Maya sites in terms of
its beauty and drama, but its distance
from Cancun and the Riviera Maya
helps assure that it is less crowded, at
least relatively. The especially decorative
style of Uxmal and other Puuc Maya
sites also makes it of special interest.
Although much of Uxmal has yet to be
excavated and restored, the following
buildings in particular merit attention: At
125 feet high, the Pirámide del Adivino is the tallest and most prominent
structure at the site. Unlike most other
Maya pyramids, which are stepped and
angular, the "Pyramid of the Magician"
has a softer, more refined round-corner
design. This structure was rebuilt five
times over hundreds of years, each time
on the same foundation, so artifacts
found here represent several different
kingdoms. The pyramid has a stairway
on its western side that leads through a
giant open-mouth mask to two temples

Uxmal is an example of the Puuc architectural style.

at the summit. During restoration work in 2002, the grave of a high-ranking Maya official, a ceramic mask, and a jade necklace were discovered within the pyramid. Ongoing excavations continue to reveal exciting new finds, still under study. As with most ruins in Yucatán, climbing is prohibited. West of the pyramid lies the Cuadrángulo de las Monjas, often considered to be the finest part of Uxmal. It reminded the conquistadores of typical convent buildings in Spain (*monjas* are nuns). You may enter the four buildings, each comprising a series of low, gracefully repetitive chambers that look onto a central patio. Elaborate symbolic decorations—masks, geometric patterns, coiling snakes, and some phallic figures—blanket the upper facades. Heading south, you'll pass a small ball court before reaching the Palacio del Gobernador. Covering 5 acres and rising over an immense acropolis, the palace lies at the heart of what may have been city's administrative center. It faces east while the rest of Uxmal faces west, and archaeologists suggest this allowed the structure to serve as an observatory for the planet Venus. The Cuadrángalo de los Pájaros (Quadrangle of the Birds) takes its name from the repeating pattern of doves, which decorates the upper part of the building's frieze. The building is composed of a series of small chambers. In one of these, archaeologists discovered a statue of the ruler Chac (not to be confused with Chaac, the rain god), who was thought to have dwelled there. A nightly sound and light show (8 pm in summer, 7 pm in winter) recounts Maya legends. The colored light brings out details of carvings and mosaics that are easy to miss when the sun is shining. The show is narrated in Spanish, but earphones (MX$39) provide an English translation. In the summer months, tarantulas are a common sight on the grounds at Uxmal. ⊠ *Uxmal* ✛ *Carretera 261, 78 km (48 miles) south of Mérida* ☎ *997/976–2064* ⊕ *www.inah.gob.mx* ✉ *MX$418, sound and light show MX$100.*

📖 Hotels

La Casa del Mago

$ | **B&B/INN** | **FAMILY** | This charming budget option with just four rooms and bright and cheery decor lies a short walk from the Uxmal ruins. **Pros:** short walk to from ruins; terrific rates. **Cons:** some noise from the road. $ *Rooms from: $55* ✉ *Uxmal* ☎ *997/976–2012, 800/235–4079 in the U.S.* 🔁 *4 rooms* ❖ *Free Breakfast.*

The Lodge at Uxmal

$$$ | **HOTEL** | **FAMILY** | The outwardly rustic, thatch-roof buildings here have red-tile floors, hand-carved doors and rocking chairs, stained-glass windows, and local weavings. **Pros:** simple yet beautiful rooms; directly across from Uxmal entrance; gracious staff; big pools. **Cons:** expensive for rustic rooms. $ *Rooms from: $175* ✉ *Carretera Uxmal, Km 78, Uxmal* ☎ *998/887–2495, 877/240–5864* ⊕ *www.mayaland.com* 🔁 *40 rooms* ❖ *No Meals.*

The Pickled Onion B&B

$ | **B&B/INN** | Owner Valerie Pickles has carved out a lovely little paradise with six bungalows and a wonderful restaurant on the outskirts of Santa Elena. **Pros:** wonderful owner; amazing rates; communal computer; food at restaurant is made from scratch. **Cons:** rustic setting is not for everyone. $ *Rooms from: $55* ✉ *Carretera 261, between Uxmal and Kabah, just after Santa Elena Centro, Santa Elena* ☎ *1997/111–7922* ⊕ *www.thepickledonionyucatan.com* 🔁 *8 rooms* ❖ *Free Breakfast.*

Chichén Itzá

120 km (74 miles) east of Mérida, 48 km (30 miles) west of Valladolid.

In 2007, this sublime Mayan city was named one of the "New 7 Wonders of the World"—a distinction that puts Chichén Itzá on par with Peru's Machu Picchu and the Great Wall of China; now more than a million people per year come from all over the world to admire it. If you want to devote more than a day to the magnificent and mysterious ruins, consider staying 2 km (1½ miles) west in Pisté, a tiny town that feels more like a base camp. Hotels, restaurants, and shops there tend to be less expensive than those just outside the ruins in the Zona Hotelera (Hotel Zone).

GETTING HERE AND AROUND

Chichén Itzá's tiny airstrip serves only private and charter planes, so virtually everyone comes by road. From Mérida, you can reach Chichén Itzá along the Carretera 180D or Carretera 180 in two or three hours respectively. For a more scenic and interesting alternative, head east on Carretera 281 to Tixkokob (a Maya community famous for its hammock weavers) and carry on through Citilcúm and Izamal. From there, drive through the small, untouristy towns of Dzudzal and Xanaba en route to Kantunil, where you can hop on the toll road or continue on the free road that parallels it through Holca and Libre Unión (both of which have very swimmable cenotes). The trip will take four to five hours.

If coming from Cancún or the Riviera Maya on a day trip, don't forget that Chichén Itzá is an hour earlier from late October to early April, but the same time the rest of the year.

👁 Sights

★ Chichén Itzá

RUINS | One of the most dramatically beautiful ancient Maya cities, Chichén Itzá (pronounced *chee-CHEN eet-ZAH*) draws over one million visitors annually. Since the remains of this once-thriving kingdom were rediscovered by Europeans in the mid-1800s, many of the travelers making the pilgrimage here have been archaeologists and scholars who study the structures and glyphs and try to piece together the mysteries surrounding them. While the artifacts here give fascinating insight into Maya civilization, they also raise many unanswered questions. The name of this ancient city, which means "the mouth of the well of the Itzá," is a mystery in and of itself. Although it likely refers to the valuable water sources at the site (there are several cenotes here), experts have little information about who might have actually founded the city; some structures, likely built in the 5th century, predate the arrival of the Itzá, who occupied the city starting around the late 8th and early 9th centuries. Why the Itzá abandoned the city in the early 1200s is also unknown, as is its subsequent role. Most visitors who converge on Chichén Itzá come to marvel at its beauty. Even among laypeople, this ancient metropolis, which encompasses 6 square km (2¼ square miles), is known around the world as one of the most stunning and well-preserved Maya sites in existence. You've likely seen photos of the immense pyramid, **El Castillo** ("Kukulkán" in Maya), but they can't capture the moment you first gaze in person upon the structure rising imposingly yet gracefully from the surrounding plain. El Castillo (the Castle) dominates the site both in size and in the symmetry of its perfect proportions. Open-jawed serpent statues adorn the corners of each of the pyramid's four stairways, honoring the legendary priest-king Kukulcán (also known as Quetzalcóatl), an incarnation of the feathered serpent god. More serpents appear at the top of the building as sculpted columns. At the spring and fall equinoxes, the afternoon light strikes the trapezoidal structure so that the shadow of the snake god appears to undulate down the side of the pyramid to bless the fertile earth. Thousands of people, from international sightseers to Maya shamans, travel to the site each year to witness this phenomenon. Make lodging reservations far in advance if you hope to join them. The question on everybody's lips is: "May I climb the pyramid?" The answer is a resounding "No." Disappointing though that response may be, wear and tear on the staircases and numerous injuries to visitors have necessitated an end to the climbing. Archaeologists are still abuzz about the 2015 discovery of a subterranean river flowing underneath the pyramid, detected via "electrical resistance survey." While the Maya would likely have intentionally constructed El Castillo over such a river cavern, will the eventual effect be that of a gigantic sinkhole that could threaten the structure's foundation? Time will tell, although experts suggest probably not yet for several generations. The interior of El Castillo houses a marvelous statue of the intermediate god Chacmool. This part of the pyramid is no longer accessible to visitors, but four other Chacmool figures are scattered around Chichén Itzá. The most visible of them stands—or rather, reclines—at the **Templo de los Guerreros** (Temple of the Warriors), just northeast of the pyramid. A Chacmool always leans back, leaving a flat spot on the belly for receiving offerings. On the **Anexo del Templo de los Jaguares** (Annex to the Temple of the Jaguars), just west of El Castillo, bas-relief carvings represent more important deities. On the bottom of the columns is the rain god Tlaloc. It's no surprise that his tears represent rain—but why is the Toltec god Tlaloc honored here, instead of the Maya rain god, Chaac? That's one of many questions that archaeologists and epigraphers have been trying to answer, ever since John Lloyd Stephens and Frederick Catherwood, the first English-speaking explorers to rediscover the site, hacked their way through the surrounding forest in 1840. Scholars once thought that the symbols of foreign gods and differing architectural styles at Chichén Itzá proved it was conquered by

Continued on page 308

The towering El Castillo pyramid, nearly 80 feet high, is the most striking structure at Chichén Itzá. Each side of the pyramid has 91 steps, which, with the addition of the topmost platform, equal 365, one for each day of the calendar year. At the vernal and autumnal equinoxes, thousands of people gather to watch as the shadow of the serpent god Kukulcán seems to slither down the side of the pyramid.

CHICHÉN ITZÁ

One of the most beautiful of the ancient Maya cities, Chichén Itzá draws some 3,000 visitors a day from all over the world. Since the remains of this once-thriving kingdom were explored by Europeans and Americans in the mid 1800s, many of the travelers who make the pilgrimage here have been archaeologists and scholars who study the structures and glyphs and try to piece together the mysteries surrounding them. While the artifacts here give fascinating insight into the Maya civilization, they also raise many, many unanswered questions.

The name of this ancient city, which means "the mouth of the well of the Itzás," is a mystery in and of itself. Although it likely refers to the valuable water sources at the site (there are several sinkholes here), experts have little information about who might have actually founded the city— some structures, likely built in the 5th century, pre-date the arrival of the Itzás who occupied the city starting around the late 8th and early 9th centuries. The reason the Itzás abandoned the city, around 1224, is also unknown.

Scholars and archaeologists aside, most of the visitors that converge on Chichén Itzá come to marvel at its beauty, not ponder its significance. This ancient metropolis, which encompasses 6 square km (2½ square mi), is known around the world as one of the most stunning and well-preserved Maya sites in existence.

(opposite) The main pyramid El Castillo is also called Temple of Kukulcán, (top) carvings of ball players adorn the walls of the juego de pelota, (bottom) Maya statue.

MAJOR SITES AND ATTRACTIONS

Rows of freestanding columns where the roof has long since disintegrated

The sight of the immense ❶ **El Castillo** pyramid, rising imposingly yet gracefully from the surrounding plain, has been known to produce goose pimples on sight. El Castillo (The Castle) dominates the site both in size and in the symmetry of its perfect proportions. Open-jawed serpent statues adorn the corners of each of the pyramid's four stairways, honoring the legendary priest-king Kukulcán (also known as Quetzalcóatl), an incarnation of the feathered serpent god. More serpents appear at the top of the building as sculpted columns. At the spring and fall equinoxes, the afternoon light strikes the trapezoidal structure so that the shadow of the snake-god appears to undulate down the side of the pyramid to bless the fertile earth. Thousands of people travel to the site each year to see this phenomenon.

At the base of the temple on the north side, an interior staircase leads to two marvelous statues deep within:

a stone jaguar, and the intermediate god Chacmool. As usual, Chacmool is in a reclining position, with a flat spot on the belly for receiving sacrifices. On the ❷ **Anexo del Templo de los Jaguares** (Annex to the Temple of the Jaguars), just west of El Castillo, bas-relief carvings represent more important deities. On the bottom of the columns is the rain god Tlaloc. It's no surprise that his tears represent rain—but why is the Toltec god Tlaloc honored here, instead of the Maya rain god, Chaac?

That's one of many questions that archaeologists and epigraphers have been trying to answer, ever since John Lloyd Stephens and Frederick Catherwood, the first English-speaking explorers to discover the site, first hacked their way through the surrounding forest in 1840. Scholars once thought that the symbols of foreign gods and differing architectural styles at Chichén Itzá proved it was conquered by the Toltecs of central Mexico. (As well as representations of Tlaloc, the site also has a tzompantli—a stone platform decorated with row upon row of sculpted human skulls, which is a distinctively Toltec-style structure.) Most experts now agree, however, that Chichén Itzá was only influenced—not conquered—by Toltec trading partners from the north.

The flat part of a reclining Chacmool statue is where sacrificial offerings were laid.

It's believed that Maya ball players had to pass some sort of ball through high stone loops.

Games may have ended with beheadings.

Just west of the Anexo del Templo de los Jaguares is another puzzle: the auditory marvel of Chichén Itzá's main ball court. At 149 meters, this ❸ **Juego de Pelota** is the largest in Mesoamerica. Yet if you stand at one end of the playing field and whisper something to a friend at the other end, incredibly, you will be heard. The game played on this ball court was apparently something like soccer (no hands were used), but it likely had some sort of ritualistic significance. Carvings on the low walls surrounding the field show a decapitation, blood spurting from the victim's neck to fertilize the earth. Whether this is a historical depiction (perhaps the losers or winners of the game were sacrificed?) or a symbolic scene, we can only guess.

On the other side of El Castillo, just before a small temple dedicated to the planet Venus, a ruined sacbé, or white road leads to the ❹ **Cenote Sagrado** (Holy Well, or Sinkhole), which was also probably used for ritualistic purposes. Jacques Cousteau and his companions recovered about 80 skeletons from this deep, straight-sided, sub-surface pond, as well as thousands of pieces of jewelry and figures of jade, obsidian, wood, bone, and turquoise. In direct alignment with this cloudy green cenote, on the other side of El Castillo, the ❺ **Xtaloc sinkhole** was kept pristine, undoubtedly for bathing and drinking.

TIPS

To get more in-depth information about the ruins, hire a multilingual guide at the ticket booth. Guides charge about MXP 750 for a group of up to 7 people. Tours generally last about two hours. 🎫 MXP 80 ⊙ Ruins daily 8–5.

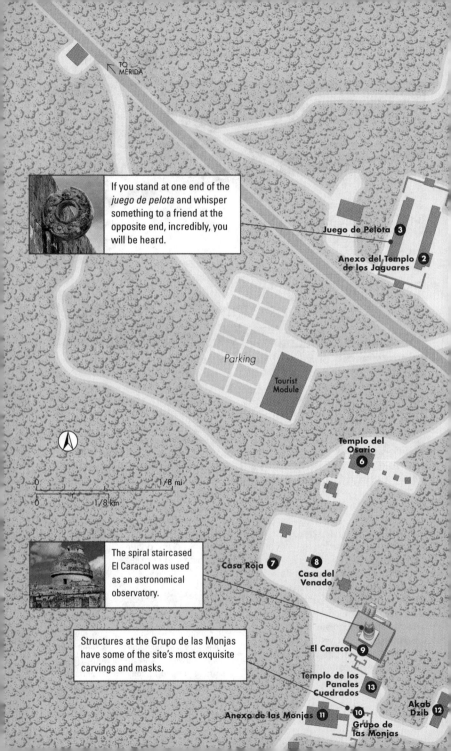

TO
MERIDA

If you stand at one end of the *juego de pelota* and whisper something to a friend at the opposite end, incredibly, you will be heard.

Juego de Pelota **3**

Anexo del Templo **2**
de los Jaguares

Parking

Tourist
Module

Templo del
Osario **6**

0 —————— 1/8 mi
0 —————— 1/8 km

The spiral staircased El Caracol was used as an astronomical observatory.

Casa Roja **7**   **8**
Casa del
Venado

Structures at the Grupo de las Monjas have some of the site's most exquisite carvings and masks.

El Caracol **9**

Templo de los
Panales **13**
Cuadrados

Akab
Dzib **12**

Anexa de las Monjas **11**   **10**

Grupo de
las Monjas

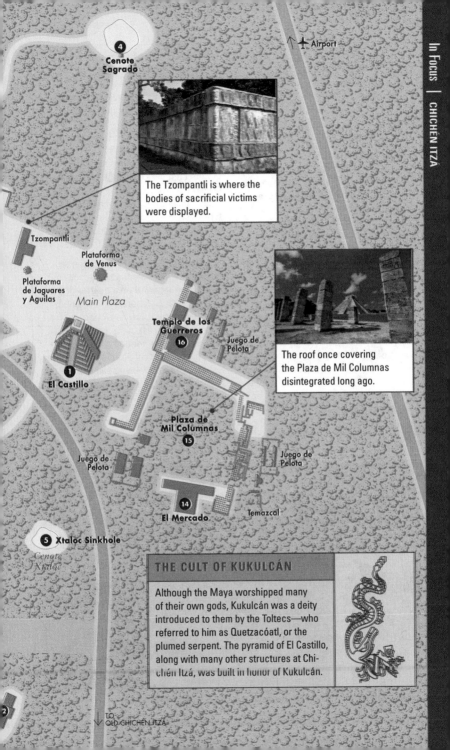

④ Cenote Sagrado

↑ ✈ Airport

The Tzompantli is where the bodies of sacrificial victims were displayed.

Tzompantli

Plataforma de Venus

Plataforma de Jaguares y Aguilas

Main Plaza

Templo de los Guerreros
⑯

Juego de Pelota

The roof once covering the Plaza de Mil Columnas disintegrated long ago.

① El Castillo

Plaza de Mil Columnas
⑮

Juego de Pelota

Juego de Pelota

⑭
El Mercado

Temazcal

⑤ Xtaloc Sinkhole

Cenote Xtaloc

THE CULT OF KUKULCÁN

Although the Maya worshipped many of their own gods, Kukulcán was a deity introduced to them by the Toltecs—who referred to him as Quetzacóatl, or the plumed serpent. The pyramid of El Castillo, along with many other structures at Chichén Itzá, was built in honor of Kukulcán.

②

TO
OLD CHICHÉN ITZÁ

Adjacent to this water source is a steam bath, its interior lined with benches along the wall like those you'd see in any steam room today. Outside, a tiny pool was used for cooling down during the ritual.

The older Maya structures at Chichén Itzá are south and west of Cenote Xtaloc. Archaeologists have been restoring several buildings in this area, including the ❻ **Templo del Osario** (Ossuary Temple), which, as its name implies, concealed several tombs with skeletons and offerings. Behind the smaller ❼ **Casa Roja** (Red House) and ❽ **Casa del Venado** (House of the Deer) are the site's oldest structures, including ❾ **El Caracol** (The Snail), one of the few round buildings built by the Maya, with a spiral staircase within. Clearly built as a celestial observatory, it has eight tiny windows precisely aligned with the points of the compass rose. Scholars now know that Maya priests studied the planets and the stars; in fact, they were able to accurately predict the orbits of Venus and the moon, and the appearance of comets and eclipses. To modern astronomers, this is nothing short of amazing.

The Maya of Chichén Itzá were not just scholars, however. They were skilled artisans and architects as well. South of El Caracol, the ❿ **Grupo de las Monjas** (The Nunnery complex) has some of the site's most exquisite façades. A combination of Puuc and Chenes styles dominates here, with playful latticework, masks, and gargoyle-like serpents. On the east side of the ⓫ **Anexo de las Monjas** (Nunnery Annex), the Chenes facade celebrates the rain god Chaac. In typical style, the doorway represents an entrance into the underworld; figures of Chaac decorate the ornate façade above.

South of the Nunnery Complex is an area where field archaeologists are still excavating (fewer than a quarter of the structures at Chichén Itzá have been fully restored). If you have more than a superficial interest in the site—and can convince the authorities ahead of time of your importance, or at least your interest in archaeology—you can explore this area, which is generally not open to the public. Otherwise, head back toward El Castillo past the ruins of a housing compound called ⓬ **Akab Dzib** and the ⓭ **Templo de los Panales Cuadrados** (Temple of the Square Panels). The latter

The doorway of the Anexo de las Monjas represents an entrance to the underworld.

The Templo de los Guerreros shows the influence of Toltec architecture.

of these buildings shows more evidence of Toltec influence: instead of weight-bearing Maya arches—or "false arches"—that traditionally supported stone roofs, this structure has stone columns but no roof. This means that the building was once roofed, Toltec-style, with perishable materials (most likely palm thatch or wood) that have long since disintegrated.

Beyond El Caracol, Casa Roja, and El Osario, the right-hand path follows an ancient sacbé, now collapsed. A mud-and-straw hut, which the Maya called a *na*, has been reproduced here to show the simple implements used before and after the Spanish conquest. On one side of the room are a typical pre-Hispanic table, seat, fire pit, and reed baskets; on the other, the Christian cross and colonial-style table of the post-conquest Maya.

Behind the tiny oval house, several unexcavated mounds still guard their secrets. The path meanders through a small grove of oak and slender bean trees to the building known today as

14 El Mercado. This market was likely one end of a huge outdoor market whose counterpart structure, on the other side of the grove, is the **15 Plaza de Mil Columnas** (Plaza of the Thousand Columns). In typical Toltec-Maya style, the roof once covering the parallel rows of round stone columns in this long arcade has disappeared, giving the place a strangely Greek—and distinctly non-Maya—look. But the curvy-nosed Chaacs on the corners of the adjacent **16 Templo de los Guerreros** are pure Maya. Why their noses are pointing down, like an upside-down "U," instead of up, as usual, is just another mystery to be solved.

Columns at Templo de los Guerreros.

the Toltecs of central Mexico. (As well as representations of Tlaloc, the site also has a *tzompantli*—a stone platform decorated with row upon row of sculpted human skulls—which is a distinctively Toltec-style structure.) Most experts now agree, however, that Chichén Itzá was only influenced—never conquered—by Toltec trading partners from the north. Just west of the jaguar annex, another puzzle presents itself: the auditory marvel of Chichén Itzá's main ball court. At 490 feet, this **Juego de Pelota** is the largest in Mesoamerica. Yet if you stand at one end of the playing field and whisper something to a friend at the other end, incredibly, you'll be heard. The game played on this ball court was apparently something like soccer (no hands were used), but it likely had some sort of ritualistic significance. Carvings on the low walls surrounding the field show a decapitation, with blood spurting from the victim's neck to fertilize the earth. Whether this is a historical depiction— perhaps the losers or winners of the game were sacrificed?—or a symbolic scene, we can only guess. (Back in Mérida, the city tourist office stages a popular demonstration of the ball game each Friday evening in front of the cathedral. No one is beheaded.) On the other side of El Castillo, just before a small temple dedicated to the planet Venus, a ruined *sacbé*, or raised white road, leads to the **Cenote Sagrado** (Holy Well, or Sinkhole), also probably used for ritualistic purposes. Jacques Cousteau and his companions recovered about 80 skeletons from this deep, straight-sided subsurface pond, as well as thousands of pieces of jewelry and figures of jade, obsidian, wood, bone, and turquoise. In direct alignment with Cenote Sagrado, on the other side of El Castillo, the **Cenote Xtaloc** was kept pristine, undoubtedly for bathing and drinking. Adjacent to this water source is a steam bath, its interior lined with benches along the wall like those you'd see in any steam room

today. Outside, a tiny pool was used for cooling down during the ritual. Older Maya structures at Chichén Itzá lie south and west of Cenote Xtaloc. Archaeologists have been restoring several buildings in this area, including the **Templo del Osario** (Ossuary Temple), which, as its name implies, concealed several tombs with skeletons and offerings. Behind the smaller **Casa Roja** (Red House) and **Casa del Venado** (House of the Deer) are the site's oldest structures, including **El Caracol** (the Snail), one of the few round buildings built by the Maya, with a spiral staircase within. Clearly built as a celestial observatory, it has eight tiny windows precisely aligned with the points of the compass rose. Scholars now know that Maya priests studied the planets and the stars; in fact, they were able to accurately predict the orbits of Venus and the moon, and the appearance of comets and eclipses. To modern astronomers, this is nothing short of amazing. The Maya of Chichén Itzá were not just scholars, however. They were skilled artisans and architects as well. South of El Caracol, the **Grupo de las Monjas** (Nunnery Complex) has some of the site's most exquisite facades. A combination of Puuc and Chenes styles dominates here, with playful latticework, masks, and gargoylelike serpents. On the east side of the **Anexo de las Monjas** (Nunnery Annex), the Chenes facade celebrates the rain god, Chaac. In typical style, the doorway represents an entrance into the underworld, and figures of Chaac decorate the ornate facade above. South of the Nunnery Complex is an area where field archaeologists are still excavating (fewer than a quarter of the structures at Chichén Itzá have been fully restored). If you have more than a superficial interest in the site—and can convince the authorities ahead of time of your importance, or at least your interest in archaeology—you can explore this area, which is generally not open to the public. Otherwise, head back toward El

Castillo past the ruins of a housing compound called **Akab Dzib** and the **Templo de los Panales Cuadrados** (Temple of the Square Panels). The latter shows more evidence of Toltec influence: instead of weight-bearing Maya arches, or "false arches," that traditionally supported stone roofs, this structure has stone columns but no roof. This means that the building was once roofed, Toltec-style, with biodegradable materials (most likely palm thatch or wood) that have long since disintegrated. Beyond El Caracol, Casa Roja, and El Osario, the right-hand path follows an ancient sacbé, now collapsed. A mud-and-straw hut, which the Maya called a *na,* has been reproduced here to show the simple implements used before and after the Spanish conquest. On one side of the room are a typical pre-Hispanic table, seat, fire pit, and reed baskets; on the other are the Christian cross and colonial-style table of the postconquest Maya. Behind the tiny oval house, several unexcavated mounds still guard their secrets. The path meanders through a small grove of oak and slender bean trees to the building known today as El Mercado. This market was likely one end of a huge outdoor market whose counterpart structure, on the other side of the grove, is the **Plaza de Mil Columnas** (Plaza of the Thousand Columns). In typical Toltec-Maya style, the roof once covering the parallel rows of round stone columns in this long arcade has disappeared, giving the place a strangely Greek—and distinctly non-Maya—look. But the curvy-nosed Chaacs on the corners of the adjacent Templo de los Guerreros are pure Maya. Why their noses point down (like an upside down "U") instead of up is, as usual, just another mystery to be solved. An evening sound-and-light show (8 pm in summer, 7 pm in winter) is presented here, with images projected onto El Castillo pyramid—it's been described as everything from stunning to cheesy. Reservations must be booked in advance through the Noches de Kukulkán website (🌐 *www.nochesdekukulkan.com*). Area tour operators can also arrange tickets. The pricey admission includes a 30-minute guided walk followed by the light show, as well as use of a translation device (original narration is in Spanish only). Assorted problems occasionally plague the equipment; if the Maya gods are smiling, the show will be on during your visit. Inquire on-site, at area lodgings, or at the Yucatán tourist office in Mérida. Because of the lateness of the hour, it's easier to take in the evening show on your own if you're staying in the immediate area. Escorted tour groups do come in from as far away as Mérida or Cancún. ✉ *Chichén-Itzá* ✣ *Off Carretera 180, 2 km (1½ miles) east of Pisté* ☎ *985/851–0137* 🌐 *www.inah.gob.mx;* 🌐 *www.nochesdekukulkan.com for sound and light show* 🎟 *MX$497, sound and light show MX$510.*

Cenote Ik Kil

BODY OF WATER | FAMILY | When you've exhausted your interest in archaeology—or are just plain exhausted—Cenote Ik Kil (meaning "place of the winds") offers a refreshing change of pace. Located across from the Doralba Inn in Pisté, this is an especially photogenic cenote to swim in. Lockers, changing facilities, showers, and life jackets are available. ✉ *Carretera 180, Km 122, Pisté* ☎ *999/437–0148* 🌐 *cenoteikkil.com* 🎟 *MX$150.*

🛏 Hotels

Doloralba Inn

$ | HOTEL | FAMILY | A longtime favorite of international travelers, this family-run spot with a small motel feel is the best budget choice near the ruins. **Pros:** close to ruins; convivial vibe and cheap prices; transport to ruins is included (return transport is not). **Cons:** small rooms; some rooms without air-conditioning; weak Wi-Fi signal. [$] *Rooms from: $64*

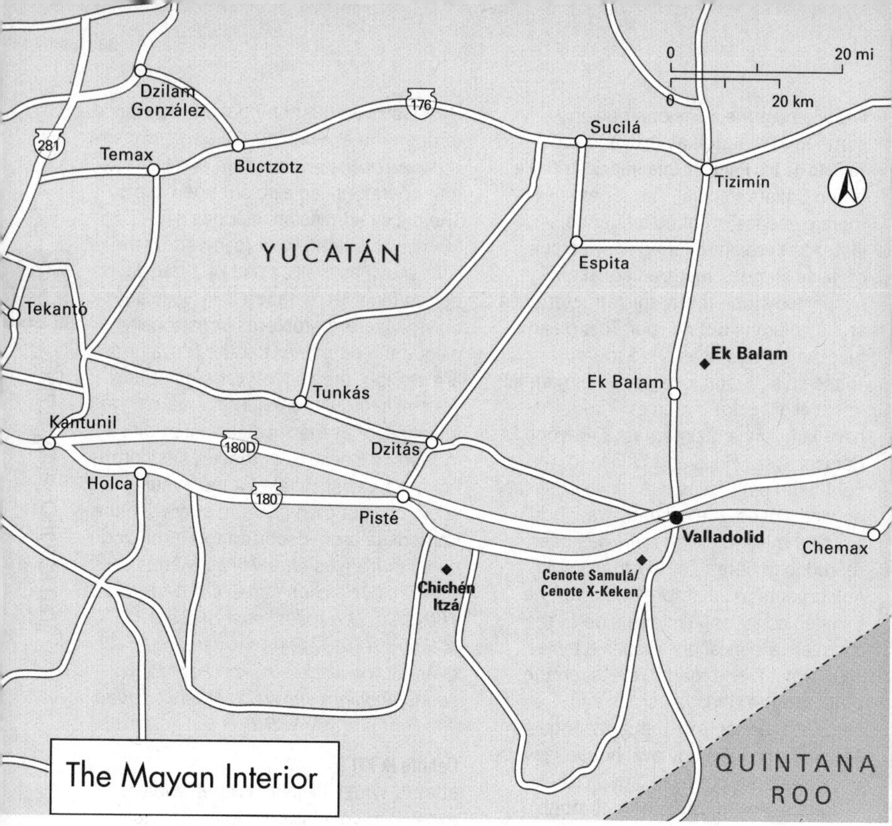

The Mayan Interior

✉ *Carretera 180, Km 122, 3 km (2 miles) east of Chichén Itzá,* ☎ *985/851–0117* 🌐 *www.doloresalba.com* 🛏 *40 rooms* 🍴 *Free Breakfast.*

★ **Hacienda Chichén & Yaxkin Spa**

$$ | **HOTEL** | This refurbished hacienda with a butter-yellow exterior has beautiful gardens and an inviting pool surrounded by palms. **Pros:** on-site organic farm; short walk from ruins; amazing spa and gardens. **Cons:** pricey; no TVs or Internet in rooms; restaurant food just OK. [$] *Rooms from: $179* ✉ *Carretera 180, Km 120, Pisté* ☎ *999/924–4222, 877/631–4005* 🌐 *www.haciendachichen.com* 🛏 *28 rooms* 🍴 *No Meals.*

Hotel Chichén Itzá

$ | **HOTEL** | **FAMILY** | Just over 1½ km (1 mile) from the ruins in the town of Pisté, this two-story hotel surrounding a pool feels like a motel in a very unlikely setting: a large grassy area edged with banana plants and other tropical trees and flowers. **Pros:** minutes from ruins; big pool; kind staff. **Cons:** mediocre food; no room service; room amenities vary (check out a few if possible). [$] *Rooms from: $60* ✉ *Calle 15 No. 45, Pisté* ☎ *985/851–0022, 877/240–5864 in the U.S.* 🌐 *www.mayaland.com* 🛏 *44 rooms* 🍴 *No Meals.*

Valladolid

161 km (97 miles) east of Mérida, 44 km (27 miles) east of Chichén Itzá, 146 km (88 miles) west of Cancún.

The second-largest city in Yucatán State, picturesque Valladolid (pronounced vye-ah-do-*leed*) has seen a big boom in popularity among travelers en route to or

Sacred Cenotes

To the ancient (and tradition-bound modern) Maya, holes in the ground—be they sinkholes, cenotes, or caves—are considered conduits to the world of the spirits. As sources of water in a land of no surface rivers, sinkholes are of special importance. Cenotes like Balancanchén, near Chichén Itzá, were used as prayer sites and shrines. Sacred objects and sacrificial victims were thrown in the sacred cenote at Chichén Itzá, and in others near large ceremonial centers in ancient times.

There are at least 2,800 known cenotes in the Yucatán. Rainwater sinks through the peninsula's thin soil and porous limestone to create underground rivers, while leaving the dry surface river-free.

Some pondlike sinkholes are found near ground level; most require a bit more effort to access, however. Near downtown Valladolid, Cenote Zací is named for the Mayan town conquered by the Spanish. It's a relatively simple saunter down a series of cement steps to reach the cool green water.

Lesser-known sinkholes are yours to discover, especially in the area labeled "zona de cenotes." To explore this area southeast of Mérida, you can hire a guide through the Yucatán State tourism office or, if you're already in Valladolid, through its city tourism office. Another option is to head directly for the ex-hacienda of Chunkanan, 3 km (2 miles) from the town of Cuzama, about 30 minutes southeast of Mérida. Here former henequen workers will hitch their horses to tiny open railway carts to take you along the unused train tracks. The reward for this bumpy, sometimes dusty ride is a swim in several incredible cenotes.

Almost every local has a "secret" cenote; ask around, and perhaps you'll find a favorite of your own.

from Chichén Itzá. (It's a far closer base for exploring the ruins than either Mérida or Cancún.) Francisco de Montejo founded Valladolid in 1543 on the site of the Mayan town of Sisal. The city suffered during the Caste War of the Yucatán—when the Maya in revolt killed nearly all Spanish residents—and again during the Mexican Revolution.

Despite its turbulent history, Valladolid's downtown contains many colonial and 19th-century structures. For a taste of local life, check out the Sunday-morning demonstrations of Yucatecan folk dancing in the main square; you can return at 8 pm, when the city's orchestra plays elegant, stylized *danzón*—waltzlike music to which expressionless couples swirl (think tango: no smiling allowed).

If you need help getting oriented, Valladolid's phenomenal municipal tourist office is open daily on the southeast corner of the square. You can also look for the bilingual tourist police dressed in spiffy white polo shirts and navy-blue baseball caps and trousers.

GETTING HERE AND AROUND

The drive from Mérida to Valladolid via the toll road takes about 2 hours; budget about 2½ hours if driving from Cancún. The tolls will be about MX$152 and MX$180 respectively. The free road cuts through several small towns where speed bumps, street repairs, and traffic increases travel time significantly. ADO (⊕ www.ado.com.mx) has direct buses from Mérida and Cancún to Valladolid, and other Mexican cities.

VISITOR INFORMATION

Oficina de Turismo. ⊠ *Palacio Municipal, Calle 40, at Calle 41, Valladolid* ☎ *985/856–2551* ⊕ *www.valladolid.travel.*

⊙ Sights

★ Casa de los Venados

HISTORIC HOME | A vintage mansion just south of Valladolid's central square contains Mexico's largest private collection of folk art. Rooms around the gracious courtyard contain some 3,000 pieces, with Día de los Muertos (Day of the Dead) figures being a specialty. The assemblage is impressive; even without it, though, the house would be worth touring. This hacienda-style building dates from the early 17th century, and restoration was engineered by the same architect who designed Mérida's ultra-modern Gran Museo del Mundo Maya (don't worry—the results here preserved its colonial elegance). Casa de los Venados opens to the public each morning for a 90-minute bilingual tour. Just show up, no reservations needed. Admission is a bargain, and all proceeds help fund local health-care projects. ⊠ *Calle 40 No. 204, Centro* ☎ *985/856–2289* ⊠ *MX$70.*

Cenote Samulá

NATURE SIGHT | Perhaps the most photographed cenote in the Yucatán, this sinkhole is located across the road from Cenote X-Keken, about 5 km (3 miles) west of the main square. A narrow stairway leads to crystal clear water where tree vines dangle overhead and hundreds of birds nest between the stalactites. Don't be alarmed by the tiny *Garra rufa* fish that nibble at your feet—they are actually eating away the dead skin cells. Guides offer tours for tips. ⊠ *On old hwy. to Chichén Itzá, Valladolid* ⊠ *MX$80.*

Cenote X-Keken

NATURE SIGHT | FAMILY | Five km (3 miles) west of the main square, you can swim with the catfish in lovely, mysterious Cenote X-Keken, which is in a cave illuminated by a small natural skylight. There are toilets and changing facilities but no lockers. Directly across the street is the equally stunning Cenote Samulá. Guides offer tours for tips. ⊠ *On old hwy. to Chichén Itzá, Valladolid* ⊠ *MX$80.*

Cenote Zací

NATURE SIGHT | FAMILY | A large, round, and beautiful sinkhole right in town, Cenote Zací—*zací* means "white hawk" in the Mayan language—is sometimes crowded with tourists and local boys clowning it up; at other times, it's deserted. Leaves from the tall old trees surrounding the sinkhole float on the surface, but the water itself is quite clean. If you're not up for a dip, visit the adjacent handicraft shop or have a bite at the popular, thatch-roof restaurant overlooking the water. We recommend paying the extra MX$30 to rent a life vest here. ⊠ *Calles 36 and 37, Valladolid* ☎ *985/856–0721* ⊠ *MX$30.*

Ex-Convento e Iglesia San Bernardino

CHURCH | Five long blocks away from the main plaza is the 16th-century, terra-cotta Ex-Convento e Iglesia San Bernardino, a Franciscan church and former monastery. The church was actually built over Cenote Sis-Há, which served as a clean water source for the monks. You can view the cenote through a grate in the well house where much of the original stone still remains. If the priest is around, ask him to show you the 16th-century frescoes, protected behind curtains near the altarpiece. The lack of proportion in the human figures shows the initial clumsiness of indigenous artisans in reproducing the Christian saints. ⊠ *Calle 41A, Centro* ☎ *985/856–2160* ⊙ *Closed Sat. and Sun.* ⊠ *MX$40.*

Iglesia de San Servacio

CHURCH | On the south side of the town's main plaza stands the large Iglesia de San Servacio, sometimes spelled "San Gervasio." Although many refer to it as a *catedral*, it is not the seat of the diocese—that's in Mérida. Its limestone exterior is impressive, but the interior is

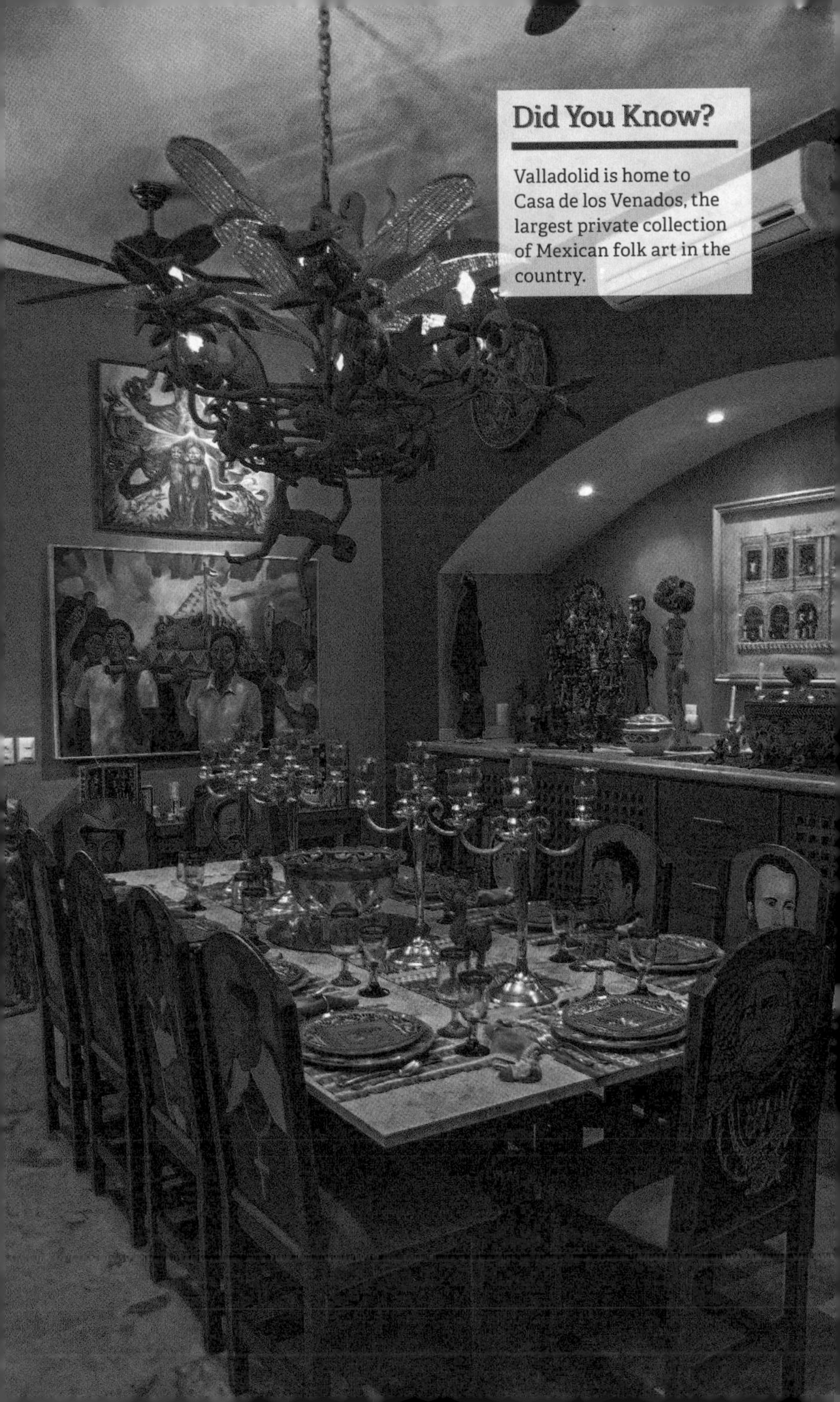

Did You Know?

Valladolid is home to Casa de los Venados, the largest private collection of Mexican folk art in the country.

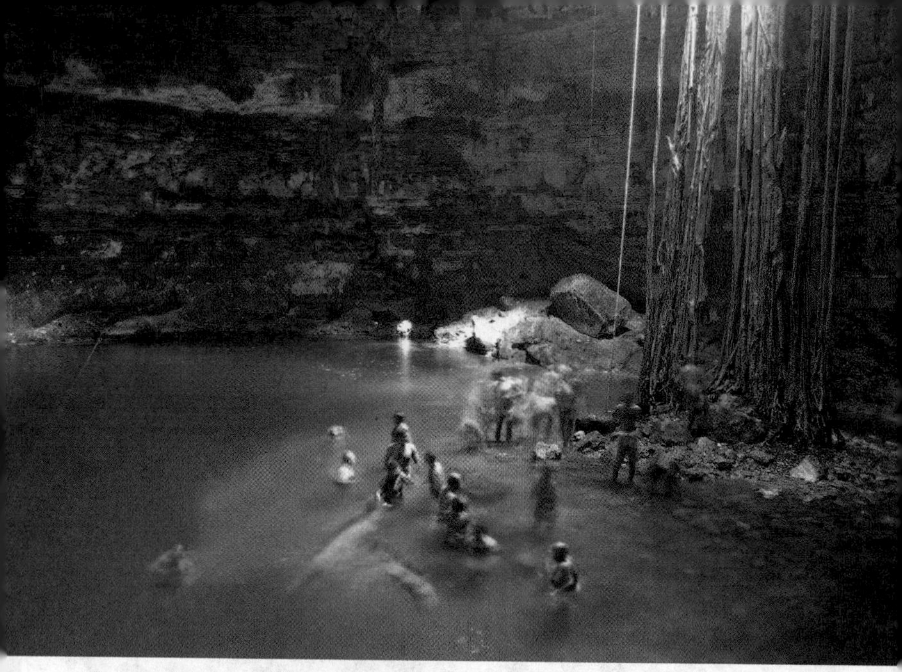

You can swim in Cenote X-Keken (for a price).

rather plain. The church makes a stunning anchor for the plaza when illuminated at night. ✉ *Calle 41, between Calles 40 and 42, Valladolid* 🎫 *Free.*

🍴 Restaurants

Casa Italia

$$ | **ITALIAN** | **FAMILY** | If there were a "Best Pizza in Mexico" contest, we'd nominate this restored colonial gem a couple of blocks north of the main square. Lots of reds and yellows brighten the interior, and the outdoor patio overlooking Parque de la Candelaria becomes prime real estate on beautiful evenings. **Known for:** impressive variety of quality pizza; good wine selection; fun vibe on outdoor patio. [$] *Average main: MP220* ✉ *Calle 35 No. 202J, between Calles 42 and 44, Centro* ☎ *985/856–5539* 🌐 *www.casaitalia.uzi-menu.com/* 🕒 *Closed Sun. No lunch.*

The Coffee Bike Station

$ | **BAKERY** | This cozy place just off the main square serves a great variety of lattes, espresso, tea, and chai, accompanied by pastries, veggie sandwiches, and frittatas. Get here early for the breads and muffins, baked fresh daily. **Known for:** fresh-baked goods; bike rental; vegetarian cuisine. [$] *Average main: MP150* ✉ *Calle 40 and Calle 43, Valladolid* ☎ *985/856–4496* 🕒 *Closed Sun. No lunch Sat.*

El Atrio del Mayab

$ | **MEXICAN** | This elegant colonial house on the south side of the main square specializes in hearty Yucatecan cuisine. *Pollo X'catik* (chicken baked in butter cream) and the city's eponymous dish, *lomitos de Valladolid* (cubed pork loin in a tomato-chile sauce), are menu highlights. If you're not feeling quite so adventurous, you can choose from *mar y tierra* (meaning, basically, surf and turf) options. **Known for:** local flavors; stylish setting; lush courtyard. [$] *Average main: MP170* ✉ *Calle 41 No. 204A, Centro* ☎ *985/856–2394* 🌐 *restaurant-atrio-del-mayab.business.site.*

Hotels

★ Casa Tía Micha

$$ | **B&B/INN** | More than a century old, this colonial home has been beautifully transformed into a five-bedroom, two-suite hotel that is owned and operated by "Micha's" grandchildren. **Pros:** homemade breakfast; friendly staff; clean rooms; secure parking. **Cons:** some rooms are dark; some street noise. [$] *Rooms from: $120* ✉ *Calle 39 No. 197, between Calles 38 and 40, Centro* ☎ *985/856–0499* 🌐 *www.casatiamicha.com* 🛏 *5 rooms* 🍴 *Free Breakfast.*

Ecotel Quinta Regia

$ | **HOTEL** | Mixing the colonial with modern Mexican, Ecotel Quinta Regia's whitewashed rooms are accented with a brightly colored wall, wrought-iron ceiling and wall fixtures, and hand-carved furniture; the nicest standard rooms have orchard-view terraces, while junior suites have balconies (overlooking the parking area), small kitchens, a living-dining area, and spa baths. **Pros:** Wi-Fi throughout; recently remodeled; lively palapa bar. **Cons:** 15-minute walk to central plaza; some rooms overlook the parking area; bland restaurant. [$] *Rooms from: $44* ✉ *Calle 40 160A, at Calle 27, Valladolid* ☎ *985/856–3472* 🌐 *www.ecotelquintaregia.com.mx* 🛏 *99 rooms* 🍴 *No Meals.*

El Mesón del Marqués

$ | **HOTEL** | On the north side of the main square, this well-preserved, 17th-century house was built around a lovely, open patio and has comfortable rooms with air-conditioning, Wi–Fi, and safes. **Pros:** free parking; 24-hour room service; nice outdoor areas; great downtown location. **Cons:** food could be better; mostly shaded pool; rooms lack charm of public areas. [$] *Rooms from: $78* ✉ *Calle 39 203, between Calles 40 and 42, Centro* ☎ *985/856–3042* 🌐 *www.mesondelmarques.com* 🍴 *Free Breakfast* 🛏 *80 rooms.*

Did You Know?

Valladolid is renowned for its *longaniza en escabeche*—a sausage dish made with pork, beef, or venison, served in many of the restaurants facing the square. While you're here, also be sure to sample *xtabentún* (pronounced eesh-tah-ben-*toon*), a liqueur that combines anise, honey, and rum.

★ Mesón de Malleville

$$$ | **B&B/INN** | The Coqui Coqui hotel group brings a contemporary feel to this luxurious property filled with vintage and handcrafted decor. **Pros:** exquisitely decorated; intimate; private and discreet atmosphere. **Cons:** expensive; lacks services and amenities of larger properties. [$] *Rooms from: $250* ✉ *Calle 41A No. 225, Valladolid* ☎ *985/856–5806* 🌐 *www.coquicoqui.com/valladolid-meson-de-malleville* 🛏 *4 suites* 🍴 *No Meals.*

Shopping

Yalat Arte Mexicano

CRAFTS | Located on the main square, this small shop sells clothing, crafts, jewelry, pottery, and masks from southeast Mexico. ✉ *Calle 41 No. 204, between Calles 40 and 42, Centro* ☎ *985/856–1969.*

Ek Balam

30 km (18 miles) north of Valladolid.

The large Ek Balam ("black jaguar") site was known to 19th-century archaeologists; however, excavation and mapping didn't really get underway until the 1990s, making this one of the "newest" rediscovered Mayan complexes.

GETTING HERE AND AROUND

If you don't have your own vehicle, *colectivos* (shared taxis) to Ek Balam leave from Calle 44 between Calles 35 and 37 in Valladolid throughout the day; the fare is MX$50 per person. You'll pay a private taxi driver MX$300 to MX$350 for the round-trip and an hour's wait.

Sights

Ek Balam

RUINS | The ruins at Ek Balam are best known for the amazingly well-preserved stucco panels on the Templo de los Frisos. A giant mask crowns its summit, and its friezes contain wonderful carvings of figures often referred to as "angels" (because they have wings)—but which more likely represented nobles in ceremonial dress. As is common with ancient Maya structures, this temple, styled like those in the lowland region of Chenes, is superimposed upon earlier ones. The temple was a mausoleum for ruler Ukin Kan Lek Tok, who was buried with priceless funerary objects, including perforated seashells, jade, mother-of-pearl pendants, and small bone masks with movable jaws. At the bases at either end of the temple, the leader's name is inscribed on the forked tongue of a carved serpent. (Mayan culture ascribed no negative connotation to the snake.) A contemporary of Uxmal and Cobá, the city may have been a satellite city to Chichén Itzá, which rose to power as Ek Balam waned. This site is also notable for its two concentric walls—a rare configuration in the Maya world—that surround the 45 structures in the main sector. They may have provided defense or, perhaps, symbolized the ruling elite that lived within. In addition, Ek Balam has a ball court and many freestanding stelae (stone pillars carved with commemorative glyphs or images). New Age groups occasionally converge here for prayers and seminars, but the site is usually quite sparsely visited, which adds to the mystery and allure. This is one of the few Maya sites where visitors are permitted to climb the structures. Be aware, though, that the trend in the Yucatán is to prohibit such activity, so the situation could change at any time. Some visitors report a dizzying sensation on descent here; for safety's sake, we recommend not climbing the structures. ✉ *30 km (18 miles) north of Valladolid, off Carretera 295* 🌐 *www.inah.gob.mx* 🎫 *MX$413.*

Hotels

Genesis Eco-Oasis

$ | **HOTEL** | Close to the Ek Balam ruins, this simple retreat is modeled on local dwellings; cabins of stucco, wood, and thatch surround a casually maintained open area with a ritual sweat lodge, meditation room, and bio-filtered swimming pool. **Pros:** close to Ek Balam; intimate and eco-friendly; cultural programs. **Cons:** pitted road to hotel; early-morning crowing roosters; sometimes difficult to make phone reservations. [$] *Rooms from: $65* ✉ *2 km (1 mile) northwest of Ek Balam* ✥ *Turn left on last rd. before entrance to Ek Balam ruins. Continue 2 km (1 mile) northwest toward Ek Balam village and follow signs to Genesis* ☎ *985/101–0277 cell* 🌐 *www.genesisretreat.com* 🛏 *9 cabins* 🍴 *No Meals.*

★ Casona Los Cedros

$$ | **B&B/INN** | Located a half-hour from Ek Balam in the low-key town of Espita, the contemporary cool Casona Los Cedros is a convenient base to explore this part of the state. **Pros:** intimate setting; stylish design; excellent restaurant. **Cons:** 30 minutes from Ek Balam; location may be too quiet for some. [$] *Rooms from: $268* ✉ *Calle 26 199, Espita* ☎ *999/249–2191* 🌐 *casonaloscedros.com* 🛏 *10 rooms* 🍴 *No Meals.*

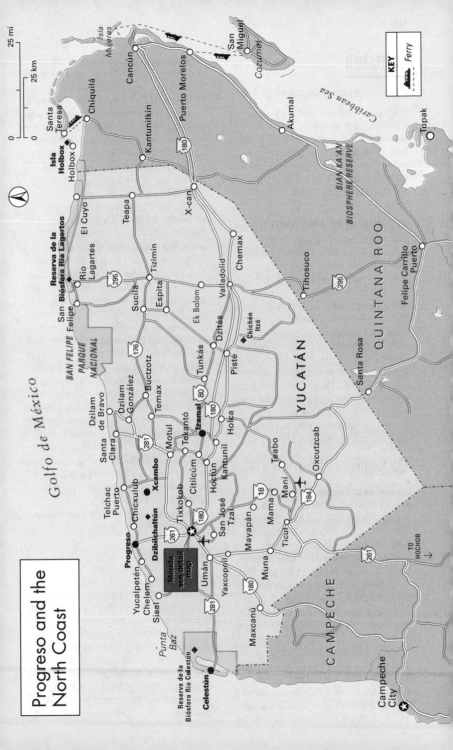

Progreso and the
North Coast

Celestún

90 km (56 miles) west of Mérida.

Think pink when someone says "Celestún." The estuaries of this biosphere reserve are home to an amazing flock of flamingos. The gateway to it, a tranquil fishing village of the same name, sits at the end of a spit of land separating the Celestún estuary from the Gulf of Mexico.

GETTING HERE AND AROUND

Every Mérida tour operator offers Celestún excursions several times per week. If you'd rather come independently, you can drive—a spiffy highway gets you there in under an hour—or take a second-class bus from Mérida's Noroeste Terminal (Calle 67 at Calle 50); there are multiple departures each day, and the round-trip fare is about MX$80. Within Celestún, moto-taxis are your best bet; they charge about MX$20 around town and MX$40 to go out to the boats from the central plaza. Make sure you establish the fare before you get on, as sometimes drivers will try to charge foreign tourists significantly higher rates.

⊙ Sights

Reserva de la Biósfera Ría Celestún

NATURE PRESERVE | Celestún is the point of entry to the Reserva de la Biósfera Ría Celestún, a 146,000-acre wildlife reserve with extensive mangrove forests and one of the largest colonies of flamingos in North America. Clouds of the pink birds soar above the estuary all year, but the best months for seeing them in abundance are November through March. This is also the fourth-largest wintering ground for ducks of the Gulf-coast region, and more than 365 other species of birds, plus a large sea-turtle population, make their home here. Mexican and American conservation programs protect the birds, as well as the endangered hawksbill and loggerhead marine

tortoises, and species such as the blue crab and crocodile. Other endangered species that inhabit the area are the ocelot, the jaguar, and the spider monkey. The park is set among rocks, islets, and white-sand beaches. There's good fishing here, too, and several cenotes that are wonderful for swimming. Most Mérida travel agencies run boat tours of the *ría* (estuary) in the early morning or late afternoon, but it's not usually necessary to make a reservation in advance. To see the birds, hire a fishing boat at the entrance to town (they hang out under the bridge leading into Celestún). A 75-minute tour for up to six people costs about MX$1,200; a two-hour tour costs around MX$2,500. Although more expensive (MX$990 per person), local tour expert Alex specializes in ecotours and donates a portion of the proceeds to the Celestún Conservation Program (call Hotel Eco Paraíso to book). Popular with Mexican vacationers, the park's sandy beach is pleasant during the morning but tends to get windy in the afternoon. And, unfortunately, mosquitoes gather in great numbers on the beach at dawn and dusk, particularly during winter months, making a walk on the beach uncomfortable. Most hotels offer mosquito netting around the beds, but bring along a good cream or spray to keep the bugs away. ⊠ *90 km (56 miles) west of Mérida, Celestún* ☎ *998/916–2100 tours booked through Hotel Eco Paraíso.*

🏖 Beaches

Playa Celestún

BEACH | FAMILY | This village may not have the classic beaches of the Caribbean, but it does have several kilometers of lovely coastline, perfect for long walks and seashell collecting. There are no crowds, even at the main beach in town, and the water is a pretty emerald-green color. The nicest stretch is at Hotel Eco Paraíso, home to 5 km (3 miles) of white sandy beaches, where turtles nest from April through July and bottlenose dolphins can be seen swimming. The waters are usually tranquil until late afternoon; when winds pick up, this isn't the best place for a dip—but it's perfect for relaxing or kayaking (rentals are available at the hotel). There are no lifeguards on duty, so ask hotel staff about rip currents and incoming swells. **Amenities:** food and drink; water sports (through the hotel). **Best for:** walking. ⊠ *Celestún.*

Hotels

Casa de Celeste Vida

$$ | **B&B/INN** | Owned by Canadian expats, this three-bedroom guesthouse is directly on the beach, making it one of the best values in town. **Pros:** less than a mile from town; isolated beach; gated property with secure parking. **Cons:** two-night minimum stay; credit cards not accepted; no air-conditioning; mosquitoes can be a problem. Ⓢ *Rooms from: $105* ⊠ *49E Calle No. 12, Celestún* ☎ *988/916–2536* ⊕ *www.hotelcelestevida.com* ⇥ *3 rooms* ❒ *No Meals.*

Dzibilchaltún

16 km (10 miles) north of Mérida.

◉ Sights

Dzibilchaltún

RUINS | **FAMILY** | Meaning "the place with writing on flat stones," Dzibilchaltún (dzi-bil-chal-*toon*) isn't a place you'd travel miles out of your way to see. But since it's not far off the road, about halfway between Progreso and Mérida, it's convenient and, in its own way, interesting. More than 16 square km (6 square miles) of land here is cluttered with mounds, platforms, piles of rubble, plazas, and stelae. Although only a few buildings have been excavated to date, scientists find Dzibilchaltún fascinating because of the sculpture and ceramics

from all periods of Maya civilization that have been unearthed. The area may have been settled as early as 500 BC and was inhabited until the time of the conquest. At its height, there were around 40,000 people living here. The site's most notable structure is the tiny Templo de las Siete Muñecas ("temple of the seven dolls"). It's a long stroll down a flat dirt track lined with flowering bushes and trees to get to the low, trapezoidal temple exemplifying the late preclassic style. During the spring and fall equinoxes, sunbeams fall at the exact center of two windows opposite each other inside one of the temple rooms. Studies have found that a similar phenomenon occurs at the full moon between March 20 and April 20. Another attraction is the ruined open chapel built by the Spaniards for the indigenous people. Actually, to be accurate, the Spanish forced indigenous laborers to build it as a place of worship for themselves: a sort of pre-Hispanic "separate but equal" scenario. One of the best reasons to visit Dzibilchaltún, though, is Xlacah Cenote. The site's sinkhole, with crystalline water the color of smoked green glass, is ideal for a cooling swim after walking around the ruins. Before leaving, visit the small but impressive Museo Pueblo Maya, which contains the seven crude dolls that gave the Temple of the Seven Dolls its name. It also traces the area's Hispanic history, and highlights contemporary crafts from the region. To reach Dzibilchaltún from Mérida, drive north on Carretera Mérida-Progreso; after 10 km (6 miles), turn right at the sign for the ruins and continue another 3 km (2 miles) until you reach a village. Just after you pass the village, take your first right toward the archaeological site. If you don't have a car, you can come by cab from Mérida (about MX$350 one way) or Progreso (about MX$1,130, including round-trip transport and two hours at the ruins): alternatively, you can catch a colectivo (shared van) from Mérida's Parque San

Juan or Progreso's main dock. ⊕ *www. inah.gob.mx* ✉ *MX$142, including museum* ✿ *Museum closed Mon.*

Progreso

16 km (10 miles) north of Dzibilchaltún, 32 km (20 miles) north of Mérida.

The waterfront town closest to Mérida is not particularly historic or picturesque; nevertheless, it provokes a certain sentimental fondness for those who know it well. On weekdays during most of the year the beaches are deserted, but over Easter and in summer they're packed with families from Mérida. Progreso has also started attracting cruise ships, and twice-weekly arrivals bring in tourist traffic. The town's charm—or lack thereof—seems to hinge on the weather. When the sun is shining, the water appears a translucent green and feels bathtub-warm, and the fine sand makes for lovely long walks. When the wind blows during one of Yucatán's winter *nortes,* gray water churns with whitecaps and sand blows in your face. Whether the weather is good or bad, however, everyone ends up eventually at one of the restaurants lining the main street, Calle 19, across from the oceanfront malecón. These all serve cold beer, seafood cocktails, and freshly grilled fish. There's also a small downtown area, between Calle 80 and Calle 31, with eateries that dish out simpler fare (like tortas and tacos), plus shops, banks, and supermarkets.

Although Progreso is close enough to Mérida to make it an easy day trip, several smaller hotels that have cropped up over the past few years make it a decent alternative base for those wanting to explore more of the untouristy coast. Just west of Progreso, the fishing villages of Chelem and Chuburna are beginning to offer walking, kayaking, and cycling tours ending with a boat trip through the mangroves for about

MX$400. This is ecotourism in its infancy, and excursions are best set up ahead of time through the Progreso tourism office. Experienced divers can explore sunken ships at the Alacranes Reef, about 120 km (74 miles) offshore, although infrastructure is limited. Pérez Island, part of the reef, supports a large population of sea turtles and seabirds. Arrangements for the boat trip can be made through individuals at the private marina at neighboring Yucaltepén, which is 6 km (4 miles) from Progreso.

GETTING HERE AND AROUND

To drive from Mérida, head out of town via Paseo de Montejo and keep going north. It's a straight shot to the beach. Buses bound for Progreso leave Mérida from Calle 62, No. 524, between Calles 65 and 67.

✪ Beaches

Progreso Beach
SWIMMING | FAMILY | If you want a pristine Caribbean-style strand, you'd better look elsewhere. The primary draw of Progreso's main beach is the distinctive little beach town and its proximity to Mérida, which often leaves the sand packed with tourists and locals alike during summer weekends and holidays. Water shoes are recommended since sharp, slippery rocks lurk below the surface, making this a poor spot for diving or snorkeling. The beach is void of shade, so your best bet is to find refuge in one of the eateries lining the long *malecón* (boardwalk) that runs along the shore. Several restaurant owners rent beach chairs by the hour, but beware: Progreso's peddlers are relentless and leave only once they receive a small tip. Despite its drawbacks, the water here offers a refreshing escape from the bustling city. **Amenities:** food and drink; toilets (restaurant patrons only). **Best for:** partiers; walking. ✉ *Av. Malecón at Calle 28, Progreso.*

Restaurants

Eladio's

$ | **MEXICAN** | **FAMILY** | An outpost of lively Eladio's in Mérida, this bar and restaurant is extremely popular with cruise-ship passengers who disembark in Progreso. You can sample typical Yucatecan dishes like *longaniza asada* (baked sausage) and *pollo pibil* (citrus-pickled chicken) while seated beneath a tall palapa on the beach. **Known for:** yummy free appetizers; fresh seafood; ocean breezes. *$ Average main: MP175* ✉ *Av. Malecón at Calle 80, Centro* ☎ *969/935–5670* ⊕ *www.eladios. com.mx.*

Crabster Seafood & Grill

$$ | **SEAFOOD** | Located right on Progreso's malecon, this restaurant is a notch above its neighbors and has contemporary Yucatecan inspired decor (think: pasta tiles, tzalam wood details, and florescent pink chairs). The menu is extensive but almost everything is from the sea, including shrimp cocktails, Baja-style fish tacos, and platters of crab. **Known for:** extensive seafood menu; ocean views; stylish decor. *$ Average main: MP200* ✉ *Calle Malecon, Progreso* ☎ *969/103–6522* ⊕ *www.facebook.com/CrabsterMX.*

Hotels

While there are many Airbnb and other rental options in Progreso and its neighboring beach towns, many travelers prefer to return after a day at the beach to Merida, where the options are generally better and more extensive.

Playa Linda Hotel

$ | **HOTEL** | Located directly across from the beach, the Playa Linda has clean rooms, bargain rates, and the best view in Progreso. **Pros:** suites have an added dining area and balcony; great value; across from the beach. **Cons:** staff speaks little English; no amenities; no restaurant. *$ Rooms from: $50* ✉ *Calle 76, between Calles 19 and 21, Progreso*

☎ *985/858–0519, 999/220–8318* ⊕ *www. playalindayucatan.com* ⦿ *No Meals* ⛵ *7 rooms.*

Progreso Beach Hotel

$ | **HOTEL** | This small hotel is across from the water and close to all the restaurants along the malecón. **Pros:** swimming pool; inexpensive. **Cons:** uncomfortable beds; Wi-Fi in common areas only; sparse rooms. *$ Rooms from: $52* ✉ *Calle 21 No.150, between Calles 66 and 68, Progreso* ☎ *969/935–5079* ⊕ *www. progreso-beach.com* ⛵ *51 rooms* ⦿ *No Meals.*

Xcambo

37 km (23 miles) east of Progreso, 12 km or (7½ miles) from Telchac Puerto.

Sights

Xcambo

RUINS | **FAMILY** | Surrounded by a plantation where disease-resistant coconut trees are being developed, the Xcambo (*ish*-cam-bo) site is a couple of miles inland following the turnoff for Xtampu. Salt, a much-sought-after commodity in the ancient world, was produced in this area and made it prosperous. Indeed, the bones of 600 former residents discovered in burial plots showed they had been healthier than the average Maya. Two plazas have been restored so far, surrounded by rather plain structures. The tallest temple is the Xcambo, also known as the Pyramid of the Cross. On a clear day you can see the coast from the summit. Ceramics found at the site indicate that the city traded with other Maya groups as far afield as Guatemala, Teotihuácan, and Belize. The Catholic church here was built by dismantling some of the ancient structures, and, until recently, locals hauled off the cut stones to build fences and foundations. ✉ *37 km (23 miles) west of Progreso* ✛ *Located between Progreso and Telchac Puerto, 3*

The estuaries of Reserva de la Biósfera Ría Celestún are filled with pink flamingos.

km (2 miles) south of the coastal rd.; turn off Carretera Progreso–Dzilam de Bravo at Xtampu 🖼 *Donation.*

Reserva de la Biósfera Ría Lagartos

105 km (65 miles) north of Valladolid.

The mangroves of the Ría Lagartos Biosphere Reserve make up one of southern Mexico's most important wildlife sanctuaries. Birds are the big draw here, and with 300-plus resident and migratory species, there's plenty for avian enthusiasts to see.

GETTING HERE AND AROUND

You can make the journey from Valladolid (1½ hours by car, 2 hours by bus) as a day trip; add 1 hour if you're coming from Mérida, and 3 hours from Cancún. Buses leave Mérida and Valladolid regularly from the second-class terminals bound for either Río Lagartos or San Felipe, which is 10 km (6 miles) west of the park. (Note

that the town is called Río Lagartos, the park Ría Lagartos. *Río* means "river" in Spanish; *ría* means "estuary.")

👁 Sights

Reserva de la Biósfera Ría Lagartos

NATURE PRESERVE | FAMILY | This national park, which encompasses a long estuary, was developed with ecotourism in mind—although most of the alligators for which it and the village were named have long since been hunted into extinction. The real spectacle these days is the birds. More than 380 species nest and feed in the area, including flocks of flamingos, snowy and red egrets, white ibis, great white herons, cormorants, pelicans, and peregrine falcons. Fishing is good, too, and the protected leatherback, hawksbill, and green turtles lay their eggs on the beach at night. Booking an excursion is the easiest way to visit the 149,000-acre park and Río Lagartos Adventures (☎ 986/100–8390 ⊕ *www. riolagartosaventuras.com*) is an excellent and experienced operation. Boat trips will take you through mangrove forests to flamingo feeding grounds. Tours are priced per boat, not person, and include one-hour tours for MX$1,000 to longer tours of up to four hours for around MX$4500. Whether you are interested in a nocturnal crocodile adventure, a fishing expedition, or an expedition with plenty of time to stop on beaches accessible only to private boats, Rio Lagartos Aventuras likely has one that is the right fit for your group. Mosquitoes can gather at dusk in unpleasantly large swarms in May, June, and July. Bring repellent to fend them off. ✉ *115 km (71 miles) north of Valladolid, Río Lagartos* ☎ *986/100–8390* 🌐 *www.riolagartosadventures.com* 🎫 *MX$40.*

🍴 Restaurants

Restaurante Ría Maya

$ | **SEAFOOD** | Grab a seat in this palapa restaurant directly across from the water and watch the day's catch come straight from the docks. The menu features local specialties like ceviche, seafood soup, fish fillet stuffed with shrimp, and breaded seafood rolled into a ball and deep-fried. **Known for:** lobster and octopus in season; quality seafood; beachy vibe. [$] *Average main: $180* ✉ *Calle 19 No. 134, on the waterfront, 50 meters from the lighthouse, Río Lagartos* ☎ *986/100–8390* 🌐 *www.riolagartosnaturetours.com.*

🛏 Hotels

Hotel Punta Ponto

$ | **HOTEL** | The main draw here is the friendly, personal attention the owners lavish on guests. **Pros:** friendly staff; lagoon views—from some rooms; waterfront location. **Cons:** rooms could use a makeover; spartan accommodations; some street noise. [$] *Rooms from: $65* ✉ *Calle 9 Diagonal No. 140, Río Lagartos* ☎ *986/862–0509* 🌐 *hotelpuntaponto.com* 🛏 *10 rooms* 🍽 *Free Breakfast.*

Hotel Tabasco Río

$ | **HOTEL** | Right on the plaza, this hotel has a bright center courtyard covered with skylights that allow light to shine on the tables where breakfast is served. **Pros:** well-appointed rooms; hotel package can include meals and tours; budget friendly. **Cons:** hot water can be inconsistent; Wi-Fi in common areas only; some rooms are spartan. [$] *Rooms from: $48* ✉ *Calle 12 No 115, Río Lagartos* ☎ *986/862–0016* 🌐 *www.tabascoriohotel.com* 🛏 *19 rooms* 🍽 *No Meals.*

Hotel Villa de Pescadores

$ | **HOTEL** | The nicest choice in Río Lagartos has 12 rooms with TVs, private balconies, water views, and colorful decor; stone walls and tile floors keep rooms rather cool, but there are fans and air-conditioning for those who need an extra breeze. **Pros:** clean rooms; great views; best location in town. **Cons:** restaurant closed for dinner in low season; four floors but no elevator; weak water pressure. [$] *Rooms from: $68* ✉ *Calle 14 and Av. Malecón, Río Lagartos* ☎ *986/862–0020* 🌐 *www.hotelvilladepescadores.com* 🛏 *12 rooms* 🍽 *No Meals.*

Isla Holbox

141 km (87 miles) northeast of Valladolid.

Only 25 km (16 miles) long, tiny Isla Holbox sits at the eastern end of the Ría Lagartos estuary and is just across the state line in neighboring Quintana Roo. Fishing fans come for the ample supply of pampano, bass, and barracuda, while birders appreciate the many avian species that fill the mangrove estuaries on the island's leeward side. Beach bums love the sandy strands strewn with seashells; although the water is often murky—the Gulf of Mexico and the Caribbean come together here—it's shallow and warm, and there are some nice places to swim. Sandy streets lead to simple seafood restaurants where conch,

Most visitors access Isla Holbox by ferry.

octopus, and other delicacies are always fresh. Lodgings here range from bare-bones to beach-luxe, and hotel owners can help set up fishing and bird-watching excursions, as well as expeditions to see the whale sharks that cruise offshore June through August.

Holbox's population numbers some 2,000 lucky souls, and in summer it seems there are as many biting bugs per person. Bring plenty of mosquito repellent. Many locals use baby oil as a natural protection against no-see-ums, also known as biting midges.

Isla Holbox lies in the state of Quintana Roo and falls in a different time zone than other destinations in this chapter. Like Cancún, Holbox is an hour later than Yucatán State during the winter and the same time the rest of the year.

GETTING HERE AND AROUND

From Río Lagartos, take Carretera 176 to Kantunilkin, and then head north on the unnumbered road for 44 km (27 miles) to the port town of Chiquilá (road signs direct you simply to "Holbox"). From Cancún, take the 180 free road toward Mérida and pass through the small town of Leona Vicario; follow the signs to Kantunilkin and continue 40 km (25 miles) until you reach Chiquilá. The drive from Cancún to Chiquilá takes about three hours depending on road conditions. The road is long and pitted with potholes, so avoid driving at night. You can park at 5 Hermanos, which has covered stalls across from the port for MX$56 a day, and continue by boat to the island.

Ferry schedules vary, but there are normally crossings on the hour from around 6 am to 7 pm. The fare is MX$50, and the trip takes about 35 minutes. Speedboats will take you over for double the price in half the time. A car ferry makes the trip at 6 am daily, returning at 1 pm, but it's recommended to leave your car in Chiquilá. If you're feeling flush, Isla Holbox has a rustic airport with a shell-bordered runway that receives small airplanes. You can charter a five-passenger Cesna through AeroSaab;

round-trip airfare from Cancún, Cozumel, or Playa del Carmen will cost your group MX$14,000 to MX$16,000.

Little golf-cart taxis ply the island for about MX$300 an hour; you can rent your own for MX$200 an hour (you may be able to negotiate a better price if you're renting for several hours or traveling in low season). Some hotels also offer complimentary bikes for guests.

AIRLINE CONTACTS AeroSaab. ☎ *998/865–4225 in Playa del Carmen* 🌐 *www.aerosaab.com.*

🍴 Restaurants

Casa Nostra Roof Restaurant
$$$ | **ITALIAN** | The creative menu here developed by its Sicilian chef, Giuseppe Genovese (commonly known as "Beppe"), blends Italian, Mediterranean, and Caribbean cuisine. Locals gather for seafood pasta, grilled lobster, octopus salad, and fresh ceviche, all bathed in garlic and olive oil. **Known for:** gourmet coffee; smoked-ham pizza; authentic tiramisu. [$] *Average main: MP320* ✉ *Av. Morelos 231, at Hotel La Palapa, Isla Holbox* ☎ *984/875–2214.*

El Sushi de Holbox
$$ | **JAPANESE** | This tiny restaurant fills a void in island cuisine with the day's catch transformed into the sushi roll of your choice. Local favorites include the Holbox Rainbow made with shrimp, salmon, tuna, and sea bass. **Known for:** creative (if inauthentic) sushi; terrific sake; ginger margaritas. [$] *Average main: MP250* ✉ *Plaza El Pueblito, Av. Tiburón Ballena, top fl., Isla Holbox* ☎ *1984/132–9507* 🌐 *www.facebook.com/elsushideholbox* ⏲ *Closed Mon. No lunch.*

Mandarina Beach Club
$$$ | **ECLECTIC** | Chef Jorge Melul, a master baker, has become known on the island for his homemade breads, cakes, and pastas, made from organic, local grown ingredients. For a memorable meal, start with shrimp tempura dipped in chipotle cream or homemade pesto and then order the fish cooked in white wine and topped with spinach and pears. **Known for:** beachside setting; fresh seafood; rooftop bar. [$] *Average main: MP330* ✉ *Casa Las Tortugas, Calle Igualdad s/n, Isla Holbox* ☎ *984/875–2129* 🌐 *www.holboxcasalastortugas.com.*

🛏 Hotels

★ Casa Las Tortugas
$$ | **HOTEL** | This romantic, bohemian-chic spot has a prime location and one of the few spas on Holbox. **Pros:** on-site kitesurfing school; organic restaurant; excellent location. **Cons:** rooms don't have TVs; usually booked far in advance; not all rooms have ocean views. [$] *Rooms from: $230* ✉ *Calle Igualdad s/n, Isla Holbox* ☎ *984/875–2129* 🌐 *www.holboxcasalastortugas.com* 🛏 *21 rooms* 🍴 *Free Breakfast.*

Hotel Mawimbi
$$ | **HOTEL** | Made up of brightly painted beachside bungalows, this small hotel has rooms that are clean, simple, and tastefully decorated. **Pros:** small dogs OK if arranged in advance; suspended beach beds are great for relaxing; decent rates. **Cons:** entryway rooms lack privacy; cement floors aren't optimal. [$] *Rooms from: $160* ✉ *Calle Igualdad s/n, Isla Holbox* ☎ *984/875–2003* 🌐 *www.mawimbi.com* 🍴 *Free Breakfast* 🛏 *11 rooms.*

★ Las Nubes de Holbox
$$$ | **HOTEL** | Remotely located on the northeast side of the island, this quiet waterfront retreat is one of the most luxurious (and expensive) hotels on Holbox. **Pros:** peaceful location; bikes for exploring; unobstructed views. **Cons:** far from town; expensive; small beach. [$] *Rooms from: $250* ✉ *Paseo Kuka s/n, Esq. Calle Camarón, Isla Holbox* ☎ *984/875–2300* 🌐 *www.lasnubesdeholbox.com* 🛏 *28 rooms* 🍴 *Free Breakfast.*

LunArena

$ | **HOTEL** | If Isla Holbox is feeling like too much, stay in El Cuyo (a beach town that is a good decade behind Holbox on the path of being discovered) at this hotel, long a secret of kitesurfers with its stylish but simple rooms. **Pros:** kitchenettes; comfortable, understated rooms; hammocks with ocean views. **Cons:** restaurant is on the expensive side; El Cuyo is remote and a drive to get there; small pool. [$] *Rooms from: MP90* ✉ *Avenida Veraniega, Isla Holbox* ☎ *984/133–0810* 🌐 *lunarena.com.mx* 🛏 *10 rooms* 🍴 *Free Breakfast.*

★ Ser Casasandra

$$$$ | **HOTEL** | Rustic meets five-star at Ser Casasandra (formerly CasaSandra), an elegantly landscaped resort with winding pathways leading to two-story casitas draped in bougainvillea. **Pros:** Ayurveda treatments; good restaurant; 500-thread-count Egyptian cotton sheets. **Cons:** some rooms get kitchen noise; expensive restaurant; not all rooms have ocean views. [$] *Rooms from: $394* ✉ *Calle de la Igualdad s/n, Isla Holbox* ☎ *984/875–2431* 🌐 *www.casasandra.com* 🛏 *18 rooms, 1 villa* 🍴 *Free Breakfast.*

Villas Delfines

$$$ | **HOTEL** | This fishermen's lodge consists of 20 pleasant, palapa-topped cabins by the beach. **Pros:** nice Saturday grill (high season only); eco-friendly property. **Cons:** slightly dated rooms; Wi-Fi in common areas only; 15-minute walk to village's main square. [$] *Rooms from: $242* ✉ *Calle Paseo Kuka s/n, Isla Holbox* ☎ *984/875–2196* 🌐 *www.villasdelfines.com* 🛏 *20 cabins* 🍴 *Free Breakfast.*

Villas Flamingos

$$ | **HOTEL** | If you are looking for simplicity, tranquility, and an eco-friendly atmosphere, this is your place. **Pros:** eco-friendly property; only beach house on the island; nice pool. **Cons:** rooms could use some upgrades; rustic design is not for everyone; far from town. [$] *Rooms from: $180* ✉ *Calle Paseo Kuka s/n, Isla Holbox* ☎ *1984/875–2167* 🌐 *www.villasflamingos.com* 🛏 *30 rooms* 🍴 *Free Breakfast.*

Villas HM Paraíso del Mar

$$ | **RESORT** | Despite the thatched roofs and rustic ambience, rooms at the island's largest property—HM is a Spanish hotel chain—are loaded with everything you could want to be comfortable. **Pros:** nice breakfast buffet; large pool and Mayan sweat lodge on-site; island's only all-inclusive property. **Cons:** some rooms lack ocean views; seaweed on shore; Wi-Fi in common areas only. [$] *Rooms from: $150* ✉ *Av. Plutarco Elias s/n, Isla Holbox* ☎ *984/875–2062* 🌐 *www.villashmparaisodelmar.com* 🛏 *58 rooms* 🍴 *All-Inclusive.*

Shopping

Lolita Holbox

WOMEN'S CLOTHING | This boutique right in the center of town has an excellent selection of beach-chic essentials including wraps, swimsuits, beach bags, and flip-flops. Lolita also has jewelry and some home goods. Their men's offerings are not as extensive as their women's, but they do carry some trunks and shirts. ✉ *Avenida Damero, Isla Holbox* ☎ *984/875–2478* 🌐 *www.facebook.com/holboxlolita.*

Activities

Holbox Tours

BOATING | **FAMILY** | Hotel Puerto Holbox offers a variety of different tours, from swimming with whale sharks (offered only from June to September) and a bioluminescent bay tour (offered only on moonless nights) to sunset cruises and fishing expeditions. Most are priced per person, though the four-hour fishing expedition is 6,000 pesos, roughly $300, for a boat that holds five people. ✉ *Hotel Puerto Holbox, Av. Pedro Joaquín Coldwell s/n, Isla Holbox* ☎ *984/875–2157* 🌐 *www.hotelpuertoholbox.com* 🎟 *MX$350 for bioluminescent bay tour.*

Index

Photo Credits

Front Cover: Wildroze/Getty Images [Description: Colorful Mexican pottery and architecture on the beach in Cancun.]. **Back cover, from left to right:** Elijah-Lovkoff/iStockphoto, Delbars/iStockphoto, Seckin Ozturk/iStockphoto. **Spine:** carmengabriela/iStockphoto. **Interior, from left to right:** Simon Dannhauer/Shutterstock (1). Alexander Sviridov/Shutterstock (2-3). cancuncd.com (5). **Chapter 1: Experience Cancún and the Riviera Maya:** javarman3/iStockphoto (6-7). Aleksandar Todorovic | Dreamstime.com (8-9). Xcaret by Mexico (9). Flocutus | Dreamstime.com (9). Nialldunne24 | Dreamstime.com (10). Xan/Shutterstock (10). Grand Fiesta Americana Coral Beach Cancun (10). Lrafael | Dreamstime.com (10). Ahaswerus | Dreamstime.com (11). Yucatán Tourism Board (11). Giuseppemasci | Dreamstime.com (12). Nialldunne24 | Dreamstime.com (12). Pixelife | Dreamstime.com (12). Chad Zube/Shutterstock (12). kravka/Shutterstock (13). BlueOrange Studio/Shutterstock (13). Elvistudio | Dreamstime.com (13). Gitano Bar Tulum (13). javarman/Shutterstock (14). AlfredoAzarPhotography (14). Son of Groucho [CC BY 2.0]/Flickr (15). Elijah-Lovkoff/iStockphoto (20). Alex W/Shutterstock (20). lunamarina/Shutterstock (20). Wangkun Jia/Shutterstock (20). SL_Photography/iStockphoto (21). Byelikova | Dreamstime.com (22). Smokelmt | Dreamstime.com (22). Mexican Caribbean (22). Ivan Soto Cobos/Shutterstock (22). Mexican Caribbean (22). Izanbar | Dreamstime.com (23). Rchphoto | Dreamstime.com (23). Bophil | Dreamstime.com (23). Mexican Caribbean (23). Atomazul | Dreamstime.com (23). Guajillo studio/Shutterstock (24). S.Pereira/Shutterstock (25). Under The Sea/Shutterstock (26). Joana Villar/Shutterstock (26). Lorena Difulvio/Shutterstock (26). aquapix/Shutterstock (27). Rob Atherton/Shutterstock (27). **Chapter 3: Cancún:** Frederick Millett/Shutterstock (67). Cancun CVB (70). Thelmadatter [CC BY SA-3.0]/Wikimedia Commons (71). Guajillo studio/Shutterstock (71). JTB Photo / age fotostock (87). Marriott International (97). Courtesy of NIZUC Resort & Spa (99). Cancun CVB (107). **Chapter 4: Isla Mujeres:** Cancun CVB (111). Eddy Galeotti/Shutterstock (124). Chris Cheadle / age fotostock (134). **Chapter 5: The Riviera Maya:** YuziS/Shutterstock (137). amResorts (145). Rosewood Hotels & Resorts (154). Ken Welsh / age fotostock (158-159). La Tortuga Hotel & Spa (165). SEUX Paule / age fotostock (171). Doug Plummer / age fotostock (173). José Enrique Molina / age fotostock (174). Stefano Paterna / age fotostock (175). Ales Liska/shutterstock (175). Qing Ding/shutterstock (176). Ken Welsh/age fotostock (176). Philip Coblentz/Brand X Pictures (177). Cancun CVB (182). andrmoel/Shutterstock (193). Nataliya Hora/iStockphoto (198). urosr/Shutterstock (204). Almaplena Eco Resort & Beach Club (209). LindaVermeulen_MermaidsKissGallery (210). **Chapter 6: Cozumel:** B&Y Photography Inc. / age fotostock (215). Mark Newman / age fotostock (222). Ramunas Bruzas/Shutterstock (226). Richard Cummins / SuperStock (228). Alvaro Leiva / age fotostock (231). The Leading Hotels of the World (236). SuperStock/agefotostock (241). cancuncd.com (243). Mike Bauer/Shutterstock (244). tslane888 [CC BY 2.0]/Flickr (244). pato_garza [CC BY 2.0]/Flickr (244). tslane888 [CC BY 2.0]/Flickr (244). tubuceo/Shutterstock (246). sethbienek/Flickr (246). Julie de Leseleuc/iStockphoto (247). Jerry McElroy/iStockphoto (248). **Chapter 7: Yucatán State:** Emicristea | Dreamstime.com (255). Robert Briggs/Shutterstock (258). Anderson Czarnesky/Shutterstock (259). Mathes | Dreamstime.com (259). Brandon Bourdages/Shutterstock (269). MAISANT Ludovic / age fotostock (270). Hacienda Xcanatun (279). Manuel Manso/Hotel Julamis (280). Schaub/Shutterstock (289). Stefano Paterna / age fotostock (292). Dmitry Rukhlenko/iStockphoto (297). David Davis/Shutterstock (300). Fedor Selivanov/Shutterstock (301). Corbis (301). Richard Gillard/iStockphoto (302). Bernard Gagnon [CC BY SA-1.0]/wikipedia.org (302). José A. Granados/Cancun CVB (303). Luis CastaÕeda/age fotostock (303). Jo Ann Snover/iStockphoto (303). Fcb981 [CC BY SA-3.0]/wikipedia.org (304). Sylvain Lapensée-Ricard/iStockphoto (304). Mexico Tourism Board (305). Philip Baird/anthroartheart.org (305). Jo Ann Snover/iStockphoto (306). Markus Sevcik/iStockphoto (307). Deanna Bean/iStockphoto (307). Robert Rosenblum / Alamy Stock Photo (313). Alex James Bramwell/Shutterstock (314). Witr | Dreamstime.com (322). Adalberto Ríos Szalay / age fotostock (324). **About Our Writers:** All photos are courtesy of the writers.

*Every effort has been made to trace the copyright holders, and we apologize in advance for any accidental errors. We would be happy to apply the corrections in the following edition of this publication.

Notes

Notes

Notes

Fodor's CANCÚN & THE RIVIERA MAYA

Publisher: Stephen Horowitz, *General Manager*

Editorial: Douglas Stallings, *Editorial Director*; Jill Fergus, Amanda Sadlowski, Caroline Trefler, *Senior Editors*; Kayla Becker, Alexis Kelly, *Editors*

Design: Tina Malaney, *Director of Design and Production*; Jessica Gonzalez, *Graphic Designer*; Mariana Tabares, *Design & Production Intern*

Production: Jennifer DePrima, *Editorial Production Manager*; Elyse Rozelle, *Senior Production Editor*; Monica White, *Production Editor*

Maps: Rebecca Baer, *Senior Map Editor*; Mark Stroud (Moon Street Cartography), David Lindroth, *Cartographers*

Photography: Viviane Teles, *Senior Photo Editor*; Namrata Aggarwal, Ashok Kumar, *Photo Editors*; Rebecca Rimmer, *Photo Intern*

Business & Operations: Chuck Hoover, *Chief Marketing Officer*; Robert Ames, *Group General Manager*; Devin Duckworth, *Director of Print Publishing*; Victor Bernal, *Business Analyst*

Public Relations and Marketing: Joe Ewaskiw, *Senior Director of Communications & Public Relations*

Fodors.com: Jeremy Tarr, *Editorial Director*; Rachael Levitt, *Managing Editor*

Technology: Jon Atkinson, *Director of Technology*; Rudresh Teotia, *Lead Developer*; Jacob Ashpis, *Content Operations Manager*

Writers: Luis Domínguez, Dana Freeman, John Newton, Jeffrey Van Fleet

Editors: Kayla Becker, Alexis Kelly

Production Editor: Monica White

6th Edition

ISBN 978-1-64097-408-1

ISSN 2166-6253

SPECIAL SALES

This book is available at special discounts for bulk purchases for sales promotions or premiums. For more information, e-mail SpecialMarkets@fodors.com.

PRINTED IN CANADA

10 9 8 7 6 5 4 3 2 1

About Our Writers

 Luis Domínguez is a Riviera Maya-based freelance writer and independent journalist interested in travel, art, books, history, philosophy, politics, and sports. He has written for *Fodor's, Yahoo!, Sports Illustrated, Telemundo,* and *Homeschool Spanish Academy,* among other brands of print and digital media in North America and Europe. Luis updated the Riviera Maya, Isla Mujeres, and Cozumel chapters.

 Dana Freeman is a Vermont-based freelance writer focusing on authentic luxury, small ship cruising, and culinary travel experiences. Her work has appeared in *CNN Travel, Thrillist,* and *Yankee Magazine* and she is a regular feature writer for *ClubLife Magazine.* Her latest, "Exploring Coastal Maine" was published in June. Dana updated the Cancún chapter. Follow her adventures on Instagram @danahfreeman.

 John Newton has been an editor at *Condé Nast Traveler, Travel+Leisure,* and *AFAR* magazines and has written travel stories for many other outlets. For this volume, he contributed to the sections on the states of Yucátan and Campeche. He currently lives in San Cristóbal, a neighborhood in Mérida's historic center.

 San José, Costa Rica–based freelance writer and pharmacist **Jeffrey Van Fleet** has spent the better part of the last two decades enjoying Latin America's rainy seasons and Wisconsin's winters. (Most people would try to do it the other way around.) He never passes up the chance to visit Mexico and, in particular, the less-explored paths of the Yucatán Peninsula. Jeff is a regular contributor to Costa Rica's English-language newspaper, the *Tico Times,* and has covered Central America for United Airlines' inflight magazine *Hemispheres.* Jeff updated the Experience and Travel Smart chapters for this edition.